Musical ImagiNat

Musical ImagiNation

U.S.-Colombian Identity and the Latin Music Boom

María Elena Cepeda

NEW YORK UNIVERSITY PRESS
New York and London

NEW YORK UNIVERSITY PRESS
New York and London

www.nyupress.org
© 2010 by New York University
All rights reserved

Library of Congress Cataloging-in-Publication Data

Cepeda, María Elena.
Musical imagiNation : U.S.-Colombian identity and the Latin music boom /
María Elena Cepeda.
p. cm.
Includes bibliographical references and index.
ISBN-13: 978-0-8147-1691-5 (cl : alk. paper)
ISBN-10: 0-8147-1691-1 (cl : alk. paper)
ISBN-13: 978-0-8147-1692-2 (pb : alk. paper)
ISBN-10: 0-8147-1692-x (pb : alk. paper)
1. Music—Social aspects—United States—History—20th century. 2. Popular music—Florida—Miami—History and criticism. 3. Popular music—Colombia—History and criticism. 4. Music trade—Florida—Miami. 5. Identity (Psychology) and mass media. I. Title.
ML3917.U6C46   2010
781.64089'68861075938—dc22   2009030334

New York University Press books are printed on acid-free paper,
and their binding materials are chosen for strength and durability.
We strive to use environmentally responsible suppliers and materials
to the greatest extent possible in publishing our books.

Manufactured in the United States of America

c 10 9 8 7 6 5 4 3 2 1
p 10 9 8 7 6 5 4 3 2 1

Contents

Acknowledgments		ix
Introduction: Colombian Connections: Tracing the Boundaries of the Colombian Musical ImagiNation		1
1	*La crisis colombiana*: Contextualizing the Political Moment	18
2	A Miami Sound Machine: Deconstructing the Latin(o) Music Boom of the Late 1990s	35
3	Shakira as the Idealized Transnational Citizen: Media Perspectives on *Colombianidad* in Transition	61
4	*Florecita rockera*: Gender and Representation in Latin(o) American Rock and Mainstream Media	87
5	The Colombian *Vallenato acá y allá*: Allegory for a Musical ImagiNation	111
6	The Colombian Transcultural Aesthetic Recipe: Music Video in the "New" American Studies	134
	Afterword: U.S.-Colombian Popular Music and Identity: Acknowledging the Transnational in the National	164
	Notes	169
	References	217
	Discography	243
	Index	245
	About the Author	255

Para Jorge y Elena Patricia Cepeda,
por siempre recordarme que el sancocho es bueno
Y para Rogelio Miñana Climent,
por dejarme volar sin perderme de vista

Acknowledgments

> I was never anything but these two countries.
> —Junot Díaz

As a U.S. Latina with a doctoral degree, I am acutely and at times painfully cognizant of my privileged status as a statistical anomaly. To this end, I write these words in recognition of the fact that this text and the years of preparation leading up to its publication would not have been the same without the critical support of many cherished mentors, colleagues, friends, and family. Primero que nada, I offer my thanks and appreciation to Frances R. Aparicio, whose intelligence, mentoring, and generosity not only initially convinced me to pursue my graduate studies at the University of Michigan but who also did much to keep me there, despite all of the obstacles. I can't thank you enough for your brilliant example, friendship, and willingness to advocate on behalf of myself and countless other junior Latina and Latino scholars. Warm thanks are also due to Margarita de la Vega-Hurtado, who supported me from the very beginning and who in the process became a true friend and a generous intellectual resource for todo lo colombiano, en particular todo lo costeño. In addition, I would like to extend a very sincere thank you to former Rackham Dean Earl Lewis of the University of Michigan for the fellowship that made my time in Miami possible and to Williams College for its generous logistical and financial support throughout this process.

My lifelong love of and fascination with Miami was only enhanced by the consideration of individuals like Michael Collier and Eduardo Gamarra of Florida International University, who allowed me to participate in one of the Colombian Studies Institute's inaugural projects, as well as Natalia Franco and John Britt Hunt, who kindly shared their scholarship on the Miami Colombian community. Thanks also to Jorge Caycedo for his warm guidance and his professional wisdom through some very difficult times. And to my Miami family: Danilo Alonso, Atty Alonso, Annette Alonso, and Robert Franzino, les doy las gracias de todo corazón, y les extraño mucho.

To my Williams College colleagues in Latina/o Studies and American Studies; to the incomparable Linda Saharczewski; to the excellent Williams College Sawyer Library staff, Eric Zinner, Emily Park, Ciara McLaughlin; and to my anonymous readers at New York University Press, I offer my thanks for your enthusiasm, professionalism, and collegiality. To my students past and present, I deeply appreciate the many lessons that you have taught me, and I thank you for enjoying our YouTube and iPod classroom sessions (almost) as much as I do.

I also offer my sincere gratitude to all of the very special friends, colleagues, professional supporters, and students who, in their own unique ways and at various stages in my career, have contributed to this text and to my scholarly development as a whole. I am keenly aware that without the groundbreaking intellectual labor, mentoring, wholehearted support, and skilled technological assistance of many of you, this project would not have been possible: Carlos Alamo-Pastrana, Jorge Arévalo Mateus, Juan Baena Parra, Daniel Berlin, Holly Cashman, Mari Castañeda, C. Ondine Chavoya, Mark Clague, Arlene Dávila, Héctor Fernández L'Hoeste, Raúl Fernández, Joyce Foster, Fabiola Franco, Celeste Fraser Delgado, Luz Gómez, Michelle Habell-Pallán, Travis Jackson, Jared Johnson, Ana Nájera-Mendoza, Suzanne Oboler, Deborah Pacini Hernández, Marcela Peacock-Villada, Gail Newman, Viviana Quintero, Wendy Raymond, P. Lyn Richards, Dan Ríos, Stéphane Robolin, David Román, Clara Román-Odio, Andrés Solorza, Arturo Steely, Juana Suárez, Angharad Valdivia, Deborah Vargas, Peter Wade, Dorothy Wang, and the late Lise Waxer. Much appreciation is also due to my Williams colleagues Roger Kittleson and Carmen Whalen for their thorough and constructive critiques of an earlier version of this manuscript and, above all, for their generous mentorship. I would especially like to thank Rebecca Brown Sharayera, Janet Chang, Galo González, Cheryl González-Loesch, Cassandra González-Loesch, Rommel Guadalupe, Frank Guridy, Deborah Parédez, Mérida Rúa, Wilson Valentín-Escobar, and Armando Vargas for their invaluable friendship and unconditional support. From Ohio to Michigan to D.C. to Florida to Minnesota to Massachusetts, you have all taught me some unforgettable lessons in community and kindness. Muchísimas gracias también to Dolores Inés Casillas for being the most amazingly generous colega y hermana, for sharing my ongoing obsession with Latinas in the popular media, for understanding the unique joys and trials of life como la hija del medio, and most of all for her sense of justice, and to Annette Alonso for her willingness to transform herself into a colombiana adoptiva and to act as my second pair of eyes all around Miami, for her astute observations regarding Latinidad, but most of all for her years of unwavering friendship. Gracias, hermanas. I am so very fortunate to have crossed paths with you both.

Much love and thanks to the transnational family that inspired this project, which includes multiple generations living in Canada, Chile, Colombia, Spain, and the United States. You have taught me more about the singular intricacies of migration than any book. Mil gracias a José Miñana Costa, María Luisa Climent Catalá, y a toda mi gente valenciana por su generosidad y cariño, y por hacerme sentir en familia desde el momento que nos conocimos. Visca Valéncia! Mil gracias en especial a mi prima María Eugenia Kaspersson por su ayuda en conseguir materiales en Barranquilla, y a toda mi querida familia en Barranquilla, Ontario, Orlando, Miami, Popayán, Queens y Tulúa por su amor y apoyo a larga y corta distancia. Un abrazo bien fuerte a Jorge, Anna Cristina, Laura, Daniela, Gabriella and Jesse Báez, as well as George A. and Diane Cepeda for reminding me in so many ways, both grand and seemingly insignificant, of what is most important. Cariños también a Mico, Diego, and the dear departed pero nunca olvidada Cristina, my beloved canine writing partners. Finally: mil gracias to my parents, Jorge and Elena Patricia Cepeda, the barranquillero immigrants who have taught me the value of family and education, along with so many lessons in transnational sacrifice, and to Rogelio Miñana, for gently helping me to question it all and sort out the priorities, for patiently adjusting to the way that I dream out loud, and for simply being the best partner and advocate possible. Et vullc mes que mai. I am so grateful to all of you for your continuous support of my dreams and ideas (aun cuando temen que sí, esta vez puede que me haya sollado de verdad). No sé de dónde sacaron tanto amor, paciencia y generosidad. Pero mejor no cuestionarlo ... simplemente sigo quiérendoles harto a todos.

Every day, Manny's Van Lines makes the four-hour trip between Orlando and Miami, with one brief break at the Port St. Lucie rest stop, located approximately halfway down Florida's 95-South corridor. The journey begins around 6:00 a.m., when one of Manny's drivers picks you up at your door in Orlando, and ends several hours later (it's never just four) when you are dropped off at the door of your choosing in Miami. In March 2000, I made my first trip back to Miami in several years in order to attend a conference and to visit a friend from graduate school and her family. Once settled into Manny's Van, I people-watched my riding companions, engaged in some polite conversation, and succumbed to the highway billboard onslaught. And then I promptly fell asleep.

    I could have sworn I woke up in Barranquilla, Colombia.

    (I found out later that it was actually the Miami suburb of Hialeah.)

    I moved down to Miami a few months later.

Introduction

Colombian Connections: Tracing the Boundaries of the Colombian Musical ImagiNation

Colombia conexión	Colombia Connection
Bañada por dos mares y el Orinoco	Bathed by two oceans and the Orinoco
Café, café, café petroleo	Coffee, coffee, coffee petroleum
Ciudades amables	Friendly cities
Mujeres lindas	Pretty women
Te vas, te vas	You're leaving, you're leaving
Y no la olvidas	And you won't forget her [Colombia]
Pobre Colombia detenta	Poor Colombia holds on
Desnuda, fría y hambrienta	Naked, cold, and hungry
Diario tan descontenta	Every day so unhappy
Con la crisis turbulenta	With the turbulent crisis
Pero el bien germina ya . . .	But the good's already germinating
Germina ya	Already germinating

— Aterciopelados, *"Colombia Conexión"* (Colombian connection)

¡Oh, gloria inmarcesible!	Oh, unfading glory!
¡Oh, júbilo inmortal!	Oh, immortal joy!
En surcos de dolores	In furrows of pain
El bien germina ya	The good already germinates

—Chorus, National Hymn of the Republic of Colombia

Within violence-plagued Colombia, art and politics have drawn ever closer in recent years, seemingly in tandem with the nation's decades-old political and economic crises. Shortly after the international success of the Colombian singer-songwriter Shakira's 1998 album *Dónde están los ladrones?* (Where are the thieves?), Colombia's then-president Andrés Pastrana in fact hailed the beloved pop star, among other Colombian artists, as "emblems of a new national era" and as living examples of the work ethic and positive attitude necessary for Colombia to overcome its troubles.[1] (That a *rock en español* band like Bogotá's Aterciopelados, a group that has dedicated itself to problematizing any facile notion of contemporary *colombianidad*, would adopt a parallel perspective was most likely not what Colombian political elites had in mind, however.) The irony is that popular music *has* in a sense become Colombia's symbolic salvation, an "antidote" to the crisis both within the nation's geopolitical borders and among its U.S-based community.[2] In one such example, the track "*Colombia Conexion*" (Colombia connection), from its 1995 album, *El Dorado*, the group Aterciopelados challenges rigid, state-sanctioned notions of *colombianidad*, as evidenced in the song's structure and patriotic thematics.[3] Whereas the song's coda contains an unmistakable metatextual reference to the chorus of the Colombian national anthem ("*el bien germina ya / germina ya*"), the verses figuratively embody another means of "doing being Colombian,"[4] as they simultaneously give voice to the Colombian (trans)national subject. As it recalls both the illicit drug trade and a sense of *patria*, the pointed double entendre contained within the phrase "Colombia[n] connection" also appears in the similarly named *Conexión Colombia* portion of the popular Colombian newsweekly *Semana*. An Internet and print media feature dedicated to "connecting thousands of Colombians in the exterior with their country," "*Conexión Colombia*" showcases an ever-changing selection of Colombian musical genres, past and present. Both of these "connections" therefore foreground the centrality of popular music as an arbitrator of the "imaginary topographies" of memory, identity, and place for *colombianos*, particularly among those claiming multiple cultural and state-sanctioned citizenships.[5] Under the new Colombian legislation passed in 1991, I, like thousands of other U.S.-born offspring of Colombian immigrants, became eligible for dual citizenship. Until then, my personal claims to *colombianidad*, or "Colombianness," were rooted in both default and desire: language, music, food, wordless gestures learned from my parents, a sense of time and space molded by letters, phone calls, vacation visits, and trinkets, and an endless list of "deterritorialized memories."[6] This is a widespread experience among Latin(o) Americans residing in the United States: a singular duality marked by geographic proximity and a (neo)colonial status both past (under various European powers) and present (under the United States).

Colombians are among the latest mass arrivals in U.S. locales like Miami, the current epicenter of the Latin(o) music and entertainment industries, in which the impact of international politics on everyday life reflects the future direction of contemporary global urban centers.[7] As a city that consistently ranks among the nation's poorest, yet is often paradoxically cast among the culturally richest, Miami has been forced to parlay its most valuable "raw materials," specifically its natural beauty and multicultural citizenry, into saleable commodities. Indeed, inasmuch as issues of resources and politics figure prominently within Miami's competitive ethnoracial labor market, ethnically defined citizenship continues to present ever greater challenges to conventional notions of local and global citizenship. In sharp contrast to the models of time-space compression that dominate current debates on globalization, Florida's largest metropolis also exemplifies the continued salience of local geographies in the face of the supposed wholesale deterritorialization of communications media.[8]

The cultural labor of the racialized majority has thus assumed considerable market import in global centers like Miami, perhaps most visibly concentrated in the city's thriving Latin(o) American music industry. In part because of its broad popular appeal and its ambivalent social, cultural, and ethnoracial location vis-à-vis the mainstream U.S. music industry, today's Latin(o) music industry and its products remain something of a mystery to most academics, including many of those whose own scholarship focuses on music produced and consumed by Latin(o) Americans. A thorough cataloguing of existing publications in the the field of Latin(o) American popular music reveals a pronounced tendency for scholars to focus on genres more clearly defined as "ethnic" musical forms that possess unambiguous Latin(o) American cultural roots (such as salsa and *merengue*, among others), notwithstanding the centrality of rock, pop, and hip-hop in the everyday lives of so many U.S. Latinos, regardless of language preference. In this respect, despite the celebratory discourse of hybridity endemic to much of current Latin(o) popular music scholarship, the need to remember that "American" history is intrinsically linked to Latino history, and vice versa, persists.[9] This is a point of particular concern, given the disproportionate impact that the historiographic configuration of more "commercial" Latin(o) music has on our collective understanding of *all* Latino music and cultural expression, despite considerable scholarly reluctance to view these forms as legitimate objects of critical attention. These attitudes reflect not only a bias against the critical analysis of popular music and its overtly commercial nature but also a persistent prejudice against an artistic form consumed primarily by women. Also pertinent to the study of Latin(o) American popular music is a consideration of the complex transcultural shifts between what are often framed as purely "folkloric" musical expressions and more identifiably commercial forms. As the example of the *vallenato moderno* superstar Carlos

Vives attests, the representation of folklore as a purely static, as opposed to "lived," space belies the quotidian realities of both producers and consumers of such genres.[10]

Yet, by its very nature, popular culture conceals, rather than accentuates, its ideological and political potential. As Joke Hermes succinctly observes, "[popular culture's] very strength is that it is not a manifesto." Often framed as a simplistic question of personal preference and/or mere entertainment, popular music—and popular culture in general—embodies an inclusive invitation for self (re)invention, as it "make[s] the presence known of those who are not in positions of direct political or economic power . . . [it] provide[s], within limits, an alternative sense of community, one not provided by social institutions such as political parties, trade unions, sports clubs, or the family" (or, I would add, traditional constructs of the nation).[11]

Given music's prominent role in the diasporic experience, as well as the reality that approximately one in ten Colombians currently live outside his or her homeland,[12] popular culture in general and popular music in particular emerged as the logical object of inquiry for this study. As perhaps the most facile mark of Colombian identity besides language and as a communal site for the negotiation of commonsense notions of race, class, gender, sexuality, and nation, music provides a collective space for imagining *colombianidad* outside traditional geopolitical borders. Equally significant are the ways in which these imagined alternatives exist (if not thrive) in a context largely divorced from the scandal and shame of the drug-trafficking trade and civil war with which contemporary Colombia is primarily associated. In this way, Colombian popular music effectuates a "fantasy of [trans]national unity"[13] among the citizens of a country in which partisan politics and government have become virtually synonymous with violence and corruption in recent decades. My fascination with popular music is thereby indelibly marked by the feelings of urgency and resignation shared by many U.S.-Colombians who fear that every trip back may be their last, that permanent immigration to the United States is the only option, and that perhaps this nation bound by the weakest of states may even cease to exist in the near future. These emotions, attitudes, and the "vanishing [sense of] home" that marks them distinguish Colombia's most recent migrants from previous South American migratory waves and lend particular credence and relevancy to present research on Colombian popular music and the transnational media "memory industries" in general.[14]

An important note regarding terminology: I deliberately employ the term "U.S.- Colombian" throughout this monograph. The label "Colombian

American" has become increasingly problematic, given that as a geographic designator it is redundant (America is a continent, not a country), and all Colombians are therefore already Americans, whether or not they live in the United States. As one of Suzanne Oboler's *colombiana* informants observed: "I only know one America. Its geographical position may be North America, Central America, or South America. . . . So, if they [the United States] take the name of the entire continent for their country, what is left for ours? What is the name of the continent that Colombia is on?" However, in accord with Ella Shohat, I do not wish to promote the mistaken notion that such dual formulations signal a form of pseudo-egalitarianism, despite their frequent circulation within progressive circles.[15] In somewhat analogous fashion, I employ the term "Latin(o) music" throughout, given its ability to foreground the tensions between the designators "Latin" (the label that many of the mainstream media use) and "Latino" (a grassroots term utilized by many U.S. Latinos themselves), without erasing either. In this regard, it is vital that we consider the symbolic gaps between the category of "Latin music" and the social groups that presumably produce and consume these forms.[16]

To borrow a phrase from Lila Abu-Lughod, my role as "halfie" observer/participant/critic has required that I "travel uneasily between speaking 'for' and speaking 'from,'"[17] thereby destabilizing the standard distinction between self and other so integral to the traditional anthropological exercise. Indeed, my subject position as the U.S.-educated daughter of two *barranquillero*[18] immigrants has often come into play, particularly as this project has demanded the constant movement across physical, affective, and discursive space and has repeatedly required that I mindfully negotiate the space between two countries: that which I officially inhabit and that which I have imagined and occasionally visited since childhood. Paradoxically, my own intimate relationship to Colombian popular music and its seemingly transparent character has at times frustrated my attempts at critical analysis and demanded that I attempt to render the familiar "strange."[19] This inevitably vexed process has in turn provided convincing evidence of music's singular tendency to "conceal its processes and communicate nothing/everything 'directly.'"[20] As a Latina exposed, via mainstream U.S. media and higher education, to primarily middle-class, mainstream Anglo feminisms, I have also struggled with the "single axis framework" upon which much of U.S. feminist theory is based, in which gender and ethnoracial identity are represented as mutually exclusive constructs. Long accustomed to, though never comfortable with, the artificial choice between allegiance to my gender and fidelity to my ethnoracial subject position, I have found Colombian popular music in particular, and my (often contradictory) reactions to its overtly masculinist content, a challenging subject of study given my hybrid socialization. As a result, I do not present my readings of Colombian popular music or the transnational community from which it emerges as monolithic. Rather, I strive to avoid the tendencies toward tropicalization, methodological nationalism, and presentism existent in much conventional scholarship on Latin(o) popular music and migration.[21]

Theoretical and (Inter)Disciplinary Orientations

My critical approach toward the study of Colombian popular music, ethnoracial identity, gender, and the transnational U.S.-Colombian community is clearly indebted to the eloquent model of U.S. cultural studies put forth by José David Saldívar. Approaching culture as a "social force," Saldívar subverts the "stable, naturalized, and hegemonic status of the national" (read: white/Anglo) in his analysis of the habitual conflation of Anglo identity and mainstream U.S. culture. Ultimately, he promotes popular cultural production as a tool with which to (re)imagine the nation as a site of multiple cognitive maps and in which the traditional nation-state fails to offer any singular model of cultural identity.[22] Perhaps most notably, however, this empowering transnational re-visioning of U.S. Cultural Studies, a perspective that foregrounds Chicano and Latino cultural agency, wisely recognizes the pivotal, if at times unacknowledged, role that Latino and Chicano Studies have played and will undoubtedly continue to play in American and Area Studies' current movement toward the transnational. Indeed, this metacritical awareness of Ethnic Studies' longstanding contributions to American and Area Studies informs my readings of ethnoracial identity, gender, and the transnational throughout.

Contemporary Media Studies scholarship has likewise played a pivotal role in the conceptualization of the central problematics and recurrent themes of my research. As Stuart Hall has noted, media texts "offer a way of imposing an imaginary coherence on the experience of dispersal and fragmentation, which is the history of all enforced diasporas." It was in this fashion that the dialogic relationship among contemporary Colombian popular music, identity, social realities, and the ideological labor of media initially became apparent to me, often at junctures in which issues of race and ethnicity loomed just beneath the "'epidermic surface' of the text."[23] Per Hall, I also pursue an analytical framework that departs from traditional hypodermic models of musical and media spectatorship in that I do not assume any transparent relationship between producerly intent and individual or communal interpretation.

The contemporary globalized media industry is frequently cited and at times reviled for its vital role in the process of identity formation. Indeed, the deterritorializing effects of media can contribute to the degradation of local communities and foster "self-entertaining nomads."[24] Nevertheless, I concur with Ella Shohat and Robert Stam's claim that an increasingly multicentered media may just as easily foment the introduction of alternative discourses, representations, and cross-cultural community-building strategies. In the context of today's rapidly expanding transnational media outlets, convergence, and the increasingly dispersed nature of popular musical meaning, I assert that not only does a specifically *cross-media* stance prove critical but that this approach is further enhanced by a feminist, transnational perspective.[25]

Aside from an explicitly cross-media orientation, my analysis adheres to Teun van Dijk's sociopolitical model of critical discourse analysis (CDA). This approach foregrounds the place of public discourse, which itself is frequently shaped by mass media, in the (re)creation of and challenges to societal dominance, or a "political critique of those responsible for [discourse's] perversion in the reproduction of dominance and inequality." According to van Dijk's CDA model, discourse and dominance are linked in two significant ways: directly through the invocation of dominance in text and speech and indirectly via the influence of discourse on the minds of individuals. Differential patterns of access to everyday public discourse thus figure prominently in this relationship. Critical discourse analysis focuses on "real-world" social inequities and abuses, and specifically on the brands of quotidian expression systematically naturalized in verbal and written language. In short, CDA strives to render everyday language and the power dynamics embedded with it more concrete.[26] Such a perspective is equally applicable to the realm of musical discourse. In this respect, Susan McClary observes that music, much like other forms of social discourse, does not merely echo an immutable, external reality. Rather, as the examples cited throughout this text attest, social reality *emerges* as the product of music as discursive practice.[27]

Illuminated through the lenses of cross-media and critical discourse analysis, the prevalence of military metaphors in popular press articles on Colombian artists is exemplified by the Colombian artist Shakira's declaration that she "is not the only soldier in this battle" (figure 1.1). The metaphor emerges as a particularly disturbing motif, especially when juxtaposed against the relative media invisibility of the United States' extensive military, financial, and intelligence involvement in the Colombian conflict. Significantly, however, the employment of military metaphors is not a unilateral tendency. Not only do those in the mainstream media apply such language to Colombians, but Colombians themselves, as the Shakira example illustrates, adopt this language in their own self-depictions. To this end, I am reminded of a colleague's reaction during the initial phase of my research: he was puzzled, if not openly disturbed, by the usage of the word "war" in my description of contemporary Colombian popular music's relationship to Colombian culture and identity at large. While I certainly appreciated his critique, I left the "war" as is, for now more than ever, I find it indicative of the mindset of many *colombianos*, who, both *acá* (here) and *allá* (there), negotiate the daily social realities of a violence that they struggle to overcome, if at the very least in musical or symbolic terms.[28]

Reflective of the populace that inhabits the contact zone of Miami, *Musical ImagiNation* portrays a diasporan community whose narratives of identity are based primarily on routes as well as roots, and more often confined to the realm of the imagination than to lived experience.[29] Indeed, the very spelling of this book's title underscores the intimate and ultimately necessary relationship between a deliberately constructed sense of national belonging (what we individually and collectively *imagine* as the nation and our place in it) and the nation itself. Here, the concept of the "musical imagiNation" borrows from Arjun Appadurai's seminal work regarding the symbiotic relationship between new media and the imagination in the globalized context. As Appadurai argues, present-day transmigrants are intimately familiar with the mass-mediated imagery that dictates as much as it reflects their movements "homeward" and back. (Take, for example, the appearance of "Colombian" *telenovelas* and television channels locally produced and readily available to Miami residents and the success of primetime television series like ABC's *Ugly Betty*, NBC/Telemundo's *Sin tetas no hay paraíso* [Without tits there is no paradise], and the FOX network's reality show *Nothing but the Truth*—all of which are based on Colombian television concepts.) Furthermore, Appadurai maintains that the imagination assumes a different function in today's deterritorialized "communities of sentiment": as an "organized field of social practices, a form of work (in the sense of both labor and culturally organized practice), and a form of negotiation between sites of agency (individuals) and globally defined fields of possibility . . . [t]he imagination is now central to all forms of agency, is itself a social fact, and is the key component of the new global order."[30] Much like music itself, the Colombian "musical imagiNation" is understood, if not explicitly expressed, as both noun *and* verb.

Figure 1.1. The October 2002 cover of the popular Spanish-language magazine *Cristina (La Revista)* featuring the Colombian artist Shakira. The cover caption describes Shakira as having "Colombia behind her back" and quotes her assertion that "I am not the only soldier in this battle." Notably, Shakira is patriotically referred to in the accompanying article as "*la mujer bandera*" (the flag woman), a moniker that explicitly recalls the trope of woman as nation.

| 9

A collective activity embedded in a definitive sense of place(lessness), the "musical imagiNation" is rooted in the assertion that the Colombian political and social crisis of the late 1990s and the early twentieth-first century has profoundly shaped, if not outrightly provoked, a veritable popular music renaissance. As a result, this reawakening has rendered Colombian popular music, as the locus for the "everyday social project" of self-imagination,[31] a powerful arbitrator of memory and identity among the Colombian diaspora. The recent swell of artistic activity has precipitated significant shifts in the communal meanings attached to Colombian identity or in the novel *possibilities* now attached to it within the U.S.-Colombian community. As Hall has effectively argued, these acts of "imaginary political re-identification [and] re-territorialization"[32] have in turn facilitated the emergence of the popular artistic counterpolitics examined here.

This is to not suggest, however, that we are presently experiencing a strictly postnational moment or that transnational dynamics necessarily constitute (un)consciously resistant or celebratory processes, as some scholars have asserted. To the contrary, despite the lesser importance ascribed to the traditional nation-state in this formulation, its ongoing role in the lives of transmigrants is not to be underestimated, as the numerous critiques with regard to this aspect of Appadurai's work, particularly among social scientists, attest.[33] In this respect, I adhere to Luis Eduardo Guarnizo's position that transmigrants do not generally seek alternatives to traditional nation-state structures but rather pursue what they consider a more advantageous multiple or dual citizen status within existing governmental structures. This vision translates into a theorization of U.S.-Colombian popular culture rooted in the persistent tensions between "containment and resistance" and mindful of the fact that transmigrant identities forged "from below," while not intrinsically oppositional, are in fact quite distinct from those constructed "from above."[34] Per this perspective, contemporary transnational media and music serve as particularly rich sites for an analysis of the symbolic as well as the material impacts of the global culture industries.

Gender and the (Trans)National in the Study of Latin(o) American Popular Music

Current studies of Colombian popular music forms tend to focus exclusively on the nation's autochthonous genres (such as *vallenato*, *carrilera*, *cumbia*, *bambuco*, and *champeta*) or local manifestations of pan-Latino genres such as salsa. As the late Lise Waxer aptly noted in her review of Peter

Wade's influential *Music, Race and Nation: Música Tropical in Colombia*, even the most comprehensive contemporary studies of Colombian popular music fail to include rock. (Tellingly, until recently the industry label "Latin music" failed to encompass rock music produced and consumed by Latin[o] Americans, regardless of language.)[35] Indeed, aside from fictional works such as Andrés Caicedo's *¡Que viva la música!* (originally published in 1977), no scholarly monographs on Colombian rock music exist. Exactly why is Colombian rock, unlike the nation's other popular genres, consistently bypassed as a subject of intellectual inquiry? Is this reluctance in some part the result of a lingering sense among many Latin Americanists that within the Latin American context, rock serves as little more than an imperialist export from the "first world" to the "third"? Or might we attribute this hesitation to the long-standing stereotype of the "apolitical" popular music performer (and fan)? If so, adopting this one-dimensional depiction of rock's historic role in Latin America runs the risk of erasing rock's contestatory usages (both past and present) within the region, thereby perpetuating existing myths that portray popular-music fans as passive receptacles, and simultaneously locating rock as the sole property of the United States, as opposed to the global cultural landscape.[36] As such, the *rock en español* genre, and central Colombian figures such as Andrea Echeverri and Shakira, figure prominently in this study.

Another substantial theoretical gap looming in much existing Colombian popular music scholarship is a lack of critical attention to issues of gender. Given the irrefutable links between gender and migration, as well as the prominence of Colombian artists such as Shakira, Andrea Echeverri, Totó la Momposina, the late Soraya, and others, a consideration of music's gendered language and structures emerges as one of the primary emphases of this book. As McClary has observed, "music does not just passively reflect society; it also serves as a public forum within which various models of gender organization (along with many other aspects of social life) are asserted, adopted, contested, and negotiated."[37] To this end, my overarching interpretation of gender within Colombian popular music hinges on a major assumption of feminist popular culture studies: namely that, as its primary subjects, consumers, and creators, women experience a different relationship to popular culture than men, just as popular music constitutes the terrain upon which many of the contradictions and complexities of contemporary feminist movements are enacted.[38] These theories of gendered difference are likewise applicable to a consideration of women's relationship to the nation, as "[n]ationalism becomes . . . radically constitutive of people's identities, through social contests that are frequently violent and always gendered."

The tendency toward framing diasporic narratives in unmarked (i.e., deracinated, ungendered, declassed) fashion continues to pervade the scholarship on the subject, in effect naturalizing male diasporic experience. To this end, I perceive the Colombian nation and its diaspora as gendered constructs fashioned in part out of "masculinized memory," just as nationalisms (and *trans*nationalisms) have historically surfaced on the basis of race, ethnicity, sexuality, religion, and culture.[39]

Conventional images of women and the nation have often revolved around the representation of women as the traditional, backwards "body" of the nation, as suggested by terms such as *madre patria*, or "mother country." These depictions stand in stark contrast to those of men, who are frequently represented as the forward-moving agents of national progress. This male/female, intellect/body dichotomy is of particular relevance to the study of Latin(o) American popular music and gender, given the region's long history of feminization through colonization. As bell hooks reminds us, sexuality has long served as a source of the gendered metaphors of colonization. Furthermore, sexuality does not merely provide the colonizing metaphor; it also contributes to the colonization process (and the process of national construction) itself.[40] Thus, in the neocolonial context, women's subordinate status entails their double (or, as in the case of women of color, triple) marginalization.

A primary goal of this book is to move beyond the existing, highly descriptive Spanish-language studies that promote neat chronologies of a given genre and instead strive to achieve a representation of the contemporary *rock en español* and *vallenato* genres and marketing formats that more accurately reflects their transcultural, transnational nature.[41] Another frequent theme that arose throughout the course of my research, particularly with regard to the Colombian Caribbean, is the roundly criticized concept of "salvage anthropology," often referred to in Colombia as "*el rescate de lo nuestro*," or "the rescue of what's ours." In the years since this theoretical stance has fallen out of favor, it has been occasionally adopted, and looked kindly upon, by so-called community insiders, prompting critiques of "the differential de facto development in the post-Said era of this idea about the (moral) authority to represent."[42] My intention here, however, is not to engage in the anthropology of rescue, nor do I wish to lay claim to any authority by virtue of my communal affiliations; rather, I promote what Virginia Domínguez has artfully described as a "politics of love and rescue."[43] As such, what I ultimately aim to realize in this book on Colombian popular music and (trans)national identity is a partial "decolonization at the level of the text."[44] I purposefully label this a partial endeavor for two reasons: first, because of my inevitable intrusion as the primary interpreter, author, and editor of this study, and second, and more significantly, because this scholarship remains partial due to the insufficient input of perspectives other than my own regarding Miami's Colombian community.

Throughout this book I present a cross-media analysis that is emphatically transnational in focus and ever mindful of the subordinate status of Ethnic Studies vis-à-vis both Area and American Studies. Given the far-reaching impacts of globalization on the creation, reception, and consumption of Latin(o) American popular artistic production and media, I assert that contemporary studies of current Colombian popular culture demand a transnational framework, despite (and, indeed, because of) the "transient and transnational" character of Colombian musicians, producers, everyday consumers, and fans.[45] Furthermore, this book participates in a more general dialogue with current scholarship on inter-Latin(o) American cultural dynamics,[46] while specifically addressing the need for a more nuanced theorization of hegemonic forces that exist both within and outside the Miami-based Latin(o) music industry.

(U.S.-) Colombians and the Transnational Miami Music Industry

In *Musical ImagiNation*, I argue that Colombian popular music provides a common space for imagining and enacting Colombian identity outside traditional national borders and in ways not overtly shaped by the scandal and shame of the drug-trafficking trade and violence with which contemporary Colombia is primarily associated. Anchored in a cross-media analysis of popular music and media, I assert that the Colombian political and social crisis of the late 1990s and the early twenty-first century foregrounds Colombian popular music and the "nationalizing moments"[47] that it precipitates as a powerful arbitrator of memory and transnational identity in the United States and Colombia. Under the auspices of the Miami-driven Latin(o) music "boom" of the late twentieth and early twenty-first centuries, I focus on issues of gender, ethnoracial identity, and transnational migration in the work of the Colombian recording artists Shakira, Andrea Echeverri (of the group Aterciopelados), and Carlos Vives. As I demonstrate here, the music and the transnational public personas of each of these prominent artists highlight a sizable shift in the communal meanings attached to Colombian identity both in the United States and in Latin America.

While prioritizing questions of ethnoracial identity, gender, and migration, *Musical ImagiNation* simultaneously engages the current debates in

American, Latin American, and U.S. Ethnic Studies regarding the academic location and institutional politics of transnational research, a key scholarly debate of recent years. In the first scholarly monograph dedicated to the rapidly growing U.S.-Colombian community, I also address the more general need for interdisciplinary scholarship that addresses the U.S. population's rapidly changing demographics as it focuses on one of the largest "new" Latino communities, U.S.-Colombians. *Musical ImagiNation* addresses a noteworthy gap in existing Media Studies scholarship in its focus on the distinct complexities of Spanish-language and U.S. Latino-centered transnational media and popular culture. This book therefore proves unique in its examination of the Miami-based, transnational Latin(o) music industry at the level of both industry production and performance.

Colombia's singular geographical position as the only South American nation to possess both Atlantic and Pacific coastlines and its rugged topography have contributed to the intense regionalism within its borders, which in turn has fostered its highly diverse musical production. These geographical circumstances hampered intranational transportation and communication in Colombia until relatively late in the twentieth century, resulting in an absence of cultural homogeneity that has ultimately hindered the establishment of an "overarching framework of musical values."[48] Colombia in general and its Caribbean coast in particular have thus emerged as ideal sites of inquiry into a postmodern hybridity further complicated by the diasporic movement of bodies, cultural constructs, and expressive forms, from south to north and back again. Indeed, as James Clifford has written, "The empowering paradox of diaspora is that dwelling *here* assumes a solidarity and connection *there*. But *there* is not necessarily a single place or exclusivist nation."[49] The collective labor of reimagining one's communal ties in the Colombian milieu, a process and product that I refer to as the contemporary U.S.-Colombian "musical imagiNation," is similarly rooted in this sense of multiple (and frequently overlapping) temporal, spatial, and social realities.

While chapters 1 and 2 are intended to ground the reader in a sociohistorical context that will help in the interpretation of subsequent chapters, this text is by no means restricted to an exclusively linear reading. Chapter 1 provides a general overview of the ongoing Colombian political crisis and the related history of contemporary Colombian immigration to the United States.[50] Here, I pay particular attention to the current U.S.-Colombian community living in the South Florida-Miami region and the singular political moments[51] that have precipitated their physical displacement to the United States. Deceptively simple, in reality the phrase "political moment" encompasses the complex web of governmental, economic, and sociocultural events that expedited the emergence of an increasingly visible transnational Colombian community by the 1990s.

Chapter 2 examines contemporary representations of Latin(o) music's presence in the United States. Here I emphasize Miami's unique positionality and Colombian music's role in the Latin(o) music industry at the moment of Miami's conversion into a "post-Cuban" city, a moment in which Latin(o) popular music undergoes a critical shift from "invisibility" to a brand of "carefully regulated, segregated visibility."[52] An in-depth examination of the popular music industry during the apex of the "Latin boom," chapter 2 deconstructs the prevailing and largely superficial depictions of the Latin(o) music boom that exist in the popular media. In particular, I foreground the decontexualized, dehistoricized language and subject matter of various recordings, television programs, and popular print media produced, written, and/or performed by non-Latinos and U.S. Latino performers and industry figures alike, with an emphasis on the unique role played by the Miami based entrepreneurs Gloria and Emilio Estefan. Both explicitly and implicitly, the final four chapters are united by the notion that recent shifts within Colombian popular music itself may ultimately be read as a microcosm of contemporary Colombian society and its ongoing struggles, in both metaphoric and concrete terms. These changes have in turn contributed to an expanded understanding of present-day transnational Colombian identity, most specifically regarding notions of ethnicity, race, and gender, both during and immediately following the historical juncture popularly known as the "Latin music boom."

Chapter 3 analyzes the figure of the Colombian pop star and recent Miami immigrant Shakira. Shakira emerges as a public persona and a "radical hybrid"[53] who embodies the interstices between U.S. Latino and Latin American identities. Within the complex epistemology of *Latinidad*, I focus here on the particular moments and processes through which Shakira, a Colombian native, "becomes" a U.S. Latina and to what ends *Latinidad* is thrust upon her. Moreover, I analyze the underlying dynamics of *Latinidad* when treated both as marketing construction *and* as identity signifier. Via my readings of media discourse and Shakira's music, I trace Shakira's somewhat contradictory representation as an idealized transnational citizen at a pivotal moment in the (re)configuration of *colombianidad* and, in a broader sense, *Latinidad* itself.

Chapter 4 centers on Andrea Echeverri, the female lead singer of the Bogotá-based rock band Aterciopelados. Focusing on Echeverri's recordings, music videos performances, and popular print media, I examine the various ways in which Echeverri musically engages constructs of gender, as well as the processes by which she is in turn framed as a gendered subject within the U.S. popular media and music industry. With a focus on contemporary *rock en español* and the recent rise of "alternative" Latin(o) American rock, I trace the ways in which music video, a format traditionally understood as a locus of oppression for both women and individuals of color, is transformed into a site for "new forms of resistance and struggle" in the work of Aterciopelados.[54] I posit that Echeverri, as well as the Miami-based industry in which she maneuvers, exemplifies the music industry's current transformations in accordance with the dictates of globalization, while simultaneously underscoring the gendered/gendering nature of sound itself.[55]

Adhering to the premise that folk culture is broadly understood as a metonym for the nation, chapter 5 treats current reworkings of Colombia's traditional *vallenato* genre, once the exclusive terrain of working-class men of color, as witnessed in the best-selling recordings of the white, upper-class performer Carlos Vives.[56] As a 2002 national survey conducted by the Colombian Ministry of Culture reveals, the *vallenato* music of the nation's northern Caribbean coast, more than any other cultural manifestation and despite its humble beginnings, is what makes Colombians feel most "Colombian." Indeed, an article published in the Bogotá newspaper *El Tiempo* that very year declared that *"La cultura es costeña"* ([Colombian] Culture is coastal), thus highlighting the manner in which, over time, the cultural practices of one region have emerged as an allegory for the nation as a whole.[57] Here I engage in a dialogue with the influential scholarship of the anthropologist Peter Wade regarding music, race, and Colombian national identity, as he delineates the complex processes via which, in Colombia, "[d]iversity does not just break through the official image of homogeneity; it is contained within it."[58] Perhaps more significantly, I argue for a transnational and gender-based approach to the study of contemporary Colombian identity and cultural production. Again, it is in within this framework that the dynamics of Colombian popular music may be viewed as an allegory for the (U.S.) Colombian postcolonial condition, or, as Masao Miyoshi describes it, a moment of intensified colonialism.[59]

Chapter 6 revisits the figure of Shakira in order to assess her *Fijación oral, Volumen I* and *Oral Fixation, Volume II* double-album production and performances in terms of the Freudian metaphors that inform our interpretations of her as a pan-Arab, pan-American figure in the post-9/11 era. Specifically, I address the implications of this focus on Shakira and her *Oral Fixation*(s) at this particular moment in the political and pedagogical trajectory of Latin American, American, Ethnic, and Middle Eastern Studies. Through a cross-media analysis of Shakira's recent music video production, I illustrate how Shakira epitomizes the emancipatory possibilities embedded in the hybrid subject and the homogenized Latina popular icon. As I attest, her status prompts us to question the prevailing frameworks applied to the analysis of contemporary Latin(a) Americans in music video as a means of elucidating the present and future role of Latino Studies in the ongoing transnationalization of U.S. Ethnic and Area Studies. Against the historical and socioeconomic backdrop of the "Latin music boom," I conclude that the individual performers and the counterdiscourses that they (at times unwillingly) engender have ultimately heralded the introduction of new possibilities for imagining *Colombianidad*, mainstream U.S. identity, and the very notion of the nation, both within Latin America and among its U.S.-based diaspora.

1

La crisis colombiana

Contextualizing the Political Moment

Since its inception, the parameters of this project have been constantly defined and redefined by the very histories of violence and displacement that permeate contemporary Colombian history. My long-anticipated visit to Colombia's renowned *vallenato* musical festival had to be canceled due to threats by guerrilla groups. A later trip to Colombia was marked by yet another armed attack against my cousin and his young grandson, the fourth such act of violence against an immediate family member that my young relative had witnessed before entering the first grade. As I completed an initial draft of this text, a large group of family members quickly left Colombia to settle near my family, victims of the nation's failing economy and of increased guerrilla activity in the region where they lived. They have since returned to Colombia (where one of them was kidnapped and shortly thereafter released), only to be replaced by others. Virtually everyone I know in Colombia has had his or her daily activities curbed if not dictated to a marked degree by violence and by the economic and political crisis to which the violence is inextricably linked. And the characteristic Colombian *desconfianza*, or lack of trust, born of these circumstances follows those who relocate to the United States, in turn affecting their willingness to interact with other *colombianos* or to publicly recognize their own national identity at all. While it is a determining factor in the lack of social cohesion among U.S.-Colombians—the vast majority of whom do not participate in the illicit drug trade or other illegal activities—the general *desconfianza* that is partly attributable to the drug-trafficking stereotype has also paradoxically fortified the community's ties to the (imagined) homeland.[1] These factors and many others, familiar to so many Colombians both in South America and *el exterior*,[2] have colored not only my eventual choice of topic but also my political views and scholarly interpretations of the music, artists, critics, fans, and government officials discussed here.

As previously established, Colombians have recently emerged as the largest community of South American origin in the United States and as one of the most dynamically transnational populations of the Western hemisphere. U.S.-Colombians have already had a noteworthy impact on the inter-Latino social, cultural, political, and economic dynamics of major U.S. urban centers like New York and Miami, where Colombian record producers, composers, and musicians played a pivotal role in the so-called Latin(o) music boom of the late 1990s and the first decade of the twenty-first century. Latino Studies scholars have long noted that in-depth analyses of lesser-known yet swiftly expanding U.S. Latino communities such as Colombians illuminate our understanding of more frequently studied Latino populations such as Chicanos, Puerto Ricans, and Cubans. To this end, the expanded interest in the study of the South American diaspora testifies to the efficacy of *Latinidad* as construct.[3]

Despite the relative proliferation of scholarly monographs on U.S. Latino popular music and culture in recent years, a dearth of book-length studies documenting the cultural production of the burgeoning populations known as "new Latinos" persists.[4] Among the second- and third-largest Latino communities in major urban centers such as New York, Los Angeles, Miami, and Houston, among others, new Latino populations function as "mirrors" for larger, more established Latino communities in the same spaces and in this sense prove vital not only to the construction of individual identities but to a more nuanced understanding of *Latinidad* itself. However, the "new Latino" label, while serving as useful demographic shorthand, tends to mask not only the longstanding presence but also the multiple societal contributions of Central, South American, and certain Caribbean immigrant communities. The label thus inadvertently underscores the need to reformulate the ways in which we measure a given community's historical presence in the United States.[5] Nevertheless, while these communities are not as "new" as the 2000 Census data and much existing scholarly literature might lead one to believe, research on the U.S.-Colombians, Guatemalans, Salvadorans, Dominicans, and Ecuadorian communities subsumed under the "new Latinos" label *is* in fact new to U.S. Latin(o) music studies. This is arguably in part a result of these populations' lack of incorporation into the U.S. higher education system and elite networks of knowledge production. For these reasons, and undoubtedly for many more, in recent years the subfield of U.S.-Colombian Studies has just begun to emerge in connection to the broader fields of U.S. Latino Studies, American Studies, Ethnic Studies, Latin American Studies, and Colombian Studies.

For all these reasons, at present U.S.-Colombian Studies is necessarily a transnational endeavor, or what Michael Peter Smith has described as a "shift from place to places, simultaneously and complexly *interconnected*, by intended and unintended consequences."[6] Nevertheless, after decades of relative privilege afforded to the study of external as opposed to internal colonialism within the academy, the current rush to embrace the transnational within Latin American and American Studies, is not without its flaws. In this regard, academia's too often uncritical celebration of the transnational, both as theory and as practice, at times fails to recognize the longstanding contributions of Latino Studies (and, in particular, U.S.-Mexican border studies), to the ongoing "worlding" of American Studies.[7] Ultimately, this theoretical omission symbolically reinscribes the material inequities that permit us the luxury of forgetting that transnational migrants do not function as ethnoracial monoliths. Rather, transmigrant individuals and communities are "situated within various power-knowledge venues and occupy classed, gendered, and racialized bodies in space that immensely complicate the social structure of any kind of 'community,' transnational or otherwise."[8] Moreover, transnational communal networks are generally much longer in the making (and far more complex) than they appear to community outsiders, who at times perceive them as "overnight" phenomena. As the Colombian case well illustrates, transnational community-building practices are perhaps best understood as the socioeconomic, cultural, and psychic survival strategies of a people that has endured many years of sustained crisis.

Although Colombia has suffered due to internal conflict for decades, since the late 1980s Colombia has been further submerged in what many consider a "dirty war" involving opposing guerrilla and paramilitary factions, the state-sponsored military, drug traffickers, and *sicarios*, or hired assassins. Who fights whom and which factions are allied is not always clear, even as Colombia has come under the increasing scrutiny of international and domestic human rights organizations. Perceptions of the gravity of the current political situation vary, and, although few would deny the staggering kidnapping and murder rates, the primary source of the violence is a constant point of contention.

As a result of Colombia's internal conflict, more Colombians suffer from poverty than at any period since the worldwide economic depression of the 1930s, with an estimated 60 to 68 percent living below the poverty line. Figures from 2006 indicate a murder rate of approximately 38 homicides per 100,000 Colombians, down from the 68 murders per 100,000 inhabitants recorded just four years earlier. The numbers of journalists and union leaders murdered have also dropped significantly in recent years, according to Colombian government statistics. However, the country's labor organizers are still the target of more homicides than in any other nation in the world, a sobering fact that has not permitted the Colombian government to escape widespread international criticism for its inaction in this regard. Despite successful Colombian military operations such as the highly visible rescue of former Colombian presidential candidate Ingrid Betancourt and four U.S. citizens in July 2008, more than 700 individuals remained kidnapped prisoners of guerrilla forces as of late 2008. Between 1997 and 2007, roughly 3.8 million Colombians (about 8 percent of the country's population), at least one-third of whom were Afro-Colombian or indigenous, were internally displaced. More than 300,000 new cases of internally displaced individuals were recorded in 2007, with an additional 110,000 instances of displacement noted during the first three months of 2008 alone. Half a million Colombian refugees have also fled to neighboring countries as a result of the ongoing conflict among guerrilla, paramilitary, and government factions. Crimes such as assassinations, extrajudicial executions, forced disappearances, and torture frequently go unpunished.[9]

The inordinate amount of political violence in Colombia is further complicated by the fact that the Colombian nation is fighting a "dirty war." A large number of armed civilians have begun to act as soldiers and policemen, allowing them to commit crimes with less fear of being detected. Conversely, actual army and police force members frequently dress as civilians in order to more easily avoid legal formalities if they are arrested. In addition, members of paramilitary groups often disguise themselves as *guerrilleros* to carry out their missions. These practices constitute central strategies of any "dirty war," in which "dirty" actions "cannot be attributed to persons on behalf of the State because they have been delegated, passed along, or projected upon the confused bodies of armed civilians."[10] As a direct consequence of this violence, Colombia now claims the world's highest homicide rate of a country not at war, as well as a dismal human rights record. According to Mario Murillo, during the 1980s the armed forces and the national police were deemed responsible for approximately 70 to 75 percent of all human rights violations in the country. Since the acceleration of counterinsurgency operations in the mid-1990s, Colombian paramilitary forces have committed an identical percentage of abuses. Guerrilla forces are blamed for 20 to 25 percent of all human rights violations.[11]

With roots dating back to the mid-1960s, Colombia's two primary guerrilla factions (the FARC, or Revolutionary Armed Forces of Colombia, organized in 1964, and the ELN, or the National Liberation Army, organized in 1965) are the remaining leftist combatants in the nation's lengthy history of armed insurrection. Although both of these groups have pledged varying degrees of allegiance to the Communist Party since their inception, many scholars argue that their existence is most accurately traced back to *La Violencia* (The Violence), a period of widespread political violence during the 1940s and 1950s. While frequently represented as little more than a period of entrenched familial and organizational conflict between the rival Conservative and Liberal parties, *La Violencia* is nonetheless inextricably linked to the violence, economic crisis, and pervasive political disenfranchisement within Colombia today.[12]

As of 2004, an estimated 2,000 to 3,000 Colombian men, women, and children were participants in the ELN, an organization primarily known for its repeated sabotage of the oil pipelines located in northeast Colombia. In comparison, the FARC constitutes a far larger force and has quadrupled in size since the early 1990s, with an estimated 15,000 to 20,000 members by 2004. Today, the FARC operates on more than 105 fronts and controls more than 40 percent of Colombia's national territory. This is not to suggest, however, that the guerrilla forces are enjoying increased popularity. Rather, for rural youth in particular, joining the ranks of the FARC, the ELN, or the right-wing paramilitary squads generally known as the AUC (*Autodefensas Unidas de Colombia*) or "paras" is frequently the only viable employment option available. In the more than forty years since its inception, the FARC in particular has witnessed a significant decline in its support among the Colombia peasantry, at least partially as a result of the rise of AUC forces in the regions where the FARC once acted with impunity.[13] This perceptible philosophical shift, however, has proven far more complex; as the historian Marco Palacios observes,

> the guerrillas seem to have renounced the supreme objective of taking power for the purpose of socialist revolution. The spirit of self-sacrifice and moral Puritanism associated with the combatant of Maoist or Guevarist extraction has given way to a pragmatic and professional model. Being a guerrilla has become an organized way of life, a career, with a political track available . . . but [the guerrillas] continue to express social resentments, rebelliousness, and a political anger whose rhetoric, despite the collapse of the Soviet bloc, has some resonance in the face of a political order assumed to be unjust and rotten.[14]

By 1994, Amnesty International was able to verify the existence of a "third actor" in the Colombian conflict in their annual report on political violence in Colombia: the supposedly independent AUC. Since the group's formation in the early 1980s as a means of combating Marxist guerrilla groups, wealthy anti-Communist landowners and drug traffickers have offered the paramilitaries economic aid under the guise of eliminating the guerrilla forces, though each party has its own underlying agenda.[15] Thus, the paramilitaries have come to represent a "marriage of convenience" between the corrupt Colombian military and the factions that constitute its economic support base. The main targets of these groups' aggression are trade unionists, leftist political and social organizations, and peasants. As of 1996, the AUC's political leader, Carlos Castaño, claimed to lead a force of approximately 2,000, guaranteeing the paramilitaries national visibility by the late 1990s. By 2000, the number of AUC troops had climbed to 11,200 (a 460 percent increase in four years). As of 2003, paramilitary forces were said to number between 13,000 and 19,500.

Though historically contained within the nation's rural zones, by the 1990s the *guerrilleros* had gained various urban footholds, and, soon afterwards, paramilitary forces became active in several working-class urban neighborhoods, as well. However, while the leftist guerrillas as well as the right-wing paramilitary groups maintain some ties to the Colombian drug trade, surveys have revealed that paramilitary groups have been involved in more civilian murders and displacements than the guerrillas. As individuals suspected of supporting guerrilla activities, even those involved in unrelated localized political movements are vulnerable to paramilitary retaliation. Moreover, the paramilitary leader Carlos Castaño at one point openly claimed responsibility for 80 percent of Colombia's existing cocaine operations. As a result, in August 2001, the U.S. government officially added the AUC to its list of terrorist organizations.[16]

The alliance among the state military, right-wing paramilitary groups, and drug traffickers working to eliminate what the Colombian government has dubbed the "internal enemy" is responsible for the majority of recorded murders, and by the early twenty-first century paramilitary forces were connected to roughly 80 percent of all politically motivated killings. Despite the fact that roughly 1,000 current AUC members have also served in the Colombian military, including numerous officers, it is only in recent years that the Colombian government has endeavored to publicly condemn the AUC's actions, referring to the paramilitaries as a "terrorist" organization (a classifier of potent significance in the aftermath of 9/11).[17] As Murillo explains, the AUC's relatively late classification as a terrorist organization neatly illustrates the fundamentally political nature of such definitions:

> the presence of the guerrillas provides the state with the justification to declare states of emergency, suspend civil protections, expand the role of the military to include civilian police functions, endorse the use of torture, and wage a war against the popular movement, all while failing to implement the political and economic reforms demanded by the vast majority of the population. Again and again, this is done in the name of national security, restoring order, and defending democracy.[18]

In this context, the "internal enemy" label applied to Colombia's armed guerrillas assumes greater significance given that the bulk of international publicity, most notably that generated within the U.S. media, posits the drug traffickers and the Colombian government as opposing forces, largely neglecting to include paramilitary, military, and guerrilla factions in the equation. This pattern persists, despite the fact that the AUC has reaped considerable economic benefits from its connections to the upper end of the international drug trade and even though *both* the guerrillas and the AUC use drug-trafficking profits to provide soldiers with rations, uniforms, weapons, and the like.[19]

Significantly, Colombia is the number one Latin American recipient of U.S. military aid, accounting for nearly half of U.S. aid to the entire hemisphere, and is currently the third-largest international recipient of U.S. military aid after Israel and Egypt.[20] The amount of total U.S. military aid allotted to Colombia currently numbers nearly $6 billion. Ironically, much of the aid that Colombia receives is in theory earmarked by the United States for use against the drug trade. However, as Giraldo notes, by the late 1990s the majority of these funds were being funneled into efforts to eliminate the guerrilla forces and their popular support base. The clear result of such simplistic policies and the tendency to perceive Colombia's problems as a case of "violence in a vacuum" ultimately casts these parties as the root cause of the Colombian conflict at large, rather than the marked socioeconomic disparities, widespread corruption, and general lack of popular political representation long endured by the majority of the nation's citizens.[21]

The original "Plan Colombia" presented by former Colombian president Andrés Pastrana prior to his election in 1998 ostensibly promoted a focus on what are widely perceived as the true causes of the Colombian conflict: a glar-

Map 1.1. Political map of Colombia

ingly unequal distribution of economic development and political power, as well as the lack of access to basic human necessities endured by much of the population. In contrast, the financial provisions under the Plan Colombia aid package approved during the second Clinton administration included an ominous development: for the first time since the involvement of the United States in Central America in the 1980s, Plan Colombia permitted military aid to be openly applied not only to counternarcotics efforts but also to counterinsurgency strategies. Signed into law by President Bill Clinton in September 2000 and heartily supported by Pastrana, the first incarnation of Plan Colombia provided for $1.32 billion in counternarcotics efforts in the Andean region, including $862 million designated for Colombian military and police forces. U.S. Special Forces were also sent to Colombia for the purposes of training the nation's elite military battalions. For many Colombian human rights advocates, this escalation in the "war on drugs" has served only to increase the number of human rights abuses suffered by Colombian citizens. Furthermore, despite fervent protests by U.S. and Colombian citizens alike, Plan Colombia also called for the implementation of a controversial strategy for coca fumigation that so far has had a devastating impact on the health and environmental conditions of southern Colombia's agricultural communities. Thus, for many Colombian progressives, Plan Colombia is less about improving the lot of average Colombians and more about rendering their nation hospitable to multinational economic interests (particularly oil), while leaving the country increasingly militarized. Despite these factors, the U.S. government's 2008–2012 foreign operations budget also earmarked $415 million for Colombia, roughly 80 percent of which was intended for use by the Colombian police and military.[22]

Several theories seek to explain just why this level of violence reigns in Colombia. To some degree, all of them address the weakness of the Colombian state. As many experts on Colombia argue, given the pronounced socioeconomic, political, regional, and ethnoracial differences that divide the nation's citizens, the notion of Colombian nationhood remains tenuous at best. It has been suggested that the lack of a unifying foundational national myth is itself a contributing element in the current conflict, as the widespread belief that Colombians are inherently violent has been substituted in its place. Malcolm Deas maintains that in the case of Colombia, violence against political rivals, whether in or out of power, is possible because it occurs within a state that "has only the most tenuous claim to a monopoly on force"; as such, political violence in contemporary Colombia is best characterized as "a violence between equals, or near-equals."[23] Echoing earlier studies by *violentólogos*, Wolfgang Heinz cites not only the weak Colombian state but also limited popular political participation, lagging agrarian reform, and massive rural-urban migration as factors. A severe lack of foreign capital influx, high unemployment, widespread poverty, and an ever-widening gap between rich and poor also come into play. As a result, the state's reaction to what is treated as a crisis of public order has amounted to the continuous use of government force, a conventional solution that ultimately fails to address the root causes of Colombia's problems.[24]

Against this backdrop, a three-year period of peace negotiations with the FARC and ELN forces under former president Andrés Pastrana (1998–2002) stalled repeatedly. With the emergence, in August 2002, of the right-wing candidate Alvaro Uribe Vélez, an outspoken advocate of a *mano dura* (literally, hard hand) approach toward the nation's conflicts, peace talks were indefinitely tabled. Uribe is an overwhelmingly popular figure among nearly all sectors of the Colombian population, with the exception of progressives, many of whom accuse the Uribe government of excessive authoritarianism. Renowned for his intense work ethic, devotion to efficiency as an antidote to corruption, and direct communicative style, he has particularly capitalized on many middle- and upper-class Colombians' weariness with the guerrillas and has proposed increasingly militaristic solutions to the violence. Unlike Pastrana, Uribe has refused to negotiate with the guerrilla forces prior to their demobilization. And, while he has been criticized by several human rights organizations for his present advocacy for and his past involvement in civilian antiguerrilla patrols (acts that his critics perceive as a form of pro-paramilitarism), the Colombian president has also been widely lauded for a 20 percent reduction in the overall murder rate. By 2005, Uribe's popularity had risen to such proportions that Colombians overwhelmingly voted in favor of a constitutional amendment permitting him to pursue a second term as president, a mandate that he won handily in 2006. In combination with the harsh socioeconomic conditions that generally await Colombians in South Florida, Uribe's relative success has encouraged many Colombians to return to their country in the past few years, sparking a reverse exodus of sorts.[25] However, as the evidence here attests, the flow of individuals, cultural practices, talent, and capital from south to north is perhaps irreversibly set, despite any momentary stirrings to the contrary.

Mapping Contemporary Colombian Migration

Colombia's long-term political and civil unrest has provoked mass migration, both external and internal, of millions of its citizens, dating back to the 1960s. By the 1980s, migration had evolved into an intrinsic element of the nation's social fabric. The number of Colombians migrating to the United States has been dictated, "directly if variously," by the nation's historical, economic, cultural, military, and political ties to its northern neighbor. While their ethnoracial profile differentiates them from earlier, primarily European migratory waves, post-1965 (or "fourth-wave") migrants to the United States such as Colombians are most clearly distinguished from their predecessors by their increased experience with the historical and economic impacts of U.S. interventionism in their countries of origin. However, while the Colombian "transnational field of action" has existed for several decades, the U.S.-Colombian transnational community has only recently come to existence on a national level.[26]

Composed of individuals and families fleeing the ever-growing violence that defines everyday life in Colombia in the age of the U.S.-led "war on drugs," as well as the personal security threats posed by paramilitary groups, guerrillas, government security forces, and common criminals, migration to the United States from Colombia has grown in number as well as socioeconomic diversity in recent decades. Conservative estimates indicate that approximately 4 million Colombians had fled the country by 1999, largely to settle in the United States, with Spain, Ecuador, Canada, Germany, France, Japan, and Costa Rica as distant second choices. This has amounted to an increase of more than 60 percent in the number of Colombians living in the United States in less than a decade. By 2004, net economic remittances sent by the U.S.-Colombian community had grown to $300 million annually, a source of income for the Colombian state second only to petroleum and greater than that of coffee. The end result of this dynamic is a transnational flow both symbolic and corporal, or a "single social continuum" merging the "here" with the "there."[27]

The international media's longstanding focus on Colombia's political struggles, while justified, has unwittingly led to a decreased emphasis on the other primary impetus driving mass migration to the United States. Significantly, the U.S. government's tendency to classify Colombians as exclusively economic as opposed to political immigrants simultaneously reflects and promotes this media bias. In actuality, high unemployment rates provoked by neoliberal economic policies, the socioeconomic disconnects provoked by rising education rates, and an increased familiarity with North American styles of consumption constitute the key immigration "push" factors for rural Colombians in particular. Indeed, a substantive public dialogue regarding the labor market impacts of hemispheric trade agreements such as Nafta (North American Free Trade Agreement), Cafta (Central American Free

Trade Agreement), and the TLC (*Tratado de Libre Comercio*, or Free Trade Agreement) among the United States, Colombia, and Peru has remained conspicuously absent from post-9/11 debates on undocumented migration to the United States. In what they have characterized as the ongoing "recolonization of Latin America," Raúl Fernández and Bernardo Useche predict that the TLC, supported by President Uribe, will ultimately spur further mass migration to the United States. According to this perspective, the Colombian government's triumphant announcement of eased visa restrictions as part of the trade agreement negotiations with the United States paradoxically remains "a smokescreen in order to attempt to hide that the increase in immigration resulting from poverty will be one of the principal effects of the implementation of the Treaty." Under these conditions, the migratory patterns set in place during the 1980s and 1990s—an era during which many South American nations became "exporters of people and importers of capital"—will likely continue.[28]

As indicated, the first significant wave of Colombian migrants to the United States arrived in the late 1960s, and persons of Colombian descent in the United States are unique in the high percentage of foreign-born individuals (more than 73 percent) within that group. Linked as they are to such a current migratory influx, most of those who self-identify as Colombians or as individuals of Colombian descent need look no further than their parents' generation or their very own in order to locate their family's point of entry into the United States, with much of their extended family often still residing in Colombia. Frequently classified as "'other' Latinos/Hispanics," since 1970 Colombians have constituted the largest population of South American origin in the United States, and they are now the sixth-largest Latino group overall. Since the surge in the late 1960s, Colombian immigration to the United States has undergone several more peaks, during the late 1970s and 1980s and in the first decade of the twenty-first century. Along with Dominicans and various other Central American and South American immigrant communities, U.S.-Colombians are presently categorized as one of the "new" Latino populations that have more than doubled in size since 1990, increasing from 3 million to slightly more than 6 million individuals total.[29]

Despite the fact that even by U.S. Census accounts[30] the U.S.-Colombian population has increased considerably since the beginning of the fourth wave immigration (from approximately 32,197 individuals in 1967 to a hotly contested 470,684 in 2000), detailed English-language publications dedicated to the U.S.-Colombian population as a whole have begun to surface only in recent years, primarily in sociological studies. In keeping with general trends of post-1965 immigration to the United States, thus far the majority of Colombian migrants arrived in the United States during the 1980s and 1990s, contributing to the replacement of Europeans as the most numerous U.S. immigrant population. And while Chicago, Houston, Los Angeles, New Orleans, and New England are frequent destinations, upon arrival in the United States most Colombians, with the exception of trained professionals, tend to settle in either the Miami or the New York area. Given the historic importance of the New York Colombian community, a reported 84,454 strong in 1990 and now estimated at more than 200,000, the majority of the existing popular and academic literature focuses on the New York population.[31]

New York Colombians are concentrated in Queens, primarily in Jamaica, Elmhurst, Woodside, Sunnyside, and most notably Jackson Heights, with a smaller population living on Long Island.[32] Despite the historic prominence of the New York Colombian community, it is estimated that approximately 75 percent of all Colombians enter the United States through Miami. Indeed, a significant portion of Colombian immigrants (approximately 31 percent as of 2000)[33] now choose to settle in Miami, which now rivals New York City as the locus for studies of the U.S.-Colombian population. According to current demographic research, Colombian immigration to the United States may be loosely organized into three distinct waves. The first wave, which ran from the late 1950s to the late 1970s, coincided with *La Violencia*, the civil war between the nation's Conservative and Liberal political parties discussed earlier. While mainly consisting of young men from the lower and lower-middle classes who arrived with their families or were united with them at a later time, this initial immigratory wave spanned all socioeconomic classes and included a significant number of professionals, among them dentists, physicians, engineers, bureaucrats, and Korean War veterans. Typically urban natives from Medellín, Bogotá, and Cali, these immigrants settled primarily in the New York metropolitan area. The passage of the U.S. Immigration and Nationality Act, in 1965 led to an increase in the number of working class Colombians migrating to the United States.[34]

Following the end of *La Violencia* in the late 1950s, the Colombian migratory flow, while continuous, abated somewhat. However, throughout the 1970s, the number of semiskilled migrants entering the United States rose, just as the number of professional migrants decreased. A second wave began in the late 1970s, marked by the increased participation of migrants from all socioeconomic classes and regions. While still primarily urbanites from the interior, the migrants also included a large number of individuals from the northern coastal city of Barranquilla and from the west-central coffee-growing region, as well. Again mainly composed of adult males, this wave ended by the mid-1990s. Notably, the individuals in this group left Colombia during a relatively prosperous period of economic growth for the nation. It is therefore likely that a significant increase in drug-related violence precipitated the departure of many, and, by the mid-1980s, Colombian migratory flows in general began to benefit from the solidification of previous migrant social networks. Simultaneously, outmigration increased in response to Colombia's profound economic and political woes and to the ongoing proliferation of the illegal drug trade. Throughout this period, the number of Colombian immigrants settling in South Florida increased, and the restaurants, small businesses, and other enterprises that they established at this time facilitated the incorporation of the third wave of immigrants that followed.

The South Florida region has proven attractive to Colombian migrants for numerous reasons. These include the widespread use of Spanish in the area, the ready availability of Colombian goods and services, the Florida weather, proximity to Colombia by airplane, and migrants' familiarity with the Miami area, particularly among the middle and upper classes. Since the mid-1990s, this third wave has made its presence felt more than previous waves, especially in South Florida, a region where, for privileged transmigrants and exiles alike, access to multiple passports has become, in the words of Aihwa Ong, a "matter of confidence" as much as a "matter of convenience."[35] Impacted by political violence as well as economic recession, Colombia's most recent immigrants to the United States are often young professionals and others from the middle and upper classes, with high levels of formal education, and these immigrants have constituted a significant drain on Colombia's intellectual resources. Unlike previous waves of Colombian immigrants, these recent arrivals hail from both rural and urban locales throughout Colombia and include both young and old. The newest Colombian immigrants to metropolitan Miami-Dade, regardless of their educational level and the amount of economic capital that they possess, have also had to contend with a variety of significant obstacles, chief among them insufficient English language skills, a lack of a permanent or work visas, inadequate social support networks, and low social capital. As such, many Colombians have found few, if any, employment options and have subsequently experienced a marked drop in socioeconomic status. Nonetheless, unlike most U.S. Latino populations (with the exception of U.S. Cubans and immigrants from the Southern Cone), the socioeconomic profile and educational attainment of U.S.-Colombians typically approach those of mainstream U.S. residents.

Because of the undocumented status of 40 to 50 percent of the U.S.-Colombian population as a whole and because of the migrants' low educational levels, exact population statistics regarding Miami's current Colombian community are difficult to locate.[36] As of 2001, the Colombian Consulate in Miami estimated that approximately 458,000 Colombians were residing in South Florida, making Colombians the largest group of non-Cuban Latin(o) Americans in Miami-Dade County. Lower and lower-middle class Colombian immigrants tend to reside in the Hialeah and Fontainebleau areas of west-central Miami-Dade, as well as in the small city of Homestead, in the southern portion of the county. Middle- and upper-middle-class Colombians frequently settle in Kendall, located in southwest Miami-Dade. Especially popular during the 1980s and early 1990s, Kendall has since suffered in popularity because of its reputation as a neighborhood for drug traffickers. Miramar, Plantation, Pembroke Pines, and Sunrise (all located in western Broward County, immediately north of the Miami-Dade line), are also frequent areas of settlement for middle- and upper-middle- class Colombians, as are Boca Raton and West Palm Beach, in southeastern Palm Beach County. The wealthiest Colombians often reside in Coral Gables, Key Biscayne, Miami Beach, Brickell, and Bayshore, all in Miami-Dade, or in the Weston area of west-central Broward, whereas Jewish Colombians of similar socioeconomic status tend to settle in the northwest Miami-Dade neighborhood of Aventura.[37]

The 2000 U.S. Census cites a 60 percent increase during the 1990s in the total number of Colombians living in the United States; significantly, by 2001, accounts of Colombian *balseros* (rafters) began to surface in mainstream Colombian publications.[38] Thus, taking into account the population of undocumented Colombian immigrants, sources indicate that an estimated 5.5 million Colombians currently live outside their home country, 4 million in the United States, rendering it home to more Colombians than any other locale besides the capital city of Colombia, Bogotá. Many of those unable to secure a coveted visa to leave Colombia are forced to overstay their three-month tourist visas to the United States or apply for political asylum. Applications for political asylum by Colombians in the United States rose from 2,747 in 2000 to 7,280 in 2001. By 2000, Colombians had grown into the fourth largest population of undocumented immigrants in the United States, constituting 2 percent of the nation's total undocumented immigrant population.

Deteriorating conditions in Colombia, while rendering the return of migrants less likely, have had a second, more positive political impact on the U.S.-based community. In a break from the community's previously low rates of naturalization and political participation (indeed, an early study referred

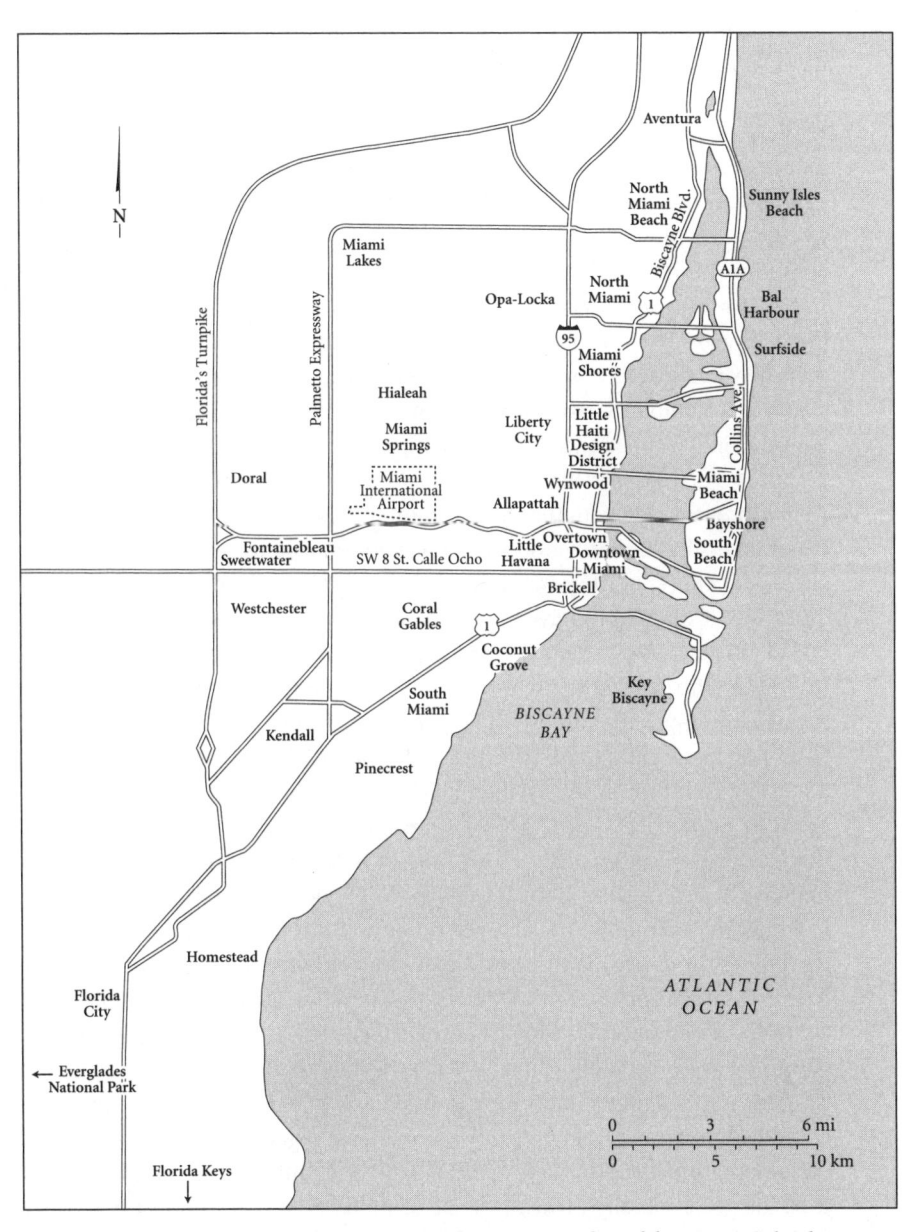

Map 1.2. Map of metropolitan Miami-Dade County. Recent studies of the Miami Colombian population indicate the existence of distinct, class-based settlement patterns, or what Michael W. Collier has described as a "patchwork quilt" of groups that demonstrates limited social interaction.

to Colombians as "aliens by choice"),[39] Colombians in the United States have begun to assert themselves politically, particularly in the aftermath of the landmark decision by the Colombian National Constituent Assembly in 1991 to grant dual citizenship to all Colombian nationals living abroad. The campaign for dual citizenship, which was spearheaded by members of New York's Colombian community, spurred numerous other electoral reforms designed in part to facilitate political participation among the diaspora. Increasingly conscious of their "double minority" status vis-à-vis both the dominant U.S. population and other, more established U.S. Latino communities, U.S.-Colombians appear to be shifting from an "almost exclusive focus on Colombia to an inclusive, translocal orientation and from traditional rigid Colombian bipartisanship to a fluid U.S. multiparty affiliation." Such actions ultimately disprove conventional frameworks that posit naturalization as a one-way phenomenon that presages migrants' wholesale incorporation into the receiving nation and their ultimate break with the "home country."[40] Many civically engaged Miami Colombians have conscientiously patterned their political strategies after the successful efforts of the powerful U.S.-Cuban political and economic lobbies. Thus, U.S.-Colombians have gradually begun to openly assert their ethnoracial identities as the "necessary place from which [to] speak,"[41] seeking a political voice with respect to the question of Temporary Protected Status (TPS). A form of temporary amnesty, TPS permits citizens from countries suffering from war or recent natural disasters to legally work and reside in the United States for eighteen months. Miami's U.S.-Colombian community has unsuccessfully pursued TPS on the local, state, and national levels since 1999, a bid that has proven increasingly more difficult in the post-9/11 era. Despite their inability to successfully lobby for favorable TPS legislation, the South Florida Colombian community has enjoyed other political gains: in November 2002, the U.S.-Colombian Juan Carlos Zapata was elected to the Florida House of Representatives for the 119th District, making him the first non-Cuban politician to represent South Florida at the state level. In addition, following the sustained diplomatic efforts of President Uribe, in 2004 Colombian citizens residing in the United States were granted access to a consular identity card, an official document that gives all Colombians, regardless of legal status, the documentation necessary to open a bank account, among other services. It is with this steadily growing sense of political and cultural capital, then, and under the growing auspices of a state-managed "transnationalism from above,"[42] that U.S.-Colombians commenced their insertion into one of South Florida's most visible money makers and sources of transcultural labor, the Latin(o) music industry.

2

A Miami Sound Machine

Deconstructing the Latin(o) Music Boom of the Late 1990s

As the Ethnic Studies scholar George Lipsitz observes, the triumvirate forces of technology, globalization, and the subsequent migration of individuals from south to north have transformed cities like Los Angeles and Miami into global, as opposed to national or regional, centers. As recently as 1980, Anglos constituted a majority in metropolitan Miami-Dade, while African Americans and Latinos represented the area's largest ethnoracial minorities. However, a mere decade later, the Anglo population was in steady decline due to "selective" white flight, the African American population (largely because of the continuous arrival of new immigrants) had remained constant, and Latinos had become the new majority. Currently, Miami-Dade County Latinos make up more than 50 percent of area residents, with blacks representing almost 20 percent. In recent years, the continuing influx of black and/or Latino immigrants from neighboring Latin America and from the Caribbean (Colombians, Haitians, Nicaraguans, and Brazilians, among others) has provoked a "change [in] the meaning of *all* racial identities" in global cities like Miami.[1] Miami's newest migrants, unlike earlier generations, are less willing to adhere to the assimilationist paradigms of the past and maintain an interest not only in the daily life and institutions of their home countries but in those of Miami, as well. As a focal point of North America's present anxieties centered on immigration, ethnoracial identity, and historic anti-Communist apprehensions, this "city on the edge" embodies "a new type of urban space, at the intersection of North America, South America, the Caribbean, crossed over by the new demographic, cultural, and economic flows between these areas."[2] Despite the demographic shifts, the U.S.-Cuban community, the ethnic group that has traditionally dominated contemporary Miami political and cultural life in the public imagination, continues to do so, most visibly within mainstream U.S. media outlets.[3] This is so despite the fact that the region's "new" Latino population, which is largely composed of South Americans, nearly equals the number of Cuban residents. The disproportionate U.S.-Cuban media presence exemplifies the organizational and institutional demands of hegemony, for, in conjunction with enhanced access to public discourse, these elites are quite literally "the ones who have most to *say*."[4]

The coverage of the 2000 presidential election results by the cable news network CNN provides a clear example of the subtle yet perceptible changes in the identity politics of South Florida. During one discussion regarding the election results still awaited from South Florida, the political analyst Robert George referred to the prime role of U.S.-Cubans in determining whether the Republican presidential candidate, George W. Bush, would win the election. In response, the CNN news anchors Judy Woodruff and Bernard Shaw offered more nuanced accounts of South Florida's most salient voting bloc:

> WOODRUFF: Much of the Hispanic vote in the state of Florida is not—we can no longer assume it's Cuban or mostly Cuban. There are more and more Hispanics in Florida who have come from different parts of Central America, South America.
>
> SHAW: Non-Cubans—let's put some faces on these people. We're talking about Peruvians, Colombians, Ecuadorians. We're talking about Panamanians, Salvadorians, Nicaraguans, Venezuelans, Chileans, and Brazilians.
>
> GEORGE: Right. You've got a—you've got a—you've got a gumbo.[5]

In the face of this demographic "gumbo," George's initial characterization of the Miami voting populace nonetheless is that which persists in the national consciousness. Indeed, Miami-Dade's myriad other populations, including the considerably less wealthy, less politically conservative, and consequently less visible sectors of the U.S.-Cuban community itself, more often than not emerge as the victims of a pervasive media silencing that is always unnatural and never neutral.[6]

Much has been made of the U.S.-Cuban economic and political dominance of Miami-Dade County in recent years, particularly in the aftermath of the Elián González controversy.[7] However, a 2000 investigative series undertaken by *El Nuevo Herald*, the Spanish-language daily published by the *Miami Herald*, to some extent challenges these deeply entrenched public beliefs regarding political and economic power. Conducted from early to mid-2000, the *Nuevo Herald* study documented the race and national origins of the individuals who at that time occupied the 1,357 positions of greatest power in Miami-Dade County in the fields of government, business, justice, higher education, the arts, and communications. According to the study, although Latinos in the region outnumbered Anglos/whites by a margin of two to one, Anglos filled more than two-thirds of all powerful positions, Latinos held one-fourth, and blacks held one-tenth; among the 406 governmental positions surveyed, Anglos occupied 51 percent of all elected or appointed positions, Latinos 32 percent, and blacks 17 percent. While these results offer a substantial rebuttal to "the myth of Cuban power,"[8] they fail to closely analyze one key result: of the 32 percent of all Latinos who filled government positions, *27 percent* were U.S. Cubans. Thus, while the perception of U.S.-Cuban dominance over Miami-Dade's Anglo population may be contested, the reality of U.S.-Cuban authority over Miami's numerous other Latino communities, specifically in the spheres of economics and culture, appears more difficult to deny, a fact that underscores the multiple, hierarchical *Latinidades* at play. In the face of (and perhaps largely because of) the continued influx of non-Cuban migration, Latino power in Miami has surfaced as a fetishized commodity to be "fought for and fought over."[9] Much like the blackness of Harlem, Miami's Latino hegemony is shaped by class and race prejudice, in which the privileged few "apply the litmus test of desirability to define the residents who are thought to jeopardize the sanctity and solidity of the collective social space."[10]

As Néstor García Canclini asserts, the hegemonic class cannot sustain economic dominance for any prolonged period by means of repression alone; *cultural power* is required, as well. In effect, by imposing sociocultural norms, legitimizing dominant structures, and camouflaging the symbolic violence that underlies forced assimilation, "cultural power not only reproduces sociocultural arbitrariness but also represents such arbitrariness as necessary and natural; it conceals economic power and aids the exercise and perception of such power."[11] Via an examination of contemporary representations of music-industry "crossover" and historical chronologies, here I problematize the prevailing and largely superficial depictions of the Latin(o) music boom in the popular media. In particular, I underscore the decontextualized, dehistoricized language and subject matter of various recordings, television programs, and popular print media produced, written, and/or performed by non-Latinos and U.S. Latino performers and industry figures alike, with an emphasis on the unique role played by the Miami-based entrepreneurs Gloria and Emilio Estefan. In this regard, I devote particular attention to the interaction of Cuban and Colombian industry figures and (to a lesser extent) that of Colombian musical genres in the context of the current Latin(o) music boom. Specifically, I focus on the popular media strategies employed in an attempt to construct (and, in some instances, contest) a historical chronology of the "boom." What do labels like "crossover" signify in this context? And, as Arlene Dávila notes, while in some instances non-Latinos may seek to "colonize" Latinos culturally, economically, and politically, how do inter-Latino media dynamics illuminate the ways in which Latinos enact power differentials upon *each other*?[12] Thus, I probe the larger questions of agency, identity, and, ultimately, economic and cultural capital that arise upon close examination of the politics of Latino representation in the current Miami music industry.

The youth of the Latino population (more than one-third of the roughly 45 million U.S. Latinos are under eighteen years of age, and the teen population is expected to increase by 62 percent by 2020), combined with its spending power (by 2011 Latinos will funnel more than $1 trillion a year into the economy, more per capita than any other U.S. consumer group), has made it the latest object of the popular music industry's attentions. And, despite a persistent overall downtown in music industry sales, Latin(o) music sales hit 650 million in U.S-recorded product in 2005. This Latin(o) music boom, nevertheless, cannot be attributed solely to increased spending on the part of Latino consumers. Rather, industry sources are noting that a majority of the current growth in Latin(o) music sales is taking place in "American" (read: Anglo/white) music stores. However, analyzing popular culture (in this case, popular music) solely in terms of "units sold" masks the identity politics and power struggles at hand. As Keith Negus reminds us, "Music is not simply received as sound but through its association with a series of images, identities and associated values, beliefs and affective desires. Marketing staff are acutely aware of this and strategically attempt to create these links—between the music and image, and between the artists and consumer."[13]

The motivations underlying the Latin(o) boom are indeed multifaceted and encompass the possibilities for economic gain as well as the increasing consumer influence and visibility of U.S. Latinos within the public sphere. As Frances Aparicio observes, this greater Latino media presence is likely symptomatic of a greater cultural and historical crisis of sorts, a movement away from the status quo that ultimately materializes in a mainstream attraction toward the so-called "Other":

Is this Latino-mania, then, another instance of cultural fixation on the Other, an attempt to displace the unsettled and unsatisfying paradigms of the internal self, as the men's movement fueled by Robert Bly has clearly evinced? Or is this phenomenon a direct consequence of the growing power, cultural contributions, and intellectual and artistic strength of Latinos/as, a more democratic latinization of the United States from within? Is it neither or both?[14]

Indeed, the case of the Latin(o) music boom highlights the flawed logic underlying the mainstream media's (and, to a lesser extent, the Latino-centered media's) insistence on consumerism as an antidote to racism and prejudice.[15]

In the past several years, a majority (if not all) of the numerous popular publications that have devoted space to the discussion of Latin(o) or what is often referred to as "Latin-tinged" music's rising popularity among non-Latino audiences have also offered their interpretations of the "boom's" appeal to mainstream audiences. Magazine cover stories with titles like "The Making of Christina Aguilera" index the self-conscious nature of the boom's media construction, while its accompanying photo illustration of Aguilera in a half-human, half-cyborg pose, created with the aid of digital mesh computer graphics, exemplifies the industry's mindful recipe for "[t]he [b]uilding of a 21st [c]entury [s]tar."[16] Such self-reflexivity, however, does not routinely materialize, as media representations more often than not uncritically mirror existing stereotypes regarding U.S Latino and Latin American performers' locations with respect to mainstream audiences. For example, in the *New York Times* article "A Country Now Ready to Listen," the journalist Peter Watrous describes Latin American nations as "places that only a few years ago saw the world through virtually pre-Columbian eyes." He then hypothesizes that "Americans [are] longing for music more rooted in a certain place and produced more honestly,"[17] hinting at a latent Anglo attraction to the "primitivistic Other." This subtext in turn permeates the narrative of Jennifer López's video for the single "Waiting for Tonight," whose action takes place in a jungle setting, as well as Ricky Martin's performance at the February 2000 Grammys, during which, surrounded by "African tribal drummers," he danced and sang from within a ring of fire. An analogous echo of the dominant gaze surfaces in the one-hour September 1999 television special "Latin Beat," hosted by the ABC news correspondent John Quiñones (a Chicano journalist, whose presence, along with its "news" format, imbues the program with an air of credibility), that chronicles the current popularity

A Miami Sound Machine | 39

Figure 2.1. "Building a 21st Century Star." *Time* magazine, March 6, 2000.

of Latino musicians. Rife with euphemisms and stereotypical references—Quiñones cites the "heat," "intoxication," and "spice" embodied in Latin(o) music, among other descriptors—and apparently oblivious to the historic presence of many Latino communities in what is now U.S. territory, "Latin Beat" characterizes Latin(o) music as "hitting the States like a tropical storm," in a coded reference to the supposedly ephemeral, dangerous element of the music. Throughout the broadcast, U.S. Latino performers are presented to viewers as museum pieces or "digested interpretations"[18] and labeled accordingly (Ricky Martin, Jennifer López, and Enrique Iglesias are respectively introduced as "Exhibit A," Exhibit B," and the "Third Exhibit"). The quasi-legal language utilized in the presentation of the performers/"exhibits" permits the public/"jury" to determine Latin(o) music's legitimacy and currency within the mainstream, as it simultaneously depicts the managment of diversity in the service of whiteness.[19] In retrospect, "Latin Beat" could be interpreted as an hour-long promotion for the "crossover acts" managed by the Miami-based Estefans, as all the artists profiled, with scant exception, had already released or were in the process of preparing English-language albums in collaboration with them.

The Rise of "Latin Hollywood": The Latin(o) Music Industry, 1990s-Present

Yo sólo quiero pegar en la radio	I just want a radio hit
Estoy ya cansado de estar endeudado	I'm already tired of being in debt
De verte sufriendo por cada centavo	Of seeing you suffering for every cent
Dejémoslo todo y vámonos para Miami	Let's leave it all behind and head for Miami
Voy a lo que voy, a volverme famoso	I'm going for what I want, to get famous
A la vida de artista . . .	and live an artist's life . . .
Apenas lleguemos llamamos a Emilio . . .	As soon as we get there let's call Emilio . . .

—Bacilos, "*Mi primer millón*" (My first million)

Not coincidentally, the Estefans' rise to prominence within the Latin(o) music industry, as referenced in the lines composed and sung by the Colombia native and Bacilos lead singer Jorge Villamizar,[20] occurred in tandem with Miami's development as the epicenter of the Latin(o) American entertainment and media industries. The ongoing influx of Colombian nationals into the South Florida region, including many of Colombia's most renowned recording artists, musicians, and producers, contributed not only to Miami-Dade's rapidly shifting demographics but also to the further consolidation of power within the Miami industry. Economic turmoil, *guerrilleros*, and state-sponsored violence aside, it has become increasingly difficult for Colombian artists hoping to "make it big" to do so solely within the confines of their native country. And the transnational entertainment conglomerates, long invested in the "mining" of third-world music as a raw resources, are often happy to oblige them in their move to the North, demonstrating that present-day migratory practices are ruled as much by multinational corporations and trade policies as they are by the life choices of individual migrants.[21] However, Miami's "hostile takeover" of the Latin(o) market is far from novel, given the music industry's historic tendencies toward gross internal polarities with regard to salary, employment stability, and geography.[22]

Lacking colonial roots and virtually an "instant city" since its incorporation in 1896, Miami has long held a space in the domestic and international popular imagination because of its historical association with tourism and the leisure culture, an association from which its alternative name, the "Magic City," is derived.[23] For Juan León, Miami, as a prefabricated modernist project, has always radiated the tropics, albeit "doubly denatured":

> First, Miami does not lie within the tropical zone. It is not, geographically speaking, tropical but rather sub-tropical. Secondly, the city is not the ambiguously signifiying Tropics of the Euro-American tradition, but rather a transformed version of it, a Tropics manufactured entirely by a modern state within its own borders and for its own purposes.[24]

Miami's ties to tourism and leisure within the global popular imagination, as well as its longstanding geographic and cultural links to Latin American and Caribbean states, particularly Cuba, have contributed in some fashion to the city's current status as the nucleus of the Latin(o) music industry. Given its pan-Latin, pan-American bearings (in aesthetic as well as commercial terms), the Miami industry is unique in that it does not depend upon geographical ties and is thus more reflective of contemporary transnational dynamics and globalization.

In the era following the Cuban Revolution, Miami began to supersede its previous status as a tourist destination, emerging as a city vital to U.S. national security interests in the fight against Communism and drug trafficking in the hemisphere. Indeed, Miami's "Latinization" surfaced as an unintended byproduct of the U.S. government's battle against communism in Latin America and the Caribbean.[25] As a regional showcase for the successes of capitalism, Miami has since come to symbolize for many the triumph of U.S.-sponsored capitalism over Communist Cuba and has emerged as a center for the postmodern political right.[26] Global politics, however, is not the sole force facilitating the Latin(o) music industry's centralization in Miami; global success is simultaneously dependent upon the prosperity of *local* social networks.[27] To this effect, the strength of South Florida's U.S.-Cuban business community and its longstanding practice of conducting its business largely within the ethnic enclave has played a crucial role in the music industry's movement toward Miami, as attested to in the example of the U.S.-Cuban Emilio Estefan, Jr., currently the industry's preeminent producer and businessman, as well as the self-proclaimed creator of the "Miami Sound."

Miami's status as the epicenter of the contemporary Latin(o) music scene, particularly during the so-called Latin(o) music boom, is also the end result of numerous broader music industry shifts that took place during the 1980s and early to mid-1990s, themselves part and parcel of a conscientious local effort to capitalize on the region's cultural "diversity."[28] While consistently ranking among the poorest cities in the country (alongside other majority-minority urban centers like Detroit), Miami is simultaneously cast as a city "rich" in culture and therefore strives to package its abundant Latino culture as a marketable resource. Rooted in a distinctly Latin American notion of racial democracy, the discourse of multiculturalism in circulation among Miami entertainment-sector elites ultimately offers "a positive spin on the unequally distributed new prosperity" of "Latin Hollywood."[29]

Although the groundwork for the city's eventual development into the epicenter of the transnational Latina(o) American entertainment and media industries was laid in the mid-1970s, beginning in the 1980s, the predominant record companies or "majors," underwent a key transformation. As a result of this shift, they no longer acted solely as straightforward musical producers and distributors and instead served as global conglomerates in the business of "integrated entertainment" and cross-marketing, which included stakes in marketing, record chains, television, cable, and satellite services, among other ventures. Local entertainment figures also cite the popularity of the television series *Miami Vice* (1984–1989), the success of the band Miami Sound Machine, and the renovation of South Beach's Art Deco District as key mid-1980s elements of the "new Miami" that was to emerge.[30] In anticipation of the predicted growth of the U.S. Latino population and the subsequent surge in buying power among Latinos, many of the majors also began to create separate departments dedicated to Latin(o) music during this period and made efforts to expand their Latin(o) recording catalogs. By the early 1990s, Miami's Latin(o) media had become further internationalized, due to increased satellite capacity, the opening of Latin American cable companies to U.S. investors, U.S. government efforts to decrease satellite signal pirating, and the rapid establishment of cable television in Latin America.[31]

Moreover, since the late 1980s the majors have all simultaneously operated as both national and global corporations. By means of consolidation, affiliation with, or acquisition of companies that had previously limited their dealings to a national context, the U.S.-based majors have gained national footholds in Latin America and elsewhere. (Many Latin American countries, however, do possess their own national recording industries specializing in the promotion of locally produced and performed genres. Several also occasionally promote "crossover" acts.) In part because of the considerable growth of the U.S. Latino population (more than 45 million individuals as of 2008) and its increased spending power (estimated to reach $1 trillion by 2010),[32] the U.S. Latino market has emerged as a focus of both mainstream and Latin American industry marketing efforts. More than ever, Latin(o) music has developed into a joint production realized between and within U.S. and Latin American corporate structures. By means of Soundscan technology, industry data now often incorporate U.S Latinos into the greater Latin American music market (which is also tabulated as part of the North American market), illustrating the links between the two markets, although Soundscan's usage within the Latin(o) music market has proven problematic at best.[33]

In recent years, major transnational corporations like BMG, EMI Latin, Sony Discos, Universal/Polygram, NARAS, WEA, and Warner-Chappell have opened offices in Miami. The Box Music Network, MTV Latin America, and Galaxy Latin America have also established themselves in the city, in a testament to the Miami entertainment industry's aggressive efforts to attract more of the Latin American market. And, while Miami is still not considered an ideal market for music sales, the rapidly increasing number of production and recording facilities in the area offers proof of its reputation as a prime production site.[34] This concentration of businesses and corporations tied to the Latin(o) music industry has in turn fostered an increase in the number of domestic and especially international talent migrating to the region. As James R. Curtis and Richard F. Rose note in their study of the Miami Sound as an "attractive force," the accessibility of recording studios often functions in tandem with the development of contemporary place-specific music or musical scenes, as music necessarily emerges from nonrestrictive (if not conducive) social conditions.[35] Cross-marketing of music industry products is also facilitated within the Miami region, given the abundance of U.S. and Latin American television stations, radio outlets, and print media located in the area. By the late 1990s, the entertainment industry had developed into the area's most rapidly growing business sector and had became part of Miami Beach's core cultural economy. Miami thus constitutes a vital "geolinguistic node" or "cluster" of media and entertainment institutions, all conveniently located within a relatively limited area.[36]

Despite the fact that the Miami cultural and business environment offers many advantages to the majors, its geographic location does have one consistent drawback: Latin(o) division staff working there must navigate the added difficulties presented by Miami's physical distance from the majors' headquarters in Los Angeles or New York. Latino division employees, many of whom are bilingual, bicultural Latin(o) Americans, who must deal with their company's mainstream distribution division elsewhere are therefore required to negotiate existing cultural and linguistic barriers that are further compounded by geographical circumstances. Insofar as these personal and political barriers are later reinscribed in the company's overall economic and management strategies, Miami's geographic and cultural distance from most of the continental United States influences Latin(o) music offerings to some degree via comparatively limited distribution routes and the like.[37] Nonetheless, lower overhead costs, geographic proximity to Latin America and the Caribbean, and the presence of an ever-increasing, low-wage and largely nonunionized immigrant workforce have contributed to Miami's attractiveness in comparison to Los Angeles and New York.[38] As a result of these combined historical, geographic, political, and socioeconomic factors, by the mid- to late 1990s, Miami had materialized as the undisputed "Latin Hollywood" for two continents.

Recasting the "Miami Sound" in the Age of the Gramilio

Further evidence of the industry dominance exercised by Gloria and Emilio Estefan's Crescent Moon Studios, a Miami-based Sony affiliate that by 1999 was grossing $200 million a year,[39] is found in prevailing popular media constructions of the historical chronology of Latin(o) music in the United States, in which Emilio Estefan is often credited as the primary creator of the "Miami Sound" or "a form of Latin pop, a mellow version of salsa mixed with elements of American rock and jazz" that is attributed to the unique musical innovations of U.S.-Cubans. Unlike more traditional Latin(o) music forms, the Miami Sound disregarded a *montuno* section in favor of two or three large musical sections that were repeated several times and that normally consisted of a verse and a bridge. Anchored by an off-beat 3-2 *clave* rhythm, this "original" Miami Sound employed Latin percussion and horn lines; while largely sung in Spanish, songs were at times performed in English, as well.[40]

With regard to the Latin(o) music industry's preeminent figures, these chronologies cede a disproportionate amount of credit for current crossover successes to the Estefans and their company, as well as to Ricky Martin's live performance at the 1999 Grammys. Martin's performance is often depicted as the "beginning" of the current Latin(o) music boom, as was apparent during the televised 2000 Grammy Awards ceremony. In a paternalistic gaze that was evident throughout the broadcast, each time a Latino took the stage to perform, present, or accept an award during the ceremony, cameras panned to the Estefans' seats in the audience in order to capture their reactions. The camera's gaze established an unspoken visual economy in which less established and powerful Latin(o) music industry figures were rendered subject to the approval of Emilio and Gloria Estefan; most notably, it registered Gloria Estefan's apparent shock upon viewing Jennifer López's now infamous green Versace gown.

During the portion of the same broadcast dedicated to showcasing musicians of the year's Latin(o) boom, Gloria Estefan was recognized by the actor Jimmy Smits as the "notable exception" among the U.S. Latino artists who had struggled for Anglo acceptance in preceding years. Ricky Martin's ongoing representation as the central figure of the current Latin(o) boom made possible by the Estefans' efforts, a role fervently embraced[41] by the Estefans, as the self-described "*first* people to combine the two [U.S. and Latin American] cultures" and who produced a musical blend of "hamburger with rice and beans," was further reified in a later comment by the singer Christina Aguilera. Aguilera cited Martin's February 24, 1999, Grammys performance as a watershed moment; more Latino recording artists had been signed to major contracts in the year after Martin's performance than ever before.[42]

Such widely held assumptions overwhelmingly fail to acknowledge the echoes of previously well-known Latino entertainers at work in both music industry constructions and Anglo receptions of current performers like Martin. Mainstream interpretations of today's "Ricky" are inevitably informed by the collective memory of the "other Ricky," or Ricky Ricardo, the alter ego of the Cuban actor and musician Desi Arnaz on the television show sitcom *I Love Lucy* (1951–1957). While rarely recognized, Arnaz's underlying presence in media depictions of Martin, despite the several decades between them, testifies not only to the general dearth of Latino performers occupying the mainstream historical consciousness but, more significantly, to the effectiveness of efforts to render the long, complex web of Latino contributions to "official" music histories short and simplistic. As chronological gaps that disproportionately privilege Estefan's and Martin's roles within Latin(o) American musical history while simultaneously erasing those of others such as Rafael Hernández and La Lupe (to name but a few), the hegemonic silences constructed in such popular media representations of the Latin(o) music boom could well be interpreted as "structural silencings," or the ongoing presence of institutional frameworks that facilitate such prevailing chronologies, in spite of their anachronistic nature. Such strategies run expressly counter to the goals of critical historiography, or what Ali Behdad describes as "not the recollection of the past but its excision, in order to invent an alternative future."[43]

Following nearly twenty-five years of incremental change and protest on the part of Latino consumers and others, the National Academy of Recording Arts and Sciences (NARAS) took an initial step toward recognizing the vast diversity within Latin(o) music, with the addition of a lone Grammy award category for "Latin Music" in 1975; prior to that time, Latin(o) music had previously been subsumed under the rubric of "ethnic and traditional" music. In 1983, three more Latin(o) Grammys were added, for "Best Mexican American," "Best Tropical," and "Best Latin Pop," and in 1997 an award for "Best Latin Rock" was included, as well, offering further evidence, as Deborah Pacini Hernández observes, of the industry's tendency to classify Latin(o) rock not as a subset of English-language rock music but rather as a variation of other Spanish-language music such as salsa and *ranchera*. The next year, NARAS deemed the "Best Mexican American" category too broad and added a Grammy for "Best Tejano"; by 2000, the Grammy for "Best Tropical" had been split into awards for "Best Salsa" and "Best Merengue." Aside from the limited number of Grammys designated for performers of Latin(o) music, television audiences had scant opportunity to see these artists as they received their awards: until recently, virtually all Grammys for Latin(o) music were awarded off camera.[44] The same year, the Latin Academy of Recording Arts and Sciences (LARAS) organized the first Latin Grammys, held on September 13, 2000. All albums released within the previous year on which more than 51 percent of the lyrics were in Spanish or Portuguese were eligible for consideration. The latter requirement, as well as the staging and the selection of performers and presenters for the Latin Grammy's inaugural telecast, underscored the prevailing ideological and performative construction of "Latin music" as a haphazard grouping of genres defined almost exclusively by their linguistic content. Deceptively facile, categorizing Latino(o) music on linguistic rather than (or, ideally, in addition to) historical, cultural, and sociopolitical grounds performs another function: it perpetuates a belief in Latin America as the geographic and artistic center of Latin(o) musical "authenticity." Notably, while many perceived the Latin Grammys as a step forward for those in the Latin(o) music industry, others interpreted the awards as a sign of the music's segregation from the mainstream.[45]

The first Latin Grammy awards were televised live on CBS from the Staples Center in Los Angeles, not Miami, because of a now-defunct law barring Miami-Dade County from dealing with those who conduct business with Cuba (in this case, the Latin Academy of Recording Arts and Sciences, or LARAS). The event was hailed as the first multilingual broadcast on a major U. S. network, as well as the first opportunity for recordings produced in Spanish- and Portuguese-speaking nations outside the United States to receive Grammy nominations. Despite the impossibility of staging the ceremonies in Miami, Emilio Estefan's presence was felt; that year's nominations were announced at one of his Miami restaurants, he led the field with six nominations, and he was simultaneously honored as the Latin Academy's person of the year. Gloria Estefan received three nominations.[46]

Both before and after the inaugural ceremonies, complaints arose regarding the Estefans' perceived control over the Latin(o) music industry in general and the Latin Grammys in particular (dubbed the "Gramilios" by their detractors). Prominent industry figures, most notably renowned the Puerto Rican trombonist, composer, and arranger Willie Colón, asserted that, as result of the industry's gradual move to Miami and the subsequent restrictions imposed by the more conservative, anti-Castro members of the U.S.-Cuban community such as Emilio Estefan, a virtual boycott of musicians with conflicting political views had begun:

> The censorship imposed by Latino corporate culture, a majority of which is Cuban exiles, and their wanting to only use musical compositions controlled by them, has resulted in generic content lacking in social commitment outside of the acceptable Anti-Castro message *à la* [U.S.- Cuban salsa performer] Willie Chirino. We can't be involved in politics, but they can. If I had been like others, if I had avoided social controversy [in my music], I would be enjoying myself alongside Gloria Estefan and others.[47]

By referring to the Estefans as the "Cuban-American mafia" in various public statements, Colón expressed his frustration not only with what he views as the Estefan's hegemony over the Latin Grammys (the bulk of the

Figure 2.2. Estefan (foreground), in a pose reminiscent of the "Miami mafia" label, appears with Santander (inset) in the popular weekly *Miami New Times*. Celeste Fraser Delgado, "Los Producers," *Miami New Times*, September 6, 2001.

nominations and awards were granted to the Estefans directly, the artists they work with, or their affiliate Sony Discos) but also, in a broader sense, with proponents of a Cuba-centric salsa origins myth.[48] Estefan and the Academy were also charged with marginalizing Mexican regional music (despite its status as the industry's highest-selling genre); few Mexican regional artists received nominations or were invited to perform, with the notable exception of the *ranchera*/banda artist Alejandro Fernández, who was under contract to the Estefans. In response to these criticisms, Emilio Estefan has publicly accused Colón of being a leftist Castro supporter. Regarding the separate yet related charge that the Latin Academy had virtually ignored Mexican regional music, Estefan maintained that the Latin Grammys had positively impacted the industry as a whole by boosting record sales worldwide. Paradoxically, he continued to reiterate his belief that politics and music should not mix and expressed his hope that the next Latin Grammys ceremony would be held in Miami.[49] Thus, the disproportionate emphasis on Latin(o) pop "crossover" stars at the 2000 Latin Grammys, a crucial component of the LARAS project, facilitated the promotion of a "non-threatening, non-politicized Latino middle class that is far removed from any immigrant experiences or sensibilities," a point of view that may be interpreted as a scarcely coded reference to middle-class aspirations.[50]

A Miami Sound Machine | 49

During the same period, Estefan became embroiled in a highly publicized lawsuit filed against him in July 2001 by the producer and songwriter Kike Santander, employed by Estefan Enterprises, Inc., who charged Estefan with withholding royalties, falsely claiming production credits, and committing a breach of contract. (Estefan promptly filed a countersuit, also alleging breach of contract.) A native of Cali, Colombia, who migrated to Miami in 1995, Santander first became known as the songwriter and coproducer (with Emilio Estefan) of Gloria Estefan's Grammy-winning 1995 album *Abriendo puertas* (Opening doors), which was based on a variety of Colombian rhythms (*vallenato, cumbia, chandé,* and *curralao*) and instrumentation (accordion, *caja vallenata,* and *guacharaca*), in combination with primarily Cuban sounds. Following his work on *Abriendo puertas,* Santander rapidly became regarded as the Miami industry's premier hit-making songwriter and a top producer. He also emerged as among the first to consistently incorporate Colombia's autochthonous genres into mainstream Latin(o) hits, including the Mexican star Thalía's 1995 *vallenato* smash "*Piel morena*" (Dusky skin). An accomplished, versatile musician, Santander performed on many of the tracks that he produced and wrote as an employee of Estefan Enterprises, winning multiple awards in the process and introducing audiences and industry insiders to the tri-ethnic base unique to Colombian popular music.[51] Juan Vicente Zambrano, another Colombian staff producer who worked for Estefan Enterprises, also began to receive industry recognition around this period, primarily for his work on Carlos Vives's *vallenato moderno* albums. Soon afterwards, non-Cuban genres, particularly the Mexican and Colombian styles, present in Shakira's later albums, became a regular feature of Estefan's productions, thereby expanding the musical repertoire, at least in practice, of what had previously been known as the "Miami Sound." By April 2002, the most public legal battle of Emilio Estefan's career had ended in a settlement between Santander and Estefan Enterprises, Inc., the exact terms of which remained confidential.[52] Santander then began devoting his energies to the Santander Music Group, his newly created production and publishing companies, while Estefan's Crescent Moon Records joined with Spain's Gran Vía Musical conglomerate and Sony Music Europe to launch Sunnyluna Records, aimed at producing and marketing Spanish-language music worldwide, with primary target markets in the United States, Spain, and Latin America.[53]

However central his role, Santander (and, to lesser extent, Zambrano) was not the sole early proponent of the Colombian-inflected music nor the Colombian performers currently being recognized in the musical trade papers as the "new wave" of Latin(o) music. Earlier pioneers, such as Phil Manzanera, a

British-Colombian *rock en español* producer, contributed significantly to the "Latin Alternative" genre. By the early 1980s, industry trade papers were beginning to note the presence of uniquely Colombian genres in the United States.[54] Concurrent with the steady increase in Colombians migrating to the Miami metropolitan area, by the late 1980s major Colombian salsa bands like Grupo Niche became aware of the viability of the untapped Miami-based Colombian market and began including successful U.S. stops on their tours; the internationally known *salsero* Joe Arroyo soon followed. (As early as 1983, however, notices of Colombian *vallenato* and salsa concerts were appearing in major New York publications, because of that region's larger and more established Colombian community. A few U.S.-based *vallenato* bands, most notably Iván Cuesta y sus Baltimore Vallenatos, were also recording and conducting brief tours.)[55] Shortly afterward, Richard Blair, a British engineer, mixer, and producer, arrived in Colombia, hired by the famed British musican Peter Gabriel to produce a record by the legendary *costeña* performer Totó la Momposina. Once in Colombia, Blair inserted himself into the country's key musical networks, establishing ties with Andrea Echeverri of Aterciopelados, Carlos Vives, and Iván Benavides (of Carlos Vives's band La Provincia and, later, Bloque), among others. Aside from his production work on Aterciopelados's first album, *Con el corazón en la mano* (With heart in hand), and Vives's hit *La tierra del olvido* (The land of forgetting), Blair established the Sidestepper project in 1997. Designed as a collaborative homage to the local musicians Blair had met while living in Colombia (his initial visit had stretched out into a three-year stay, though he now spends a portion of his time living in Miami), Sidestepper's inaugural production became the album *Logozo* (1999), a fusion of Afro-Colombian rhythms and electronic experimentation, followed by *No Grip* (2000), and *3 a.m. (In Beats We Trust)* (2003). All of the Sidestepper recordings enjoyed considerable critical acclaim and solid commercial success. As albums that were widely distributed throughout the United States and Europe, Blair's collaborations with Colombian musicians and artists also figured in the rise of Colombian music's visibility and popularity beyond the borders of Latin America, thus underscoring the centrality of the networks uniting musicians, producers, and market considerations in the creation of popular music.[56]

"Columbus Effect(s)" and the Politics of "Crossover"

Nevertheless, as a cultural signifier, the mainstream conflation of the Miami Sound with an exclusively U.S.-Cuban sound has persisted, for as a "place-specific" music it is charged with real and symbolic meanings that may hold significance for both residents and nonresidents of these cities. Viewed externally this spatio-musical association may serve as an important component in shaping the perceptions and images that "outsiders" have of the places in question, regardless of whether they have actually been there or not.[57]

In this way, more than twenty years later, this early description of what was then recognized as the (U.S.-Cuban) Miami Sound continues to reign, largely unchanged, as *the* Miami Sound in many ears, despite the more multilayered, polyphonic musical realities of today's Miami musical scene, which is influenced by scores of different racial and ethnic communities. In a sense, the symbiosis and the subsequent conflict between Santander and Estefan symbolize the growing influence of non-U.S.-Cuban musical genres and executives in the greater Miami industry.

Most mainstream popular media chronologies and categorizations thus continue to conflict with the research of the numerous scholars whose works on Latin(o) popular music in the United States and in Latin America contest the discrete time frames imposed by widely viewed programs such as the 1999 Grammys.[58] One such study, Ruth Glasser's *My Music Is My Flag*, in which she states her intent to "reevaluate the structure of ethnic history in general and the place of ethnic cultural expression within it," explores the interplay of power, history, and the silences imposed upon contestatory accounts and provides compelling evidence of the long-standing impact of Latino musicians on U.S. popular musical forms.[59] Unlike John Storm Roberts, whose book *The Latin Tinge*, a widely cited text on Latin(o) popular music, elides the role of female participation in the twentieth-century Latin(o) music industry, Glasser traces key Latinas' roles in the dissemination of Latin(o) popular forms. Most notably, she focuses on the role of Victoria Hernández, the sister of the Puerto Rican composer Rafael Hernández, thereby challenging prevailing mainstream histories that erase women's contributions, if not much of U.S. Latino musical production in general, the example of Gloria Estefan notwithstanding. As witnessed in the careers of veteran performers like the Peruvian Susana Baca, the Cuban Rubén González, and the Nuyorican Marc Anthony, among others, most Latin American and U.S. Latino performers who perform primarily in Spanish are, upon winning contracts with major English-language U.S. labels, repackaged as "debut artists" and "discoveries" of mainstream record companies, in a brand of "sonic tourism" reflective of what Wilson Valentín-Escobar terms the "Columbus effect."[60] This ability to recontextualize and in essence "resemanticize" Latin(o) American artists provides a lesson in the importance of "discovery" and nomenclature:

The naming of the "fact" is itself a narrative of power disguised as innocence. Would anyone care to celebrate the "Castilian invasion of the Bahamas"? . . . Naming the fact thus already imposes a reading and many historical controversies boil down to who has the power to name what. . . . Once discovered by Europeans, the Other finally enters the human world.[61]

Moreover, the industry's insistence upon grooming many of its artists to perform primarily in English or to alter musical arrangements to appeal to non-Latino tastes exemplifies the common hegemonic practice of dismantling and subsequently resemanticizing popular culture for profit.[62]

On a symbolic plane, a more astute examination of groups such as Cuba's Buena Vista Social Club, which has enjoyed considerable commercial success as a creation of the Anglo musician and producer Ry Cooder, offers an alternative reading of Latin(o) music's popularity. Indeed, both Wim Wenders's documentary on the Buena Vista Social Club and the group's 1999 U.S. tour were marked by their ahistorical, decontextualized character. Lacking any references to race, gender, class, or, most notably, U.S.-Cuba relations, the documentary in particular serves to reinscribe the romanticized, tropicalized[63] vision harbored by many U.S. leftists of post-Castro Cuba, in particular, and of Latin America in general. As Tanya Katerí Hernández suggests, the Buena Vista Social Club narrative functions as a powerful social tool aimed at the perpetuation of unequal power relations, in large part because of its insistent claim that "socialist Cuba does not appreciate the talent of its populace in a way like a White North American like Ry Cooder can."[64] Through its consumption of the Buena Vista Social Club's music, the U.S. mainstream public is afforded the opportunity to engage in an unproblematized encounter with the Other. This encounter not only perpetuates facile prescriptions for multicultural harmony but also conforms to dominant media representations of Latin(o) America, which are so often devoid of any commentary on subject position or neocolonial dynamics. This constitutes the

> "absent" but imperializing "white eye"; the unmarked position from which all these "observations" are made and from which, alone, they make sense. This is the history of slavery, and conquest, written, seen, drawn and photographed by The Winners. They cannot be *read* and made sense of from any other position. The "white eye" is always outside the frame—but seeing and positioning everything within it.[65]

In this context, Valentín-Escobar's concept of the "Columbus effect" proves especially illuminating, particularly in reference to the Buena Vista Social Club's charismatic singer, the now-deceased Ibrahim Ferrer.

According to Valentín-Escobar, the Columbus effect implies a "discovery" of sorts, necessarily followed by a process of appropriation. History, culture, identity—in essence, *being* itself—commences at the moment of discovery,[66] enabling a seventy-three-year-old artist like Ferrer, with decades of performing experience in Cuba, to be reborn as the recipient of the Latin Grammy for Best New Artist of 2000. In many senses, the Buena Vista Social Club perhaps appeals to many because it echoes "the Cuba of the past," or the pre-Columbian spaces described by Peter Watrous in the *New York Times*, thereby provoking a nostalgia for that which no longer is or that which offers, in the words of García Canclini, "the opportunity to both be different from the rest and establish symbolic relations with simpler life-styles, a yearned-for nature, or the Indian artisans who represent that lost closeness."[67] (García Canclini speaks here with specific regard to Mexico's large indigenous population, though his premise rings true in the Cuban case as well.)

Consumed with recording the music of elderly Cuban performers for the benefit of audiences outside the island, Cooder engages in the fruitless anthropological rescue of the "popular" (the popular that often serves as a euphemism for the primitive)[68]—fruitless because the popular, never "pure" to begin with, is constantly subject to processes of transformation, not extinction. Cooder's dealings with the group reflect what Michel-Rolph Trouillot identifies as the two common historical tropes: the first, "formulas of erasure"; the second, "formulas of banalization."[69] In short, the apolitical, anachronistic character of the Buena Vista Social Club's recordings and appearances serves to obliterate Cuba's longstanding history as a (neo)colonial possession, while the deliberately simplified arrangements of the musical standards that they perform[70] can be perceived as pandering to the tastes of consumers unknowledgeable regarding the richness of Afro-Caribbean rhythmic stylings. While the performers in the Buena Vista Social Club are ultimately reinscribed as colonial subjects in this scenario, Valentín-Escobar pinpoints another, equally disturbing dynamic underlying Cooder's avowed faith in the superiority of Buena Vista's "uncorrupt" music: the suggestion that diasporan Latinos, particularly those located in transnational locales such as Miami, New York, and Los Angeles, are incapable of producing "authentic" music.[71] Cuban music's current popularity in the United States, however, does not signal a new trend. During the 1920s and 1930s, Cuban music was in such demand stateside that Latino musicians were frequently generically referred to as "Cuban musicians," regardless of their national origins.[72] More recently, changes in what was known as the "Trading with the Enemy Act" in 1988 (an act that had barred Cuban music and musicians from entering the United States) had the unexpected effect of (re)introducing Cuban music not into Latino music circles but into those of so-called world music, whose consumer base is largely non-Latino.[73] Entangled in a complex web of politics and economics compounded by prevailing notions of racial and cultural authenticity, Deborah Pacini Hernández argues, the ongoing embargo against Cuba has in turn paradoxically enhanced the allure of Cuban music among world music consumers, "endowing it with the seductiveness of the forbidden."[74]

The same hegemonic impulse wielded upon Latin American and U.S. Latino artists via the Columbus effect is also embodied, as we shall see, in designators such as "crossover." Within the context of the current Latin(o) music boom, who defines "crossover"? And what remains unspoken in the often-invoked language of crossover, a politically loaded term that does not persist, however, without considerable protest from key figures in the U.S. Latin(o) music industry? And, finally, what possibilities, if any, do mainstream definitions of crossover allow for the recognition of bicultural identities?

Reebee Garofalo delineates the roots of the term "crossover," specifically its basis in the music industry's historical presumption that each musical genre corresponds to its own distinct consumer group, absent any overlap. (For example, folk music was designated for southern, rural whites, rhythm and blues for blacks, and pop for the white, northern, urban middle and upper classes, otherwise known as the "mainstream.") "Crossover" thus "refers to that process whereby an artist or a recording from a secondary or specialty marketing category . . . achieves hit status in the mainstream market . . . its most common usage in popular music history clearly connotes movement from margin to mainstream."[75] As a result, the segregationist marketing ideologies and business practices propelling the notion of "crossover" as it refers to particular artists and/or their recordings have had a lasting impact on public perceptions of musical production and history. As Garofalo notes,

> the identification of music with race, which has tended to exclude African American artists and others from certain marketing structures in the music industry, makes the task of unearthing an accurate history of U.S. popular music quite difficult and encourages serious underestimates of the degree of cross-cultural collaboration that has taken place.[76]

The case of the popular music phenomenon Christina Aguilera, a singer of Irish and Ecuadorian descent whose 1999 English-language album *Christina Aguilera* debuted on the *Billboard* charts at number one and eventually sold more than 6 million copies,[77] raises crucial questions regarding the situational nature of identity and the politics of crossover within the male, Anglo-dominated U.S. recording industry. In the months immediately preceding her February 2000 Grammy win for Best New Artist of 1999, Aguilera's record company launched an aggressive campaign to resituate her within the U.S. market not as a phenotypically Anglo singer with an ambiguously "foreign-sounding" last name but rather as a teenage U.S. Latina preparing to re-release a series of her previous hits plus some original tracks, recorded this time in her newly acquired *español*. Targeted at U.S. Latino consumers, BMG/RCA's highly visible campaign to manipulate Aguilera's public persona included cover stories with accompanying photos in widely read Latino publications like *Hispanic* and *Latina*, the previously mentioned *Time* cover story, and a performance at the Latin Grammys of "*Genio atrapado*," the Spanish-language version of her previous number-one hit "Genie in a Bottle."

Although the majority of the press coverage regarding Aguilera's Spanish-language album largely failed to address the questions of phenotype, skin privilege, and language politics that many U.S. Latinos grapple with on a daily basis, Aguilera's December 1999 interview with *Latina* magazine disclosed a bit more with regard to the way in which Aguilera locates herself. In response to inquiries about her (dyed) platinum blonde, blue-eyed appearance, Aguilera asserts that "[Latinas] come in all shapes, sizes, and colors." And while the rationales dictating her foray into Spanish-language music are never explicitly expressed in the article, Aguilera shares that "A lot of my fans are young girls, and they go, 'You're someone young Latin women can look up to,' because there really aren't many. . . . It's not like I was *born* in Ecuador. . . . Still, I have those roots."[78] Foremost, Aguilera's response provokes multiple readings that on one hand display what might be termed an "insider's" sensitivity to the complexities of Latino phenotype ("[Latinas] come in all shapes, sizes, and colors"). Simultaneously, in the statement "It's not like I was *born* in Ecuador," she reveals her own lack of awareness regarding the very nature of U.S. Latino identity. Aguilera's limited concept of *Latinidad* is predicated upon national and territorial, as opposed to primarily political, cultural, and historical, factors and sharply contrasts with a more politicized vision of U.S. Latino identity as "imbued with social, cultural, and political values that are resilient against the homogenizing impulses of the economically and politically dominant society."[79] (It is also interesting to note that

Aguilera self-identifies here as a role model for "Latin" girls, as opposed to young Latin*as*, thereby using the terminology more often favored in the mainstream Anglo press.)

While many Latino music fans do profess a certain amount of skepticism regarding the motives underlying this abrupt shift in marketing strategy, questions of agency must be taken into account. Not only is the public not privy to the particulars of Aguilera's contract with BMG/RCA; we also know little more than the barest details regarding her personal relationship with Spanish, which she was ironically learning with the aid of the text *Spanish for Gringos*.[80] Thus, Aguilera's very public experience reflects the larger, more private efforts among numerous U.S. Latino youth to reclaim Spanish and foregrounds the questions of linguistic colonialism and unequal access to Spanish for many U.S.-educated Latinos. Aguilera's ties to her allegedly abusive Ecuadorian father (Aguilera's parents divorced when she was very young, and she and her younger sister subsequently lived exclusively with their mother) also remain out of the public eye. In terms of the Latin(o) music industry at large, her experience demonstrates the ways in which those raised outside of the U.S. Latino community can partake of Miami's transnational, pan-Latino character.[81]

As their repeated representation as fin de siècle fad artists attests, Latino performers and other performers of color have had to contend with an industry that has historically and systematically categorized their music in opposition to an unmarked, white pop norm. (Incidentally, the March 2000 cover of *Hispanic* magazine featured Aguilera and bore the caption "Latin Pop: Just a Fad?") As Suzanne E. Smith notes in her cultural history of Motown, shifts in the way in which industry designators such as "pop" and "rhythm and blues" were applied to Motown artists' recordings directly reflected the amount of crossover success a particular group had achieved. However, insofar as the media and industry were concerned, Motown performers' race ultimately overrode any consideration of musical styles: "The Motown sound was always 'brown,' regardless of the company's diverse musical output and its popularity with multiracial audiences."[82] As evidenced by the title ("Latin Music Goes Pop!") of *Time*'s May 24, 1999, cover story on the Latin(o) music boom, the label "pop music," during the Motown era as now, functions as a euphemism for Anglo/"white" music, which in turn affords artists greater access to ostensibly more affluent white audiences and thus higher sales. "Crossover status," therefore, is not exclusively a reflection of ethnoracial, gender, and generational dynamics; economic factors also undeniably play a critical role in the industry's desire to broaden its consumer base.[83]

While consumers and music executives no longer employ the term, constructions of categories of "race music" persist, repackaged in R&B, hip-hop, and Latin(o) forms, among others. Racial gatekeeping within the U.S. popular music industry, however, extends beyond the subtext legible in *Billboard*'s market categories or the pretenses visible in the layout of music stores. As the Puerto Rican author Esmeralda Santiago observes with regard to Latino artists with large Anglo followings, "this is still the white face of the Caribbean." Indeed, the "ethnic ambiguity" of white/light Latino artists testifies to the potentially pragmatic character of hybridity and representational vagueness. According to this scenario, Latino performers with the ability to transcend U.S. phenotypical fault lines are more likely to gain positive mainstream media exposure.[84] Thus, as within the music industry, phenotypical considerations have not escaped the media's notice, as the following comments describing Ricky Martin suggest: "His voice isn't great. But he's got the looks, he's got the energy, and he's got the backing. . . . And he's not *too* Latin."[85]

In other words, the popular media recognize that part of Martin's (as well as López's, Marc Anthony's, and Aguilera's) appeal to mainstream audiences is the *appearance* of "whiteness." Furthermore, mainstream media representations of the Latin(o) music boom as a crossover phenomenon rely on the assumption that "crossing over" to pop music is the ultimate goal of all Latino artists, a status that, once achieved, they should gratefully and passively accept: "Latinos are the fastest-growing demographic in the U.S., and as a rule, they tend not to complain too loudly when one of their own crosses over."[86] This presumption that "America" is synonymous with English and whiteness reigns as the veiled premise upon which much media coverage of Latin(o) music is constructed, as the following quote regarding the Nuyorican artist Marc Anthony illustrates: "It's good to be the king . . . of salsa. But it's taken some fancy crossover moves and an English-language hit to get America talking about Marc Anthony."[87] The question thus emerges: to just *which* America is Anthony's interviewer referring? Such representations, however, do not go uncontested within the Latino community, as one article, subtitled "*Ricky siempre será nuestro*" (Ricky will always be ours), observes: "what do you do when something that was so personal becomes so public?"[88] For his part, Anthony has repeatedly rejected the crossover label in both print and television interviews on the grounds that it fails to encompass the bicultural nature of U.S. Latino identity.[89] Demonstrating a parallel line of reasoning, the actor and *salsero* Rubén Blades has been more openly critical of the concept of crossover, stating: "I hate the word 'crossover' with a passion because it is a racist term for people who can't accept the mixture that has already taken

Figure 2.3. To many, Martin's frequent exposure in the mainstream media appeared to herald a new, more inclusive aperture within U.S. popular culture. *Time*, May 24, 1999.

place."[90] In more covert fashion, popular magazines aimed at U.S. Latinos have responded to the assumptions posed in more mainstream publications, establishing a dialectics of contestation of sorts. The Latino-produced magazine *Mía*, for example, "answered" *Time*'s May 24, 1999, "Latin Music Goes Pop!" cover story with its own cover bearing the phrase "Música Latina: Did It

Really Go 'Pop'!?", a title that simultaneously questions the profundity of pop music's influence on "traditional" Latin(o) musical forms and the sincerity underlying Latin(o) music's appeal to mainstream audiences. As Fiol-Matta argues, Latino identity in this context supplies "an available script for the process that made these artists over, transforming them into images promoting a globalized, but not progressive, understanding of *latinidad*."[91]

As the preceding discussion regarding the contested chronologies of Latin(o) music and the dynamics of crossover underscores, media representations of the Latin(o) music boom are rife with contradictions and to a great extent reveal dominant attitudes toward the Latino cultural "invasion" that many of these performers embody. In sum, a not-so-subtle form of xenophobia emerges when one examines closely the various textual representations of the boom and the growing U.S. Latino population's predicted impact on the monoracial, monocultural "America" encoded within them, as titles such as "*¿Se Habla* Rock and Roll? You Will Soon: A Musical Invasion From South of the Border" and "Watch Out: The Rhythm Is Gonna Get You, Too"[92] suggest. In this light, I have problematized the largely decontexualized, dehistoricized nature of the Latin(o) music boom's numerous representations and have worked toward dismantling the covert assumptions underlying the widely employed media designator "crossover." As chapter 3 elucidates, it is in part the "Miami Machine" itself that later rendered the international success of Colombian artists like Shakira possible; Carlos Vives, too, has certainly benefited from its marketing strategies. Moreover, the element of "crossover" that we witness here in what comes to be known as the Latin(o) boom's "first wave" proves central to the construction of the "second wave" that I discuss in chapter 4. As the forceful examples offered by the Estefan empire and the Buena Vista Social Club under Ry Cooder attest, the aptly named Columbus effect is hardly confined to an exclusively vertical (north to south/south to north), out-group trajectory. Akin to the inter-Latino dynamics outlined by Dávila, the Estefan case in particular illuminates yet another brand of tropicalization,[93] as yet unnamed: the largely unspoken, though longstanding, brand of in-group discrimination that the various U.S. Latino communities at times visit upon one another.

3

Shakira as the Idealized Transnational Citizen

Media Perspectives on Colombianidad in Transition

> Like many of the spanglish [sic] generation, Shakira is a walking, living, breathing, singing contradiction. Born and raised in Colombia, she lived for bands like Led Zeppelin, The Cure, The Police, the Beatles and Nirvana. Rock was her first musical love, but her Arabic culture was her life. . . . Despite the fact that she was once named the queen of the Barranquilla carnival and was crowned by Colombian salsa great Joe Arroyo, Shakira is above all a rock chick.
>
> —Ed Morales, "Fade to Blonde"

In the most elementary sense, transnationalism entails the "the social practices of 'transmigrants' and their organizations" and may include habitual activities that involve regular travel and a certain degree of predictability, as well as activities dictated by more extraordinary circumstances, such as natural disasters or political events. In a more official capacity, a transnational dynamic emerges when, in response to a large immigrant population, government officials in a nation set out to reconfigure the nation-state's borders in order to include even those residing outside the state's physical boundaries. The result, a "deterritorialized transnational nation-state," encompasses the immigrants themselves as well as their descendants.[1]

It is essential to bear in mind that the dynamics of transnationalism are not limited to the bodily movement of individuals. Cable television, for example, has emerged as a key means by which the transnational flow of cultural values, images, and ideals is facilitated between Latin America and the United States as well as within Latin America itself. In recent press articles, both Latin American recording artists and music industry figures cite the prodigious growth of cable television within Latin America over the past several years as a driving force behind the rise of numerous market-generated categories and genres, such as the ongoing *rock en español* movement. For U.S. Latinos, expanded access to Latin American/U.S.-owned channels such as Univisión and Telemundo has translated into increased exposure to music videos, soap operas, news, and the like from both continents, thereby informing their perceptions of Latin American culture while simultaneously exposing Latin American viewers to the lives of U.S. Latinos in the north.[2] Whether real or imagined, such increased familiarity reflects a widespread shift in Colombia's literal and figurative borders, a shift replete with endless "scripts [being] formed of imagined lives, their own as well as those of others living in other places." Today's media play a central role in contemporary identity production through their ability to "facilitat[e] an engagement with distant peoples, [and] . . . 'deterritorialize' the process of imagining communities."[3]

Transmigrants must not be simply viewed as unbounded social actors lacking social, political, and cultural constraints within the local context. Indeed, conceptualizing transnational communities in such an indistinct manner threatens to render the "boundaries of transnationality" meaningless and fails to recognize the vast differences in the degree of social, political, and economic mobility afforded to diverse individuals. As such, Michael Peter Smith and Luis Eduardo Guarnizo's efforts to better define the parameters of transnationalism, or what one might term the "limits" of contemporary Latin(o) American transnational identity, inform the analysis at hand: just when and how does a "Latin American" become a "U.S. Latino"? How is *Latinidad* impacted when it is simultaneously cast as both social identity *and* a media/ marketing tool? And via what means do political elites actively aim to "constitute the scope and meaning of 'transnationalism?'"[4]

Clearly, the process of identity formation does not depend solely on the individual; in sum, "the One cannot be conceived of without the Other."[5] For Latin(o) American immigrants and their U.S.-born offspring, identity formation entails a perpetual dialectics of negotiation with longstanding beliefs regarding belonging and the national body. As Stacey Takacs suggests, "immigrants do not belong 'naturally' to the national family—that is, they have not inherited citizenship as a birthright—so they must be *naturalized*." Control over immigration translates into control over the national identity, as not all immigrants enjoy the same "degree of legitimization."[6] Indeed, many U.S.-born offspring of Latin(o) Americans bear the same "unnatural" categorization, often externally imposed upon them, as their parents. As such, the inherent difficulties underlying (un)conscious attempts to compartmentalize Latin(o) America's vast diversity point to the creation of yet another ethnic label, the concept otherwise known as *Latinidad*.

In this context, the internationally known singer and songwriter Shakira emerges as a primary example of a public persona who at times occupies the interstices between the Latin American and the U.S. Latino contained within the rubric of *Latinidad*. As one of the most visible performers of the most recent so-called Latin(o) music boom, and as what Angharad Valdivia has termed "a radical hybrid,"[7] Shakira, through her music and through her public persona, shapes both in- and out-group notions of what it means to be not only Latina but also *colombiana*. Furthermore, her multiple subject positions (as Lebanese-Colombian, Caribbean-Colombian, female, popular performer, and recent U.S. migrant) contribute to a sense of *Latinidad* and *colombianidad* both within and outside U.S. borders. Like many young "third-world" women native to countries to which world markets flock in search of cheap labor, and whose factories subsequently employ a disproportionate number of young females in low-paying jobs, Shakira's career trajectory embodies the crossroads of globalization's ethnoracial, gender, and class ideologies, as her media presence simultaneously demands that we take into account the most "visible" of human categories, namely gender and race. In this respect, Shakira represents a very public, albeit highly privileged, example of the intricacies of *Latinidad* and "flexible citizenship."[8]

Both within and beyond Colombia's physical borders, the increasingly aggressive marketing of Shakira's image and music, a phenomenon that has provided much of the U.S. mainstream with its first view of Colombian culture beyond the drug wars, has arguably "reconfigured the meaning and value of contemporary citizenship" among *colombianos*, in addition to sparking a reconsideration of the ways in which the transnational Colombian community constructs and relays its understandings of in-group membership. Given her multiple positionings, a closer examination of Shakira's persona elicits a number of questions: within the complex epistemology of *Latinidad*, in what moments and through what processes does Shakira, a native of Colombia, "become" a U.S. Latina? How is *Latinidad* shaped when treated both as marketing and media construction *and* an identity signifier? And to what ends is *Latinidad* thrust upon Shakira? Via my readings of cross-media discourse and music, I address these questions as I trace the "competing discourses of agency"[9] embedded in Shakira's somewhat contradictory representation as an idealized, transnational citizen at a pivotal moment in the (re)configuration of *colombianidad* and, in a broader sense, *Latinidad* itself.

As an inhabitant of Miami, a city whose "'local' life and culture . . . have decidedly international dimensions,"[10] Shakira, like much of Miami's majority Latin(o) American population, exemplifies the erroneously implied relationship between citizenship and culture in which culture is intrinsically linked to difference: "full citizenship and cultural visibility appear to be inversely related. When one increases, the other decreases. Full citizens lack culture, and those most culturally endowed lack full citizenship."[11] In contrast, if we embrace the related notion that cultural citizenship is not necessarily contingent upon full legal citizenship in the traditional sense,[12] Shakira may be interpreted as enacting the experience of multiple citizenships and multiple identities. Living her public and private lives "like two quantum particles in two places at once," Shakira therefore embodies the brand of "strategic mitosis," or contextually bound identity shifts, that defines life in the United States for many Latin(o) Americans.[13]

If the Colombian "transnational field of action" has long existed, the U.S.-Colombian transnational community has only recently come to existence at the national level. Driven to immigrate for reasons of personal safety as well as because of the crushing economic recession of the late twentieth and early twenty-first centuries, Colombia's most recent immigrants to the United States distinguish themselves in that they are mostly young professionals and other well-educated individuals from the middle and upper classes. As previously discussed, these recent arrivals differ from previous immigrants in that they hail from both rural and urban locales throughout Colombia and include both the young and the old. The character of this latest wave of immigrants thereby calls into question the prevailing tendency to portray transnational activity as the exclusive realm of the marginalized,[14] when in fact examples to the contrary, Shakira among them, abound.

In light of recent studies that touch on the social stigmas often attached to Colombian identity in the United States,[15] members of the transnational elite like Shakira differentiate themselves from less prosperous community members in at least one fundamental sense: Shakira is free to enjoy the luxury of declaring her Colombian identity in a public forum. As Nina Glick Schiller and Georges Eugene Fouron assert, "[t]ies are one thing; *public identities* are something else."[16] Simply stated, Shakira's widespread fame and economic success in essence override the stigma attached to her *colombianidad* within the U.S. context. Conversely, it is common, in both formally documented and anecdotal cases, to learn of Colombians who have lied about or concealed their national identity for fear of discrimination as they seek basic employment and services. This point is of particular salience in Miami and in other pan-Latino, pan-ethnic urban centers, where the myriad Latin(o) American nationalisms and their attendant stereotypes function as highly fetishized commodities.

Shakira Rides the Migration and Media Waves

Shakira Isabel Mebarak Ripoll was born to a New York-born father of Lebanese descent and a mother of Catalonian parentage on February 2, 1977, in Barranquilla, Colombia, a Caribbean port city of particular influence in Colombia's popular musical development. (Colombia's northern Caribbean coast, where Barranquilla is located, is commonly referred to as *La Costa*, or the Coast. Its inhabitants, therefore, are known as *costeños*.) Since its inception, Colombia has been characterized by an intense regionalism among its citizens, as exemplified in the complex, often contentious relationship between the more economically developed interior regions (*el interior*) and the northern Caribbean provinces (*La Costa*), with a contingent emphasis on the supposed cultural, linguistic, and racial superiority of the nation's inland regions. The entrenched character of these historic cultural tensions is perhaps best illustrated by Colombians' overwhelming tendency to identify and ally themselves primarily according to their regional, rather than their national, affiliations.[17] For many Colombians, Shakira's local or regional identity is therefore not necessarily subsumed by her more current, globalized "Latina" identity.[18] Shakira's *costeña* identity is of particular relevance; indeed, the act of reading Shakira's gendered, class, and ethnoracial locations *into* media texts about her sheds crucial light on the manifold identity politics at play.

Shakira's first public performance as a child was in a Middle Eastern dance recital, and she began composing original songs at age seven.[19] Influenced by Colombian pop and folk music, U.S. rock, disco, and the Arabic music that her father brought into the family home, at age thirteen Shakira released her first album, *Magia* (Magic), which consisted primarily of pop ballads, as did her follow-up work, *Peligro* (Danger), released in 1993. Following the commercial failure of *Peligro*, she pursued a brief acting career in Bogotá, most notably as the protagonist of the 1994 soap opera *El oasis* (The oasis). However, it was not until the release, in 1996, of *Pies descalzos* (Bare feet), based on a fusion of pop, rock, reggae, dance music, and ballads, that Shakira began to receive musical recognition outside Colombia.

Historically, Shakira's star began rising at a moment in which Colombian popular music in general was riding a wave of favorable recognition, both on its own and as part of the greater so-called Latin(o) music boom. Those who wrote about the subject, in both Latino and mainstream Anglo media outlets, however, more often than not uncritically attributed Colombia's recent artistic achievements to a "new" musical renaissance within the nation. This misconception, which hints at prevailing paradigms of neocolonial "discovery," was not lost on the U.S.-Colombian music critic Leila Cobo, who maintains that the emerging Colombian sound was not a new one but rather a unique treatment of an existing folkloric musical base.[20] Notably, much of the current praise for Colombian popular music has been reserved for the nation's pop and/or *rock en español* artists, the rock genre's relative lack of popularity within Colombia notwithstanding.

In some of the earliest articles published on Shakira in the U.S. popular press, she was referred to as "Lebanese-Colombian," whereas in more recent pieces she has been exclusively described as Colombian or simply Latina. Interestingly, Shakira has publicly disagreed with critics who observed that her vocal style, aptly described as a "rangy and robust mezzo spiked with yodel-like shadings,"[21] is connected in some way to her Lebanese heritage. Ironically, she has achieved considerable critical and commercial success with her live performances and with her recordings of "*Ojos así*" (Eyes like yours), which draw heavily from Middle Eastern rhythms and instrumentation, as well as the Arabic language itself. In the period following the September 11, 2001, attacks on New York City and Washington, D.C., media coverage of Shakira, particularly within the Spanish-language press, began more frequently to reference her Lebanese roots and their impact on her music and performance style. Shakira appeared on the December 2001 cover of *Cristina (La Revista)* with the statement "*No todos los árabes somos terroristas*" ("Not all of us Arabs are terrorists") superimposed across her image (figure 3.1). Her compositions, while undoubtedly drawing on a variety of musical traditions, draw almost exclusively from non-Colombian genres, such as Mexican mariachi ("*Ciega, sordomuda*" [Blind, deaf and dumb]) and reggae ("*Un poco de amor*" [A bit of love]), among others. In light of these examples, then, it appears that Shakira, as a *costeña, colombiana-libanesa*, woman, and recent immigrant to Miami, alternatively embraces and rejects the multiple characterizations that are imposed upon her both in the popular press and by her fans.

It may be tempting for cultural critics to interpret Shakira's predilection for nonautochthonous genres as a commercial strategy aimed at attracting a broader range of listeners. Nevertheless, Barranquilla's long history as

Figure 3.1. The caption below Shakira's photograph reads "Not all of us Arabs are terrorists." *Cristina (La Revista)*, December 2001.

Colombia's port of entry for foreign musical influences bears mention in this regard. Barranquilla and the smaller coastal city of Cartagena have long been viewed as the primary hosts to Colombia's musical vanguard, both imported and from within the nation's borders.[22] Founded in 1533, Cartagena became a major distribution point in the trans-Atlantic slave trade. An estimated one million slaves passed through its port, explaining the prevalence of African influences in the region's musical production.[23] However, following the construction of a rail connection between its port and Colombia's interior regions, in 1871, Barranquilla gained importance, ultimately surpassing Cartagena to the west and Santa Marta to the east as the region's commercial and industrial nucleus.

Barranquilla was home to Colombia's first radio station, La Voz de Barranquilla (The voice of Barranquilla), which began operating in 1929, as well as its second record company, Discos Tropical, founded around 1945, after Discos Fuentes was founded in Cartagena, in 1934. In particular, Barranquilla's status as a musical center may be traced to two of the city's historical institutions, the *tiendas* (stores) and the *carnaval* (carnival). The *tiendas*, or local convenience stores, provide customers with a seating area in front of the store at which they may gather, listen to the radio, and dance. The popularity of the *tiendas*, in turn, has rendered heavy radio rotation a must for musical acts hoping for success in Colombia. In addition, Barranquilla's renowned *carnaval* has typically served as a musical gathering point for the rhythms of Barranquilla and those of neighboring coastal settlements.[24] And, while both institutions have suffered from declining influence in Colombia in recent years, Jorge Arévalo-Mateus's account of the Carnaval de Barranquilla held in Queens, New York, each year underscores the relative vitality of these musical traditions among the U.S.-based Colombian population.[25] Large waves of European and Middle Eastern immigration to the Colombian Caribbean (primarily Italians, Syrians, Palestinians, and Lebanese) also made significant contributions toward shaping the region's unique musical identity. And, while Barranquilla's immigrants were not generally members of the elite in their countries of origin, in time they came to form a substantial portion of the city's entrepreneurial class; examples include Emilio Fortou, founder of Discos Tropical, and Elías Pellet Buitrago, founder of La Voz de Barranquilla.[26] Non-Colombian music, particularly Cuban, Mexican, and North American genres, has tended to enter the nation through Barranquilla, its primary physical and cultural port.

Given Shakira's roots in the Colombian Caribbean, her choice to perform and market herself as a *rockera* is noteworthy in and of itself. After releasing two albums full of pop ballads by age fifteen, she continued to move away from typically Caribbean genres such as *cumbia*, salsa, and *vallenato* and instead proceeded to record her own rock and pop compositions with the U.S.-Colombian producer Luis Fernando Ochoa, a long-time resident of Los Angeles.[27] As a *costeña* artist already overwhelmingly associated with the Latin(o) American youth market, and to some extent limited to that very market, Shakira made a decision to pursue a career as a *rockera* that was in many ways significant. For, while *rock en español* albums produced by local artists sell rather well outside Colombia's borders, within the country *rock en español* has yet to emerge as a major commercial genre; even the best-known bands, such as Bogotá's Aterciopelados, have until recently sold no more than 30,000 units within their own country.[28] Perhaps as a result of her predilection for non-Colombian genres, Shakira's music is considered to have broader marketing potential. And, although cultural hybridity, including musical hybridity, arguably constitutes the core of Latin(o) American identity, Shakira's particular brand of musical hybridity has often led music critics and executives to describe her work as somehow "less Latin" and more accessible to non-Latinos, in a sense reifying the boundaries between "Anglo" and "Latino" musical spaces.

Becoming a U.S. Latina/colombiana

With the success of *Pies descalzos*, Shakira caught the attention of Miami-based Sony Discos. Shortly afterward, she relocated to Miami to begin working with Emilio Estefan and his wife, the singer Gloria Estefan. Historically, Miami has played a role of singular importance to *barranquilleros*, particularly those from the middle and upper classes, for many of whom the pan-Latino metropolis embodies *"lo que quisiéramos que Barranquilla fuera"* ("what we wish Barranquilla was").[29] Thus, as a *barranquillera/costeña*, a Latin American, and a recording artist and composer aiming to appeal to both the Anglo and the Latino markets, Shakira, by relocating to Miami in the late 1990s, appeared to take the logical next step in her career trajectory. There, in a nod to her transnational status, she was selected as one of the most important figures of the year 2000 in both Miami and Colombia,[30] offering one of few hopeful images of Colombian culture in a sea of international media tropes largely limited to unilateral commentaries regarding the ongoing "war on drugs." The result of Shakira's inaugural collaboration with the Estefans, 1998's *Dónde están los ladrones?* (Where are the thieves?) triumphed in the Anglo, U.S. Latino, and Latin American markets, establishing

Shakira as the best-selling Latin(o) American recording artist in the world, having sold approximately 10 million records in Spanish and Portuguese in Latin America alone.[31]

Shakira's most visible live appearance in support of the *"Ojos así"* single, the most popular song from *Dónde están los ladrones?*, took place at the September 2000 Latin Grammys. The performance was choreographed around a display of traditional Middle Eastern dance movements. During another performance, the August 12, 1999, taping of her MTV Latin America Unplugged special ("unplugged" in the sense that it was a performance devoid of the usual battery of electronic studio equipment) in New York City, Shakira's choice of words at a key moment in the concert highlighted the sense of *Latinidad* that united her otherwise eclectic urban audience. In the bows and acknowledgments that followed a reworked performance of her hit *"Ciega, sordomuda"* (Blind, deaf, and dumb), a song whose structure is unmistakably influenced by the Mexican mariachi genre (and on this occasion performed in conjunction with the Miami-based mariachi group Los Mora Arriaga), Shakira accepted the audience's applause. She then paused a moment before shouting, *"¡Viva México! ¡Viva Colombia!"* and then *"¡Viva nuestra Latinidad!"* (Long live our Latinness!). It is at this juncture, among others, that Shakira "became" a U.S. Latina.[32] Not unexpectedly, each of Shakira's cheers directed specifically to Mexico and Colombia was met with considerable enthusiasm by the audience, but neither received the welcome accorded her final reference to *Latinidad*. As Simon Frith states, one of popular music's primary functions is to aid fans in fashioning a self-definition, which in turn produces what he terms the "pleasure of identification—with the music we like, with the performers of that music, and with the other people that like it. And it is important to note that the production of identity is also a production of non-identity—it is a process of inclusion and exclusion."[33]

That the crowd reacted so affirmatively to Shakira's words at the concert taping was in essence an expression of a sense of identity, in this case a common *Latinidad* that goes beyond links forged through shared musical tastes; it encompasses the identity politics enacted outside the concert space. For, as the ever-present Latin American flags waved at Latin(o) music concerts across the United States indicate, "only music seems capable of creating this sort of spontaneous collective identity, this kind of personally felt patriotism"[34] (or, I suggest, a shared sense of *Latinidad*, however fleeting). It is worth noting that nearly two years after the original taping of the concert, MTV's U.S. programming division elected to broadcast "Shakira Unplugged" (without subtitles) on its flagship English language network, making it the first Spanish-language program ever broadcast on the channel. The decision to air "Shakira Unplugged" was undoubtedly multifaceted in its aims and was intended to draw in bicultural, U.S. Latino viewers as well as MTV's more musically curious, if monolingual, audience members. In effect, it constituted an attempt to prime the channel's Anglo audience for Shakira's upcoming English debut.

Work on Shakira's follow-up English-language debut, initially based on translations of her existing hits, began in 1999, with the backing of Sony executives eager to emulate the success of "crossover" artists like Ricky Martin. It is interesting to note, moreover, that Gloria Estefan acted as Shakira's primary collaborator on the initial translation project, an arrangement that reflected Estefan's status as the literal and figurative conduit for Latina voices in the Miami music industry. In view of the Estefans' substantial, some would say hegemonic, hold on the Miami-based Latin(o) American music industry, Shakira's recent career has been portrayed as having been "edit[ed] by Gloria Estefan."[35] After several months of recording, however, the project was abandoned at Shakira's insistence in favor of an attempt to release an album of entirely new material written in English by Shakira herself, who had yet to compose any songs in English. Given the growing pressure on the music industry from large-scale retailers that were attempting to manage consumer consumption and the industry's resulting unwillingness to promote "risky" projects or artists,[36] Shakira's abandonment of the translation project stirred considerable interest within Miami industry circles. Her subsequent decision to no longer employ Emilio Estefan as her manager was met with astonishment, although Freddy DeMann, former manager of both Michael Jackson and Madonna, was soon hired in his place. In November 2001, amid a mainstream media blitz, *Laundry Service* was released and quickly achieved platinum status, outselling both *Madonna's Greatest Hits—Volume 2* and Britney Spear's *Britney*, both released in the same two-week period.[37] (Interestingly enough, Madonna and Britney Spears happen to be the two Anglo performers to whom Shakira was most frequently compared in the U.S. mainstream media at the time.) *Laundry Service* was considered the first major "crossover" album by a Spanish-dominant recording artist and ultimately sold more than 3.3 million copies in the United States and more than 13 million globally. In total, Shakira had sold 26 million units worldwide by this point in her career.[38]

Juxtaposed with the overtly commercial and, as many Latin(o) American fans claim, "inauthentic" recordings of Latin(o) American artists such as Ricky Martin and Gloria Estefan, Shakira's market positioning assumes a unique space. Hovering between the linguistic and cultural advocacy of Colombian groups like Aterciopelados and what is perceived by many as the musical opportunism of U.S. artists like Christina Aguilera, in many senses the very nature of Shakira's music and her public persona appear to defy facile categorization. For, while Shakira is featured in mainstream articles with titles like "The Making of a Rocker" (which suggests an Adornian notion of contemporary popular music performers as mere products of a globalized culture industry), she is simultaneously cast as a "true" artist who moves away from "packaged pop" and lends a much-needed voice to women.[39] As Juana Suárez argues, however, the "seductive globalizing force" of the Miami recording industry has for the most part eliminated the possibility of promoting a politicized artistic agenda for artists like Shakira.[40]

A thorough survey of the crowd, easily numbering a few thousand, that attended a South Beach (Miami) record-signing event in 2001 to promote *Laundry Service* revealed that Shakira's U.S. audience, much like her Colombian audience, is still primarily composed of adolescent girls.[41] *Laundry Service*'s thematic departure from Shakira's previous Spanish albums, however, has not gone unnoticed by the artist's longstanding Latin(o) American fan base. Accustomed to the relatively politically and socially topical compositions of *Dónde están los ladrones?*, as well as to the naturally black hair and more modest attire that Shakira affected during her previous media appearances and concerts, many of her Latin(o) American fans have at times reacted negatively to what they perceive as the singer's increasingly "anglicized" image (one Miami magazine, for example, quoted a group of young U.S. Latinas shouting out in Spanish "Don't forget about us!" to Shakira at the South Beach promotional appearance).[42] It is vital to contextualize these shifts in appearance and performing style, however, within the contemporary U.S. and global music industries. Indeed, in recent years, industry dictates have rendered it increasingly difficult for artists to mediate the delicate balance between the creative processes inherent to musical production on one hand and the overwhelming pressure to generate a commercially successful "product" on the other. As John Lovering notes, "the emphasis on selling (and reselling) rather than producing music is directly connected to the massive concentration of capital in the industry and the pressure to realize profits."[43] (Small wonder, then, that Shakira's new management team appeared to encourage her to cultivate an aesthetic more "familiar" to mainstream, monolingual U.S. audiences.) Shakira's status as a hot commodity was reflected quite literally in the creation of a line of *Laundry Service* Barbie dolls in her image. According to the toy giant Mattel, Shakira was selected as a model for the dolls because of her "multicultural appeal," an ironic fact given the near-identical appearance (minus a few wardrobe items) of the Shakira doll and the sleek-haired blonde, impossibly busty Anglo Barbie of old.[44]

The Transnational Media Writes Shakira: Gender, Genre, and Latina Sexuality

Despite Shakira's efforts to artistically and commercially separate herself from the latest incarnation of the Latin(o) music "boom" of the late 1990s, her representation within the U.S. mainstream media traces a pattern similar to those of most Latin(o) American artists. For much of the U.S. mainstream public, "third-world" and specifically Latin(o) American artists continue to embody the racial, ethnic, and cultural hybridity so often absent in official renderings of the U.S. national body. And, as the recent U.S Latino population boom has finally engaged the attentions of U.S. industry marketing strategists, it has also provoked a newfound "appreciation" of sorts and, in turn, fed a false sense of global cultural egalitarianism. As Bruce Orwall wrote in *The Wall Street Journal*, Shakira's imminent introduction to the U.S. mainstream offers the latest proof of a greater paradigm shift at hand, in which the "U.S. culture industry" looks to the South (Latin America), as opposed to the West (Europe), for the " next latest thing." Yet, Orwall's depiction of music industry efforts to market "a *mongrel global culture* that isn't necessarily born in the U.S.A.," immediately followed by the reassuring observation that "even when that entertainment doesn't come originally from America, *it is still influenced by it*,"[45] nonetheless hints at latent anxieties over the threat of hybrid/ "mongrel" subjects and their cultures. Ironically enough, the Colombian media expressed concern that Shakira and her upcoming English-language recordings, unlike those of market competitors Jennifer López and Christina Aguilera, would not be bicultural *enough* for U.S. audiences.[46]

Given Shakira's myriad musical and linguistic influences (to date, she has recorded entire albums or portions of albums not only in Spanish but also in Portuguese, Arabic, and English), this worry appeared laughable, but, as Angharad Valdivia and Ramona Curry's analysis of the Latin American superstar Xuxa's failure to capture a mainstream U.S. audience underscores, the fear that Shakira wouldn't "make sense" to U.S. Anglos was perhaps justified.[47] As Valdivia and Curry emphasize, the seemingly trivial media commentaries regarding the physical appearance of female performers, particularly comments related to hair styles and weight loss or gain, often allude to a host of covert anxieties. In the highly visible cases of Jennifer López, Christina Agu-

Figure 3.2. Cartoon depiction of Shakira from the September 2006 issue of *Latina* magazine. This drawing exemplifies the gendered, racialized undertones of popular Latin(o) American representation, as well as the multidirectional character of her media critiques.

ilera, and Shakira, for example, each woman has grown successively thinner and blonder since her emergence in the U.S. market. It is as if by means of hair dye and weight loss (and, in Aguilera's case, brilliant blue contact lenses, as well) these Latin(a) American women have sought to mitigate their reception within the U.S. mainstream conscience, in essence manipulating the visual in a way that renders them more "user-friendly" to non-Latinos. Indeed, the exotic/erotic nature of Shakira's performances, specifically her dance style based on Middle Eastern belly dance movements, has emerged as a primary hallmark of her publicity campaign. As such, Shakira's belly has emerged as the primary site of her difference and her (quite literally) embodied media coverage, a fact rendered more salient by the increased international emphasis on the Middle East and its cultures in the post-9/11 context. Shakira, referred to in the English-language media as a "*bomba* shell" who has made a "hip-shaking English debut," has embraced the notion that her dancing ability is somehow part and parcel of a uniquely Latin(o) American genetic inheritance. In interviews, she has remarked that her ability to move her body is "something that is in my DNA" and that "no one told me how to move my hips," reinforcing the popular belief in an inherent link between Latina corporality and hypersexuality, as well as the traditional mind/European, body/"Latin" binary.[48] (Significantly, a few years later, Shakira's single "Hips Don't Lie" earned the distinction of becoming the most-played song in U.S. radio history.)

This apparent inability on the part of the U.S. mainstream media to extricate Shakira's public persona from more stereotypical paradigms of Latina identity and corporality (a situation that she and her management team have themselves perpetuated to some degree) manifests itself as well in the constant parallels drawn in the English-language press between Shakira and the Anglo performer Britney Spears—a comparison that, curiously enough, does not appear in the Spanish-language press. As Deborah Parédez notes, such comparisons "strategically invoke Latina sexuality as means by which both to mark its excessiveness and to contain it."[49] Unlike most mainstream media journalists, however, who tend to categorize Shakira as a substitutive entity (such as "a new"/"another" Madonna, Spears, or Alanis Morissette), Latin(o) Americans at her November 2001 South Beach appearance indicated that they viewed Shakira as an additive cultural force capable of maintaining multiple, simultaneous identities: "She *preserves* Colombian culture and *adds* to American culture, making it richer."[50] The younger Spears, well known at the time for her close relationship to her mother, who was also her touring companion, was perhaps even better known for her early statement that she intended to remain a virgin until marriage. In the few years since, however, Spears's increased tendency to favor skimpy clothing while performing, in addition to a highly publicized romantic relationship, led the U.S. media to report on her "virginity pact" (or lack thereof) with a noticeable degree of sarcasm, if not outright criticism. Ironically, as a teenage star in Colombia, Shakira made a similar public vow to maintain her virginity until she married, "barefoot, in an intimate ceremony, dressed in white and virgin at the ocean's edge,"[51] a statement common within Colombian public discourse, if not in private practice; more than thirty years of age, she still travels with her parents on tour and shares a home with them in Miami Beach. As Súarez observes, the notion of family (and, more specifically, Shakira's protection of and dependence on her family) has long been central to the construction of her public persona. Widely photographed moments like her visit with Pope John Paul II and her parent's constant presence lend Shakira an air of the "good girl" who just happens to be a rock star (and sex symbol) and may also have the net effect of softening any social critiques present in Shakira's music.[52] Notably, this widespread depiction also presents her with the opportunity for an embedded, and potentially more subversive, critique.

Since her earlier public declaration, however, Shakira has in more recent interviews remained silent on the subject of her virginity, despite interviewers' repeated efforts to provoke some sort of comment. The disproportionate amount of media attention dedicated to Shakira's sexuality (a dynamic that may be equally ascribed to the popular media, industry marketing trends, fans, Shakira, and her own management team) underscores a seeming inability to evaluate young female artists, particularly non-Anglos, on the basis of their musical attributes rather than their physical appearance and sexuality. Thus, in another sense, and perhaps more significantly, this practice highlights the well-entrenched acceptance of *marianismo* (or the "Madonna/whore" complex) that informs Shakira's framing within the transnational media.

Conversely, Frances Negrón Muntaner and Dolores Inés Casillas offer a more U.S. Latina-centric, though no less politicized, reading of Latin(a) American corporality within the U.S. popular media. Specifically, in contrast to Anglo feminist interpretations that tend to monolithically interpret media attention to the physical appearances of popular Latin(a) American entertainers, particularly Jennifer López, as merely another sexist, racist display, these analyses posit alternative readings of López, in which "the big rear end acts both as an identification site for Latinas to reclaim their beauty and a 'compensatory fantasy' for a whole community."[53] These interpretations, in keeping with Michel Foucault's belief that "we must not think that by say-

Figure 3.3. *La evolución de Shakira* (Shakira's evolution). Note the usage of the term "evolution," which connotes a positive change or, more specifically, a form of personal advancement. The featured vignette is from the February 2002 issue of *People en Español*.

Figure 3.4. "How a Catholic Schoolgirl Seduced America." Cover image from the April 11, 2002, issue of *Rolling Stone* magazine. During that month, Shakira graced the covers of two widely distributed U.S. magazines (*Blender* being the other), both of which proclaimed her ability to successfully "seduce" her way onto the "American" music scene.

ing yes to sex, one says no to power,"[54] also hint at the longstanding notion of sexuality as a weapon of the weak. Curiously, a common motif in two recent English-language cover stories on Shakira is the use of a cover photo of Shakira on which is superimposed a caption referencing her "seduction" of America (see figure 3.4). In both accompanying articles, Shakira declares her desire to "seduce" the United States, which she explicitly goes on to distinguish from any desire to "conquer" the country. This word choice stands in stark contrast to an earlier interview in the July 2001 issue of *Latina* magazine, in which she rather pointedly expressed her plan to "conquer" the world through her music.[55] In these later examples, the more overt, even militaristic vocabulary exemplified in verbs such as "conquer" is abandoned in favor of the more covert, feminine discourse of seduction. Thus, seduction here acts by "forwarding the strengths of weakness" within an oppositional framework in which "power comes to be defined not by domination, but by the manipulations of the dominated."[56] This interplay of power and seduction, then, gives rise to a complex media dialectic, or the containment of Latino "excess" by means of commodification; once commodified, Shakira earns permission to "seduce" her way into the U.S. mainstream popular imagination.

Moreover, the U.S. media's tendency to mediate Shakira's introduction to the U.S. mainstream public via constant comparisons to well-known female Anglo pop and/or rock stars, such as Spears and the Canadian Alanis Morrisette, signals the deeply entrenched belief in rock as an inherently European or U.S. genre. Indeed, the apparent need for constant references to female Anglo performers as a means of "explaining" Shakira suggests that journalists have little faith in the mainstream audience's ability to conceptualize the existence of successful, female, Latin(a) American *rockeras* (rock singers/musicians). The contrived and historically gendered division of "pop versus rock," exemplified by the fact that Shakira was awarded *both* the rock and the pop Latin Grammys for the same album at the September 2000 ceremony, is clearly present in media representations of Shakira.[57] Shakira's perceived merit and very identity as a *rockera* is thereby informed by a popular media and an industry both dominated by male assessments of female ability and physical attractiveness. Notwithstanding the overwhelmingly positive (and voluminous) press coverage that she receives in Colombia, and although she publicly labels herself a *rockera*, Shakira has been criticized for her lack of credibility within the genre. Indeed, while one cover story in the Colombian news magazine *Semana* praised her in one paragraph for losing weight and dying her hair blonde, in the next paragraph the authors cited her lack of validity among rock fans, citing comparisons to several other Latin(o) American rock acts (all male, with the notable exception of Andrea Echeverri), thus delineating the ways in which "'community' can be site both of support and oppression." In a similar vein, the *rock en español* critic Ernesto Lechner categorizes Shakira as a "so-called Latin rock star" whose arena shows are "lots of fun." As Lechner notes, "Any *rock en español* fan worth his salt will tell you that [Shakira does not belong] in the defiantly unique aesthetic of the movement ... concentrate on the bands and solo artists who have made a *serious* contribution to Latin alternative as an innovative field."[58] Lechner's statements are problematic on several counts: first, the lexicon clearly indicates that Lechner's imagined fan/reader is male; moreover, the veracity of his categorization is thrown into question by the seeming boundlessness of the *rock en español* category itself.

Nevertheless, the gendering of rock reflected in this media coverage is neither a product of its primordial maleness nor a reflection of some predetermined masculine sensibility. Rather, the cultural association between rock and masculinity exemplified in Lechner's commentary is best understood as an artifice that is *actively* perpetuated through the everyday activities and ideologies of the global rock industry.[59] The vast majority of the popular press coverage on Shakira, both in Colombia and in the United States, is generated by male critics, which may well have impacted her portrayal within the press as a latter-day Lolita of sorts. Within the context of rock journalism, the potential impact of "men writing women," or what we might alternatively term the "discursive impacts" of (neo)colonialism,[60] is not to be underestimated. The *Rolling Stone* reporter Rob Sheffield's article "Shakira Sinks Her Colombian Flag," for example, describes Shakira as the "recently blonde, frequently dressed, belly-dancing, CHARO-channeling Colombian love machine ... not to be confused with ... anything involving your moneymaker or the shaking thereof." Here, Sheffield conflates Spain (as embodied by the campy 1970s entertainer Charo) with Latin America, *Latinidad* with an inherent, unbridled sexuality ("Colombian love machine"), and a host of Latin(o) boom stars (Ricky Martin and Jennifer López come to mind) with an emphasis on one's rear end ("moneymaker") and the commercialization thereof. He also hints at prevailing stereotypes linking Colombian identity to drug trafficking: "Why, Colombia hasn't had such a major impact on American popular music since the EAGLES broke up!," thereby reducing Shakira's contributions, if not those of all contemporary Colombian musicians, to the realm of illicit narcotics use.[61]

Sheffield's article also foregrounds what he perceives as the excessive character of Shakira's work on *Laundry Service*. When he writes that "her actual music can strip the paint off a passing car" and that "she's just a louder, pushier, version of what she thinks an American pop star should sound like,"[62] he reinscribes longstanding beliefs regarding *Latinidad* as a culture of excess. Frank Kogan's *Village Voice* review of *Laundry Service* adopts a similar, if less pronounced, attitude toward Shakira's vocals on the album, as he criticizes her inability to sing or write "soft songs"; in fact, two-thirds of Kogan's article is dedicated to his musings on the state of Shakira's voice.[63] The emphasis in both reviews on what these male critics label a "weakness" in Shakira's work—ironically, the very *strength* of her voice—serves as a prime example of the ways in which patriarchy often works to undercut the power of women's public voices. As Aída Hurtado notes in her comparative analysis of women's discursive styles, the communicative stylings of women of color, differing as they so often do from those of white women and (most significantly) those of white men, can serve as an alternative form of political power.[64] As such, the sheer power and forcefulness of Shakira's voice, or, more specifically, the vocal timbres in which she expresses herself, may at the very least be read as a threat to the established gatekeepers of U.S. mainstream popular culture.

Female journalists, especially those who write for the Spanish-language market, also tend to perform more traditional readings of Shakira, focusing for the most part on the minute details of Shakira's romantic life. Shakira herself did little to dispel these more traditional depictions of Latina female identity in press interviews promoting *Laundry Service*, a "crossover" album that ultimately sold 13 million copies worldwide. References to her search for her *príncipe azul* (literally, blue prince, or the colloquial Spanish for Prince Charming) and her actual fiancé, Antonio de la Rúa, son of Argentina's ex-president, predominated. Echoing the chorus of the ballad "Underneath Your Clothes," the second single released from *Laundry Service*, Shakira repeatedly described herself as a "good girl" worthy of de la Rúa's love[65] and as a woman of "very developed" maternal instincts."[66] Moreover, as she framed herself almost exclusively in terms of her roles as a girlfriend and future wife/mother, Shakira explicitly separated herself and her work on *Laundry Service* from any sort of overtly feminist or political agenda: "It's not *feminist*, my position in these songs, it's more *feminine*."[67]

Shakira Writes Herself

Shakira's media portrayal as a talented if somewhat apolitical artist, however, is belied by the latent critiques present in one of her previous Spanish-language compositions. "*Se quiere se mata*" (Wanted, killed), the final cut on the 1996 album *Pies descalzos*, for example, offers commentary regarding the issue of abortion in overwhelmingly Catholic Colombia. Packaged as a simply structured, synthesizer-driven pop song (indeed, the song's thematic and musical dissonance is one of its central features), "*Se quiere se mata*" chronicles the story of Dana, an upper-class teenage girl who accidentally becomes pregnant by her boyfriend. Employing a third-person narrative voice, Shakira tells of how the young woman, anxious that neither her family nor the neighbors learn of her pregnancy, makes a visit to the doctor in order to "*acabar con el problema*" (get rid of the problem). As the song progresses, we note a perceptible shift from the modulated vocal tones with which Shakira recounts the young lovers' story to the more urgent vocals and rhythm of the final verse. It is the final verse that openly communicates the song's, and perhaps Shakira's, opinions about abortion: "*Fuiste donde el doctor a acabar con el problema / hoy tu vecino está en casa dándose un buen duchazo / y tú dos metros bajo tierra viendo crecer gusanos*" (You went to the doctor to get rid of the problem / today your neighbor's at home taking a nice shower / and you're six feet under watching the maggots grow).[68] This narrative shift to the second person "you," in striking contrast to the rest of the song's third-person perspective, speaks directly to Dana's fate and the consequences of her lack of access to a safe abortion, as well as to Shakira's invisible interlocutor. In the musical narrative, not only do Dana and her unborn child meet an untimely end; the neighbor "taking a nice shower," blissfully divorced from the everyday struggles of contemporary youth, figuratively recalls the song's other "death": the death of an open, collective discussion regarding adolescent sexuality and reproduction. The embedded critique in "*Se quiere se mata*" of the attitudes and beliefs endemic to bourgeois Colombian mores thus functions as a clear example of the "Pandora's Box" of sexualities in rock. Simply stated, by virtue of its female-centric theme, the song runs counter to rock's established use as a terrain within which men are free to express a largely heterosexual identity absent the "messiness" of pregnancy, disease, child care, and abortion or a locus within which rock is a site for the "exscription" of the feminine. As Sheila Whiteley argues, "such stereotypes do not only situate the body as the seat of subjectivity, they equally situate it as the target of power and social control."[69]

In the final analysis, however, "*Se quiere se mata*" proves the exception among Shakira's earlier recordings, which as a rule tend to avoid overt political commentary. Inspired by the real-life theft of a suitcase containing the only existing copies of her most recent compositions, Shakira titled her first U.S.-produced album *Dónde están los ladrones?* (Where are the thieves?).[70] Ultimately, the album's title query evolves into a sly reference to the political corruption and general social mistrust that pervade contemporary Colombian society. It is a corruption in which Shakira recognizes her own complicity both visually (the album cover features a photo of her, soot-covered

Figure 3.5. Album cover, *Dónde están los ladrones?* Sony Discos, 1998.

palms up, literally caught with her hands "dirty") and lyrically ("dónde están los ladrones / dónde está el asesino / quizá allá revolcándose / en el patio del vecino / . . . y qué pasa si son ellos / *y qué pasa si soy yo* / el que toca esta guitarra / o la que canta esta canción" [Where are the thieves / where's the murderer? / maybe he's there wallowing around / on the neighbor's patio . . . and what happens if it's them / *and what happens if it's me* / the one that's playing this guitar / or the one that's singing this song]) (see figure 3.5).[71] Shakira's 2001 English-language album *Laundry Service* represented a considerable departure from *Dónde están los ladrones?*, both musically and thematically, in its reliance on power ballads and more traditional romantic themes.

A "New [Trans]National Era": Another Facet of Latinidad

More often than not, the ways in which Shakira is written within the transnational popular media, particularly within the U.S. mainstream press, contradict her alternative media portrayal: that of the idealized, transnational *colombiana*. Significantly, in the case of Shakira, this construction has served to advance state-sponsored notions of civic responsibility, as a brief glance back over her earlier career chronology indicates. The watershed moment of Shakira's career thus far occurred during the September 2000 inaugural broadcast of the Latin Grammys, described in the Colombian media as a "second-class award," in which she was awarded Grammys for Best Female Pop Performance and Best Female Rock Performance.[72] However, it was not until February 2001, when Shakira received the "traditional" Grammy for Best Latin Pop Album, that her public persona began to undergo radical changes in the Colombian and, to a lesser extent, the U.S. media.

Once "discovered" by the public and music industry figures north of Miami, Shakira began to be referred to in the principal pages of Colombia's newspapers as "unstoppable," "good news from Colombia," and the "national pride," among other terms of praise.[73] In fact, shortly following the international success of *Dónde están los ladrones?*, Colombia's then-president, Andrés Pastrana, cited Shakira, among other Colombian artists, as "emblems of a new national era."[74] Later, in a further reflection of the ongoing union of art and politics, (trans)nationalism and symbolism enacted within Colombia's public sphere, Pastrana presented Shakira with the title of Colombia's "national goodwill ambassador."[75]

As demonstrated in the case of Shakira, highly transnationalized states have taken to cultivating these extra-official, largely symbolic public figures in the hope that individuals abroad will develop and/or maintain their economic and social ties to the homeland. Thus, even when concentrated at the local level, or what might aptly be described as transnationalism with a "small t," cross-border dynamics constitute "a product of interchange and the strategic behavior of people in local settings."[76] In this regard, transnationalism is employed as a means of community management and governmental instrumentality.[77] Specifically, Shakira's quasi-official status provided the much-criticized Pastrana government with a precious link to its citizens, both in Colombia and abroad. This is just one example of how national institutions and political practices are increasingly molded by globalization and the global economy and how, as a result, previous constructions of national identity continue to rapidly lose currency.[78]

This move marked the beginning of an increasingly transnational dynamic that culminated in the Colombian government's aforementioned 1991 approval of dual Colombian-U.S. citizenship and the subsequent coining of phrases like "*colombianos en el exterior*" ("Colombians in the exterior") to refer to Colombians living outside the nation's geopolitical borders.[79] The same year, Colombians *en el exterior* were also granted the right to vote in the country's national elections. In 1997, Colombians transnationals were allotted a congressional seat. To date, the majority of the congressional representatives have been residents of the New York or Miami metropolitan regions, and their participation in Colombian-U.S. politics consistently belies the notion of the passive transnational citizen. These ongoing developments thus indicate a distinct movement toward a bicultural, transnational politics, accompanied by a concomitant shift from a pan-Latino to a U.S.-Colombian-centered communal identity.[80]

Arguably, since Colombia's approval of dual citizenship in 1991, a move that has provoked a shift in the ways in which all those who self-identify as Colombians conceptualize *colombianidad*, no one else has come to publicly symbolize the state-sponsored construction of the idealized, transnational Colombian citizen in the broad sense that Shakira has. Here we witness another facet of *Latinidad*: while Shakira is herself free to accept *Latinidad* by means of numerous symbolic acts and thereby "become" a U.S. Latina and/or U.S.-*colombiana*, at times *Latinidad* is thrust upon her, largely for the political and economic gain of others.

However, individual concepts of identity and communal belonging are by no means limited by state-imposed parameters. Much like other contemporary transnationals, U.S.-Colombians have devised their own unique means of "being Colombian" within the United States. For example, as Shakira's very public and repeated use of the phrase "¡*Viva Colombia!*" (Long live Colombia!) at internationally televised awards ceremonies and concerts attests, she appears acutely aware of her position among Colombians everywhere. One major Colombian newspaper quoted her as stating, following her February 2001 Grammy win, "I know what this means for my country."[81] The fact that Shakira, like most Latin(o) American award winners at the mainstream Grammys, dedicated her award to an entire nation testifies to the clearly delineated element of difference that these artists embody in comparison to popular music's dominant genres, performers, and linguistic codes. In contrast, within the context of the Latin Grammys, these public displays of national pride fulfill the aims of both the Latin Academy of Recording Arts and Sciences (LARAS) and its advertisers, entities that strive to attract a larger audience by offering fare of as broad appeal as possible.[82]

Furthermore, it is likely that, for Shakira herself, her fabricated role as the idealized, transnational Colombian affords her access to a higher status than would have been accorded her and an alternative power hierarchy that perhaps would not have been available to her had she remained in Colombia, given her gender, age, and regional affiliations. Issues of power and gender are particularly salient here, in light of evidence that Latin(a) American female migrants, unlike their male counterparts, tend to report an improvement in their gender status upon relocating to the United States. As George Lipsitz observes, "[g]lobalization does not just change relations between countries, it also upsets relations between genders." It is in this sense, then, that liberation for one group can signify oppression for another.[83]

Thus, the ways in which Shakira's fellow *colombianos*, both in the United States and in Colombia but particularly in the United States, recognize and validate her *individual* artistic and commercial standing provide the transnational Colombian community at large with a vital *collective* context for expressing statuses and identities not always available to them in the United States.[84] As Gordon Matthews argues, "understanding the nature of individuals' sense of commitment or lack of commitment to the nation and the states is as essential as understanding larger institutional and historical forces in comprehending the interrelation of nation and state in the world today."[85] In this regard, Shakira's public persona operates as a quasi-oppositional rendering of the (trans)national body politic that is of significant import, given her multiple subject positionings. Thus, for Shakira, a U.S. Latino identity cannot be conceived of without a Latin American identity, and vice versa. As a process of both interpellation and representation, the work of identity formation necessarily entails a negotiation of the autobiographical and the biographical.[86] Therefore, while highly visible and, indeed, universally marketable, transnational figures like Shakira are certainly free to embrace *Latinidad* and a concomitant U.S. Latina identity, by the same token, *Latinidad* may be just as easily be imposed upon them from the outside.

4

Florecita rockera

Gender and Representation in Latin(o) American Rock and Mainstream Media

Florecita rockera   Little rock blossom
Tú te lo buscaste   You asked for it
Por despertar mi pasión   By arousing my passion
Encendiste mi hoguera   You lit my fire
No tienes perdón   There's no forgiving you
Te pondré en una matera   I'll put you in a flower pot
— Aterciopelados, *"Florecita rockera"*

Fresh-cut flowers, along with coffee, emeralds, and cocaine, figure among Colombia's principal exports. Therefore, it seems entirely suitable—though perhaps merely coincidental—that *"Florecita rockera"* (Little rock blossom), as sung by the lead singer of Aterciopelados, Andrea Echeverri, has emerged as one of the defining anthems of the Colombian rock movement. When read in isolation, *"florecita"* may well simply reference a primary cash crop; read in conjunction with *"rockera"* (female rocker), however, this flower assumes an entirely different meaning. Relying on lyrics heavy in plant and floral imagery juxtaposed against a punk/ska backdrop, *"Florecita rockera"* unites the seemingly disparate worlds of the stereotypically "feminine" and hard-core punk music.[1] As evidenced in the song's opening verse, in which Echeverri inquires *"Cómo echarte flores/ Si eres un jardín?"* (How can one give you compliments [literally, throw you flowers]/ If you're already a garden?"), *"Florecita rockera"*'s first-person narrative is replete with colloquial Colombian phrases that reference not only nature in its physical forms but also recall another, supposedly "natural" phenomenon: the gender dynamics underlying the (ostensibly heterosexual) mating ritual. *"Florecita"*'s first-person narrative voice, that of Echeverri, is notably a woman's voice, effectively leading us to question the perspective from which she performs. Initially, it

| 87

is difficult to distinguish whether Echeverri is taking on a disapproving tone (as she directly addresses her complaints to the "*florecita*" in the first person) or whether she is simply ironically parroting the criticisms she herself has received as a fellow *florecita*. As in much of Aterciopelados's repertoire, the self-referential character of Echeverri's delivery and composition ultimately serve to dull the sting of would-be insults.

It is not until the song reaches its ska-inspired bridge that "*Florecita rockera*" offers listeners a bit of clarity, as Echeverri openly assumes the "masculine" role of sexual aggressor that she has hinted at all along, affirming: "*Soy el picaflor / Que chupará toda tu miel*" ("I'm the Casanova [literally, hummingbird] / That will suck up all of your honey"). If we read through "*Florecita rockera*"'s lyrical double-speak, it becomes apparent here that Echeverri is not merely physically occupying the traditionally masculine space at the front of a rock band. Rather, by declaring herself a *picaflor*, she is also intent on challenging the naturalness of the societal gender norms that have long dictated the rules of the heterosexual mating game and subverting the traditional role of female vocalist as the mediating instrument of messages constructed by men, for men.[2] It is this willingness to challenge audience's preexisting notions regarding gender and *rock en español* that has enabled Andrea Echeverri to offer an alternative vision of contemporary Colombian gender dynamics against the back drop of the transnational Latin(o) music boom and the emergence of music video in Latin America.

My reading of Andrea Echeverri and her music focuses on *rock en español* as it pertains to issues of marketing and gender within Colombian rock. Colombian *rockeras* like Andrea Echeverri are gaining increased visibility at a moment in which Colombian popular music in general is riding a wave of favorable recognition, independently as well as under the auspices of the greater so-called Latin(o) music boom. Significantly, much of the current praise for Colombian popular music has been reserved for the nation's pop and/or *rock en español* artists, despite the genre's relative lack of popularity within Colombia itself. Of further note is the fact that the media focus on Colombian *rock en español* (a genre that, like its U.S. and European counterparts, has historically excluded women), largely centers on Shakira and Echeverri, the lead singer of the Bogotá-based band Aterciopelados. As Sheila Whiteley states, "[r]ock's function is to confer masculinity: to enter the domain of rock is a male rite of passage."[3] Echeverri's femaleness and national origins are therefore constantly foregrounded in the popular press; for as a *latinoamericana*, she embodies the double bind of gender and ethno-racial identity. With musical and thematic content that highlights Colombia's ethnoracial and ideological diversity, Echeverri and the band that she leads have carved out a unique space for women's voices in *rock en español*. Her preference for the rock idiom, long known as a "difficult-to-police" medium (hence its attraction for those women seeking to access a culturally "masculine" mode of musical expression),[4] thus renders Echeverri a particularly salient subject of inquiry regarding gender dynamics in the Latin(o) American rock sphere.

Echeverri, and the Miami-based industry in which she maneuvers, also exemplifies the music industry's current tranformations in accordance with the dictates of globalization.[5] Therefore, via an examination of Echeverri's recordings, music video performances, and an analysis of popular print media, I consider issues of gender and representation within the greater contemporary Latin(o) music boom and the Miami music industry. In particular, I examine the ways in which the popular media represent Andrea Echeverri as a gendered subject to mainstream U.S. consumers. I also elucidate the means by which Echeverri herself engages in an "aesthetics of transgression"[6] in order to musically articulate the quotidian gender dynamics of contemporary Colombia and beyond.

Much of contemporary writing on rock is done within a context in which white male U.S. or European identity functions as the unspoken, unmarked point of reference. As Norma Coates explains, this attitude is apparent in much of male-produced journalistic and academic writing's tendency to "relate to 'women in rock' as men in rock plus and minus a few crucial anatomical parts."[7] That said, my analysis constitutes an effort to clarify just how the popular music media mold our perceptions as they simultaneously construct an illusion with respect to Andrea Echeverri's positionality as a Colombian *rockera*. It also strives to dismantle the limiting tropes of "latinization" that inform most media depictions of Latin(a) American performers of *rock en español*.[8]

Rock en español, Colombian Style: From the 1950s to the "Second Wave"

For artists and musicians coming of age in Bogotá, the 1980s marked a period of rapid cultural transnationalization. Then as now, Bogotá, long the hegemonic epicenter of Colombia's highly regionalized political, economic, and cultural geography, served as home to the nation's nascent rock movement. As Pilar Riaño-Alcalá observes, *bogotano* youth of this generation were distinguished by a particular dynamic of appropriation of cultural products and a different manner of defining their relationship with the world (we-they). These youth, as much as they can be fascinated by technological novelties, fashions of "development," of the agendas of radical movements, still maintain and activate in their expressive realm the "parent" culture, the popular culture: a parent culture that provides them with a universe of the senses where the melodramatic, the romantic, and the past mediate everyday experiences.[9]

Many of *rock en español*'s current generation of performers, several of them, like Andrea Echeverri, now in their thirties and forties, have expressed an overt rejection of this rigid leftist doctrine of their adolescence, which deemed local genres the only legitimate avenues of musical expression. Instead, most contemporary U.S. Latino and Latin American rock aesthetics and ideologies reject the implied relationship between cultural identity and patrimony.[10]

Drawing primarily from Anglo rock stylings and forms, early incarnations of *rock en español* began to appear in Colombia, as in much of Latin America, as early as the late 1950s. Disc jockeys from Radio Caracol (Cadena Radial Colombiana) began incorporating U.S. rock selections as novelty items in their playlists around 1958. For the rather insular Colombia of the 1950s, rock music served as a "revolving door to the global community." The ever-changing ebb and flow of the Colombian rock scene that emerged from these beginnings mirrored the nation's rapid urbanization and the dramatic demographic shifts that occurred in the decades that followed.[11]

If the 1960s marked an era of festivity associated with Colombian rock, the postintroductory period spanning the years from the 1970s to the 1990s signaled various transformations in rock's production and reception. Much as they were for the Mexican rock of the era, the 1970s were a time of underground activity for Colombian *rockeros*, as more cheaply produced local genres such as the *vallenato* claimed precedence. As expressed in the 1977 novel *¡Que viva la música!* (Long live music!), written by Andrés Caicedo, a native of Cali, Colombia, for many Colombian youth of the era, rock was still viewed as a mere imperialist import associated with a bourgeois mindset. Thus, the female protagonist of Caicedo's novel eventually rejects rock music (which she associates with the English language), and local musical genres altogether in favor of salsa, which for her embodies the creative expression of the Latin(o) American popular classes: "I swelled up with life, my eyes swelled as I remembered how much I had understood the lyrics in Spanish, the culture of my country, I let out a great yell born of the sun within: 'Down with Yankee cultural penetration!'"[12] In this sense, Caicedo's protagonist reflects prototypical youth attitudes of the period and, more specifically, an individual "at a point of cultural crisis that ranges from a [perceived] lack of cultural tradition to dependence on foreign culture."[13] Because of its emphasis on Colombia's cultural fragmentation at this specific historical juncture, namely the euphoric rewriting of Latin America engendered by the literary boom, *¡Que viva la música!* is considered by many Colombia's first postmodern novel.[14] However, Caicedo's perspective represents a marked contrast from the 1980s youth culture that was to follow, in which so-called native and foreign musical genres coexisted in less Manichean fashion.

To the north, the 1980s also heralded the rise of music video, which, along with digital music downloading, constituted the music industry's most important innovation of the second half of the twentieth century. Film and television's appropriation of popular music culture via the introduction of MTV into North American homes in 1982 marked a new era in the entertainment industry's integration, expansion, and concentration. This development, in turn, wielded a singular impact on the configuration of social space; unlike radio,

> music television is national; it spans the map as if there were no boundaries, no regions, no borders, encouraging us to see music as a transnational product emanating from an abstract space. Its symbolic landscape fills a vacuum that has been left by its own suspending of music from "real space," which, like real time, is a concept related to the human body. Video frames the song, encloses it in a shared symbolic (but not physical) space, and invites us to enter that space, or rather, to invite it into our own. Then we go out and buy the records.[15]

MTV therefore emerged as a "new [transnational, transcultural] language," and the idiom further expanded with the launch of Miami-based MTV Latino on October 1, 1993. Merely one year later, MTV Latino had become the leading cable network in South America.[16]

Also during the 1980s, rock began to re-emerge and to earn a broader audience among all Colombians. The rock music of the late 1980s distinguished itself from the strain of *rock en español* that arose in the mid-1980s, which was heavily influenced by the punk scene and was therefore attractive to struggling musicians because of its relative technical simplicity and minimal equipment demands. (Indeed, by mid-decade the term "*el rock en tu idioma*" [rock in your language] had emerged.) Latin American universities, home to much student political activism during the period, shared the art-based educational philosophy that formed the bedrock of European higher education. The educational and political contexts that gave rise to English punk music therefore contributed to the flourishing of *rock en español* in the mid-1980s. By now beyond mere translation and mimicry of U.S. and European pop and rock standards, the nascent Latin American musical groups of the period, among them Aterciopelados, began to cultivate popular music that "neither forgets Latin America's rich popular and folk traditions nor adapts them passively. These groups adopt and adapt *mambo, bolero, cumbia*, and *carrilera*, but they do so critically."[17] In this regard, the developmental trajectory of Latin American rock resists simplistic models of cultural imperialism and instead delineates the ingenious merging of global and local mass cultural forms. It was not until the 1990s, though, that Colombian rock bands began to engage in sustained musical experimentation and efforts to expand their audiences beyond the nation's borders. It is at this stage, then, that Colombian *rock en español* is perhaps most accurately conceptualized as a truly indigenized musical and cultural art form. Neither Latin American nor North American (though at times musically, if not lyrically, indistinguishable from expressive forms associated with the latter), *rock en español* surfaced as a third space. This space offered an alternative site of self-expression to young Colombians who had matured under the weight of potent foreign cultural influences while experiencing the simultaneous pull of the family, the Catholic church, and the educational institutions that demanded their loyalty to local culture.[18]

However, to speak of a unified "*rock nacional*" (national rock) in the Colombian context, as is done in Argentina and Mexico, is likely unfeasible, despite rock's increased popularity and ongoing artistic development within Colombia and beyond. The reason for this is Colombia's historical lack of a solidified official culture, in addition to a rather unstable record of rock music production. Perhaps contributing most to this dearth of a consolidated national rock culture is Colombia's entrenched regionalism; notably, Colombian rock production has centered almost exclusively in the interior industrial cities of Bogotá and Medellín. Rock's greater popularity in the interior regions is also clearly reflected in the playlists of each city's radio stations: as of the late 1990s, approximately 50 percent of the FM stations in Bogotá and Medellín were dedicated to rock, while only about 9 percent of Barranquilla's FM stations played rock music. To some extent, this was a result of the Caribbean region's longstanding predilection for genres such as salsa and *merengue*.[19] In sum, the pathways traced by Colombian rock recall those traveled by the nation itself:

> In many respects, the variety of [rock] genres and the abundance of almost individual statements confirm the lack of cohesiveness in Colombian society. It is exceedingly hard to suggest a common, collective spirit in Colombian rock. Rock in Colombia is Colombian by association; it is far from being national in its cultural disposition and background.... In Colombia, nation and state allude to very different spaces.[20]

Despite these obstacles, Colombian rock experienced considerable growth in both the national and the international arenas through the late twentieth and early twenty-first centuries. Moreover, as current and future Colombian groups continue to incorporate autochthonous rhythms, instruments, musical genres, language, and social themes into their rock compositions, a more clearly recognizable pattern of rock development has begun to surface, if only in a more informal sense. More recent Colombian artists (Aterciopelados, Bloque, and Juanes being some prime examples) have tended to prioritize local forms and thematics in their work. Thus, despite the U.S. media's simplistic characterization of *rock en español* as "a sonic shift away from regionalism [that] points to a new global Latin identity,"[21] Colombian rock and, in a more general sense, MTV Latino will likely continue to serve as prime sites for the transnational rearticulation and reinvention of Latin(o) American identity.

Though still relatively dwarfed within Colombia by the popularity of national genres such as *vallenato*, *cumbia*, and pan-Latino forms like salsa, in the U.S. sales of *rock en español* music increased fivefold from the mid- to the late 1990s, though the music industry has accomplished little in terms of formal recordkeeping on the genre.[22] During the same period, led by acts such as Carlos Vives, Shakira, Bloque, Ehkymosis, Aterciopelados, Juanes, and the late Soraya, Colombian popular music enjoyed a marked increase in the popularity of its hybrid pop and rock forms abroad. Soon afterward, with the advent of the "first wave" of successful Latin(o) music acts in 1999, some U.S. music executives, newly awakened to the untapped potential of the U.S. Latino market and the existence of non-Latino publics eager for "new forms of community and pleasure,"[23] began preparations to launch a so-called second wave[24] of popular Latin(o) musical releases. These executives ostensibly reasoned that even if these second-wave acts performed in Spanish, their guitar-based sounds and general music aesthetic would render them more familiar to mainstream audiences than other Latin(o) forms such as *merengue* or *banda*. (Tellingly, until recently the industry had not even included Latin[o] American rock music under the rubric "Latin music," regardless of the language in which it is sung).[25] It is crucial to remember that the labeling of many of these second-wave *rock en español* groups as "alternative" or "Alterlatino" above all denotes an industry-generated marketing category, rather than suggesting any shared set of aesthetic or artistic values. The category "alternative" is rather unspecific in musical terms[26] and therefore in this context is analogous to the broader category of *rock en español* itself. Thus, the current interest in marketing bands like Aterciopelados as "alternative" groups is best interpreted as a reflection of the U.S. industry's assessment of product distribution patterns rather than any shared musical characteristics.

Declaring themselves the "custodians of culture," high-level industry executives such as Arista's Jerry Blair and BMG Latin's Leslie José Zigel lauded this second wave as more sophisticated, urbane, and "authentic." The second wave was epitomized by groups like Aterciopelados, which was described as "an Andean rock band with an unpronounceable name that sings exclusively in Spanish and bears no resemblance whatsoever to Ricky Martin and Jennifer López."[27] Aterciopelados was also featured in the publication "Ricky, Listen to These Numbers; Move Over Martin, Tell López the News . . . ", which proclaims, "We're in the middle of a Latin-music renaissance that has nothing to do with trendy pinups and pop stars. While hunks and babes like Ricky Martin and Jennifer López may be a feast for the eyes, a host of more substantial Latin stars have been pleasing the ears."[28]

The "custodian of culture" attitude embodies the U.S.-based Latino entertainment industry's ongoing ethnoracial division of labor. In short, this division dictates that, although Latinos are needed on the creative end for the "authenticity" or "subcultural capital" that they provide (both of which are largely defined and contained per dominant standards), it is still mostly Anglo males who enjoy expanded access to industry networks and wield greater cultural capital in general.[29] In the spring of 2001, Aterciopelados became the focus of an agreement between the record labels BMG Latin and Artista records as part of a marketing campaign to promote the band to both mainstream and Latino audiences, with a particular emphasis on U.S. Latinos between fourteen and twenty-nine years of age. And, although most industry executives did not expect this second wave of Latin(o) and Latin American acts, including Aterciopelados, to outsell the pop-based first wave, the rapid growth of the U.S. Latino youth population demanded their attention. (Indeed, the audience at one Aterciopelados performance in Miami that I attended consisted of an overwhelmingly bilingual, bicultural, and middle-class U.S. Latino audience roughly eighteen to thirty years of age).

In particular, the promotional campaign directed at recent second-wave *rock en español* releases exemplifies the contradictory discourse via which the mainstream rock media attempts to contain, as it simultaneously "celebrates," the presence of not only women but also non-U.S. and European acts within the industry. For, while the potential commercial success of the "next big thing" may represent economic gains for the U.S.-based music industry, it also embodies a significant threat to the overwhelmingly masculinist leanings of rock itself[30] (and, I would add, to its predominant ethnoracial composition). On some level, this latest marketing strategy, primarily engaged in the promotion of Latin American acts, consists of defining second wave Latin American-based groups in opposition to their earlier, bicultural, bilingual U.S. Latino counterparts of the first wave, thereby reinscribing existing myths regarding the gap between Latin American and U.S. Latino musical and cultural purity, linguistic or otherwise. These artists and their music have in turn been framed as a welcome "alternative" not just to what are typically encoded as Anglo genres but also to the previous Latin(o) music wave, perpetuating a false dichotomy of authenticity.[31] The construction of the authenticity myth is not merely unilateral, however, as the mainstream Latin American press in turn attempts to construct *rock en español* as a uniquely southern phenomenon, policing the boundaries of authenticity by representing acts like Aterciopelados as the first true (i.e., direct from Latin America, not U.S. Latino) *rock en español* bands marketed in the United States.[32] Perhaps most significant, as products of highly visible marketing campaigns designed to project a ready-for-consumption corporate prototype of the "ideal" U.S. Latino, these myths of authenticity, which predicate themselves on simplistic, stereotypical constructions of *Latinidad*, contribute to the anachronistic notion of the United States as the site of a greater Latino historical vacuum. Moreover, as Arlene Dávila states, adopting a solely Latin-American-centered marketing approach has relegated U.S. Latinos to the role of *Latinidad*'s consumers, yet never its producers.[33] As this second wave was being constructed, Andrea Echeverri began to emerge as a global alternative music star during an era in which the U.S. mainstream media increased its interest in and access to Latin America performers (in large part a product of the Latin[o] music boom of the late 1990s), which in turn translated into increased media coverage of Echeverri as a gendered subject.

Gender and Representation in the U.S. Rock Media

By means of her distinct public persona and musical style and the multiple significations with which she is subsequently invested, Echeverri contests her audience's often unquestioned belief in rock as a fundamentally male, Euro/U.S.-centric genre. However, the gendering of rock is neither a product of its primordial maleness nor a reflection of some pre-determined masculine sensibility. Rather, as noted in my discussion of Shakira in chapter 3, the cultural association between rock and masculinity must be understood as an artifice that is actively perpetuated via the everyday activities and ideologies of the rock "scene." (Here I take the liberty of employing Sarah Cohen's notion of a musical "scene" in a more expanded sense, utilizing it in reference to the larger rock culture maintained not only by the musicians themselves but also by industry producers, promoters, and so forth.)[34] Through its reliance on commonplace notions of gender roles and music, the rock media also reinscribes longstanding assumptions about women's relationship to and within rock. As articles with titles like Tim Padgett's "Tough as Males,"[35] which examines the role of women in Latin American rock, attest, the association between masculinity and rock persists to such an extent that women's artistic credentials within rock are in large part a reflection of their ability to measure up to the genre's masculine standard, or to be as "tough as a male."

Much in the same way in which the juxtaposition of *lo cachaco* versus *lo costeño* is enacted within Colombian culture,[36] Andrea Echeverri is framed within the media as a veritable anti-Shakira of sorts, as suggested in the *Miami Herald*:

> A star of the *rock en español* scene, she's fond of hitting the stage in a washed out T-shirt and baggy parachute pants. Forget the accouterments of the typical Latin girl act. Echeverri . . . works it in piercings and tattoos. She's an unstudied, soulful, hard-core Olive Oyl look-alike who doesn't need eyeliner, lipstick or lacquered hair to whip a crowd into a frenzy.[37]

Repeatedly described as articulate and politically aware, Echeverri has enjoyed an artistic success and a persona that are posited as evidence of Colombia's emerging "modernity." Again, one may choose to read this in opposition to Shakira, who in the mainstream media appears to embody a more stereotypical notion of Latin(a) American identity, replete with its concomitant reliance on depictions of hypersexuality, *marianismo*, "natural rhythm," and so forth. Perhaps because of her widely known association with more progressive attitudes regarding gender roles, references to Echeverri's sexuality are essentially absent from her press coverage both in the United States and abroad. In fact, the 2001 announcement of her out-of-wedlock pregnancy, still a major social taboo in largely Catholic Colombia, passed without fanfare in *El Tiempo*, one of the country's leading newspapers.[38] However, the transnational media's continual casting of Echeverri in such terms during her pregnancy also speaks to the popular representation of the pregnant female and/or mother as a nonsexual, if not asexual, figure.

As the previous discussion attests, rock criticism, while indeed serving as a means of ascribing legitimacy to the medium, can also play a significant role as a gatekeeper and shaper of public tastes. For, while not its sole agent, the critic occupies the central role of the "architect" of formal reception. In essence, the critic acts as a (singular) individual speaking for (plural) individuals, in what Marcia Citron terms "a collectivity born of individuality."[39] Historically speaking, written musical critiques, which can be traced back to eighteenth-century Europe, emerged in response to the need to legitimize music in the face of a decline in the royal patronage of art music and music's subsequent movement into the public domain. (I would in fact argue that the need to legitimize looms even greater with respect to today's popular music.) Then as now, the overwhelmingly male profession of musical critic affords its members the luxury of engaging in "one-way communication [with] countless individuals, who function as respondents twice-removed: the critic, as a respondent to the performance or work, is creating a work for other respondents."[40] (This is not, however, to suggest that listeners are entirely passive. They, too, create new works, unfettered by temporal or historical considerations, much less compositorial intentions, via the act of listening or other forms of engagement with music as aural and/or visual text.)[41]

The systematic exclusion of female music critics, moreover, can be attributed not only to discriminatory practices but also to ideology. As Citron states, the role of critic implies authority, judgment, mind, and wisdom— all, incidentally, characteristics that women have historically been perceived as lacking. Simply put, without these traits women cannot dispense or control knowledge; thus, "the ideological has laid a foundation for the practical," and the end result has been a dearth of female critics that continues to this day.[42]

> We are modern people. . . . But we have links to the past.
> —Andrea Echeverri, "Sounds of Magical Realism"

Unlike Shakira, Andrea Echeverri, now in her early forties, did not begin to pursue a musical career until her early twenties, when she met her future Aterciopelados bandmate Héctor Buitrago, then a bassist with the hardcore band La Pestilencia, at an informal jam session in Bogotá. At this point, La Pestilencia had gained recognition as one of Colombia's premier punk-influenced rock groups. Punk, which emerged in Colombia around 1979, had flourished in the nation's harsh urban settings throughout the 1980s. For Echeverri, as well as for many other aspiring female musicians, both then and now, punk's blatant subversion of the preference for "expert" or "professional" (and primarily male) musicians proved key, as it opened the door for female musicians who might otherwise not have gained entrance to traditionally male-dominated musical networks. Punk was also the first rock-based genre not to rely exclusively on love songs, which translated into a different type of feminine voice heard on recordings and the radio. In 1990, Echeverri and Buitrago began their musical collaboration, melding his hardcore roots with her experience learning traditional Colombian folk genres and guitar in her parent's home. Along with other musicians, including Charlie Márquez and Andrés Giraldo, Echeverri and Buitrago formed the group Delia y los Aminoácidos (Delia and the amino acids), which eventually became Aterciopelados. The group's surprise first hit, the punk-inspired tune "*Mujer gala*" (Party girl), was released in 1993, and shortly afterwards Aterciopelados recorded its first album, Con el corazón en la mano (With heart in hand). Its subsequent album, 1995's El Dorado (The gilded one), sold 200,000 copies, more than any other album by a Colombian rock band in history at the time.[43] As in the case of most lead singers, particularly women, Echeverri has been the focus of the majority of Aterciopelados's media coverage. Along with Buitrago, she serves as the band's primary composer (other than Buitrago and Echeverri, the group's lineup of musicians is in constant flux), its sole female musician, and ultimately the band's public "face" and most recognizable member.

As Juana Suárez argues, Aterciopelados merit categorization as a feminist band not merely because of Echeverri's presence but because of its vested interest in engaging in frank discussion regarding the female subject in contemporary Colombian society. The group's ongoing commentary, rooted in its consistent attack of misogyny vis-à-vis the reification of feminine corporality, encompasses a wide variety of themes, such as government corruption and the nation's historic union of church and state. The end result is a insightful critique of Colombia's so-called national culture.[44]

The daughter of two Bogotá dentists, Echeverri was raised in a conservative bourgeois environment and earned a fine-arts degree in ceramics at the prestigious Universidad de los Andes. In contrast, Buitrago, the son of two shopkeepers, grew up in a working-class Bogotá neighborhood. Echeverri has often humorously referenced Colombian upper-class mores in her music and performances, as in the song *La estaca* (The stake), a tune inspired by the *carrilera*, a genre based on verbal insults and threats. The song's rumbling bass line and off-tempo drumbeat, embellished with a smattering of acoustic guitar riffs, initially appears to approximate a traditional *carrilera*. However, *La estaca*'s unexpectedly raucous electric chorus reveals the punk roots of its performers. The video for *La estaca* features Buitrago, Echeverri, and another male guitarist performing the song as they slowly move through the streets of Bogotá on a truck bed. Echeverri sports a fluorescent orange pageboy wig, exaggerated makeup, debutante's white ballgown, and plastic tiara; her choice of dress, locale, and melodramatic vocals functions not only as an ode to the popular and the kitsch, which Aterciopelados have described as their primary aesthetic influences, but also as a humorous reference to her past as an upper-middle-class *niña bien*, or good girl. In a general sense, the group's consistent incorporation of popular signifiers contests the reigning belief in Latin American popular culture as that which is exclusively confined to rural or peasant spaces. By underscoring and ultimately exploiting the uneven distribution of sonic and physical space in this context, Echeverri effectively renders herself the author of Bogotá's streets. Moreover, her pointed exaggeration of the visual "discourse of femininity" not only subverts conventional notions of femininity itself but also acts as a powerful tool for confronting these same paradigms.[45]

The deployment of Bogotá's streets as a backdrop for Aterciopelados's music videos, however, is not unique to *La estaca*. Throughout its existence, the group has continuously employed the capital's public spaces for a variety of videos (i.e., "Florecita rockera" and "El álbum" [The album]), underscoring the band's energetic mixture of traditional/popular/folk elements and the more modern sights and sounds of punk, rock, trip-hop, electronic and lounge cultures. This is more than a mere visual acknowledgment of the band's hybrid musical roots, however; as Peter Wade states in his research on gender and violence, in Colombia sharp distinctions are drawn between what are considered gender-appropriate behaviors within the domestic and those that are acceptable in public. In this way, popular music, and music video itself, functions as yet another stage upon which everyday, gendered power differentials that distinguish the private (the "feminine") from the public (the "masculine") are realized. Within this quotidian framework, masculine control over the definitions of propriety enables the naturalization of imparities based on gender and race. Thus, within the Colombian context, "the street . . . is associated with live performance, male activity and rebellion, and with the public spaces that women are not supposed to frequent."[46] Under these deeply engrained cultural ideologies, a woman *on* the street (*mujer en la calle*) is swiftly transformed into a woman *of* the street (*mujer de la calle*).

Echeverri's visual and sonic reclamation of the street transforms it into what Lisa A. Lowe has termed an "access sign," or a system of signs in which "the privileged experiences of boys and men are visually appropriated . . . [t]he female musicians appearing in the videos textually enact entrance into a male domain of activity and signification."[47] This video, along with several of Aterciopelados's other releases, thereby breaks with the conventional notion of the streets, and the masculine youth leisure culture that the streets embody, as the exclusive training ground of male adolescents, for whom the streets typically serve as a first taste of the gender-biased social privileges that await them in adulthood.[48]

The song "*Cosita seria*" (Serious little thing), a popular single from the band's third album, also critiques the societally driven gender norms that afford Colombian men the freedom to physically and verbally dominate women in public spaces. Beyond its straightforward opening beats and clean, sharp tones, the song offers the first hints of the group's later forays into sampling and the incorporation of electronic effects. Her vocals punctuated by thick, pulsating electric guitar chords and occasional measures of Afro-Latin drumming throughout, in "*Cosita seria*" Echeverri recounts her experiences as the target of sexualized male street commentary, as well as her reaction to this brand of unsolicited objectification: "*El muy bestia no respeta / yo me voltié y le di en la jeta*" (The brute doesn't respect / I turned around and gave it to him in the mouth), followed by the chorus, in which she declares herself someone to be reckoned with (a "*cosita seria*"), who isn't afraid to say what she has to ("*no tengo pelos en la lengua*"). At the song's end, Echeverri tells of a man who has his foreskin removed as punishment for making vulgar comments to women on the street, concluding: "*y aunque un poco exagerado yo pienso / se lo había buscado*" (And even though it's a bit much, I think / that he asked for it).[49] Thus, the frequent video images of Echeverri in Bogotá's public spaces, in addition to the band's overt lyrical references, challenge existing gender norms within *rock en español*.

The centrality of the music video format to Aterciopelados's and, more specifically, Andrea Echeverri's artistic development is not to be underestimated. Music video served as a means for the group, which has been framed as a very "Colombian" band, to disseminate its music beyond Colombia's borders and to gain an international following. The video format simultaneously provides the group with the means to construct a specific visual narrative in conjunction with its instrumentation and lyrics. For female artists in particular, music video has furnished the opportunity to win industry support and to convey a singular textual vision. However, from its inception, MTV Latino, the only MTV global affiliate headquartered in the United States and a prime site of "media glocalization and indigenization,"[50] has relied heavily on the same rigid gender norms that permeate its English-language sister channel, MTV. In the case of Aterciopelados, its heavy rotation on MTV Latino has translated into a fan base that extends far beyond the group's original Bogotá audiences, while simultaneously earning its videos a reputation for representing a consistent departure from traditional gender paradigms in music video. Indeed, the majority of MTV Latino videos feature exclusively male bands and male performers, while videos featuring female performers are invariably directed by men. And, much as in the U.S. heavy metal context described by Robert Walser, women are frequently represented in video narratives revolving around traditional heterosexual relationships (which constitute MTV Latino's standard fare) as figures in a veritable adolescent male "dreamworld."[51]

Conversely, while the video format imparts increased visibility to female musicians (arguably a mixed blessing, given the resulting pressures on female performers to conform to rigid beauty standards), for female fans it can also signify the introduction of novel identity discourses. These discourses may in turn foster innovative opportunities to identify with female musicians.[52] In this regard, Lowe argues that, in some cases, the role of female musicians within the video format may be recast to women's advantage, as female musicians utilize the medium as a means of subverting traditional modes of female representation and enlist viewers, particularly females, in "authorship activity." Popular culture, and specifically television, therefore reveals its contestatory potential in not only marking the presence of the disempowered but also constructing alternative communities.[53]

A video clip by Aterciopelados based on the 1998 single "*El estuche*" (The box) provides one such example. In this video, Echeverri appears as a fashion model of sorts, outfitted in a series of costumes (Puritan, Medusa, and mermaid) as she slowly turns, encased in a bell jar. As a scientific tool employed for the protection and display of fragile objects and for the control of experimental atmospheres in general, the bell jar provides a stark visual cue for "*El estuche*"'s commentary on women's relationship to the beauty myth:

> *No es un mandamiento ser la diva del momento*
> *para qué trabajar por un cuerpo escultural*
> *acaso deseas en ti todos los ojos*
> *y desencandenar silbidos al pasar . . .*
> *el cuerpo es sólo un estuche*
> *y los ojos la ventana de nuestra alma aprisionada*
>
> (Being the diva of the moment's not a commandment
> Why work for a statuesque body?
> Maybe you just want all eyes on you
> and whistling to break out as you pass by . . .
> the body's simply a box
> and the eyes a window to our imprisoned souls)[54]

The song itself, which begins with a series of exaggerated trumpet slides that lend it a playful feel, quickly settles into a marked electronic bass/snare line that continues unchanged throughout. The rhythm, like the song's central message, does not vary. *El estuche*'s brief didactic chorus ("*Mira la esencia no las aparencias*" [Look at the essence, not appearances]) dominates the tune by virtue of its simplicity, layered harmonies, and constant repetition. Another recurring auditory and visual image is that of a box/vagina, which is slowly opened to reveal various treasures in the form of jewels or the solar system itself, as Echeverri sings: "*si abres el estuche lo que debes encontrar / es una joya que te deslumbrará*" (if you open the box what you should find / is a jewel that will dazzle you). In a final gesture reminiscent of a Frida Kahlo self-portrait, Echeverri-as-mermaid "opens" her chest to reveal the aquatic world within, replete with exotic fish and clear blue ocean waters. As the song and its accompanying video underline, societal emphasis needs to rest on the human interior ("*lo que hay dentro es lo que vale*" [what's inside is what counts]), and all other considerations, particularly female measurements, are merely arbitrary: ("*90-60-90 suman 240 / cifras que no hay que tener en cuenta*" [90-60-90 make 240 / numbers not worth taking into account]). Embedded in Aterciopelados's critique of unidimensional female corporality constructed for the sole purpose of heterosexual male pleasure is an alternative definition of feminine strength.[55] As a cleverly crafted song and video, *El estuche* utilizes the music video genre itself as a means of not only foregrounding but also subverting the aesthetics imposed upon women in the MTV Latino format. Simultaneously, "*El estuche*" underlines music video's potential for providing an expressive context in which "style is reclaimed for girls and richly articulated as a symbolic vehicle of female expression."[56]

Aside from their inventive employment of music video, Aterciopelados's compositions, when taken alone, also offer an oppositional perspective of gender-biased social mores. Produced by the British Colombian Phil Manzanera, *Miss Panela* (Miss brown sugar), from the group's 1996 hit album *La pipa de la paz* (The peace pipe), chronicles the story of two individuals embroiled in two stereotypically "Colombian" institutions: beauty pageants and drug trafficking. Beginning with Héctor Buitrago performing the standard opening *vallenato* cry of "*¡Con sentimiento, compadre!*" (With feeling, buddy!), "*Miss Panela*," while not completely abandoning the conventional *vallenato* archetype of the scheming, heartbreaking woman, offers a slightly redemptive perspective. The story of a newly rich drug trafficker who becomes obsessed with earning the affections of a materialistic beauty queen, "*Miss Panela*" relates how the man's newfound love ultimately betrays him to U.S. drug enforcement officials:

> *conquistar la reina fue sólo lo que pensó este mal*
> *amor lo obsesionó*
> *dando malos pasos nuevo rico se*
> *volvió tanto*
> *billete lo confundió*
> *no importó a quién por encima le pasó hasta que al*
> *fin la coronó*
> *le siguieron el rastro y la DEA lo agarró esa mujer*
> *lo delató*
>
> (Conquering the queen was all that he thought about
> The bad love obsessed him
> In illegal ways he became nouveau riche so
> So much money
> Confused him
> It didn't matter whom he stepped on until
> He finally crowned her
> They followed his trail and the DEA grabbed him
> That woman
> Turned him in)[57]

Despite his subsequent incarceration, he never suspects his beauty queen lover, who continues to enjoy his wealth: "*enamorada pero del billete ella lo exprimirá*" (in love only with money, she'll take him for what he's worth). Ironically, the purest of Colombian popular cultural symbols, the young beauty queen, turns out to be not so pure (or sweet, despite her name) after all, and in the song's melancholic, accordion-filled closing, both lovers are condemned: he to a prison sentence, she to an unhappy existence based on ill-gotten gain. Thus, "*Miss Panela*," while not a *vallenato* song per se, offers a slightly revisionary perspective on the Colombian popular culture that *vallenato* embodies.

Another Aterciopelados composition from the same album treats less specifically "Colombian" themes. "*No necesito*" (I don't need), whose spare arrangement, ambling bass line, and liberal use of the wah-wah pedal belie its strident message about individuality, assumes another layer of meaning entirely, as sung by Echeverri:

>*No necesito su aprobación tengo por*
>*dentro un medidor*
>*que va marcando grados de satisfacción*
>*no necesito su aprobación,*
>*que me censuren tiene su bemol*
>*pero mi metro va por dentro*
>
>(I don't need their approval I have
>A measure inside
>That goes marking degrees of satisfaction
>I don't need their approval,
>Let them censure me
>It's their problem
>But my ruler's inside)[58]

For the duration of "*No necesito*," Echeverri continues to assert her belief in a more realistic, if not pessimistic, worldview, culminating in the final verse: "*y desde mi casa en el aire todo me huele / a que se pudrió*" (and from my house in the air everything smells / like it has rotted). Here, Echeverri's "*casa en el aire*" references yet another, more famous "house in the air" of Colombian popular music: that of the classic *vallenato* tune "*La casa en el aire*," by the renowned composer Rafael Escalona and most recently performed by the *vallenato* superstar Carlos Vives:

Te voy a hacer una casa en el aire,
solamente pa' que vivas tú
después le pongo un letrero bien grande
de nubes blancas que diga
"Ada Luz" [bis]

Cuando Ada Luz sea una señorita
y alguno le quiera hablar de amor,
el tipo tiene que ser aviador
para que pueda hacerle la visita

(I'm going to build you a house in the air,
Just so that you live there
Then I'll put a really big sign on it
Of white clouds that says
"Ada Luz" [repeat]

And when Ada Luz is a young woman
And someone wants to court her
The guy's going to have to be a pilot
In order to visit her)[59]

In Vives's uptempo, contemporary rendering of the same song, the male singer relates his desire to construct a beautiful, idealized home in which to protect his beloved daughter. In contrast, in the *casa en el aire* that Echeverri describes, the house and its surroundings are literally and figuratively rotten. By extension, so are the dreams of domestic harmony with one's very own "Prince Charming/*príncipe azul*" at the core of traditional societal gender roles so often relayed to young women and girls. Here, Echeverri's ironic metatextual reference erases the masculine perspective of the father who seeks to (over)protect and isolate his daughter and in effect treat her as a possession in a "heavenly" home, distanced from all potential male suitors. As in many of Aterciopelados's compositions, preexisting cultural symbols are musically juxtaposed to ironic effect.[60] "*No necesito*"'s intention is to interrogate, not romanticize, traditional gender dynamics and to promote a vision of woman as individual beyond the domestic sphere. In this sense, Aterciopelados's compositions contrast sharply with many of the overriding themes present in Colombian popular music, particularly the societal convention of the *príncipe azul* that is often present in the recordings of more mainstream artists such as Shakira.

As such, Aterciopelados is expressly known for creating "music which is critical of its own material [and] critical of the social situation within which it arises."[61] As Carmelo Esterrich and Javier Murillo note, one of the group's primary artistic goals is to highlight the misogynistic elements of Colombian culture through the use of Colombian music itself and, in many cases, through the use of its most markedly "masculine" genres such as the aforementioned *vallenato* music of the Colombian Caribbean.[62] The net effect of this performance of *vallenato* standards and incorporation of *vallenato* elements, as in the case of the band's cover of the 1980s hit "*Baracunátana*," is one of subversion. The song was originally composed from a male, heterosexist perspective; "*baracunátana*" is actually the (untranslatable) name given to a woman who is accused of running away with another man: "*anoche te vi había otro que te chequeaba / montaste su moto te brindó chicle también / galleta / prendió su motoneta y te marchaste con el mono / de jean el overall y la chaqueta*" (last night I saw you, there was another guy checking you out / you got on his motorcycle, he offered you gum / and a cookie, too / he started it up and you took off / with the jean-jacket, overall-wearing blond).[63] The song was a hit in both its initial *vallenato* and in its *vallenato*-rock versions; its highlight is its raucous, slang-filled chorus, which consists of insults directed at the ostensibly unfaithful *baracunátana*. "Liar," "scum," "whore," and "bitch" are only a few of the epithets leveled at the fictitious girlfriend in the chorus; although the slang employed is so localized and generational that it is difficult for any one individual to comprehend all of it, the song never fails to attract a willing crowd of participants of both sexes, no matter where it is played in Colombia. This rearticulation of popular Colombian (and largely misogynist) vulgarities engenders a sense of familiarity among many of its interlocutors and retains the potential to counteract the original composition's more hegemonic lexicon.[64] Thus, within the context of the song's overtly misogynist perspective, Echeverria's revocalization of the traditional male lead is rendered doubly significant, as here Aterciopelados reinscribes not only the male-dominated *vallenato* genre[65] but also the coastal/interior dichotomy that pervades much of Colombian cultural discourse.

Defining itself both musically and visually as a uniquely Colombian band has been a hallmark of Aterciopelados's musical production since the group's inception. Notably, the group's belief in music as the antidote to Colombia's problems related to its self-conceptualization has increasingly emerged as the aesthetic tie that binds its recordings. This musical and thematic aesthetic manifests itself most notably in 2001's *Gozo poderoso* (Powerful joy), which was produced entirely in Colombia. For the recording, the group employed only Colombian musicians, despite the difficulties presented by

Figure 4.1. Photo of Echeverri taken from a feature story on the promotion of Aterciopelados's 2001 *Gozo poderoso* album to mainstream U.S. audiences. Echoing the media coverage of Shakira and other Latin(o) American artists, a slightly militaristic tone is evident, as the group is portrayed as engaging in a "Velvet Offensive." Celeste Fraser Delgado, "Velvet Offensive," *Miami New Times*, June 21, 2001. Photograph by Steve Satterwhite.

mounting violence, the ongoing financial crisis, and the mass exodus of many of the country's top professionals and skilled workers. Throughout the subsequent press junkets for the album, Buitrago and Echeverri repeatedly described *Gozo*'s production as an act of national solidarity, declaring the album "our position regarding the exodus that our country is suffering."[66]

Perhaps in part because of the group's preference for Colombian musical genres, themes, and colloquial speech, Aterciopelados has also had to contend with a U.S. mainstream press and marketing machine that insists on categorizing Colombian artists and, to a lesser extent, Latin American artists in general as products of "magical realism" and/or *macondismo*. Ana María Ochoa explains that *macondismo* is best understood as an ideology that celebrates magical realism, an artistic device that (re)frames Latin America as "decipherable, beyond the code, and as a place whose very disjunctures are, in and of themselves, identifying characteristics." Thus, the discursive links between Echeverri and *macondismo* illustrate the dominant media's propensity for locating "third-world" women in alternative spatial and temporal orders, as if they were "living on another planet, in another time."[67] In this regard, the current rush among music industry giants to define and market the local references longstanding issues of power and control, a veritable "crisis occasioned by the repositioning of dominant cultures among them-

Florecita rockera | 107

selves as well as with the 'others.'"[68] Uninformed marketing campaigns aside, in 2001 Aterciopelados received three Latin Grammy nominations and won one award, for best rock album by a duo or group.[69] However, these were not the group's first nominations; it was previously nominated (though not for any Latin Grammys, which were awarded separately beginning in the fall of 2000) for the albums *La pipa de la paz* (The peace pipe) (1995) and *Caribe atómico* (Atomic Caribbean) (1998). As Suárez notes, Aterciopelados's Grammy nominations, like those of other Colombian artists, accentuate "the ambivalences of globalization and the cultural logic of capitalism: on one hand, they privilege the record market of the majors, but on the other they also facilitate the diffusion of local groups and singers."[70]

By the summer of 2001, Aterciopelados had become the first Spanish-language act ever to land on *Billboard*'s alternative music chart, as well as the first to appear on the widely viewed *The Tonight Show with Jay Leno*, suggesting a concerted effort not to employ English in the group's music. (Regarding her feelings about singing in English, Echeverri has stated that "I think about singing in English sometimes. . . . As a Colombian, I would love to tell Americans what I think of them dumping pesticides on our crops to kill cocaine. They kill everything").[71] Later that fall, *Time* magazine's music critics named them "one of the ten best bands on planet Earth." The appearance on a major U.S. television program marked the apex of a four-month promotional campaign conducted by the combined forces of Arista and BMG Latin in support of Aterciopelados. However, by the end of 2004, *Gozo poderoso* had sold a mere 70,000 copies in the United States, and by the time the group released its follow-up album, the greatest hits collection *Evolución* (Evolution), in 2003, the Anglo company Arista was no longer involved in Atercopelados's media promotion.[72]

The fascination among some mainstream U.S. critics with Aterciopelados in general, and Echeverri in particular, did not entirely subside, however. Echeverri's first solo album, *Andrea Echeverri* (2005), for which all the songs were composed by the singer and produced by Buitrago, marked what many Latin(o) music critics viewed as a considerable departure from Echeverri's previous work. Written and recorded in the period following the birth of the singer's daughter, Milagros, *Andrea Echeverri* is organized into two sections: *canciones de cama* (bedtime songs) and *canciones de cuna* (crib songs) and features a streamlined visual, if not musical, aesthetic far removed from the kitsch-inspired allusions to Colombian popular culture that dominate Aterciopelados's earlier recordings (see figure 4.2). The shifts in thematic focus and visual layout for *Andrea Echeverri* prompted many longtime Ater-

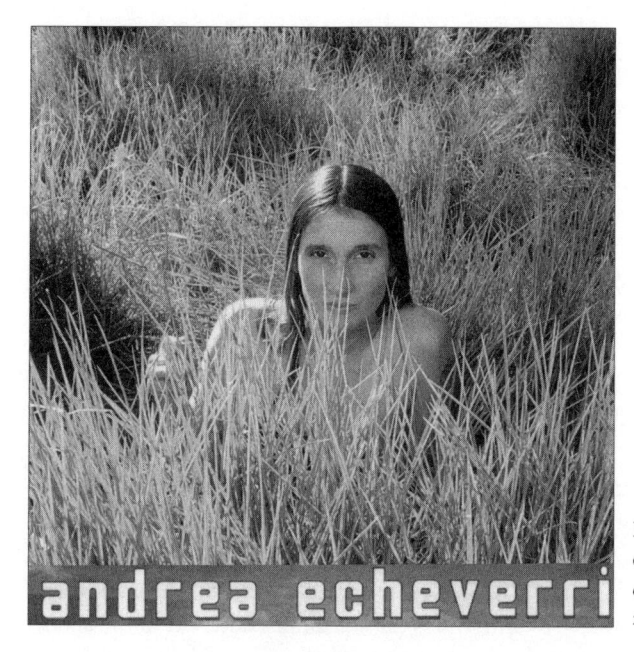

Figure 4.2. Album cover, *Andrea Echeverri*. Nacional Records, 2005.

ciopelados fans to view the album with skepticism, as well. As the broadcast journalist Noah Adams offered, "Echeverri's solo debut trades political anthems for songs about motherhood,"[73] a remark that highlighted both fans' and critics' tendency to treat heterosexual motherhood and political engagement as mutually exclusive constructs a priori, as suggested by the verb "trade." While on a superficial level the album's content appears a rather simplistic celebration of motherhood and heterosexual romance, recordings such as "*Lactochampeta*" give the lie to such unidimensional readings:

> *Chúpate la tetica*
> *Tómatela todita [bis]*
> *Así así durito y con ritmo y con ritmo*
> *Sacía todos tus apetitos conmigo bebé*
> *Toma de mí lo que quieras*
> *Pon tu boquita en mi pezón y con la encía haz*
> *Presión*
> *Como chupas de rico*
>
> (Suck the titty
> Take it all [repeat]

Florecita rockera | 109

Hard like that and with rhythm with rhythm
Satisfy all your appetites with me baby
Take what you want from me
Put your little mouth on my nipple and press with your gum
You suck so well)[74]

When read as a traditional text minus musical accompaniment, *Lactochampeta* appears little more than a facsimile of the hypererotic lyrics typical of the *champeta* genre of Colombia's Caribbean Coast.[75] "*Lactochampeta*," however, constitutes Echeverri's pointed answer to traditional *champeta* discourse, as the electronic echo effects and her vocal delivery accentuate in the recorded version. Plainspoken and tender, Echeverri's vocals not only contradict the song's seemingly pornographic content but also provide a sharp contrast to the heterosexist, male-centric discourse at the core of much *champeta* music. The constant repetition of the phrases "*chúpatela*" (suck it) and "*desocúpatela*" (empty it) disrupts the conventional portrait of the apolitical, asexual maternal figure as it simultaneously underlines the sensuality inherent in the act of breastfeeding. Far from signifying a trade of politics for motherhood, "*Lactochampeta*" instead exemplifies the same skillful manipulation of sonic and lyrical irony that are a hallmark of Echeverri's work with Aterciopelados.

Critical analysis of her recordings with Aterciopelados, popular press coverage, and videos affirms that Andrea Echeverri and her music exemplify the ways in which the male-dominated Latin(o) music industry, in combination with the mainstream media, impacts our readings of gendered subjects in the era of a globalized "Latin Hollywood" media landscape. In spite of this, Echeverri, largely through her use of the music video format and her lyrical choices, manages to contest standard gender paradigms. As recent media coverage of Aterciopelados and Colombian rock (referred to in an article as "The *Other* Plan Colombia")[76] suggests, Echeverri and her band's success offer an alternative vision of contemporary gender dynamics within the rock industry. Moreover, in a broader sense, Aterciopelados proposes a more affirmative, though certainly not unrealistic, articulation of transnational Colombian reality in general. For, while the mainstreaming of Latin(o) American artistic self-expression may well function in part as a gatekeeping mechanism guided by and for the political and economic interests of the dominant sector,[77] it also simultaneously provides a unique vehicle by which Latin(o) American fans, and particularly *colombianas* everywhere, can reimagine themselves and their communities.

5

The Colombian *Vallenato acá y allá*

Allegory for a Musical ImagiNation

> I think the only vestige of identity left us is vallenato. It is the pride that is left us. . . . The medium for expressing what we think, what we want, what we dream is vallenato.
> —Tomás Darío Gutiérrez, "Colombia Strikes a New Note"

In his 1996 video for "*La cachucha bacana*" (The cool cap),[1] the Colombian musician Tulio Zuluaga performs an updated version of the late composer and musician Alejo Durán's *vallenato* classic, in contemporary scenes that feature Zuluaga alongside various male musicians and female backup singers. In keeping with *vallenato* custom, Zuluaga begins his performance by verbally acknowledging the song's composer, Durán ("Alejo, for you buddy"). He also provides visual recognition of Durán's contribution to 1990s *vallenato* via an intermittent series of vintage clips of Durán performing the same piece decades earlier. Numerous contradictory elements emerge from Zuluaga's video for "*La cachucha bacana*" that ultimately point toward distinct tensions between Colombia's present and past. In the mestizo Zuluaga's rendering, the contemporary technological advances of color television are contrasted with the dated black and white images of the late Afro-Colombian Durán, hinting at what the anthropologist Peter Wade[2] terms the *blanqueamiento* (whitening) of Colombia in the post-Independence era:

> Models of modernity and progress were not abandoned; rather, racial mixture and black and indian populations were harnessed to them. . . . Blacks and especially indians were romanticized as part of a more or less glorious past, but the future held for them paternalistic guidance towards integration, which also ideally meant more race mixture and perhaps the eventual erasure of blackness and indianness from the nation. The mestizo was ide-

alized as of bi-ethnic or tri-ethnic origin, but the image held up was always at the lighter end of the spectrum. *The future would bring, almost magically, a whitening of the population through race mixture.*[3]

Zuluaga's rendering of "*La cachucha bacana*" may thus be read as a postmodern allegory that tenuously unites past (embodied in its visual references to Colombia's "mythical" indigenous ancestors, its rural roots in the form of a cow, and archival footage of the late Durán) and present (as evidenced by the singers' urban attire and their technologically advanced instruments). Gender also arises as a salient factor in Zuluaga's video, as the female backup singers, positioned as a collective, largely ornamental element of the piece, are juxtaposed against the individual male figures foregrounded throughout the video. In a more global interpretation, the bridge upon which the entirety of the video's action is realized recalls the often-cited Janus-face metaphor for nationalism, as it exists in a sort of "in-between space," looking simultaneously to the past ("tradition") and the future ("modernity.") This interstitial positioning ultimately echoes the *vallenato*'s status as a product of Colombian regional folklore recently incorporated into the broader framework of Latin(o) and so-called world musics. In a contemporary conflict for cultural capital waged within and through the strains of the Caribbean *vallenato*, the decidedly tri-ethnic, working-class male origins[4] constructed around the *vallenato* appear to have given way to the genre's emerging white and, to a lesser extent, female voices in the symbolic struggle to (re)shape Colombian identity and collective consciousness. In part because of the genre's frequent association with the *costeño* Nobel laureate Gabriel García Márquez, one of the genre's most noteworthy supporters, the violence and *macondismo* with which Colombia is typically associated "stand as mirror images of identity—a mirror in which the reflection of the one by the other silences the catastrophic dimension of the contradictions as their mutual excesses constitute each other."[5] Thus, in both visual and musical terms, Zuluaga's video, and the *vallenato* genre itself, may ultimately be read as an allegory for contemporary Colombian society both within the nation's physical borders and among its U.S. diaspora.

Departing from a neo-Gramscian vision of popular culture as a product of active consumption, here I engage in an exploration of the *vallenato*'s past and present trajectories with regard to race and national identity. Given the historical tendency to view "folk culture" as the embodiment of the nation, genres like the *vallenato* have long formed part of middle-class efforts to "imagin[e] the past to make the present." As today's *vallenato* illustrates, elite appropriations of folk culture or popular forms thereby frequently risk the valoration of an "empty, impossible category . . . [and] an active denial of the actual lived cultures of working people, both rural and urban."[6]

Contrary to popular press reports, no lone individual, including the Colombian musician and actor Carlos Vives, may be credited with the current globalized popularity of Colombian *vallenato* music in the *vallenato moderno* format. The multilayered process of appropriation instead constitutes the product of numerous individuals of all classes. Propelled by individual needs (and, ultimately, hegemonic values), the process of appropriation is open to different interpretations, depending upon one's socioeconomic status. Nevertheless, its "common structure[s] of meaning" persist intact.[7] Therefore, any analysis of Colombian popular musical forms must focus not only on the cultural objects themselves but also on the production, circulation, and divergent meanings that consumers ascribe to these popular artifacts.[8] In particular, I assert that the *vallenato*'s recent recasting as a pan-*colombiano* phenomenon coincides in a more global sense with the escalation of political violence in Colombia since the mid-late 1990s and the subsequent increase in Colombian migration to the United States. I examine the *vallenato*'s ongoing resemanticization, or, as Fernando Ortiz terms it, metalepsis,[9] through the lenses of race, gender, and transnationalism, with particular emphasis on the genre's contemporary ethnoracial dynamics.

Admittedly, the connections among race, gender, transnational dynamics, and the *vallenato*'s ongoing resemanticization are extremely difficult to measure, if not impossible to quantify. Recent scholarly investigation of corporality and the carnevalesque[10] provokes some key questions with regard to *costeño* musical production and race: who are the objects of the *vallenato*'s discourse? Its subjects? Who is afforded the right to "sing the nation"? And what types of gatekeeping mechanisms are at work within the *vallenato*? My intention here, however, is not so much to outline the "what" or the "how" but rather to begin to theorize the "why." As such, in an effort to begin to understand the role that race plays in the *vallenato*'s resemanticization, I trace the genre's transcultural commodification from an oral art form relegated to the margins of Colombian popular artistic production to its incorporation as a vital marker of *colombianidad* within the pan-Latino, transnational musical repertoires of musicians and consumers in the United States and Colombia.

Furthermore, I discuss the processes through which the *vallenato*, once a visual and auditory signifier of coastal mestizo identity as embodied by black, mulatto, and *zambo* performers like Alejo Durán, has realized its current pan-Colombian status via the representations of white, upper-class cul-

Figures 5.1-5.2. The late Alejo Durán (above), one of *vallenato*'s all-time greats, and Carlos Vives (opposite), the genre's current preeminent superstar. Album cover, Alejo Durán, *Álbum de oro (Gold Album)*, Discos Victoria, 1997; album cover, Carlos Vives, *Déjame entrar (Let Me In)*, EMI Latin, 2001.

tural brokers such as Carlos Vives.[11] While I draw from various scholarship on Colombian racial constructs and music, my analysis dialogues primarily with the British anthropologist Peter Wade's recent scholarship on music, race, and Colombian national identity. Specifically, I adopt his assertion that the twentieth-century movement through which Colombia's coastal music came to replace Andean forms as the nation's representative genre(s) involved a series of racialized shifts. However, I maintain that these shifts have also necessarily encompassed Colombia's gendered, classed, and diasporan communities (a critical fact as yet overlooked in existing research), thereby simultaneously mirroring (and contributing to) existing notions of *colombianidad*. Most important, I expand upon Wade's highly suggestive, though underdeveloped, assertion that *costeño* music's (or, more specifically, the *vallenato moderno*'s) countrywide popularity is somehow linked to an increase in violence within Colombia in recent years. I promote a revised perspective on the *vallenato* and, in a broader sense, Colombian popular music, based on the conceptualization of popular artistic production as a measure of a community's sociopolitical "pulse" or the aforementioned "political moment," as well as a means of recasting the collective consciousness. Again, in this sense, *vallenato* and the larger category of Colombian popular music function as allegories for the current (U.S.-) Colombian political moment.

As mandated in the 1886 Constitution, in Colombia as in much of Latin America, state-sponsored strategies aimed at achieving national unity were primarily integrationist in character, with *mestizaje* perceived as a tool of

The Colombian Vallenato acá y allá | 115

democratization.[12] Latin American elites of the era looked to the United States and Europe to inspire their nation-building projects, often at the expense of the popular classes. These close cultural ties with Europe and North America thereby inflected the ruling classes' attitudes about race; regional civil wars and democratic institutional defeats, among other difficulties, were attributed to the racial inferiority of the masses. Per the U.S. example, mass European immigration and the segregation and/or extinction of blacks and indigenous peoples appeared the most viable solution to these issues. Anchored in the belief that their racial superiority justified their rule, elites adopted theories on race that profoundly shaped Latin American public policy, particularly with regard to education, immigration, and matters specifically affecting the region's indigenous populations.[13]

Over time, the 1886 Colombian Constitution came to perpetuate a dynamic in which the recognition of indigenous diversity was all but erased through the widespread adoption of the belief in Colombia as a singularly mestizo nation. Framed as an inherently democratic ethnoracial category, *mestizaje* and the equality of rights associated with it were thus perceived as incompatible with the preservation of non-mestizo identities.[14] In contrast, the sweeping reforms introduced in the nation's 1991 Constitution were ostensibly designed to ensure unity through the very conservation of individual ethnoracial diversity itself, as they simultaneously emulated the racialized shifts in national identity already under way.

Yet, even in the wake of such a radical constitutional measure and in the face of an Afro-American population that constitutes somewhere between 20 percent and 45 percent of the total population (second in proportion only to that of Brazil), the wholesale erasure of the Afro-Colombian presence persists.[15] As an orally based expressive form, *vallenato* music has historically been met with disdain by many *costeño* elites, particularly in the nation's interior, which has long been perceived as Colombia's intellectual and cultural nucleus. *Vallenato* musical discourse, initially identified as a "low" discourse about "physicality, presence, and appearance," has also historically been associated with dancing, thereby perpetuating existing stereotypes that link blackness, sexuality, and music in the Colombian social imaginary.[16] Conversely, Carlos Vives's longstanding promotion of Caribbean *vallenato* music, while undeniably lending the *vallenato* unprecedented exposure on the international front, may paradoxically be read as yet another example of the public nullification of Afro-Colombian and Afro-Caribbean contributions to global popular culture. Covert racial critiques of Vives are often embedded in public discussions regarding the contemporary *vallenato*'s alleged lack of authenticity. Is Vives's prominence, then, a mere indicator of the genre's "whitening"? Notably, just as Vives acknowledges the criticisms that are often leveled at him by *vallenato*'s more traditional practitioners, he responds by promoting his brand of *vallenato* as a tool of pan-Caribbean unity, a means of "bringing Colombian music closer to the rest of the Caribbean."[17]

Clearly, the *vallenato*'s performative face did not shift from black or brown to white in a vacuum, nor are such changes unique among Colombian (or Latin American/Caribbean) musical genres, whose recasting as "folkloric" is part and parcel of their discovery as commodities.[18] Much like the cultural manifestations detailed in the study of other working-class expressive forms,[19] many Afro-*costeño* musical genres have traced a similar "fringes-to-center" trajectory, followed by the subsequent emanation of seemingly "newer" musical styles. Such a progression, as Wade notes, "seems to indicate a desire for musical distinctiveness that has no qualms in opting for openly black and African associations. Some working-class *costeños* are keeping one step ahead of the musical game, as it were: as *costeño* music is nationalized and becomes mainstream, new forms are appropriated, setting up new distinctions which nevertheless recall previous ones in their moral connotations."[20] The process of recuperation and, ultimately, commodification that has ensued as part of the *vallenato*'s developmental trajectory has signaled a meaningful permutation in the constitution of *all* Colombian identities, regardless of regional or ethnoracial differences. Questions of cultural ownership have centered on *costeño* cultural practitioners' claims to regional genres, which are in conflict with those of industry marketers who conceptualize the same forms as inherently "Colombian." Moreover, Wade rightfully claims that, "[i]n any event, this is now a Colombia associated with heat, tropicality, sabor, and the Caribbean—in a word, with La Costa."[21]

A member of Colombia's white, upper-class minority, Carlos Vives was born in coastal Santa Marta in 1961. He initially rose to fame as an actor in various soap operas and eventually went on to record two albums of low-selling pop ballads with Sony Discos. In 1992, however, he accepted the lead in *Escalona*, a *telenovela* set in the 1940s that chronicled the life of the legendary *vallenato* composer Rafael Escalona.[22] The *telenovela* soon spawned a series of *Escalona* soundtrack albums, the first of which became the best-selling album in the history of Colombian music. The commercial success of the *Escalona* album marked an unexpected emerging pattern among Colombian middle-class consumers: the most popular *vallenato* albums were not those dealing with contemporary themes but rather retooled versions (albeit remakes employing updated instrumentation, rhythms, and technology) of standards culled from the the genre's "Golden Age."[23] For Vives as for many bourgeois Colombians, the wildly popular series signified the first sustained contact with the *vallenato* in quite some time, thereby constituting a form of cultural recuperation on both the individual and the collective levels. (Without engaging in any sort of reductionism in this regard, I suggest that nostalgia for Colombia, while in itself an incomplete explanation, did in fact emerge as a significant factor in the *vallenato*'s subsequent migration to the U.S.-Colombian population.) This nostalgic impulse figured prominently in the 1990s-era resurgence of a postmodern longing for such "modernized" traditional forms. When Vives informed the record label Sony Discos of his desire to continue recording *vallenato* music, however, he was swiftly released from his contract. In 1993, then, he recorded *Clásicos de la Provincia* (Classics from the province) on his own label, Gaira Productions. The international hit "*La gota fría*" (The cold drop) became the album's most successful single, with the entire album eventually selling more than a million copies. His follow-up disc, a mix of old standards and original compositions entitled *La tierra del olvido* (The land of forgetting) (1995) was also widely popular. In contrast, his final album produced entirely on the Gaira label, *Tengo fe* (I have faith) (1997), sold relatively poorly. Upon completion of *Tengo fe*, Vives and his family permanently relocated to Miami, although Gaira Productions continued to maintain its offices in Colombia. His first Miami-produced disc, *El amor de mi tierra* (Love for my land) (1999), also signified his inaugural collaboration with Emilio Estefan and Kike Santander,[24] who subsequently produced the album *Déjame entrar* (Let me in) (2001) and who served, among several others, as producers for the album *El rock de mi pueblo* (My people's rock) (2004). The success of these production partnerships has arguably contributed considerably to the increasingly global reach of the Miami-based Latin(o) music industry, along with the *vallenato*'s transformation from a markedly regional genre into a transnational popular phenomenon.[25]

The Historical and Regional Roots of the Vallenato

While I provide a rough sketch of its musical features, I prefer to define the *vallenato* in "extramusical" terms,[26] rather than take the more conventional approach of classifying genres within strictly stylistic parameters. Although it has gained widespread popularity outside of Colombia's coastal region in only approximately the past forty years, *vallenato* music was performed as early as circa 1880, making it a contemporary of the *bolero* genre.[27]

Vallenato (literally, *nato del valle* or "valley native") music traces its roots back to the Caribbean town of Valledupar, on Colombia's northern Atlantic coast. It emerged from the combined musical traditions of *La Costa*'s indigenous, African, and European communities in a process of "mutual accommodation,"[28] or the inevitable ethnoracial blending, or *mestizaje*, that results from material and institutional conditions. Subject to white rule, or, in Consuelo Araújo de Molina's words, "excluded from the decisions yet submitted to them," the work songs, folkloric myths, legends, and fables that arose in part from this "latent rebellion" against light-skinned elites constituted the precursors of the *vallenato* music that came to be recognized as a separate genre only as recently as the 1940s.[29]

Vallenato music is divided into three schools, all corresponding to various departments within the Caribbean region: the *vallenato-vallenato* (performed in the central and southern zones of the Guajira department), the *vallenato-bajero* (played in the Magdalena department and banana-growing region), and the *vallenato-sabanero* (performed in the departments of Bolívar, Sucre, and Córdoba). The genre is based on four distinct rhythms or genres: the *son, paseo, merengue,* and *puya,* ranging from the slow *son* to the rapid *puya,* with the *merengue* and *paseo* being the most commonly performed today.[30] The first *vallenato* rhythm to be played on the accordion, the *puya* is generally associated with more sarcastic thematic material, while the closely related *merengue* distinguishes itself from the *puya* by virtue of its more narrative function. The *son*, characterized as a more nostalgic style, is recognized for its use in Colombian slave laments. Finally, the multithemed *paseo* style is noted for its Spanish influences, as expressed in its narrative form (*paseos* are employed in descriptive, picaresque, and romantic themes) and in its strophic structure. Both of these latter genres are generally employed as vehicles for the display of musicians' poetic skills.[31] In sharp contrast to its origins, the most popular rhythms of the *vallenato moderno*, which can be traced back to the inclusion of Afro-Cuban percussive techniques in the 1960s, have evolved into a genre more dependent on rhythm than on lyrics, an evolution that has arguably rendered the *vallenato* more global in its reach. Perhaps more important, as Vives's renderings of the *vallenato moderno* demonstrate, it is quite possible to have it "both ways"—the global does not erase the local, and vice versa; rather, the two forces shape each other.[32] In this regard, Vives, like many popular artists located within the subjective and shifting category of world music, assumes a dual role: that of cosmopolitan world citizen and representative local artist. Running counter to the tide of logic that deems popular music more parochial in its spatiality,[33] Vives and his ironically named band La Provincia (The province) have nonetheless managed to meaningfully insert their music into the larger pan-Caribbean popular corpus while simultaneously retaining their *colombianidad*, thereby avoiding the "placelessness" associated with many contemporary popular genres.

Traditional *vallenato* arrangements typically include the accordion, the *caja vallenata*, the *guacharaca*, and the *gaita*; in keeping with oral tradition, compositions are generally learned by ear.[34] In essence, the genre's instrumentation reflects the tri-ethnic ancestry of its creators, while the terminology associated with the *gaita* in particular also foregrounds the gendered nomenclature of the instruments. The *gaita*, reportedly invented by the Chimila Indians of the old Valle de Upar province,[35] is a flute fashioned from the long tubes of the *cardón* plant. Lacking any sort of vibrating reed, *gaitas* are classified as either *hembra* (female, containing five fingerholes) or *macha* (male, containing two fingerholes, with one always stopped with wax). The *vallenato*'s other indigenous instrument, the *guacharaca*, is a rasp made of a slender palm trunk known as *caña de lata* that is scraped using a metal fork, or *trinche*. The double-headed drum, or *caja*, recalls the *vallenato*'s African roots and is similar to the Cuban *bongó*; *vallenato* musicians play the *caja* by holding it on the knee and beating it with two sticks.[36] However, for many musicians, the accordion serves as the genre's defining musical element. Generally speaking, a *vallenato* ensemble's accordionist also serves as lead singer, although in recent years this custom appears to have been become less prevalent, as in the case of Carlos Vives. Contemporary versions of the *vallenato*, such as those performed by Vives, Amparo Sandino, and the group Moisés y la Gente del Camino, may incorporate electric guitars, synthesizers, and other technologically advanced elements and thus are sometimes referred to as *vallenato techno* or *vallenato moderno*.[37]

In the traditional *vallenatos* performed in the past by musicians and composers like Alejo Durán, Leandro Díaz, and Rafael Escalona, lyrical themes and uses vary. While many of the *vallenato*'s themes are considered timeless and are in fact transmitted across generations, other compositions, notably the recent *vallenato de protesta* (protest *vallenato*) recall a more specific time frame.[38] In the past, traditional *vallenatos* were also often utilized for musical "duels" or *piquerías* between composers (Vives's immensely popular 1993 recording of Emiliano Zuleta's classic, "*La gota fría*," is an example) as well as for the romantic *serenatas vallenatas* or *vallenato* serenades still occasionally performed in rural coastal zones.[39] These early *vallenato* duels likely served the purpose of permitting musicians to assert their masculinity and thereby gain an alternative form of social prestige while living as marginalized subjects in an openly racist, classist society. However, in thematic terms, the *vallenato* has only somewhat retained its "newspaper-esque character," musically relating events and histories of importance to *costeños* and frequently referencing regional myths, geographical spaces, and individuals.[40]

In effect, the heavy reliance on orality in Colombian Caribbean culture has produced a music whose marked orality has not diminished in spite of massive rural-to-urban migration.[41] Indeed, from the beginning, the *vallenato*'s emphasis on orality has engendered a code of sorts among its regional audience and producers. Much like rap and salsa, the *vallenato* not only constitutes a source of communal pleasure but also serves as a collective lexicon for communities that otherwise lack such a code.[42] *Vallenato* orality and, in a broader sense, *costeño* orality, in turn function as a brand of countermemory, or what George Lipsitz describes as

> a way of remembering and forgetting that starts with the local, the immediate, and the personal . . . counter-memory looks to the past for the hidden histories excluded from dominant narratives . . . [and] forces revision of existing histories by supplying new perspectives about the past. Counter-memory embodies aspects of myth and aspects of history, but it retains an enduring suspicion of both categories.[43]

In this context, *vallenato* (counter-)memory assumes a productive, rather than consumptive, character and as such figures prominently in the ongoing construction of the Colombian musical imagiNation. As a visit to any *vallenato* concert will reveal, the specialized, highly specific lyrics of *vallenato* standards (and, to a lesser extent, newer *vallenato* compositions) prove challenging to memorize, despite the frequent usage of repetitive call-and-response patterns. Therefore, audience participation in the fullest sense demands an in-depth, "insider's" knowledge of *costeño* culture. The *vallenato*'s emphasis on highly localized subjects simultaneously reflects and reinscribes the tendency toward regionalism among Colombians within Colombia and among the diaspora alike. In this respect, Carlos Vives and most *costeños* experience multiple subjectivities indicative of their "incongruous position vis-à-vis the nation to which they belong politically and the Caribbean region to which they belong culturally."[44]

The deep-seated character of Colombian cultural regionalism likewise surfaces in conventional musicological histories, which typically focus on questions of regional and ethnoracial origins. Accordingly, scholarly debates centering on Andean versus Caribbean genres inevitably tend to mirror discussions of Colombian identity in general, complete with a facile emphasis on the nation's tri-ethnic origins consistently juxtaposed against an ever-present discourse of sameness and difference.[45] Nevertheless, the representative status assigned to popular music from the interior began to fade somewhat in the 1940s, following the founding of Discos Fuentes and Discos Tropical on the coast and the record industry's move in the 1950s to Medellín, the commercial nucleus of the Antioquia region. During this period, *costeño* genres (such as *porro*, *cumbia*, and later on, *vallenato*) experienced a marked surge in popularity, while the foreign musical genres that typically entered Colombia via its Caribbean ports continued to enjoy success. The rise of *costeño* musical genres simultaneously signaled Andean music's demise as the reigning musical symbol of national identity—just as Colombian Caribbean music, seemingly in spite of its associations with heat, poverty, sexuality, and blackness, assumed a predominant representative role.[46]

Race and Ownership in the Vallenato

No importa si es blanco   It doesn't matter if he's white
si es pobre y famoso   if he's poor and famous
si al fin lo que vale   if in the end what matters
es que cante sabroso   is that he sings with feeling
              —Carlos Vives, "*Carito*"

While in the preceding composition Vives speaks from his privileged subject position as a white, upper-class male, the song nevertheless correctly identifies race as a salient factor contributing to the contemporary *vallenato*'s resemanticization. In Colombia as well as in Latin America in general, a basic three-level system of racial classification reigns in which notions of black and white occupy opposite ends of the social spectrum, while the vast majority of individuals fall into the "international" category of mixed, or mestizo.[47] Latin America's regional racial signifiers are also far more amorphous than those in the United States. As the popular Latin American refrain "*el dinero blanquea*" (money whitens) recalls, phenotypical attributes do not necessarily determine one's racial classification. Economic factors figure prominently in the formation of racial signifiers, rendering identifications such as "black" and "indigenous" more malleable.[48] The malleability of Colombian racial and ethnic identity is further enhanced by the added dimension of class, in which the financially motivated "search for whiteness" is inextricably linked to questions of class. Thus, for many *costeños*, the term "*negro*" is in fact synonymous with the lower class.[49]

Prior to Colombian slave emancipation in 1852, the coastal city of Cartagena served as a major port in the trans-Atlantic slave trade. There, as throughout the Atlantic coast, miscegenation among Europeans, indigenous peoples, and Africans produced a highly mixed population. Consequently, a racial lexicon and system of social stratification based on variables such as skin color and social class, among others, developed among *costeños*. By the beginning of the twentieth century, the term "*blanco*" had come to signify a member of the dominant class, regardless of phenotype, while labels such as "*claro*" were employed to refer to those whose skin was light but who were of lower socioeconomic standing; intermediate categories also emerged. This interweaving of discrimination and tolerance with blackness, indigeneity, and *mestizaje* thus occurred within an elite project of Colombian national identity that vigorously promotes a vision of mestizo (mixed) nationhood. While blacks and indigenous peoples are potentially included in this paradigm (although in different ways), they may also both be excluded as non-mestizo and therefore categorized as "mixed" peoples.[50]

Undoubtedly, the high rates of race mixture on the Atlantic coast have contributed to the perpetuation of the myth of racial democracy.[51] However, despite their undeniable contributions to the formation of *costeño* culture, Afro-Colombians are largely absent from official Colombian histories, a reflection of the differential institutional treatment afforded to Colombia's black and indigenous populations.[52] Indigenous Colombians have historically been conceptualized as the Other, while Afro-Colombians have assumed a far more nebulous status that dates back to the colonial period. Official attitudes dictated that Colombia's indigenous peoples be available for exploitation as well as protection; in contrast, blacks, while enjoying limited (albeit uneven) legislated privileges, were deemed more in need of institutional control than of protection. Indigenous peoples therefore possessed an institutionalized identity and, by extension, enjoyed a position marginally superior to that of blacks. Nevertheless, both groups have long suffered from discrimination in the region, as recent governmental attempts to control or instrumentalize Colombian ethnoracial identity evince.[53]

Thus, *La Costa* and its African cultural influences have been historically posited as inherently more "musical" and less "civilized" than the nation's interior regions, echoing predominant stereotypes regarding the intersection of music, blackness, and sexuality.[54] Nonetheless, these pejorative connotations have not deterred elite Colombian artists from partially assimilating the *vallenato* (and, before it, the related *cumbia* genre) for marketing purposes. Such strategies recall the bourgeois tactics of appropriation and reform (as opposed to outright repression), in conjunction with capitalist demands on the meanings attached to popular culture.[55] As Raymond Williams argues, these repeated, predictable cycles of appropriation that have occurred throughout musical history are best addressed by theories of transformist hegemony, or nationalist attempts to foment cultural unity and sanction diversity by "assimilating elements of that heterogeneity through appropriations that devalue them or that deny the source of their contribution."[56]

In a more nuanced addendum to his previous scholarship on the whitening of Colombia and the differential treatment afforded to Colombian blacks and indigenous peoples, Wade's more recent work on national identity and race challenges existing paradigms of the relationship between Colombian elites and ethnoracial minorities. To this end, he cites the prevailing trend within the study of Latin American musical genres and their sociopolitical contexts toward presenting elites as a group intent on homogenizing resistant minorities. Hence, within this scenario, the discourse of diversity always emanates from outside the official discourse on national identity and music, thereby presenting an unproblematic, unrealistic version of events.[57] On the contrary, Wade characterizes these social dynamics as far more intricate:

> Diversity is necessary to nationalist ideas, partly because it is only *vis-à-vis* diversity that unity can be imagined, but also because diversity almost always involves power relations. Just as in colonial power relations the coloniser's sense of domination is fed by a narcissistic desire for the submission of the subordinate other, so the nation builders define their own superiority in relation to the diversity they observe and construct—and desire. *Distinction as excellence depends upon distinction as differentiation; discrimination as refined and superior taste depends on discrimination against those defined as inferior and different.*[58]

Colombia's emphasis on the interior as the epicenter of cultural power that "not only reproduces sociocultural arbitrariness but also represents such arbitrariness as necessary and natural; [that] conceals economic power and aids the exercise and perception of such power"[59] is longstanding. The racial and cultural divides present in Colombian life are also evidenced in the "*cachaco/costeño*" dichotomy present in everyday Colombian speech and further paralleled in the deliberate, top-down construction of cultural

Figure 5.3. *El rock de mi pueblo* (My people's rock), Vives's recent fusion album. EMI Latin, 2004. While at times presenting an overly simplistic view of racial dynamics in terms of its visual iconography as well as its musical content, *El rock de mi pueblo* has proven to be Vives's most musically ambitious work to date.

diversity, as evidenced in the 1991 Colombian Constitution and the states's so-called acts of cultural recuperation.[60]

In contrast to many left-wing critiques, Colombian cultural policy has therefore sought not to erase ethnoracial difference but rather to *capitalize upon and seemingly benignly promote its very presence* in an effort to maintain the asymmetries feeding long-entrenched hierarchies. Indeed, many of these government-sponsored initiatives and acts of recuperation merely reinscribe the anthropological rescue of the popular. In these initiatives, the difference on display invariably focuses on black and indigenous subjectivities, thereby underlining the status of whiteness as the unmarked norm against which all other Colombian ethnoracial identities are measured.[61] Related debates regarding the politics of musical appropriation across cultural and ethnoracial lines are not unique, however, as David Byrnes and Ry Cooder's work with Latin American artists and Paul Simon's forays into South African and Puerto Rican music demonstrate. As Deborah Pacini Hernández has observed in this regard, elite artists who achieve success performing formerly maligned genres have introduced a new dimension to the debate: how might Cultural Studies approach the situation when the artist "transgressing boundaries" is from the same country, if not the same socioeconomic or ethnoracial background, as those whose work is appropriated?[62]

Beyond Valledupar's Borders:
The Commodification of Contemporary Vallenato

In a partial reflection of the secondary status accorded to the role of political economy in most cultural analyses of music and identity, comparatively little information exists on the nature of the Colombian music industry. The current dearth of publications on this topic is further underscored by fact that one of the central issues arising from debates on musical commodification, that of authenticity, frequently arises in conversations regarding the music industry and its products.[63] In sum, the *vallenato*'s ongoing commodification and resemanticization are fundamentally traceable to an overall struggle for cultural capital, as evidenced by the "revisibilization" of an historically invisible country ravaged by violence. The genre's commodification and its very legitimization thus present the possibility of an alternative *colombianidad*, a significant departure from previous, state-sponsored notions of self. Along these lines, new technologies such as the Internet, including Web sites such as *Semana* magazine's *Conexión Colombia* (see chapter 1) have emerged. These new mediums have, in turn, played a prime role in the promotion of previously unknown hybrid subjectivities, subsequently reflecting and facilitating the Colombian diaspora's engagement in transnational and/or multiple identities.

The *vallenato* has also garnered another brand of "validation through visibility," in the form of the willingness of entertainers like Vives to embrace a historically nonwhite genre. As an elite cultural mediator, Vives participates in a complex series of mediations in which an expressive form is first adapted by a member of the dominant community with ties to a marginalized population. He in turn interprets the form, in this case the *vallenato*, for elite audiences relatively estranged from Colombia's marginalized communities. However, these elite concessions may ultimately merely serve to placate Othered communities, to the benefit of the dominant classes. Thus, the cultural capital that is apparently accessible to all really "belongs" only to those who possess the material means to acquire it.[64] Vives's privileged position as cultural mediator is not lost on many in the Latin(o) American or mainstream U.S. popular media. His role in the *vallenato*'s dissemination is frequently likened to Elvis Presley's exploitation of the blues throughout his rock and roll career; "like the King, he is a white man singing with a black feel who has sold millions of records."[65] Eagerly engaging in this comparison and seemingly oblivious to the explicit critique of gender, race, and class hegemony embedded within, in interviews Vives has discussed the connections between blues and rock in terms of their analogous relationship to *cumbia*, a genre that he labels the "mother" of *vallenato*, and to *vallenato*. In recent compositions Vives has cited the shared social, cultural, and geographical matrices uniting the Mississippi and Magdalena Rivers and, by extension, the cities of New Orleans (a site associated with the zydeco, another accordion-based genre) and Barranquilla. This circular thematic is incorporated into the song "*Décimas*," from *Déjame entrar* (2001):

Cartagena a San Juan	Cartagena is like San Juan
Santo Domingo y La Habana	Santo Domingo and Havana
... a Santa Marta, Sevilla	... like Santa Marta, Sevilla
Taganga a Taganguilla	Taganga is like Taganguilla
... y la ciudad de Neworlín	... and the city of New Orleans
se parece a Barranquilla	is like Barranquilla[66]

Similar references resurface in the 2004 recording "*Santa Marta-Kingston-New Orleans*." "*Santa Marta*," a rolling bass- and harmonica-laden departure from Vives's previous albums, appears on *El rock de mi pueblo*, a work whose very title communicates an explicit reclamation of rock as an always/already pan-American hybrid expressive form. Somewhat ironically given Vives's positioning as the postmodern Elvis of Colombian popular music, the comparatively greater rock, blues, and gospel (and, ultimately, pan-African American) underpinnings of "*Santa Marta*" and *El rock de mi pueblo* signal a historical recognition, albeit ethnoracially sanitized, of the common circum-Caribbean historical and cultural nexus. Just as Vives has recognized the musical and historical union of these various Afro-diasporic forms in practice, however, he has also discursively distanced them from one another in subsequent interviews, particularly in his commentary regarding the imperative among Colombian artists to remain "faithful" to local genres.[67] Such critiques, which he has occasionally directed at fellow *costeño* artists and at Shakira in particular, arguably undercut the potentially oppositional content of his endeavors in pan-American musical performance and composition.

Within this context, the practice of naming (whether the self, others, or geophysical spaces) in the *vallenato* provokes a variety of questions regarding the veracity of artistic claims to authenticity. Beyond its symbolic contribution to communal affiliation[68] as a shared text to which most *colombianos* can relate in some fashion, the potential impact of this seemingly unmediated version of "home" merits further consideration. In contrast to the notion of music as a mobile life form, the myth of cultural authenticity embraces the concept of musical genres as static, isolated forms of property whose movement is nearly always unidirectional, in which dominant appropriate cultural forms borrow from the dominated. This is not to suggest, however, that the dynamics of cultural appropriation and/or transmission are inherently uniform or one-sided but rather that they are dialectical in nature. As such, despite (or perhaps because of) the boundaries established around them, commodified musical forms such as the *vallenato* may benefit in part from the "eroticization of difference" and a submerged identification with marginalized Others that ultimately augments the appeal of selected racialized cultural commodities among dominant consumers.[69] In the song "*Malas lenguas*" (Gossipers; literally, Bad tongues) from *Tengo fe* (1997), Vives indirectly indexes these issues and their connection to broader questions of authenticity and their location within the commercial Latin(o) and "world music" spheres :

De esas costumbres	Of all the customs
que hay en mi tierra	that exist in my country
pensaba yo de las malas lenguas [. . .]	I thought about the gossipers [. . .]
No se preguntan	They don't ask themselves
no saben nada . . .	they don't know anything . . .
Y son los dueños de la palabra	And they're great talkers
y dicen tener siempre la razón	and they always think they're right
Que si soy de Santa Marta	About whether or not I'm from Santa Marta
O si soy de Valledupar . . .	Or Valledupar . . .
Soy libre	I'm free
Puedo cantar	I can sing
Pregúntale	Ask

A Leandro Díaz ...	Leandro Díaz ...
[C]anté con Francisco el Hombre	I sang with Francisco the Man
en la serranía	in the mountains[70]

Here, Vives references his less conventional approach to the *vallenato*, as he argues that despite his seemingly nontraditional appearance and approach to the genre, he is in fact a legitimate *vallenato* performer. To Vives, hailing from the birthplace of the *vallenato* (Valledupar), much less one's racial identity, is not as important as what's in one's heart, as he asserts his right ("*Soy libre / Puedo cantar*") to represent Colombia as a *vallenato* musician, regardless of his origins. However, upon defending his place in the genre, Vives swiftly falls into the type of *vallenato* posturing that is based on one's knowledge of certain people and places ("*Pregúntale / A Leandro Díaz*"; "*canté con Francisco el Hombre*"),[71] thereby to some extent engaging in the same superficial tests of authenticity as his detractors, just as he fails to recognize the skin, gender, and class privileges that facilitate his insertion into (and self-selected departure from) *costeño* and global popular music networks.

Many *vallenato* scholars, such as Rocío Cárdenas Duque, Daniel Samper Pizano, and Pilar Tafur, have lamented the *vallenato moderno*'s commercial success and the genre's commodification, claiming, in the words of Cárdenas Duque, that the music is "losing its artistic meaning," a terse nationalistic argument against the potential impacts of globalized media.[72] Statements such as these, however, are problematic on numerous counts. First, they negate the possibilities for incorporating differing perspectives into the *vallenato* via the introduction of women and others new to the genre in a public forum. Second, Cárdenas Duque appears to be denouncing the *vallenato*'s commodification not because it perhaps signifies a loss of artistic agency for Afro-Colombian musicians and composers (indeed, race, gender, and class critiques are absent from her commentary) but rather because it has quite literally hastened artistic production and therefore compromises artistic standards.[73] Her comments also recall the flawed reasoning that often arises in discussions of musical syncretism in the Caribbean. Given that as an *already* syncretic musical form the *vallenato* suffered from a lack of "purity" before it was ever even "discovered" by record producers, how do we explain the critiques regarding the *vallenato*'s ever-increasing commercialization and its subsequent further lapse into "inauthenticity"? Furthermore, via what processes, and to what ends, is the *vallenato*, a musical form that fits squarely into European, African, and indigenous musical paradigms, solely subsumed under the overarching category of "black" music?

In the final analysis, such perspectives on authenticity merely serve to reinscribe existing beliefs about a mythical past in which women in particular were content with an ostensibly passive existence limited to the private sphere. "*La celosa*," (Jealous woman), a popular *vallenato* standard originally composed and performed as a *paseo* by Alejo Durán, clearly exemplifies the gendering of the private and public spheres in Colombian society:

Cuando salga de mi casa	When I leave the house
Y me demore por la calle	And hang out on the street
No te preocupes Anita . . .	Don't worry, Anita . . .
Negra no me celes tanto	Honey don't be so jealous
Déjame gozar la vida [bis]	Let me enjoy life [repeat]
Tú conmigo vives resentida	You're resentful of me
Pero yo te alegro con mi canto [bis] . . .	But I'll cheer you up with my song [repeat] . . .
Cómo tú ya me conoces	How well you know me
Te agradezco me perdones	I am grateful; pardon me
Si regreso un poco tarde	If I return a little late
Cuando llegue yo a mi casa	When I get home
Quiero verte muy alegre	I want to see you really happy,
Cariñosa y complaciente	affectionate, and agreeable
Pero nunca me recibas con desaire	But you better never greet me angrily
Porque así tendré que irme nuevamente [bis]	Because then I'll have to leave again [repeat][74]

Vives's recording of "*La celosa*" functions as a musical *parranda costeña*, or *costeño* party. The piece opens slowly with the strums of a guitar, but once the initial strains of the accordion break through, the "party" begins. Like many *vallenato* compositions, *La celosa*'s strophic structure encourages audience participation; its melody line is clearly delineated, and hand claps are employed not only as a means of engaging listeners but also as an economical form of percussion. The insider/outsider dynamic so fundamental to the evolution of the *vallenato* is retained here, as Vives and his fellow performers continuously call out the names of coastal towns and their inhabitants. As the song draws to a close, so does the party; the performers bid each other farewell, and "*La celosa*" ends as it began, with spoken dialogue.

The voices that frame the beginning and the ending of "*La celosa*" are undeniably masculine, as are the (c)overt dialogues that adorn the piece function on numerous levels: between the performers at the moment of recording itself, between *"La celosa"*'s performers and its listeners, and between the listeners themselves and other citizens of the Colombian musical imagiNation. Women's voices are muted throughout this public, high-volume conversation. Notably, the voices that Vives invites to participate are exclusively masculine, thus contributing to the piece's overall privileging of male dialogue and public expression while simultaneously invoking the historically gendered boundaries of musical performance. Through its use of the racializing term *"negra"* (a popular term of endearment in many Caribbean societies), *"La celosa"*'s lyrics evince Latin(o) popular music's tendency to portray dark-skinned women as objects of male sexual desire.[75] Moreover, Anita, the object of the song's discourse, does not speak; she waits at home for Vives, the narrator, to appear. As in his live performances, Vives ends *"La celosa"* with some laughing remarks to his colleagues: *"Tengo otra canción que está peor, tengo otra canción que realmente está peor"* ("I have another song that's even worse, I have another song that's really worse"), indicating his fundamental awareness of the gender dynamics at stake in *"La celosa."*[76]

In many respects, the deconstruction of the gendered notions of subject/object within *vallenato* offers fertile ground for ongoing discussions regarding cultural constructs of authenticity, particularly with regard to the genre's transition into the *vallenato romántico* (romantic *vallenato*) format. How do the *vallenato*'s meanings and representations differ when performed by Amparo Sandino, a former backup singer in Carlos Vives's band La Provincia, and by male duos such as Diomedes Díaz and Iván Zuleta? Like Gloria Estefan's *vallenato* or *vallenato*-hybrid recordings, Sandino's lyrics depart from the traditional *vallenato*'s collective, politicized themes and focus exclusively on issues of love and romance from an individual perspective (though it is important to note that, regardless of gender, contemporary *vallenato* favors romantic themes in general). For example, virtually all of the selections of Sandino's 1996 solo debut album, *Punto de partida* (Point of departure) may be classified as "love songs," with the exception of the album's final selection. By the same token, Gloria Estefan's aforementioned recording *Abriendo puertas* (1995), a montage of Cuban and Colombian musical genres, never departs from the stereotypically feminine themes of heterosexual romantic love and idealized familial existence.

The *vallenato*'s historical trajectory thus mirrors that of salsa, in which the more socially conscious lyrics of the genre's earlier phases have been displaced by the more benign salsa *romántica*, or romantic salsa. Significantly, musical historiographies of the Caribbean have largely failed to incorporate women; if they are recognized, it is solely as performers of the romantic *bolero* genre.

Thus, while in recent decades some of the most successful and innovative salsa artists have been women, with few exceptions they have been relegated to the category of the so-called salsa *monga* (limp salsa) subgenre, which emerged in the 1980s in opposition to the exclusively masculine salsa *dura* (hard salsa) of the 1970s.[77] Arguably a response to the increased visibility and participation of female artists in the genre, such an explicitly gendered, and overtly phallic, Manichean dynamic predominates *vallenato* music, as well. And, while not as historically entrenched as the divisions between salsa *monga* and salsa *dura*, the *vallenato romántico*'s gendered and racialized status has ultimately led to its common portrayal as feminized, whitened, and therefore less "authentic."

Apart from any beliefs regarding cultural authenticity, control of musical production is a deciding factor in the overall process of commodification. Hence, the right to engage in instrumentalism, or the "picking and choosing" of a cultural product's characteristics in an effort to establish cultural boundaries, ultimately affords music producers the ability to define the parameters of artistic expression. Indeed, the influence of the predominantly male producers of Latin(o) music needs to be taken into account, and, despite consumers' tendency to conflate the role of composer with that of performer (and both with overarching musical trends), the centrality of the music industry's role in supporting such dichotomies is undeniable. Conversely, the music industry's investment in the rise of the *vallenato romántico*, parallel to that of salsa, has also functioned as a means of globalizing a genre previously marked by its engagement in localized political themes.[78]

Undoubtedly, in traditional as well as contemporary *vallenato*, women are often the subjects of *vallenato* discourse, if not the agents of its dissemination. This is not to suggest that the romantic themes currently being interpreted by some female *vallenato* performers lack merit or that having women, particularly Latin(a) Americans, perform male-coded genres is not in and of itself a considerable advance within the public sphere. Rather, it is always more "socially acceptable and politically innocuous"[79] for a woman to sing about her love life than for her to sing about more overtly politicized topics. Again, much like salsa *romántica*, contemporary *vallenato* forms cannot be summarily dismissed as inauthentic. It bears repeating that the location of cultural forms is fluid, just as their very significations are constructed outside the forms themselves. It is also worth noting the critical and often disconcerting parallels between the distinct pragmatic functions attached to ethnoracial and gendered difference within the Colombian context and the strategic deployment of ethnoracial and/or migrant status within the project of

U.S. national identity.[80] Regardless, and indeed perhaps in spite of, their often profoundly problematic representations of *mestizaje*, gender, and national identity, for many younger Colombians, and certainly for numerous Colombians in the diaspora, the *vallenato moderno* and *vallenato romántico* forms resonate with the hybrid subjectivities activated in the wake of the deterritorialized nation-state. We must therefore recognize commodification's critical role in the *vallenato*'s general resemanticization, as well as its transnationalization, across multiple racialized, gendered nexus of articulation into a vibrant synecdoche for *colombianidad* in Latin America and abroad. As the individual and collective artistic trajectories of Colombian recording artists such as Carlos Vives, Andrea Echeverri, and Shakira evince, contemporary Latin(o) popular music also serves as a productive platform for engaging in a metacritical analysis of transnational studies in the present-day academy.

6

The Colombian Transcultural Aesthetic Recipe

Music Video in the "New" American Studies

> [P]opular culture, commodified and stereotyped as it often is, is not at all, as we sometimes think of it, the arena where we find who we really are, the truth of our experience. It is an arena that is *profoundly* mythic. It is a theater of popular desires, a theater of popular fantasies. It is where we discover and play with the identifications of ourselves, where we are imagined, where we are represented, not only to the audiences out there who do not get the message, but to ourselves for the first time. As Freud said, sex (and representation) mainly takes place in the head.
>
> —Stuart Hall, "What Is This 'Black' in Black Popular Culture?"

After decades of relative privilege afforded to the study of external as opposed to internal colonialism, the current rush to embrace the transnational within Latin American and American Studies, while largely a welcome development, also proves somewhat problematic. I refer specifically to the enthusiastic critiques leveled by numerous scholars regarding the need for American Studies to "go global." As Felicity Schaeffer-Grabiel and others have observed, to uncritically accept the apparent novelty of such logic is to disregard the longstanding contributions of Latino Studies (and, I would add, Ethnic Studies in general) as inherently transnational intellectual and political projects. Perhaps more significant, to engage in such a move in unreflexive fashion runs the risk of eliding the intrinsically transnational character of U.S. Ethnic Studies vis-à-vis American Studies and thereby erasing, as is so often done in the globalized labor market, the intellectual labor and contributions of women and of communities of color in general. Emory Elliot has remarked that "[S]ome institutions and administrators may be too ready to embrace a seemingly new idea without recognizing the continuing value of what is already in place, if it appears to 'solve' a lingering discomfort with departments established through activism."[1] In a similar vein, I would argue that to ignore the inherently (trans)national character of Latino Studies entails reinscribing the hegemonic paradigm of "American exceptionalism" upon which American Studies was originally founded—for, much like Arab American, Native American Studies, and Asian American Studies in particular, Latino Studies is rooted in ongoing historical conflicts centered on racism, migration, imperialism, and colonialism.

From an International or Latin American Studies perspective, to disregard the fundamentally transnational character of Latino Studies or, as is most commonly done, to locate the transnational exclusively in "nondomestic" fields of inquiry is to participate in the artificial division of the Latin American and the U.S. Latino, itself an act of historical amnesia and a standard tool of colonization. As Ella Shohat notes, the scholarly fixation on the "elsewhere" ultimately discounts the "co-implicatedness" of U.S. political and cultural interventions in the global context. Indeed, such moments point to the need to affect American Studies from within, without conducting yet another colonizing move.[2] For Area and Ethnic Studies, while distinct, are not strictly oppositional scholarly pursuits, given that domestic issues such as racism and internal colonialism possess decidedly international dimensions. However, the case of the internationally known singer and songwriter Shakira offers a significant counternarrative to such limited conceptualizations of American, Ethnic, Middle Eastern, and Latin American Studies and to the transnational elements inherent to each of these rather unstable academic categories. Both literally and figuratively, Shakira's movements embody the translocal nature of her artistic influences and media persona. While undeniably provocative in its incorporation of classic Middle Eastern dance gestures emphasizing the hips and abdomen, Shakira's hybrid aesthetics simultaneously contest traditional, straightforward readings of the relationship between gender, ethnoracial identity, sexuality, and power in music video.

I maintain here that the thematic and aesthetic foundations of Shakira's most recent recordings, *Fijación oral, Volumen I* (2005) and *Oral Fixation, Volume II* (2005) can be divided into roughly three broad categories, all of which foreground the mouth as the epistemological hinge upon which the human experience swings: sex, food, and language. I reference the obvious Freudian allusions afoot in the album and its iconography, with particular emphasis on the ways in which these motifs and others emerge as key components of Shakira's recordings, music videos, and press coverage. As José David Saldívar argues, any comprehensive examination of culture must take into account both its symbolic and its material facets. I note this because, significantly, more than a century after their initial arrival on the Colombia's Caribbean coast, the Middle Eastern community has arguably had its broadest material impact in the region's culinary sphere.[3] An "Arab plate" (*plato arabe*) is present on nearly every restaurant menu, and the culinary integration of the Middle Eastern and the *costeño* is such that most Colombian cookbooks include recipes for dishes like hummus, kibbeh, tabboule, and almond rice, most of which are frequently presented as regional or national specialties. Nevertheless, Shakira is not the first Latin(a) American to embark on this precise sensorial exploration of the mouth as erogenous zone. Acclaimed authors such as the Chilean Isabel Allende, the Mexican Laura Esquivel, and the U.S.-Cuban Dolores Prida, in addition to the aforementioned Carmelita Tropicana (herself a tongue-in-cheek reference to the legendary Carmen Miranda), have also published erotic cookbooks, novels, and theatrical pieces in which they offer their own unique interpretations of the ways in which the Latina mouth (as both subject and object) becomes the simultaneous site of dominant stereotypes, cultural baggage, and individual pleasure.

As the most visible member of Barranquilla's well-established Arab community, Shakira has described herself as a combination of "quibbe crudo and plátano frito" ("raw kibbeh and fried plantain").[4] This characterization neatly reflects the transcultural aesthetic recipe upon which her artistic identity is based. Building on my previous commentary regarding the interstitial character of Shakira's subject position and its subsequent impact on notions of "Latino" and "Latin American" identity among the growing U.S.-Colombian transnational community, I posit that Shakira's personal history, artistic production, and media presence provide a fruitful example relevant to the ongoing (re)conceptualization of American, Latin American, and transnational studies.

My consideration of Latin(a) American music video in general and Shakira's work in particular departs from a brief consideration of the history of women in music, specifically pop and rock, followed by a discussion of the role of women in music video during the early days of music television (MTV) as well as now. This analysis is grounded in the overarching concerns of feminist and media music criticism, in particular the musical and media "commonsense" of ethnoracial identity, gender, and sexuality. My cross-media examination of Shakira's music videos, print media presence, television appearances, and recordings addresses the methodological and thematic gaps in existing scholarly approaches to gender, race, and sexuality in contemporary music video. Simultaneously, I argue for a more nuanced metadisciplinary engagement with the location and politics of transnational studies within the academy.

Music Video and New Media: Reclaiming a Site of Critical Analysis

The methodological challenges presented by the study of music video mirror those that face scholars of popular music. Dependent on multiple layers and moments of meaning, both of these performative categories demand exhaustive critical attention to a variety of interdependent, distinct, and simultaneous elements, such as rhythm, tempo, lyrics, color, texture, and timbre. They are then communicated and framed by the various codes of performance and star texts that circulate in the mass media. Given the increasingly dispersed nature of popular musical meaning in the age of media convergence, a feminist, cross-media approach has proven essential. As Jillian Báez observes, such a framework

> examines issues of power and agency across difference, understanding that identities are not monolithic and can be contradictory or competing. Transnational feminism additionally highlights the fluidity, mobility, and also immobility of people and cultural products . . . [and] leaves room for women's resistance and agency within dominant global structures.[5]

This approach differs from the predominant theoretical paradigms of much present music video scholarship and film studies, namely the tendency to privilege the visual codes of music video at the expense of musical or aural analysis. In this respect, Susan McClary asserts that, while film soundtracks have generally been understood as cinematic elements that exercise a covert affective impact on viewers, the aural elements of music video assume a far more active role: "the *music* in music videos is largely responsible for the narrative continuity and affective quality in the resultant work, even if it is the visual images we remember concretely."[6] (Or, as Jody Berland affirms in more succinct terms: "A single can exist [technically, at least] without the video, but the reverse is not the case").[7] Early proponents of cross-media music video analysis maintained that the artificial split between popular music's aural and visual realms elides a fundamental historical feature of the pop universe: namely that the visual has *always* formed a central function of the popular apparatus, via record covers, print media, and the like.[8]

To date, numerous scholars of popular music have also commented on the gendered nature of the perceived boundaries between the rock and pop genres. These arbitrary distinctions reflect the social fear of music's status as a primary conduit for the channeling of desire and the definition of sexual appeal, processes that inform and simultaneously reflect the manner in which popular music is consumed, marketed, and produced.[9] Given Western culture's longstanding binary between the body (coded as feminine) and the mind (coded as masculine), in conjunction with music's frequent categorization as a corporal/feminine activity, male musicians have long policed the borders of musical participation. These exercises in containment, often a response to masculine fears of being perceived as feminine or effeminate, have typically translated into attempts to constrain female participation in musical performance and production (the idea being that a cultural practice in which women do not participate can hardly be perceived as "feminine").[10]

As Susan Fast contends, in this respect rock music has traditionally constituted a safe site for heterosexual male self-expression, a place where overt expressions of sexually transgressive and emotionally charged behavior are socially sanctioned. Conversely, the freedom to publicly enact one's sexuality is not as readily available to women. Female musicians have historically been forced to contend with the stereotype that they are somehow sexually available to both fans and/or music industry executives. Such attitudes are directly linked to music's ability to influence listeners in ways over which they have negligible relational control. These gendered, raced, and classed constructions have, in turn, wielded considerable material and symbolic impacts on the ability of most female artists to garner commercial and/or critical recognition for their efforts, particularly in the realm of "rock" music. Paradoxically, the few women who have achieved commercial success in the rock market are often simultaneously targets of criticism, as the following *New York Times* review of Shakira's *Oral Fixation, Volume II* succinctly reveals: "If her songs hadn't become international pop hits, Shakira would have been lauded as an innovator in Latin alternative rock."[11] Similarly, a slide show on the popular website msn.com mused that "Shakira's gigantic popularity sometimes obscures the fact that she's one of Latin pop's most progressive and adventurous artists."[12] As explicated in these stark phrases, media logic dictates that once Shakira has submitted herself to the lure of pop commercialism (as if rock musicians were not interested in earning a living, as well), and particularly when her fan base consists primarily of women and young girls (whose musical proclivities lack the legitimacy afforded to those of male fans), Shakira and her music are at times deemed beyond the pale of "alternative" rock forms, or rock by any means. While the previous quotation was taken from a review written by a well-known male popular music critic, the erroneous association of pop with vapid commercialism also persists among Shakira's longstanding Latina reviewers: "I *do* think her music is becoming more commercial than ever. It's almost as if, in wanting to sell her music to as many people as possible, she's sacrificed a bit of her identity—a bit of what made me fall for her in the first place."[13] Exhibiting some of the possessive sentiments expressed by many popular music fans, this passage also foregrounds the unique challenges and tensions faced by popular female musicians of color who are not U.S. natives or artists whose original fan base consists of a marginalized segment of the United States or the Americas at large.

Notably, the majority of work on gender and sexuality in rock and pop music video to date has been overwhelmingly restricted to the analysis of mostly heterosexual female artists hailing from the United States or Great Britain. This limited conceptualization of who makes popular music echoes the "narrow-casting" strategies of MTV's initial phase, in which adolescent rock video fans were almost exclusively imagined as male, white, heterosexual, and English-speaking. In this regard, the singular possessive "my" in the iconic "I Want My MTV" advertising campaign proved anything but false advertising, as in its nascent stages the channel did in fact encapsulate the personal vision of a sole individual: Bob Pittman, the young U.S. cable executive who has been described as the driving force behind MTV's inception.[14] The immense popularity of a few African American artists such as Michael Jackson eventually altered the racial politics of MTV's content and ultimately opened the door for more artists of color and for rap musicians in particular. Critical engagements with race, ethnicity, and the transnational in music video scholarship have nevertheless comparatively lagged behind such developments. Locked into a vision of race, ethnicity, and national origins that hinges on binaries of black/white and "American"/British *or not* (with queerness relegated to an unacknowledged silence), this scholarship reinscribes the reigning corporate vision of MTV's early days, just as it figuratively erases the increased presence of Latinos, Asian-Americans, non-European/U.S., and openly queer music video artists.

Such an uneven focus also unwittingly perpetuates the longstanding myth that rock in particular is the singular purveyance of the United States and Great Britain, as it simultaneously reflects the colorblind, Anglo-centric, and nation-bound terms of existing scholarly debates on female music video. Nonetheless, these works have contested overriding perspectives of music videos as monolithically sexist, homophobic popular texts and of female music video stars as industry pawns entirely lacking in agency. As typified in the groundbreaking work of Lisa A. Lowe and her influential theory of access and discovery signs, this approach has reframed our understanding of the role of women in early music video via its emphasis on the liberatory potential of the medium.[15] Specifically, Lowe has argued that the integral role of lip-synching in popular music video signaled a strategic opportunity for female artists historically restricted to the role of lead of secondary vocalist. Accordingly, what was once perceived as an artistic limitation was now recast as a potential advantage:

> In narrative videos, the soundtrack provided by the female vocalist can operate like a narrator's omnipotent voice-over to guide the visual action. Sometimes, she manages to literally put words in the mouths of other characters (sometimes male) through the use of a common music video device whereby a selected lyrical phrase is lip-synched as though it were dialogue.[16]

The inclusion of female musicians on MTV also impacted the gender composition of the live performances offered by the same artists, as concert events once frequented almost exclusively by male fans rapidly grew into sites for female fan gatherings as well.[17] A more critically sound approach thus emerged with regard to questions of audience agency, as scholars such as Andrew Goodwin argued for more measured theories of audience manipulation that straddle the line between an overly optimistic view of viewers' ability to contest "intended" encoded discourses and the "hypodermic needle" assumption that intended discourses always achieve parallel results.[18] These are the theoretical parameters that define the early 1990s or the "golden age" of music video scholarship, a period that also parallels what many consider to be the apex of MTV's power and influence. (This is not to discount the comparatively greater geographical reach of MTV in the current context, however.)

Perhaps not unexpectedly, much of the foundational Cultural Studies, Media Studies, and musicological research on music video reflects the Western European, U.S. Anglo, and, to a lesser extent, male heterosexual roots of the genre's performers, producers, distributors, and core content. Since this period, relatively little research has been published that focuses exclusively on music video,[19] despite dynamic structural shifts in MTV's structure and scope. Principal developments include a marked growth in the number of video directors and performers who are female, openly queer, and/or of color; MTV's meteoric rise into an inter/transnational, multilingual and multicultural phenomenon; and the channel's ability to achieve greater vertical integration with the aid of new technologies such as the Internet and cellular telephones. While at first glance these transformations appear to constitute welcome advances in the MTV's historical trajectory, it is crucial to interpret them in a fashion mindful of the ways in which media representations of ethnoracial hybridity are often strategically employed within late capitalism as a means of economically addressing various audiences simultaneously. As Angharad Valdivia states, "Although both bodies and cultural forms mean different things in different places, they nonetheless travel across regional and national boundaries, with accompanying changes in meaning and status." In short, she suggests that we consider "the tensions and pains of hybridity—the fact that it is not all fun and profits,"[20] within a globalized mass media context defined by increased visibility for some marginalized subjects though not necessarily improved media access, control, or financial gain for all.

As previously discussed, the early 1990s also heralded a key moment in the active reframing of Miami's media image. This regional revival was in part a result of the slick packaging and broad appeal of television programs such as *Miami Vice* (a show that was ironically initially conceptualized under the title *MTV Cops* and that owed much of its visual and sonic aesthetics, not mention several noteworthy guest stars, to the music video format). In the years that followed, Miami continued to attract an increasingly diverse group of Latin American popular music and media stars, among them Shakira and her fellow countryman Carlos Vives. For those Colombian artists who chose not to immigrate to the United States for political or personal reasons, such as Aterciopelados, Miami nonetheless served as a key tour destination and the site of one of their largest fan bases.

Just as to some extent the development of Miami into the "Latin Hollywood" of the Americas may be traced to the global dispersion of music video aesthetics, the emergence of music video itself has been inextricably linked to the fate of the international recording industry. However, the emergence of music video is perhaps best characterized as a cable television, not a music industry, phenomenon. The initial steps toward the development of music television proved far too risky a venture for a U.S. music industry suffering an unprecedented drop in sales at the end of the 1970s, following several years of windfall profits. Broadly speaking, the struggling music industry was reluctant to commit money to a format that many deemed of negligible artistic merit and longevity. While what today's viewers recognize as music video is rooted in a lengthy history of similar efforts to combine the aural and musical mediums, the emergence of MTV, in 1982, can be attributed particularly to the unique confluence of the following five events: (1) increased consumer access to cable television services, particularly in the United States; (2) shifts in the consumption patterns of rock and pop music fans; (3) the ongoing recession in the music industry, coupled with the industry's concerns about competing audiovisual leisure outlets, such as videotape recorders; (4) the rise of "New Pop" in Great Britain and a concomitant shift in pop music ideologies; and (5) transformations in the pop music performing and recording processes.[21] Yet, despite the distinct character and unparalleled dissemination of contemporary music television and critics' insistence on categorizing music television as the "new medium" of its era, the deployment of pop music performance as a promotional vehicle is hardly novel. A case in point is Steven Levy's forceful, if inaccurate, characterization of MTV as a purely commercial entity whose resounding success among an "artificial community" of mindless consumers portends the death of "true" (1960s) rock culture. Most notable is his faithful adherence to masculinist musical scales of value, as evidenced in the dichotomy he posits between 1960s rock performance (which signs as male, heterosexual, ostensibly noncommercial, and therefore artistically superior) and early music video (and its association with a devoted fan base, commerce, and increased visibility for female and/or queer performers, mostly "feminine"/feminized characteristics deemed inherently inferior). Moreover, if we embrace the notion that the union of (popular) music and commerce is scarcely original, it then follows that song itself, or the union of music and lyrics, is perhaps best understood as yet another, albeit older, mode of multimedia expression. Significantly, this approach demands that we rethink today's predominant media paradigm (namely the stark historical representation of the divisions between "old" and "new" media and the correlation of the latter with more passive, static forms of interaction)[22] in favor of recognizing the inherently shifting nature and active potential of *all* media formats, both "old" and "new." Per this logic, the music video format continues to occupy a role of singular importance in the global recording industry, notwithstanding the introduction of various forms of so-called new media. The primary difference is merely one of location: whereas today's music fans dedicate much of their video consumption to clips viewed on Internet sites like *YouTube* and *MTV Overdrive*, earlier devotees of the genre viewed them almost exclusively on cable television.

As an integral force in the global popular cultural context, music video therefore fulfills multiple and often overlapping roles: "[s]tanding at the nexus of film, television, and advertising, the music video [is], at times, each one, and as combination album cover, photo shoot, and promotional appearance, also something fundamentally new: a form of visual art equally dedicated to the huckster's come-on and the artist's sincere appeal."[23] Calls for an approach to music video that valorizes the economic and the artistic on equal terms have thus proven popular among many scholars of the genre.[24] However, in a vertically oriented media culture in which it is often difficult to know "what is designed to promote what"[25] and, perhaps more important, in the face of cultural hierarchies that treat the commercial and artistic aspects of the music industry as mutually exclusive entities, the dangers of dismissing the potential of music video as a subject of rigorous critical analysis, particularly with regard to class, race, ethnicity, gender, and sexuality, persist. Nonetheless, as Sue Wise observes, "Feminist biography . . . is much less about *who* is the chosen subject, and much more about *why they are chosen* and *how we go about looking at them*."[26] In a similar vein, I argue for a scholarly approach to music video anchored in cross-media, transnational feminist analysis that simultaneously moves away from dehistoricized conceptualizations of the relationship among American, Ethnic, and Area Studies, ever mindful of the fact that "[w]hile culture is produced everywhere, only some locales enjoy the power to project their products around the world."[27]

On the Union of Quibbe Crudo and Plátano Frito: The Lebanese Migrants of the Colombian Caribbean

As the musical and industrial nucleus of Colombia's northern Caribbean coast (popularly known as *La Costa,*), the port city of Barranquilla has historically served as the destination of choice for the majority of the region's immigrant population. A significant number of the migrants who settled in the region during the twentieth century, especially between 1890 and 1930, hailed from Syria, Palestine, or Lebanon. As in the rest of Latin America both then and now, Colombia's population of Middle Eastern origin is predominantly Lebanese and mostly Christian, largely from the Maronite, Orthodox, or Catholic Churches.[28] However, while the Middle Eastern immigrant populations in many areas of Latin American and the Caribbean have achieved considerable prominence, relatively few academic studies of these communities exist. Ignacio Klich and Jeffrey Lesser attribute this dearth partially to the fact that, despite the vitality among Latin Americanists of ongoing scholarly debates regarding notions of race, the field of Ethnic Studies remains relatively new. The perceived status of the Middle Eastern immigrant population as "permanent foreigners," a perception fed by the community's adherence to many premigratory customs, has also contributed to a deficit of scholarly attention. In this respect, scholars of Lebanese migration have noted that Lebanese nuclear family formations, as well as gender dynamics and culinary customs, remained intact long after migration. Other logistical factors, such as linguistic barriers, lack of support from Middle Eastern governments, small concentrations of immigrant populations, and difficulty accessing materials have also led to a reduced focus on Middle Eastern migrants in Latin America. Significantly, the Middle Eastern population's inclusion within the "white" category, though marginal, has driven some scholars of race in the Americas to categorize them as part of the Latin American elite and thus not a rich object of study. As Nadine Naber has argued, the seemingly ambiguous nature of Arab-American ethnoracial identity ("American" may be understood here in the broadest sense) has contributed markedly to Arab Americans' historical invisibility. Indeed, the consequences of being labeled "white" rather than "nonwhite" are far reaching and affect both individual and community access to resources, political power, and general societal visibility. Arab-Americans' official status as "white" has also weakened the group's claims for protection from discrimination, as it has simultaneously erased a longstanding history of discriminatory practices against the community.[29]

The longstanding nomenclature used to refer to Latin American citizens and migrants of Middle Eastern origin, or *"turcos"* (Turks), implies a range of signifiers ranging from the overtly prejudicial to the benign and ultimately reflects the community's frequently liminal status within local and national networks. Even as Arab and other Middle Eastern migrants were cast as economic desirables because of their relatively rapid ascent to the business class, they also aroused suspicion among local elites, who saw them as neither black nor white. This impression was likely enhanced by the popular perception of Islam as "intrinsically nonwhite," despite the early migrants' Christian background, and thereby exemplified the ongoing tendency to racialize Middle Eastern migrants and their descendants on the basis of religion rather than biology or phenotype.[30] As a result, the Middle Eastern communities of Latin America were frequently targets of twentieth-century public discourse regarding migration policy.[31] Lebanese migrants, who constitute the largest group of Middle Eastern immigrants to Latin America, were spurred to emigrate by several factors in their country of origin, among them improved education and exposure to the outside world. Religious and political unrest, a desire to avoid military conscription, and the Lebanese civil war of the 1860s also contributed to increased migration rates. Attracted by the general economic and social advances that perhaps awaited them in the Americas and by the possibility for social mobility and economic prosperity in the Colombian Caribbean in particular, a significant number of Lebanese migrants began to arrive in Latin America during the second phase of Lebanese migration. This period roughly spanned the period from the second half of the nineteenth century to the beginning of the twentieth.[32] Nevertheless, the mixed reception received by these migrants has not deterred some scholars from describing the path of Lebanese assimilation in Latin America in terms reminiscent of the myth of racial democracy.[33]

Then as now, the Lebanese migrants arriving on the Colombia's Caribbean coast have fulfilled a central role in the region's development, particularly in the city of Barranquilla. As the nation's chief port, Barranquilla, prior to the arrival of the Lebanese, had already become home to numerous immigrant communities, including Italians, Americans, French, Germans, Jews, and Cubans. The city's highly diversified immigrant population, in addition to the tri-ethnic (indigenous, African, and European) roots of its natives, provided the Lebanese newcomers with relatively greater room to maneuver than was available in Colombia's other major urban centers. In time, the Arab and Jewish populations of *La Costa* came to constitute the largest immigrant communities and subsequently wielded the most lasting impact on the region's development. While often exclusively represented as itinerant peddlers who swiftly advanced to opening small family businesses and, ultimately, larger commercial houses, the Lebanese migrants of the Colombian Caribbean also participated to a lesser extent in agriculture and industry. Their influence was felt not only in the realm of commerce but also in the cattle trade and political spheres. Nevertheless, the success of some in the Lebanese community provoked varying degrees of hostility among *costeño* natives and likely contributed to the introduction of migration quotas in 1937 that restricted the entry of various nationalities, among them the Lebanese.[34]

Despite the subsequent decrease in the steady flow of Lebanese immigrant to Colombia's northern shores, the political, artistic, economic, and culinary influence of Barranquilla's Lebanese immigrant community continues, several generations later. Notably, for many Colombians in *el exterior* (the exterior) as well those who remain in the country, the descendants of Lebanese migrants such as Shakira have come to embody alternative modes of understanding Lebanese identity in the (trans)national arena. Shakira's characterization as a hyphenated Latin(a) American has extended to her U.S. media coverage, as well, as magazine article titles like "The Two Sides of Shakira" attest.[35] Increased media awareness of Latin American's hybrid subjectivities beyond the traditional "Spanish + African + Indigenous" formula, however, has proved a double-edged sword, particularly in the post-9/11, Latino-phobic U.S. context. A boldfaced cover story caption from *Blender* magazine offers a telling, if sarcastic, example of implicit mainstream fears in this regard: "She [Shakira] can curse in Arabic, owns the best hips in music, and dates a president's son. Now she wants to make America sing in Spanish. The rest of the world already belongs to Shakira. Are you sure you want to stand in her way?"[36] The faulty logic upon which the author's commentary hinges is apparent, as Shakira is cast as the sum of three parts: her ability to swear in the language of a "terrorist" culture, her male romantic partner, and her corporality. Moreover, according to the feature article, "America" (in the narrowest sense of the word) and, by extension, "Americans" (read: European-Americans) do not speak Spanish, and, as a Latina of Lebanese descent and a recent immigrant, Shakira, like most "third-world" migrants, seeks to (culturally, linguistically, geographically, racially) "conquer" the United States. Finally, this brief caption implicitly suggests that the Latino and Middle Eastern "invasions" constitute a significant, if inevitable, threat to the mainstream "American" way of life.

Although rarely so explicit, echoes of an analogous tension between fixation and disavowal surface in additional contexts. In an uncanny, if unintentional, reference to the biblical iconography of her album cover for *Oral Fixation, Volume II*, audience reaction to the "forbidden fruit" of Middle Eastern dance and music was markedly more enthusiastic than the reception accorded her other songs at a fall 2006 Boston concert by Shakira. As in most live venues, Shakira waited until the encore to perform her most popular songs, "*Ojos así*" (Eyes like yours) and "Hips Don't Lie," perhaps the compositions most musically, linguistically, and choreographically influenced by Middle Eastern performative styles. From my seat on the main floor of the T. D. Banknorth Arena, the irony of watching a Lebanese-Colombian perform these numbers in front of a sold-out audience of rapt, cell-phone-light-waving U.S. fans (the traditional concert lighters a casualty of post–9/11 increased security restrictions) did not escape me.[37] Clearly, within the context of the international "war on terror" and the ongoing political struggles over Latin American migration in the U.S. context, Shakira's appeal seemed ever more paradoxical. However, as the November 2006 dedication of a six-ton, fifteen-foot iron statue of Shakira in her hometown of Barranquilla, the success of her Colombia-based charity Fundación Pies Descalzos,[38] and her 33 million-plus international record sales indicate, the fascination with Shakira as artist and star text has assumed global proportions.

Figure 6.1. Exhorting potential consumers to "Speak English [and] "Live Latin," the print advertisement for the cable channel Sítv offers striking photographic evidence of the connections between Latino sexuality, racial mixture, and language in the U.S. popular imagination. While problematic because of its visual adherence to the U.S. black/white racial binary and the association of Latino identity with an innate hypersexuality, the text of the advertisement is nonetheless noteworthy for the way in which its supports a revised paradigm of Latino identity that ultimately breaks with a traditional, hermetic association of the Spanish language with Latino culture.

In the brief period since the success of her 2001 "crossover" album *Laundry Service*,[39] Shakira has indeed materialized as a "global" media personality and performer. As Licia Fiol-Matta indicates, the status of the globalized media figure is best understood not as the result of a spontaneous category but rather as the product of a deftly constructed marketing strategy designed to enhance multimedia communication.[40] The lexicon of globalization is often foregrounded in Shakira's media representations, as she is alternately described as "the embodiment of globalization, the digital-age demolition of national boundaries," "a sweetly upbeat face of globalization," "a truly global artist," and "the Colombian conquistadora of global pop."[41] Straightforwardly, if superficially, interpreted as benign commentaries on the international appeal of Shakira's performances and persona, such depictions also evince the myriad strategies through which her "multi-ethnic background is employed by the record company's image-makers as a transnationalizing and globalizing agent... [i]f identity politics was never an issue, why then does so much care go into Shakira's manufactured imagery?"[42] While to a degree productively mindful of the constructed nature of identity in the (trans)national music industry and media, this perspective nonetheless fails to "avoid the twin pitfalls of euphoria and melancholy"[43] associated with Manichean approaches to globalization as it simultaneously performs a wholesale erasure of Shakira's individual agency. Just as she is framed in terms of a globalized narrative, Shakira, much like Andrea Echeverri of Aterciopelados, is simultaneously localized through the pervasive trope of *macondismo*. Obliquely realized through constant references to the author Gabriel García Márquez[44] (a fellow native of the Colombian Caribbean), the formulaic allusions to *macondismo* in Shakira's media coverage fulfill various separate, if somewhat contradictory, functions. In the broadest sense, the repeated connections between García Márquez and Shakira, while not necessarily pejorative, demonstrate the limited scope of most journalists' knowledge of Colombian culture. (Are there no other Colombians to whom she might be compared?) Furthermore, the links to García Márquez, a universally revered figure of world literature, elevate Shakira from pop star status to the realm of "high" literary culture and in this respect gesture toward the globalized cosmopolitanism hinted at in much of Shakira's media coverage. Finally, the nods to *macondismo* provide a measure of subtextual psychological solace regarding the "natural order" of center/periphery relations. Restoring dominant consumers' faith in historical depictions of the primitive Latin(a) American steeped in the culture of disorder, excess, and superstition, these allusions counterbalance any implied claims to elite cosmopolitanism and high culture associated with Shakira.

In the context of such totalizing representations, it is imperative that we pursue more nuanced readings of popular music and media reflective of the quiet counternarratives embedded in U.S. mainstream media. One such moment, a brief postconcert interview on NBC's *Today Show*, materialized during Shakira's response to host Katie Couric's question regarding the reasons for her "overnight" success among U.S. audiences. Smiling yet firm, Shakira informed Couric that her acclaim was not, in fact, something that had materialized overnight but rather represented the fruits of many years' labor in Latin America.[45] While at first glance little more than a polite reply, Shakira's response ultimately constitutes a public rescripting of her career trajectory in the face of mainstream insistence on the ethnocentric "crossover" narratives of the Latin(o) music boom. Shakira's insistence on emphasizing her professional roots in Latin America also represents a recognition of the Latin American and U.S. Latino audiences that have long constituted her primary listeners. Given the difficulties of constructing a coherent narrative or character profile from song lyrics or music video imagery alone, the metatextual hybrid star text offered in televised interviews such as this one thus provides a crucial "point of identification" for the popular music fans that play a critical role in music industry economics and representational strategies.[46]

Sights, Sounds, and Tastes

> "Look, Sammy, I'm an American, not a Colombian, and Americans don't eat tongue."
> "That just shows what a hick you are. In French cuisine tongue is considered a great delicacy."
> "Oh, yeah? But we're in America not in France."
> "We're in Jackson Heights, Colombia," I said.
> —Jaime Manrique, *Latin Moon in Manhattan*

In the preceding passage from the 1992 novel *Latin Moon in Manhattan*, the U.S.-Colombian protagonist, Santiago/"Sammy," attempts to convince his American-born nephew Gene of the culinary pleasures of tongue. Yet Gene insists on rejecting his hybrid identity ("I'm an American, not a Colombian"), as he asserts a sense of self anchored in purely geographic, as opposed to historical, political, gender, class, or ethnoracial, terms. In response to this unidimensional perspective, Sammy jokingly reminds his young nephew of their present location: "Jackson Heights, Colombia" (actually Jackson Heights, Queens), site of the largest concentration of Colombian migrants in the United States. A witty appeal to their shared hybrid subject position, Sammy's emphasis on the joys of tongue, known in Spanish as *lengua* (also the word for "language"), also reminds the reader of the love for language that he exhibits in his job as professional interpreter. In a broader sense, Sammy's argument for the delights of the tongue not only constitutes an oblique reference to the skillful "slips of the tongue" that so many bilingual, bicultural U.S. Latinos perform on a daily basis but also may be read as an implicit appeal to the manifold pleasures of orality in general. Thus, both the previous epigraph and Shakira's *Fijación oral/Oral Fixation* series elucidate the ways in which, for both of these artists, language (*lengua*), and specifically linguistic (fore)play, constitutes a central referent in their portrayal of or engagement with the multiple Americas.[47] As witnessed in her 2001 English-language record debut entitled *Laundry Service,* as well as in her frequent usage of Spanish, Arabic, French, Portuguese, German, and Italian in her music and media coverage, Shakira is, to borrow a phrase from Alina Troyano (a.k.a. Carmelita Tropicana), "very very good with the tongue." As Troyano's phrase implies, Latino cultural production, or perhaps what might be more precisely described as a Latino aesthetics, is imbued with a transcultural sensibility. In the case of Shakira, this "transcultural recipe" centers on the facts of her personal history and her star text. The final portion of my analysis focuses not only on Shakira's persona but also on the recent publicity campaign for her recent two-volume set, *Fijación oral, Volumen I* (released June 2005) and the subsequent *Oral Fixation, Volume II* (released November 2005). Here I engage in a reading of the music video for the first hit single from *Fijación oral Volumen I*, "La tortura" (The torture), a song that Shakira wrote and performed in conjunction with the Spanish pop star Alejandro Sanz. I then augment this analysis with a consideration of the music video for "Hips Don't Lie," a single written and performed with the U.S.-Haitian rapper Wycleff Jean for inclusion in an expanded special edition of the *Oral Fixation, Volume II* released in March 2006. Again, the thematic and aesthetic foundations of Shakira's recent work tend to span three overarching categories, all of which foreground the mouth as the epistemological hinge upon which the human experience swings—sexuality, food, and language. Clearly, a Freudian influence is afoot in the album iconography, in its explicit reference to the four psychosexual stages of child development (the oral, anal, phallic, and genital stages), though the emphasis here is on the initial, or oral, phase of development. As Shakira herself remarked in a promotional interview, the decision to employ this particular image was the product of a moment of free association.[48] In various engagements during the promotion of the two album series, Shakira was forthcoming about her own two-year history of psychoanalysis because of her fear of death, insisting that she herself remained "stuck in the oral stage,"[49] or what she has alternatively described as the most "primitive" stage of individual human existence. While recognizing the provocative potential of the albums' titles and iconography, she nonetheless insisted on a more expansive interpretation of orality in the context of the recordings, citing the gratification associated with food and platonic physical contact: "the word 'oral' is very vast, and that's what I like about it. Through our mouths we discover and explore the world. Our mouth is the first source of pleasure, right?"[50]

As a visual and textual point of reference in the production of popular music meaning and a guiding factor in its visualization,[51] the album cover for *Fijación oral, Volumen I* (figure 6.2), which presents Shakira in a flowing, white gown and cradling a cherubic white infant in her arms, provokes numerous interpretations. The most immediate of these are perhaps that of the virginal bride and the nurturing (heterosexual) mother so entrenched in traditional Latin(o) American Catholic mores.[52] This imagery stands in sharp contrast to the multiple signifiers (psychological and sexual) embedded in the phrase *Fijación oral* located immediately above, thereby underlining the thematic tensions between photographic image and text and female sexual agency as the simultaneous source of pleasure and sin/shame. As Freudian psychology teaches us, conflicts between the sexual self and society arise at every stage of human psychosexual development. Although in this case the visual medium could almost be mistaken for a Renaissance-era painting instead of a photograph, the album cover iconography of *Oral Fixation, Volume II* (figure 6.3) echoes similar gendered religious references in its overt allusions to Eve and woman's role as the purveyor of "original sin." Read in conjunction with the straightforward photographic imagery of her album covers, Shakira's stated desire to "attribute to Eve one more reason to bite the forbidden fruit and that would be her oral fixation"[53] may be interpreted as an attempt to complicate and/or contest the biblical justification for women's moral inferiority. Adopting Eve as a universal female archetype, Shakira embraces a "competing discourse"[54] rooted in a more traditional gender analysis, however: "Only for having stolen a simple apple, we received the punishment. Women are full of buttons, little buttons, millions of buttons. And men have just the *on* and *off* switch. Men only need food and *you-know-what*. We need so much more. We're like—what do you call them? Barrels without bottoms. There's no way to satisfy a woman, ever."[55]

Figures 6.2-6.3. Album covers for *Fijación oral, Volumen 1*. EPIC, 2005 (above), and *Oral Fixation, Volume 2*. EPIC, 2005 (opposite).

Showcasing an explicit rejection of strict English/Spanish binaries, Shakira's two-part album series and its accompanying advertising blitz at times break with several traditional mainstream marketing and linguistic conventions. Here, Shakira assumes the role of a *global* popular phenomena whose linguistic choices privilege a conceptualization of "American" identity rooted in a hemispheric/plural, as opposed to national/singular, understanding of the label. Notably, "*La tortura*," a pop/reggaetón/flamenco hybrid, was the first Spanish-language single ever aired on MTV's U.S. flagship station without subtitles or an identical, English-language version available to viewers. As polysemic, ancillary texts that "[draw] our attention simultaneously to the

152 | MUSICAL IMAGINATION

song and away from it, positing [themselves] in the place of what [the song] represents,"[56] the music videos for "*La tortura*" and "Hips Don't Lie" demonstrate the centrality of the visual in the marketing of popular music and artistic identity. Furthermore, these popular artifacts underscore the impossibility of divorcing music video imagery from other modes of visual promotion.[57] I cite these music videos as visual and aural embodiments of the multiple signifiers that Shakira addresses, both explicitly and implicitly, in her transcultural aesthetic project. My intention is not to offer a frame-by-frame analysis of the musical and visual elements of these videos; rather, I propose a feminist, transnational reading that departs from monolithic readings of gender, race, language, sexuality, and nation in the music video medium.

The Colombian Transcultural Aesthetic Recipe | 153

Reading the Transcultural Aesthetic Recipe

The music video genre offers prime evidence of the ways in which the guiding principles of popular music (namely music, lyrics, and iconography) rarely provide viewers with a coherent address. Bolstered by the disjuncture of visuals and lyrics, an indefinite temporality, and the avoidance of linear narratives, the "confusion" of music video coalesces in the first video from *Fijación oral, Volumen I*, "*La tortura*." Ground-breaking in terms of its resounding success at attracting an enormous following among MTV's mainstream, largely monolingual U.S. audience, "*La tortura*" successfully disproved the notion that, in the age of global cable channels and the Internet, lyrics (and specifically English-language lyrics) are integral to the success of a music video.[58] Read as what Kobena Mercer, after Karl Marx, has termed a "social hieroglyph," or a "commodity form which demands, yet defies, decoding,"[59] the image of Shakira that appears in "*La tortura*" deftly represents enough of a departure from her previous videos to solidify her chameleonic ability to rapidly change with the postmodern times. By the same token, in many respects the video reinscribes familiar tropes of gender and sexuality, particularly in its portrayal of the romantic triangle involving its protagonists (Shakira and Alejandro Sanz) and Sanz's anonymous live-in female partner.

Like most music videos, "*La tortura*" considers, though it does not necessarily completely engage, various themes: adultery, voyeurism, the links between food and sensuality, betrayal, and gendered power differentials. In this regard, the video generates more questions than answers. Set in a nameless Latin(o) American urban center, the loosely ordered narrative arc of "*La tortura*" centers on the relationship between Shakira, who plays the part of the sensual object of Sanz's scopophilic gaze, and Sanz, the married man who lives in the apartment building across the street.[60] While throughout much of the video Shakira appears oblivious to Sanz's constant spying (just as his sleeping partner remains aware of his infidelity), the pair engage in an adulterous affair punctuated by various encounters over meals together.

Scopophilia, or a brand of voyeurism bordering on the pathological, has long functioned as a determining organizational element for expressing sexual desire in music video. Significantly, in both "*La tortura*" and "Hips Don't Lie," Shakira serves as the object of the intense scrutiny of her heterosexual male counterpart. This fixed gaze is in turn multiplied vis-à-vis the viewing practices of her global audience, thus renewing the scopophilic act. The scopophilic gaze forms the uniting thread of both videos, a motif that is further punctuated in "*La tortura*" by the union of Sanz's line of sight with the camera's perspective. Rapidly shifting among scenes of Sanz observing Shakira, brief interludes involving the pair, and Shakira's solo dance sequences, "*La tortura*" has as its primary visual metaphor Shakira's blackened body. Clad in a short, midriff-baring tank top and a torn miniskirt, Shakira performs in Middle Eastern-inflected dance sequences that offer an intimate account of her corporal presence, as they simultaneously reference the primitive (the dancing native in a loincloth), the political (the oil fields of Iraq, now occupied by the United States), and the questionable ("racial cross-dressing").[61] In this regard, the rich textures of Shakira's solo dance sequences provoke the type of visceral response in viewers that essentially fills in the gaps left behind by the video's fragmented narrative. However, much like "*La tortura*"'s musical hooks, the video's primary visual motifs extend beyond these brief scenes.[62]

As Shakira has explained with respect to "*La tortura*," "I think there's something fascinating about stimulating the senses."[63] "*La tortura*"'s sensuous stimuli, interpreted as both an instrument of commodity promotion and an exercise in the expression of liberated female sexuality, also include numerous scenes of a mute Shakira, writhing on the floor or sliding along the expanse of a long wooden table as an amused Sanz watches on, eating from a carton of Chinese take-out as Shakira "serves herself up" for consumption. During these momentary sequences, Sanz literally and figuratively looks down on her as Shakira performs to the heavy backbeat of the song, her expression vacant, tank top hiked up about her abdomen, her navel the focal point of the camera's, and Sanz's, attention. From his habitual post at his apartment window across the street, a smugly satisfied Sanz observes as Shakira stands in her kitchen, ostensibly weeping for him. Read in isolation, these scenes recall standard feminist critiques of music video, in which the genre is charged with "[r]eproducing coded images of the female body, conventionally positioning girls and women as objects of male voyeurism, [as] effective strategies for associating male adolescent desire and male dominance."[64] Nonetheless, a more holistic interpretation of "*La tortura*" unveils a partial inversion of these codes in the presence of several "competing discourses of agency."[65] Adel Iskandar has described the imagery of Shakira's videos as a form of "demean[ing] herself for the viewer's pleasure" and, in a more general sense, as the product of "both a traditionalist and a revived Orientalism."[66] However, such a reading is plausible only given the absence of a careful consideration of Shakira's cross-media star text across time and space, as well as an understanding of the ways which the inversion of historical stereotypes is often paradoxically achieved though their very invocation. This univocal approach to Shakira's artistic production and media presence also fails to take into account feminist, transnational, or fan-based perspectives, much less tropicalization theory, itself a more contemporary reading of Orientalism specific to the Latin(o) American context.[67]

While Iskandar questions the validity of readings that attribute a contestatory function to Shakira's sensual choreography and storylines,[68] in sum refuting the possibility of "sex as a weapon," the work of Kaja Silverman offers a distinctly different perspective. In her examination of the relationship between masochism and exhibitionism, Silverman notes how "Voyeurism has been heavily coded with Western culture as a male activity, and associated with aggression and sadism. . . . However, [l]ike the child in the primal scene, the shadowy onlooker is more *mastered* than *mastering*."[69] Silverman's framework provides a compelling point of departure from which to decode the video's fleeting visual cues, as it ultimately facilitates a reading *a contrapelo* (against the grain). Aided by the fragmented narrative structure of the video (a tactic that encourages multiple viewings, thereby enhancing its commercial and promotional value), moments like the scene of Shakira standing alone in her kitchen, crying, suddenly acquire fresh meaning. On second (or third, or fourth) glance, a seemingly bereft Shakira is revealed not to be crying over Sanz but rather as teary-eyed for a more mundane reason: we discover that she is merely crying because she is chopping onions. In similar fashion, during the scene in which a Chinese takeout-eating Sanz can't quite convince Shakira to share his meal, Sanz may now be alternatively read as a scopophile who consumes his food/Shakira just as he is figuratively *consumed by her*. These moments point to a more radical analysis of the links between music, gender, sexuality, and power, departing from the realization that

> The ways in which fear of female sexuality and anxiety over the body are inscribed in the Western music tradition are obviously very relevant for the would-be (wannabe?) female musician. First, women are located within a discourse in a position of both desire and dread—as that which must reveal that it is controlled by the male or which must be purged as intolerable.[70]

Indeed, the video's final sequence depicts Shakira's overt lyrical and visual rejection of Sanz's voyeuristic attempts at control. At the end of a disjointed narrative in which she has repeatedly submitted herself up for Sanz's sexual and psychological pleasure, Shakira suddenly redirects her gaze directly into the camera, openly acknowledging Sanz's scopophilic presence for the first time. Smiling knowingly, she pointedly lip-synchs the final lyrics of "*La tortura*": "*Yo ya no voy a llorar por ti*" (I am no longer going to cry for you).[71] Defeated at the game of domination that he assumed he was winning and surprised by his (now former) lover's awareness of his voyeurism, a startled Sanz sheepishly smiles, instantaneously cognizant of Shakira's rejection. The validity of such readings, while not always feasible within the highly codified gender and racial dynamics of music video, are often occluded by the tendency to monolithically interpret music video and popular culture on the whole as misogynist terrain devoid of agency by females of color. Nonetheless, this revisionist perspective is likewise fraught with a degree of tension, for, as we embrace the belief in the expression of female sexuality as a potential site of feminist revolution, we must be equally mindful of the fact that the inverse, or *rejecting sex*, does not necessarily signify the existence of a level playing field between the genders. Clearly, Shakira does exert a measure of power within the context of the video. However, this power does not entirely free her from the subjugating gaze of the heterosexual pornographic imaginary, once more reminding us of the need to pursue a more nuanced reading of agency among females of color in the music video context.

"*En Barranquilla se baila así*" (In Barranquilla We Dance Like This)

While a popular music milestone in and of itself, the widespread commercial success of "*La tortura*" was overshadowed by the release of "Hips Don't Lie" in the spring of 2006. With "Hips Don't Lie," Shakira earned the distinction of becoming the first artist to reach the number one spot on *Billboard*'s Top 40 and Latin pop singles charts. During the same period, she appeared as a frequent guest on widely viewed mainstream broadcasts such as MTV's *TRL (Total Request Live)* and *American Idol*,[72] further evidence of the diverse character of Shakira's fan base. A "pseudodocumentary" designed to advance audience's idealistic fantasies about the music industry,[73] the video for "Hips Don't Lie" was released as a bonus track on a revamped version of *Oral Fixation, Volume II*, in an attempt to remedy the album's slower-than-anticipated initial sales. Performed and written in conjunction with the noted U.S.-Haitian hip-hop artist Wycleff Jean, "Hips Don't Lie" was essentially a remake of Jean's 2004 single "Dance Like This," featuring Claudette Ortiz and included on the *Dirty Dancing: Havana Nights* soundtrack. Beginning with a hook-laden horn section sampled from the 1992 hit "*Amores como el nuestro*"

(Loves like ours), by the Puerto Rican *salsero* Jerry Rivera, and buttressed by a chorus that borrows from the 1985 carnival anthem "*Baila en la calle*" (Dance in the street), by the Dominican Luis "Terror" Díaz , "Hips Don't Lie" exemplifies the postmodern reliance on the liberal use of sampling, just as it reflects the longstanding cross-fertilization of African American and Latin(o) American musical styles.[74] As both a popular historical text and a lesson in the divergent impacts of globalization, the music video for "Hips Don't Lie" furthermore demonstrates the deft employment of Colombian, Caribbean, and African American "home genres" (primarily *cumbia* and rap) as a basis of introduction for the seemingly "new" (Latin[o] American rock/pop; the Middle Eastern presence in Latin America). Tied to the necessity to encourage repeat viewing, the focus on these ostensibly new signifiers,[75] as well as the video's liberal exploitation of well-worn stereotypes, renders "Hips Don't Lie" a fertile object of inquiry for the new American Studies.

The video opens to the crisp metallic cadences of multiple trumpets, accompanied by a slow-motion street shot of carnival revelers. Punctuated by Wycleff Jean's calls for "No Fighting," Shakira first appears against a dark backdrop with her back to the camera, seemingly bare to the waist except for an elaborate crystal design, shifting her hips in a series of Middle Eastern–inspired dance gestures. Faintly reminiscent of a map of the circum-Caribbean, the crystal markings on Shakira's body quite literally recall the historic trope of woman as nation. Mute throughout the video's initial sequences, Shakira is nonetheless metatextually inserted into the song before the singing even commences, as Jean calls out her name. In response, Shakira continues her hybrid dance performance, alternating between belly-dancing in front of the black backdrop and a brief series of robotic poses conducted against a shadowy yellow and blue-striped wall. Read in conjunction with her red clothing, the color palette of the latter scene alludes to the red, yellow, and blue hues of the Colombian flag, just as it constitutes a synesthetic reference to the music's up-tempo beat and marked bass line. In virtually all of the opening scenes of "Hips Don't Lie," Shakira begins with her back to the viewer, alternatively pressed up against a dark backdrop or a brightly painted wall in a liminal pose. In contrast, Wycleff Jean and the anonymous musicians who accompany him face forward from the onset, occupying the camera's lens with an energy and authority indicative of Jean's status as the artist who sets the initial lyrical tone of the performance.

As the song progresses, however, the gendered spatial organization is subverted. The music video's carnivalesque iconography, with Shakira at its center, assumes a more substantial role in the narrative action. Barefoot, with relatively little makeup and unkempt brunette locks, Shakira appears in her "natural" state, as she performs various cultural stereotypes associated with Latin America, the circum-Caribbean, and specifically the Colombian Caribbean. Facilitated by the digital reproduction techniques that have rendered the manipulation of sound and image across time and space possible, the settings for "Hips Don't Lie" shifts among a dusty, dirt-floored street space with spectators boxed on two sides, a maze of lilac gauze curtains, and a humble "third-world" bar. The video also exhibits a steady thematic and geographic progression from the general to the specific, or from the Caribbean to the Colombian to the *barranquillera/o*. Analyzed against the backdrop of its celebratory references to Barranquilla's famed carnival and the amicable chemistry between its star performers, however, the complicated questions of race, ethnicity, gender, nation, and language at the core of "Hips Don't Lie" are easily elided. Central to this reading is the video's heavy reliance on dance performance, reflective of dance's ability to instruct us as to "how the music is to be experienced in the body."[76] Imbued with the "authenticity" provided by its street setting, Shakira's subject position as a Barranquilla native, and the presence of a largely black supporting cast, the multiple dance sequences in "Hips Don't Lie" mirror the rhythmic and melodic progressions of the song itself. They guide the viewer through the arduous process of deciphering the video's aural and visual signifiers.[77]

The kinesthetic mappings included within the video's continuous dance numbers illustrate the myriad possibilities for decoding movement-based texts, ranging from the notion that in contemporary "ethnic" cinema "[s]waying the hips—or 'going native'—becomes a collectively desired fantasy of the upper-middle class" to the belief in Latina and/or queer dance performance as a decolonizing strategy.[78] Shakira's dance performances exemplify both scenarios: at times her movements appear little more than a choreographed response to Wycleff Jean's exhortation that she "Let me [Jean] see you move like you come from Colombia," in a echo of the "DNA-level multiculturalism"[79] cited earlier. Conversely, Shakira's gestures arguably assume a less reactive tone as she commands her listeners in Spanish to "*Mira, en Barranquilla se baila así/¡Sí!*" (Look, in Barranquilla we dance like this/Yes!), a phrase subsequently mimicked by Wycleff Jean.[80] Lacking any translation beyond that implied by the dancers' physical gestures, Shakira's inclusion of the Spanish phrase and her specific invocation of Barranquilla subverts, however superficially, the relationship between linguistic/geocultural center and periphery familiar to most monolingual Anglo-Saxon viewers.

For the duration of "Hips Don't Lie," Shakira employs not only dance but also space, race, and language as effective means of staking a claim to Latin(a) American authenticity. In this regard, the video's street setting, ostensibly reminiscent of the public revelry of the *carnaval barranquillero*, facilitates our engagement in the celebratory fantasy.[81] As Rafael Pérez-Torres comments regarding the ways in which Shakira transforms Latin American iconography into "an object of pleasurable consumption," "Hips Don't Lie" "suggests a perfectly postmodern portrait of Colombian culture as a source of endless delight, divorced from the violence and political crisis" of everyday Colombian existence.[82] However, while Pérez-Torres correctly identifies the influence of commodity exchange in the decontextualized nature of the video's visual and aural thematics, to some degree the iconographic "conflation" that he critiques is better understood as a virtually inherent product of Barranquilla's profoundly hybrid cultural patrimony. The presence of numerous *marimondas* (traditional masked figures from Barranquilla's carnival) throughout the video, most of whom may be phenotypically read as Afro-Colombian, provide another case in point. Like most supporting cast members in music video, the location of the *marimondas* is rather nebulous, with the exception of one iconic figure, a young, Afro-Colombian girl dressed in a vivid, full-skirted red dress and disguised in a white skull mask. With unruly long black curls that mimic the natural state of Shakira's own hair, the adolescent *marimonda* retraces Shakira's gestures in other ways as well, copying her dance moves in the occasional frame. The carnivalesque juxtaposition of the "two Shakiras" (one black, one phenotypically light/white), underscores a portrayal of Colombian racial identity at once liberatory and troubling; while the parallels drawn between the young *marimonda* and Shakira suggest a fruitful engagement with and an internalization of Afro-Colombian culture that extends beyond the merely epidermal, it also highlights a relational dynamic in which white/light subjects always occupy the (literal, symbolic) center, just as Afro-Caribbean individuals/objects are relegated to the (literal, symbolic) margins. The deployment of linguistic signifiers in "Hips Don't Lie" reflects a similar politics of authenticity. Significantly, however, it is Wycleff Jean, and not Shakira, who adheres to a more traditional, hermetic depiction of the relationship between language and hybrid subjectivity. In one of the song's most persistent lyrical hooks, Jean declares that "I never really knew that she could dance like this/ She makes a man want to speak Spanish/*Cómo se llama* (*sí*)/*Bonita* (*sí*)/*Mi casa* (*sí*, Shakira, Shakira)/ *Su casa*" (I never really knew that she could dance like this/She makes a man want to speak Spanish/What's her name? (Yes)/Beautiful woman (Yes)/My house (Yes, Shakira, Shakira)/Her house).[83] While reinforcing the essentialist belief that Latin(o) American identity is inextricably linked to the Spanish language, Jean's emphatic statement also ironically belies the fact that perhaps 95 percent of the song is actually uttered in English—a choice more reflective of global marketing concerns than of the aesthetic directives of the musical composition. When read in isolation from an analysis of his live performances, his cosmetic use of stock Spanish phrases also suggests an incorporation of Latin(o) American signifiers more indicative of promotional dictates than of an attempted expression of cross-cultural solidarity. Though limited to an invocation of the quasi-homophonic phrase "Don't you see baby/ *así es perfecto*" (Don't you see baby/It's perfect like that),[84] Shakira's own conceptualization of language hints at an understanding of quotidian Latino linguistic practices that is absent from her previous work, which relied on more rigid binaries of language and identity.

Along similar lines, the overarching thematic premise of the "Hips Don't Lie" video, or the carnivalesque union of races, cultures, genders, and classes in the pursuit of shared public revelry, triggers multiple, if at times antithetical, interpretations. Metaphorically and figuratively mapped onto the light/"white" body of Shakira and the darker body of Wyclef Jean, the multicultural and multiracial Caribbean diasporas that the central protagonists represent are united by their love of music and dance, exchanges that foreground the relational, syncretic nature of pan-Caribbean culture. However, these common cultural preferences are superseded by the collective burden of the oppression faced by both groups with respect to U.S. migration policy, unequal power relations between the "third world" and the "first," and the circulation of negative stereotypes. These parallels offer the promise of cross-cultural, ethnoracial, and class solidarities, as Jean explicitly states in his extended rap performance near the close of "Hips Don't Lie": "She's so sexy/Every man's fantasy/A refugee like me/back with the Fugees from a Third World country/ . . . Why do the CIA wanna watch us?/Colombians and Haitians/I ain't guilty, it's a musical transaction/No more so we snatch ropes/ Refugees run the seas 'cause we own our own boats." Through his purposeful use of the signifier "refugee," here Wyclef Jean engages in an act of reclamation, as he simultaneously expands the term's literal definition to encompass all those who arrive in the United States as migrants of second-class status. Implicitly juxtaposing the prejudicial treatment of poor black Haitians against the preferential treatment accorded Cuban refugees, who are popularly imagined as exclusively white, Jean reminds audiences that all *balseros*, regardless of their political, economic, or racial status in the eyes of the U.S.

government, are "boat people," as well. While flawed in its idealistic glossing over of the multiple internal sites of difference that distinguish U.S. immigrant communities, Jean's message nonetheless proves an integral part of his ongoing artistic attempts to politically empower migrants by reminding them of the fact that they "own [their] own boats."[85] In this light, the "musical transaction" invoked in the clever coda at the rap's close levels a subtextual wink at the seemingly irreconcilable demands of music industry promotion and artistic and political expression.

Toward A Transnational Feminist Reading of Latin(a) American Music Video

Since MTV's inaugural broadcast, in 1982, the music video format has irrevocably altered the ways in which audiences experience, interpret, and consume popular music in the United States. Employing previous writings on the representation of women in music video and popular music as a point of departure, I advocate for a cross-media consideration of an increased industry presence for women, people of color, and/or queer individuals in the genre. To a lesser degree, I also delineate the role that the advent of MTV as transnational empire and overarching trends toward media convergence play in our understanding of Latin(a) Americans in music video. Specifically, Shakira's recent hit videos for "*La tortura*" and "Hips Don't Lie" are offered as prime examples of transnational, pan-Caribbean, and female-centered performance in the present media context. While not entirely free of traditional modes of gender and sexual representation, Shakira's performances in these pieces provide both a literal and a figurative retracing of migration routes and transnational exchanges, as well as fresh sonic and visual evidence of an alternative means of marking musical and, ultimately, transcultural and transnational time.

What are the implications of this focus on Shakira and her *Oral Fixation*(s) at this particular moment in the political and pedagogical trajectory of Latin American, American, Ethnic, and Middle Eastern Studies? As the large-screen image of her belly-dancing torso framed by a row of waving Colombian flags suggests,[86] Shakira's artistic production and star text prompt us to reconsider traditional notions of Latin America as a place where people immigrate *from*, and/or as a space where the racial and cultural equation is a relatively simplistic matter of "Spaniard + African + Indian." This reformulation in turn contests and simultaneously expands the existing parameters of Latin American, U.S. Latino, Middle Eastern, and Arab American identity. As the work of Middle Eastern Studies scholars has shown, the Middle Eastern-origin communities of Latin America constitute "radical hybrids" that do not lay claim to solely one ethnicity, but that profess allegiance to "multiple ethnicities that operate in both parallel and intersecting planes."[87] Furthermore, as a native of Barranquilla, Shakira's transculturated aesthetic sensibility in particular disrupts traditional Ethnic and Area Studies notions of the "border"/"border crosser" in which a port city, and not an exclusively land-based geopolitical divide, provides the basis for the Arab/African/European/Indigenous contact zone in question. Shakira's star text and artistic production thus furnish a figurative road map for analyzing the points of convergence and divergence between what are traditionally presented in Academia as separate fields. This road map is of particular import to Middle Eastern Studies, Latin American, and U.S. Ethnic Studies, and the ways in which ethnoracial difference is theorized within and between these inter- and multi-disciplinary fields. Much like U.S. Latinos, Arab migrants in Latin America and the United States have been traditionally framed as perpetual foreigners. Moreover, Middle Eastern and Latino populations, given the challenge that they represent to existing black/white racial binaries,[88] have historically offered (and continue to offer) a vexing challenge to government bodies looking to encourage the "right" sort of migration and/or engage in neat racial taxonomies, as in the long-standing political debates over U.S. migration reform. As Steven Salaita's commentary on the location of Arab American Studies both before and after September 11, 2001 illustrates, the Arab American community's rapid shift from "invisible to glaringly conspicuous" has introduced a host of daunting challenges to an academic field that has only recently begun to systematically analyze the linkages between Arab American, Ethnic Studies, and Area Studies in particular.[89]

Afterword

U.S.-Colombian Popular Music and Identity:
Acknowledging the Transnational in the National

Nosotros de rumba　　　　We're partying
Y el mundo se derrumba　　And the world is crumbling
　　　—"Descarga" ("Explosion"), Bloque

At the end of virtually any sizable Latin(o) musical event in Miami, a modest cluster of Colombian street vendors appears, waiting outside to hawk *arepas* (corn cakes) and *chuzos* (meat skewers) to the gathering crowds. More so than usual, on this early September evening, they are expecting a crowd of fellow Colombians to spill out of the downtown Miami Arena at the close of the evening's concert by Carlos Vives. They (and we) are not disappointed. As the sound system fades out, chants of "¡Colombia! ¡Colombia!" bounce off the building's concrete walls and out into the humid Florida night, a testament to the somewhat paradoxical reaffirmation of national identity in the context of ever-shifting transnational communal affiliations. It was a satisfying ending: Vives closed his concert with a three-song encore featuring "*La tierra del olvido*" (The land of forgetting), a plaintive guitar and harmonica tune, considerably more down-tempo and sedated than the rest of the evening's performance. Ostensibly a patient ode to a far-away lover, "*La tierra del olvido*" narrates the pain and longing provoked by distance. Reread in reference to Colombia, however—the country that Vives professes in interviews to "never forget"—the song also adopts the optimistic perspective of an individual who perceives displacement and the cultural hybridity that results from it not as deficits but rather as part of the inevitable evolution and expression of one's multiple subjectivities. I am reminded: for many, to be *colombiana* or *colombiano* during this particular historical moment means to reach for music as one of the few hopeful, polyphonic representations of one's identity. Tongue in cheek though it may be, the popular Colombian bumper sticker quoted in the epigraph ("We're partying / And the world is crumbling") succinctly reflects the central role that Colombian popular music and the *parranda* (party) occupy in these ever-evolving constructs of the (trans)nation.

Like the chanting crowd streaming out all around me, I revel in the momentary brush with collective power that such a concert can provide. To this effect, Simon Frith writes that "It is when the validity of a social group is in dispute that music becomes politically important, as a way of authenticating it.... Under certain circumstances, then, music becomes a source of collective consciousness which promotes group cohesion social activities that in turn wield political consequences."[1] For the transnational Colombian community, the shared power that Frith identifies is frequently expressed in starkly material terms. As the examples of Shakira recast as transnational goodwill ambassador and the tragic 2001 murder of the *vallenato* scholar and icon Consuelo Araújonoguera by FARC guerrillas attest,[2] Colombian popular music is indeed vested with political meaning in the most concrete of fashions.

According to this logic, the ongoing shifts within Colombian popular music itself echo those of contemporary (U.S.-)Colombian society and its ongoing internal struggles with respect to the politics of ethnoracial identity, gender, and transnational migration. As Latin(o) Americans, Shakira, Carlos Vives, and Andrea Echeverri are consistently framed in terms of their perceived locations vis-à-vis these very categories. Their respective artistic and media trajectories reflect the divergent, though inextricably linked, processes underlying the development of an expanded understanding of Colombian identity both within the nation's geophysical borders and among its U.S.-based diaspora. Indeed, the ever-increasing visibility of these performers and others like them within the U.S. popular mainstream will continue to carve out alternative routes of representation for U.S.-Colombians. Conversely, their artistic production is perhaps just as likely to contribute to the perpetuation of traditional cultural norms regarding gender, sexuality, ethnoracial identity, and the (trans)nation.

In this context, I retain a certain curiosity, if not a bit of healthy skepticism, regarding the Colombian government's burgeoning interest in the instrumentalization of (U.S.-) Colombian identity, given the state's ongoing attempts at managing *costeño* popular musical forms and the often uneven mutual expansion of "first-" and "third-world" national borders into each other.[3] Such state-sponsored efforts aimed at promoting any singular, idealized identity, as is particularly evident in the case of Shakira, inevitably fail to consider the potential impacts of fan or consumer culture, much less the perspectives of

Figure A.1. A cover story from Colombia's premier newsweekly celebrates Vives's return (*regreso*) to Colombia for a brief concert tour, as its language foregrounds the transnational cycle (south to north, north to south) at the core of Colombian transnational identity. *Semana*, December 2, 2002.

166

those who experience transnationalism from below. As Néstor García Canclini affirms, "there will be no truly popular cultural policies [nor, I would add, academic studies] as long as the producers do not play a leading role."[4] In this respect, studies of popular culture and media that lack the appropriate historical, social, and political frameworks contribute to the all-too-prevalent vision of popular culture and its consumers/fans as entities disconnected from the rest of society[5] and, more important, erase its primary producers. Despite its status as a pervasive social force in the daily lives of many Latin(o) Americans and others, "commercial" Latin(o) popular music remains markedly understudied. This gap in the scholarly corpus in turn negatively impacts our collective understanding of *all* Latino popular music and cultural expression. It also promotes existing beliefs in pop and rock in particular as exclusively masculine, Anglo-American products and in folklore as a purely static expressive form. Music's thematic elasticity, or, more specifically, its facility for communicating explicit ideologies in a manner that is still open to interpretation and often read as universal, renders it a compelling political tool in the formation of national, "subnational," and localized scholarly geographies.[6] It similarly provides critical public and private forums for the construction and dissemination of discourses of ethnoracial identity, gender, sexuality, class, and nation. It is through this union of the artistic and the political that the U.S.-Colombian musical imagiNation provides a most potent vehicle for challenging not only reigning affective hierarchies but also, as the examples of Shakira, Echeverri, and Vives testify, longstanding ways of conceptualizing international borders and political alliances as well. An unexpected—though no less potent—product of Colombia's ongoing political and economic crises, the transnational Colombian musical imagiNation affirms the central role of popular culture (specifically, popular music and media) in the lived experience of transmigrants and their offspring. Resolutely anchored in the collective cultural labor of (re) imagining transnational Colombian identity, the U.S.-Colombian musical imagiNation simultaneously reflects the distinct material conditions of *colombianos* everywhere and the unique sociohistorical specificities of the so-called Latin music boom and its aftermath. For the artists profiled in the preceding pages, it also encompasses (albeit at times unintentionally) an attempt to contest and in turn rearticulate Latin(o) American gender, ethnoracial, and geospatial norms.

As a community that has barely begun to establish a distinct collective identity within the U.S. popular imagination under the "new Latinos" rubric, U.S. Colombians are finding that the political moment of the late twentieth and early twenty-first centuries is steadily materializing through the subfield of U.S.-Colombian Studies. In turn, U.S.-Colombian Studies has just begun to emerge from the fields of U.S. Latino, American, Latin American, and Colombian Studies, all of which are currently progressing (or, in the case of U.S. Latino Studies, resolutely maintaining its existing foundation) toward a transnational scholarly framework. As the recent artistic and commercial success of Colombian recording artists and musical genres evinces, artists such as Echeverri, Shakira, and, to a lesser extent, Vives realize that one of the most effective means of combating violence is through the creation of alternative (though not always/already resistant) cultures. The U.S.-Colombian musical imagiNation that has emerged represents but one of the quotidian products of Colombia's longstanding political and economic crises. And though certainly not free of its own representational flaws and clichés, popular artistic expression has helped to make it possible for *colombianos* everywhere to carve out our own symbolic spaces within a political moment otherwise principally defined by violence.

The public personas and artistic production of Shakira, Carlos Vives, and Andrea Echeverri likewise provide us with a fertile site for engaging in a metadisciplinary discussion of the ongoing shifts within Latin American Studies. This conversation coalesces around the movement toward the consolidation of Latino and Latin American Studies within U.S. higher education and the thirst for the transnational embodied within the "new" American Studies. In this respect, Winfried Fluck remarks that analytically engaged approaches to a "global" American Studies carry considerable promise, provided that they do not entail "dissolving 'America' as an object of study into a diffuse globalism and replacing it with a new object defined hemispherically or globally. . . . It is curious to see that this is suggested at a time in which understanding the United States has become perhaps more important than ever." He correctly contends that to do so would likely signal a fatal movement away from American Studies' bedrock interpretive and political challenges.[7] However, as I have previously asserted, such institutional sea changes, when realized with a historically blind eye toward U.S. Ethnic Studies' intrinsic engagement with transnational research and activism, threaten to reinscribe the very brand of American exceptionalism that American and Ethnic Studies have long repudiated. While these developments may indeed offer valuable opportunities for the introduction of alternative research and pedagogies, undertaking these directions in decontextualized fashion is highly problematic at best, given the tendency to displace the historic struggles, contributions, and sacrifices that these movements often represent—as well as the promise that they hold for an enlightened critical understanding of present, past, and future Latin(o) American popular artistic production.

Notes

Unless otherwise noted, all translations are the author's.

INTRODUCTION

1. Aterciopelados, *Colombia conexion*, El Dorado, RCA International, 1995; National Hymn of the Republic of Colombia, lyrics by Rafael Núñez; music by Oreste Síndici, 1887; Ed Morales, "Colombia te canto: The Redeeming Power of Music," *Hopscotch* 1.4 (1999): 34; "Pastrana: 'Shakira, nuestra embajadora internacional,'" *ElTiempo.com*, 23 Feb. 2001 <http://www.eltiempo.terra.com.co/23-02-2001/rock_pf_5.html>.

2. See Martha Ellen Davis's article "An Antidote to Crisis," *Hemisphere* 11.3 (2002): 4–7, for a brief account of the psychological role that popular music has played within South Florida's Colombian community.

3. Aterciopelados, *Colombia conexión*. Referencing natural phenomena (the Orinoco River), former political leaders (Gaitán, Galán, Rojas Pinilla), musical genres (*bambuco, torbellino, cumbia, guavina*), and other points of reference, *Colombia conexión* presents an abridged history of the Colombian nation familiar to many of its local citizens and diaspora. According to Juana Suárez, Aterciopelados's inventory of national icons also references the self-reflective stance of many contemporary Colombians regarding the veracity of their national symbols. Juana Suárez, "Sites of Contention: Colombian Cultural Production at the Threshold of a New Millennium" (Ph.D. diss., Arizona State University, 2000), 120.

4. The phrase "doing being Colombian" is borrowed from Ana Celia Zentella's notion of "doing being bilingual" (itself inspired by the work of the sociolinguist Peter Auer). To me, "doing being Colombian" implies the skillful, constantly shifting identity work realized by bicultural, and often by bilingual, individuals. Ana Celia Zentella, *Growing Up Bilingual* (Malden, MA: Blackwell , 1997).

5. "Conexión Colombia," *Semana*, 11 Nov. 2002: 17; Martin F. Manalansan IV, *Global Divas: Filipino Gay Men in the Diaspora* (Durham, NC: Duke University Press, 2003), 12.

6. Jesús Martín Barbero, "Latin America: Cultures in the Communication Media," *Journal of Communication* 43.2 (1993): 27.

7. John F. Stack, Jr., "The Ethnic Citizen Confronts the Future: Los Angeles and Miami at Century's Turn," *Pacific Historical Review* 68.2 (1999): 314. The multiple ways in which one may read "Latin(a/o) American" reflect the inherently context-bound, highly individualized nature of identity. As such, I use the shorthand term "Latin(a/o) American" at various points in this text when I wish to simultaneously reference both U.S. Latinos and Latin Americans. Otherwise, I employ the terms "Latino" and "Latin American" in accordance with their more standard usages. For further discussion of the significance attached to these labels as well as other, related nomenclatures, see Suzanne Oboler, *Ethnic Labels,*

Latino Lives: Identity and the Politics of (Re)Presentation in the United States (Minneapolis: University of Minnesota Press, 1995), and Daniel Mato, "On Global and Local Agents and the Social Making of Transnational Identities and Related Agendas in 'Latin' America," *Identities* 4.2 (1997): 167–212.

8. Stack, 310, 314; John Sinclair, "'The Hollywood of Latin America': Miami as Regional Center in Television Trade," *Television & New Media* 4.3 (2003): 212. For a quantitative discussion of second-generation U.S.-Colombians see Alejandro Portes and Rubén Rumbaut, *Legacies: The Story of the Immigrant Second Generation* (Berkeley: University of California Press, 2001); Marilyn Espitia, "The Other 'Other Hispanics': South American-Origin Latinos in the United States," *The Columbia History of Latinos in the United States Since 1960*, ed. David G. Gutiérrez (New York: Columbia University Press, 2004), 257–280; and Luis Eduardo Guarnizo and Marilyn Espitia, "Colombia," in *The New Americans: A Guide to Immigration Since 1965*, ed. Mary C. Waters and Reed Ueda with Helen B. Marrow (Cambridge, MA: Harvard University Press, 2007), 371–385.

9. Michelle Habell-Pallán, *Locomotion: The Travels of Chicana and Latina Popular Culture* (New York: New York University Press, 2005), 187. For welcome interventions in the field of *rock en español* scholarship, see Habell-Pallán, as well as Deborah Pacini Hernández, Héctor Fernández L'Hoeste, and Eric Zolov, eds., *Rockin' Las Americas: Rock Music and Rock Cultures Across Latin(o) America* (Pittsburgh: University of Pittsburgh Press, 2004).

10. Licia Fiol-Matta, "Pop *Latinidad*: Puerto Ricans in the Latin Explosion, 1999," *CENTRO Journal* 14.1 (2002): 36; Melissa A. Click and Michael W. Kramer, "Reflections on a Century of Living: Gendered Differences in Mainstream Popular Songs," *Popular Communication* 5.4 (2007): 243.

11. Joke Hermes, *Re-Reading Popular Culture* (Malden, MA: Blackwell, 2005) 4, 11.

12. "Conéctese con una causa—Migraciones," *conexioncolombia.com*, 20 Aug. 2006 <http://www.conexioncolombia.com/conexioncolombia/content/page.jsp?ID=887>; see also Mark Slobin, "Music in Diaspora: The View from America," *Diaspora* 3.3 (1994): 243–250.

13. Celeste Fraser Delgado, "What Rock and Roll Owes the Blues, Carlos Vives Owes Vallenato," *miaminewtimes.com*, 20 Dec. 2001 <http://www.miaminewstimes.com/issues.2001-12-20/music.html/print/html>. For an account of Colombian and U.S. political attitudes in recent years, see John C. Dugas, "Colombian Attitudes Toward the United States After 9/11," in *America: Sovereign Defender or Cowboy Nation?*, ed. Vladmir Shlapentokh, Joshua Woods, and Eric Shiraev (Burlington, VT/Hants, Great Britain: Ashgate, 2005), 69–88.

14. Suzanne Oboler, "Introduction: Los que llegaron: 50 Years of South American Immigration (1950–2000)—An Overview," *Latino Studies* 3 (2005): 50; John Storey, *Inventing Popular Culture* (Malden, MA: Blackwell, 2005), 85. As defined by John Storey, the "memory industry" consists of those portions of the culture industry dedicated to articulating the past.

15. Oboler, *Ethnic Labels*, 151; Ella Shohat, "Ethnicities-in-Relation: Toward a Multicultural Reading of American Cinema," in *Unspeakable Images: Ethnicity and the American Cinema*, ed. L. D. Friedman (Urbana: University of Illinois Press, 1991), 216.

16. Frances R. Aparicio and Cándida Jáquez, *Musical Migrations: Transnationalism and Cultural Hybridity in Latin/o America*, ed. Frances R. Aparicio and Cándida Jáquez with María Elena Cepeda (New York: St. Martin's Press, 2003), 1–10; Deborah Pacini Hernández, "Race, Ethnicity and the Production of Latin/o Popular music," in *Global Repertoires:*

Popular Music Within and Beyond the Transnational Music Industry, ed. Andreas Gebesmair and Alfred Smudits (Aldershot: Ashgate, 2001), 57.

17. Lila Abu-Lughod, "Writing Against Culture," in *Recapturing Anthropology*, ed. Richard Fox (Santa Fe, NM: School of American Research Press, 1991), 143. Abu-Lughod defines "halfies" as those individuals "whose national or cultural identity is mixed by virtue of migration, overseas education, or parentage" (137).

18. *Barranquillera/o* is the adjective used to refer to the natives of Barranquilla, the largest city on Colombia's Caribbean coast.

19. Horacio N. Roque Ramírez, "Rafa Negrón's Pan Dulce and the Queer Sonic Latinaje of San Francisco," *CENTRO Journal* 24.1 (2007): 274–313; see also Helmi Järviluoma, Pirkko Moisala, and Anni Vilkko, "Not Only Vision—Analysing Sound and Music From the Perspective of Gender," in *Gender and Qualitative Methods*, ed. Helmi Järviluoma, Pirkko Moisala, and Anni Vilkko (Thousand Oaks, CA: Sage, 2003), 84–106.

20. Susan McClary and Robert Walser, "Start Making Sense! Musicology Wrestles With Rock," in *On Record: Rock, Pop, and the Written Word*, ed. Simon Frith and Andrew Goodwin (London: Routledge, 2000), 278.

21. Tricia Rose, *Black Noise: Rap Music and Black Culture in Contemporary America* (Hanover, NH: Wesleyan University Press/University Press of New England, 1994), 181; see also Ella Shohat, *Taboo Memories, Diasporic Voices* (Durham, NC: Duke University Press, 2006). In her critique of current trends in the anthropological study of transnational commumunities, Nina Glick-Schiller outlines the flawed reasoning underlying the use of the ethnic group as a unit of scholarly analysis, or what she terms the reproduction of "methodological nationalism." See Nina Glick-Schiller, "Transnational Urbanism as a Way of Life: A Research Topic Not a Metaphor," *City & Society* 17.1 (2005): 51–54, as well as Peter Wade, *Race and Ethnicity in Latin America* (London: Pluto Press, 1997), 7. Here, Wade discusses the dangers of presentism, or the tendency to judge previous historical eras by the standards of the present time. I assert that this notion of presentism might also apply to one's vision of different, though chronologically parallel, cultures, in particular mainstream U.S. feminist interpretations of women's status in Latin America.

22. José David Saldívar, *Border Matters: Remapping American Cultural Studies* (Berkeley: University of California Press, 1997), ix, xiii, 14.

23. Stuart Hall, "Cultural Identity and Diaspora," in *Theorizing Diaspora: A Reader*, ed. Jana Evans Braziel and Anita Mannur (Malden, MA: Blackwell, 2003), 235; Stuart Hall, "The Whites of Their Eyes: Racist Ideologies and the Media," in *Silver Linings: Some Strategies for the Eighties: Contributions to the Communist University of London*, ed. Communist University of London (London: Lawrence and Wishart, 1981), 35; Shohat, "Ethnicities-in-Relation," 215.

24. McClary and Walser, 278; Andrew Goodwin, *Dancing in the Distraction Factory: Music Television and Popular Culture* (Minneapolis: University of Minnesota Press, 1992), 2, 24–25, 56–57. For a revolutionary analysis of contemporary media reception, see Stuart Hall, "Encoding/Decoding," in *Culture, Media, Language: Working Papers in Cultural Studies, 1972–79*, ed. Stuart Hall, Dorothy Hobson, Andrew Lowe, and Paul Willis (London: Hutchinson, 1980), 128–138.

25. Ella Shohat and Robert Stam, "From the Imperial Family to the Transnational Imaginary: Media Spectatorship in the Age of Globalization," in *Global/Local: Cultural Production and the Transnational Imaginary*, ed. Rob Wilson and Wimal Dissanayake

(Durham, NC: Duke University Press, 1996), 145. A timely discussion of the growing import of convergence phenomena in contemporary media culture can be found in Henry Jenkins, *Convergence Culture: Where New and Old Media Collide* (New York: New York University Press, 2006). Noteworthy examples of cross-media, transnational Latino feminist scholarship include Jillian Báez, "*'En mi imperio'*: Competing Discourses of Agency in Ivy Queen's Reggaetón," *CENTRO Journal* 18.1 (2006): 62–81; Dolores Inés Casillas, "A Morning Dose of Latino Masculinity: U.S. Spanish-Language Radio and the Politics of Gender," in *Latina/o Communication Studies Today*, ed. Angharad N. Valdivia (New York: Peter Lang, 2008), 161–186; Dolores Inés Casillas, "Sounds of Belonging: A Cultural History of Spanish-Language Radio in the United States" (Ph.D. diss., University of Michigan, 2006); Rosa Linda Fregoso, *MeXicana Encounters: The Making of Social Identities on the Borderlands* (Berkeley: University of California Press, 2003); Habell-Pallán; Isabel Molina Guzmán, "Gendering Latinidad Through the Elián News Discourse About Cuban Women," *Latino Studies* 3 (2005): 179–204; Isabel Molina Guzmán and Angharad N. Valdivia, "Brain, Brow or Bootie: Iconic Latinas in Contemporary Popular Culture," *Communication Review* 2 (2004): 205–221; Deborah Parédez, "Remembering Selena, Re-membering *Latinidad*," *Theatre Journal* 54(2002): 63–84; Felicity Schaeffer-Grabiel, "Planet-Love.com: Cyberbrides in the Americas and the Transnational Routes of U.S. Masculinity," *Signs: Journal of Women in Culture and Society* 31 (2006): 331–356; Angharad N. Valdivia, "Latinas as Radical Hybrid: Transnationally Gendered Traces in Mainstream Media," *Global Media Journal* 4.7, 2004 <http://lass.calumet.purdue.edu/gmj/refereed/htm>, and Angharad N. Valdivia, *A Latina in the Land of Hollywood and Other Essays on Media Culture* (Tucson: University of Arizona Press, 2000).

26. Teun A. van Dijk, "Principles of Critical Discourse Analysis," *Discourse & Society* 4.2 (1993): 249, 253, 270; Otto Santa Ana with Juan Morán and Cynthia Sánchez, "Awash Under a Brown Tide: Immigration Metaphors in California Public and Print Media Discourse," *Aztlán* 23.2 (1998): 137; Otto Santa Ana, *Brown Tide Rising: Metaphors of Latinos in Contemporary American Public Discourse* (Austin: University of Texas Press, 2002).

27. Susan McClary, *Feminine Endings: Music, Gender, and Sexuality* (Minneapolis: University of Minnesota Press, 1991), 21.

28. The tendency for Colombians to employ popular music as a form of psychological refuge is not historically unprecedented, however. During the widespread political violence of the 1940s and 1950s, Afro-Colombian musical forms from the Atlantic Coast enjoyed an enormous surge in popularity. See Peter Wade, "Racial Identity and Nationalism: A Theoretical View From Colombia," *Ethnic and Racial Studies* 24.5(2001): 845–865, as well as Marco Palacios, *Between Legitimacy and Violence: A History of Colombia, 1875–2002*, trans. Richard Stoller (Durham, NC: Duke University Press, 2006).

29. I borrow the term "contact zone" from Mary Louise Pratt, who defines a contact zone as "the space of colonial encounters, the space in which peoples geographically and historically separated come into contact with each other and establish ongoing relations, usually involving conditions of coercion, radical inequality, and intractable conflict." Mary Louis Pratt, *Imperial Eyes: Travel Writing and Transculturation* (New York: Routledge, 1992), 6; see also Storey, chapters 6 and 8, and Benedict Anderson, "Exodus," *Critical Inquiry* 20.2 (1994): 319.

30. Arjun Appadurai, *Modernity at Large: Cultural Dimensions of Globalization* (Minneapolis: University of Minnesota Press, 1996), 6, 8, 31.

31. Ibid. 4.

32. Stuart Hall, "Old and New Identities, Old and New Ethnicities," in *Culture, Globalization and the World-System: Contemporary Conditions for the Representation of Identity*, ed. Anthony D. King (Minneapolis: University of Minnesota Press. 1997), 52–53.

33. See, for example, Monisha Das Gupta, *Unruly Immigrants: Rights, Activism and Transnational South Asian Politics in the United States* (Durham, NC: Duke University Press, 2006); Robert Alvarez, Jr., *Mangos, Chiles, and Truckers: The Business of Transnationalism* (Minneapolis: University of Minnesota Press, 2005); Martin F. Manalansan IV, *Global Divas: Filipino Gay Men in the Diaspora* (Durham, NC: Duke University Press, 2003); Nina Glick-Schiller and Georges Eugene Fouron, *Georges Woke Up Laughing: Long-Distance Nationalism and the Search for Home* (Durham, NC: Duke University Press, 2001); Guarnizo and Espitia, 2001; Michael Peter Smith and Luis Eduardo Guarnizo, "The Locations of Transnationalism," introduction to *Transnationalism from Below*, ed. Luis Eduardo Guarnizo and Michael Peter Smith (New Brunswick, NJ: Transaction, 1998), 3–34; and, most notably, Aihwa Ong, *Flexible Citizenship: The Cultural Logics of Transnationality* (Durham, NC: Duke University Press, 1999).

34. Guarnizo 248; Smith and Guarnizo 23.

35. Lise Waxer, review of *Music, Race, and Nation: Música Tropical in Colombia*, by Peter Wade, *Journal of Popular Music Studies* 13.2 (2001): 237; Pacini Hernández, 59.

36. Eric Zolov, *Refried Elvis* (Berkeley: University of California Press, 1999), 9. A vivid example of the "politically passive fan" stereotype can be found in José Dávila, "Bush Whacked by Ricky Martin: The World's Most Famous Latin Hunk Grows a Brain—and a Conscience," www.miaminewtimes.com, 18 May 2007 <http://music.miaminewtimes.com/2007-05-17/music/bush-whacked-by-ricky-martin/print>.

37. McClary 8.

38. Lana F. Rakow, "Feminist Approaches to Popular Culture: Giving Patriarchy Its Due," in *Cultural Theory and Popular Culture: A Reader* (2nd ed.), ed. John Storey (Athens: University of Georgia Press, 1998), 278; Mavis Bayton, "Feminist Musical Practice: Problems and Contradictions," in *Rock and Popular Music: Politics, Policies, Institutions*, ed. Tony Bennett, Simon Frith, Lawrence Grossberg, John Shepherd, and Graeme Turner (New York: Routledge, 1993), 177.

39. James Clifford, "Diasporas," in *Internationalizing Cultural Studies: An Anthology*, ed. Ackbar Abbas and John Nguyet Erni (Malden, MA: Blackwell, 2005), 535; Anne McClintock, "Family Feuds: Gender, Nationalism and the Family," *Feminist Review* 44 (1993): 61–62; see also Joel Streicker, "Policing Boundaries: Race, Class and Gender in Cartagena, Colombia," in *Blackness in Latin America and the Caribbean*, vol. 1, ed. Norman E. Whitten, Jr., and Arlene Torres (Bloomington: Indiana University Press, 1998), 278–308, in which he similarly notes the ways in which the "mythical past" is constructed as distinctly masculine; Inderpal Grewal, *Transnational America: Feminisms, Diasporas, Neoliberalisms* (Durham, NC: Duke University Press, 2005), 84.

40. bell hooks, *Yearning: race, gender, and cultural politics* (Boston: South End Press, 1990), 57; Wade, "Racial identity and nationalism," 853.

41. For a frequently cited example of this more traditional brand of scholarship, see Delia Zapata Olivella, "La cumbia: Síntesis musical de la nación colombiana," *Revista colombiana de folclor* 3.4 (1962): 189–204.

42. Virginia R. Domínguez, "For a Politics of Love and Rescue," *Cultural Anthropology* 15.3 (2000): 363–364.

43. Ibid. 361–393. Many thanks to Mérida Rúa and Lorena García for bringing this useful concept to my attention.

44. Abu-Lughod, 143.

45. Robert Hanke, "'Yo Quiero Mi MTV!': Making Music Television in Latin America," in *Mapping the Beat: Popular Music and Contemporary Theory*, ed. Thomas Swiss, John Sloop, and Andrew Herman (Malden, MA: Blackwell, 1998), 221.

46. Recent monographs focusing on inter-Latino social dynamics and subjectivities include the work of Arlene Dávila, *Latinos, Inc: The Marketing and Making of a People* (Berkeley: University of California Press, 2001); Nicholas De Genova and Ana Y. Ramos-Zaya, *Latino Crossings: Mexicans, Puerto Ricans, and the Politics of Race and Citizenship* (New York: Routledge, 2003), and Pablo Vila, *Crossing Borders, Reinforcing Borders: Social Categories, Metaphors, and Narrative Identities on the U.S. Mexico Border* (Austin: University of Texas Press, 2000).

47. Benedict Anderson, "Exodus," *Critical Inquiry* 20.2 (1994): 315.

48. Raymond L. Williams, *The Colombian Novel, 1844–1987* (Austin: University of Texas Press, 1991) 13, 15–16; Jorge Duany, "Popular Music in Puerto Rico: Toward an Anthropology of Salsa." *Latin American Music Review* 5.2 (1984): 193.

49. James Clifford, "Diasporas," in *Internationalizing Cultural Studies: An Anthology*, ed. Ackbar Abbas and John Nguyet Erni (Malden, MA: Blackwell, 2005), 544 (emphasis in original).

50. Suzanne Oboler, "Introduction: Los que llegaron: 50 Years of South American Immigration (1950–2000)—An Overview," *Latino Studies* 3 (2005): 42–52. For an effective overview of the critical concepts amd debates associated with the notion of *Latinidad*, see Mérida M. Rúa, "Latinidades," in *Oxford Encyclopedia of Latinos and Latinas in the United States*, ed. Deena J. González and Suzanne Oboler (New York: Oxford University Press, 2005), 505–507.

51. *Mil gracias* a Margarita de la Vega-Hurtado for suggesting this concise phrase to me during the earlier stages of my research.

52. See George Yúdice, *The Expediency of Culture: Uses of Cultures in the Global Era*, chapter 7 (Durham, NC: Duke University Press, 2003); Stuart Hall, "What Is This 'Black' in Black Popular Culture?" in *Black Popular Culture*, ed. Gina Dent (Seattle: Bay Press, 1992), 24.

53. Angharad N. Valdivia, "Latinas as Radical Hybrid: Transnationally Gendered Traces in Mainstream Media," *Global Media Journal* 4.7 (2004) <http://lass./calumet.purdue.edu/cca/gmj/refereed.htm>.

54. Saldívar, 35.

55. Andrew Leyshon, David Matless, and George Revill, introduction, *The Place of Music*, ed. Andrew Leyshon, David Matless, and George Revill (New York: Guilford Press, 1998), 10.

56. John Storey, *Inventing Popular Culture* (Malden, MA: Blackwell, 2003), 2.

57. Carlos Augusto Cabrera, e-mail forwarded to the author, 14 July 2002, containing the article by Bernardo Bejarano González, "Para los colombianos, los eventos culturales son de la Costa Caribe," *ElTiempo.com*, 14 July 2002, quoted in Elisabeth Cunin, "El Caribe visto desde el interior del país: estereotipos raciales y sexuales," *Revista de Estudios Colombianos* 30 (2006): 6–14.

58. Peter Wade, "Racial Identity and Nationalism: A Theoretical View From Latin America," *Ethnic and Racial Studies* 24.2 (2001): 854.

59. Masao Miyoshi, "A Borderless World? From Colonialism to Transnationalism and the Decline of the Nation-State," *Critical Inquiry* 19.4 (1993): 750.

CHAPTER 1

1. For an analysis of common social patterns among Colombian immigrants, see Luis Eduardo Guarnizo, Arturo Ignacio Sánchez, and Elizabeth M. Roach, "Mistrust, Fragmented Solidarity and Transnational Migration: Colombians in New York City and Los Angeles," *Ethnic and Racial Studies* 22.3 (March 1999): 367–396; Luis Eduardo Guarnizo, "On the Political Participation of Transnational Migrants: Old Practices and New Trends," in *E Pluribus Unum?: Contemporary and Historical Perspectives on Immigrant Political Participation*, ed. Gary Gerstle and John Mollenkopf (New York: Russell Sage Foundation, 2001), 233. Since the early 1980s, a host of popular cinematic and print media representations touting the stereotype of the Colombian *narcotraficante* (drug trafficker) have emerged. Some of the most familiar include James Kelly's *Time* 1981 magazine cover story entitled "Trouble in Paradise"; the Brian De Palma film *Scarface* (1983); the Ted Demme film *Blow* (2001); and the more recent Billy Corben documentary *Cocaine Cowboys* (2005).

2. Within Colombian mass media, "*el exterior*" is a phrase commonly used to refer to the Colombian diaspora.

3. Mario A. Murillo, *Colombia and the United States: War, Unrest and Destablization* (New York: Seven Stories Press, 2004), 18; Andrés Oppenheimer, "Uribe's Counteroffense Working—at Least at Home," *Miami Herald*, 22 April 2007 <http://miamiherald.com>; Frida Ghitis, "The Colombian Miracle," *Arkansas Democrat-Gazette* (Little Rock), 8 July 2008 <http://www2.arkansasonline.com>; James P. McGovern, *The Suffering Continues: Internally Displaced People in Colombia*, report prepared for the Congressional Human Rights Caucus, 110th Cong., 2nd sess., 21 July 2008; Congressman Jim McGovern of Massachusetts, "Recognizing 2007 as the Year of the Internally Displaced in Colombia," H. Res. 426, 110th Cong., 1st sess., *govtrack.us*, 11 July 2007 <http://www.govtrack.us/congress/bill.xpd?bill=hr110-426>; Dugas 84.

4. The label "new Latinos" comes from Roberto Suro's Pew Hispanic Center report on the 2000 U.S. Census. In his report, Suro employs the term "new Latinos" to refer to all U.S. Latino communities (besides Mexicans, Puerto Ricans, and Cubans) that have experienced marked population growth in the past ten years, specifically, Colombians, Dominicans, Ecuadorians, Guatemalans, and Salvadorans. Roberto Suro, Pew Hispanic Center, *Counting the "Other Hispanics": How Many Colombians, Dominicans, Ecuadorians, Guatemalans and Salvadorans Are There in the United States?* (Washington, DC: Pew Hispanic Center, 2002). Notably, to date I have uncovered no academic studies of U.S.-Colombian popular culture, with the exception of Jorge Arévalo-Mateus's unpublished ethnomusicological study of *vallenato* practitioners in metropolitan New York and the work of the documentarian Roberto Arévalo. See Jorge Arévalo-Mateus, "The Colombian Costeño Musicians of the New York Metropolitan Area: A Manifestation of Urban Vallenato" (master's thesis, Hunter College of the City University of New York, 1998);

La arepa colombiana en Nueva York/The Colombian Arepa in Nuew York, DVD, directed by Roberto Arévalo (1991/2007; Atlanta, GA: Beyond Documentary, 2007); *Me duele el corazón/My Heart Aches*, DVD, directed by Roberto Arévalo (n.d./2007; Atlanta, GA: Beyond Documentary, 2007). For examples of recent noteworthy monographs in the field of Latino popular culture, consult Frances R. Aparicio, *Listening to Salsa: Gender, Latin Popular Music and Puerto Rican Cultures* (Hanover, NH: Wesleyan University Press/University Press of New England, 1998); Raúl Fernández, *From Afro-Cuban Rhythms to Latin Jazz* (Berkeley: University of California Press, 2006); Ruth Glasser, *My Music Is My Flag: Puerto Rican Musicians and Their New York Communities, 1917–1940* (Berkeley: University of California Press, 1995); Habell-Pallán; Frances Negrón-Muntaner, *Boricua Pop: Puerto Ricans and the Latinization of American Culture* (New York: New York University Press, 2004); and Raquel Z. Rivera, *New York Ricans From the Hip-Hop Zone* (New York: Palgrave Macmillan, 2003), among others.

5. Silvio Torres-Saillant, "Pitfalls of Latino Chronologies: South and Central Americans," *Latino Studies* 5 (2007): 501.

6. Michael Peter Smith, "Power in Place/Places of Power: Contextualizing Transnational Research," *City & Society* 17.1 (2005): 5 (emphasis in original).

7. José David Saldívar, *Border Matters: Remapping American Cultural Studies* (Berkeley: University of California Press, 1997) xiii.

8. Smith, 9.

9. Javier Giraldo, *Colombia. The Genocidal Democracy* (Monroe, ME: Common Courage Press, 1996), 81.

10. Giraldo 22–23; Murillo 89. For a detailed discussion of human rights in the Colombian context, see Grace Livingstone, *Inside Colombia: Drugs, Democracy and War* (New Brunswick, NJ: Rutgers University Press, 2004).

11. Marco Palacios, *Between Legitimacy and Violence: A History of Colombia, 1875–2002*, trans. Richard Stoller (Durham, NC: Duke University Press, 2006). While I question the tendency to present the contemporary history of Colombian violence and the economic and political crisis in such chronologically discrete terms, I would also underscore the numerous differences between the violence of 1940s and 1950s Colombia and its more recent manifestations. Obvious distinctions include the introduction of the international narcotics trade and the scale of outbound migration connected to the latter period.

12. Murillo 59, 70, 75.

13. Palacios 256–257, 267.

14. Ibid.; Amnistía Internacional, *Violencia política en Colombia. Mito y Realidad* (Madrid: Editorial Amnistía Internacional, 1994). Mark Chernick asserts that while drug traffickers do wield a certain amount of influence over Colombia's politicians in the form of bribes, popular media terms such as "narco-democracy" overstate the drug traffickers' political power. Drug traffickers have not flaunted their socioeconomic power in support of political alternatives; rather, they have corrupted Colombia's traditional party system in an effort to protect their own interests. These interests include halting the spread of guerrilla movements that challenge drug traffickers' local power and property. Marc W. Chernick, "The Paramilitarization of the War in Colombia," *North American Congress on Latin America* (hereafter *NACLA*) (March-April 1998): 40.

15. Hagen 29; "Peace in Colombia? This Year, Next Year, Sometime . . . ," *The Economist* 10 (April 1999): 31; "No Peace," *The Economist* (11 Oct. 1997): 38; ColettaYoungers,

"U.S. Entanglements in Colombia Continue," *NACLA* (March-April 1998): 34; Lewis Dolinsky, "The True State of Colombia," *The San Francisco Chronicle*, 22 April 2001 <http://www.sfgate.com/chronicle>.

16. Giraldo 9, 17; Murillo 67, 85–86, 89, 92, 99–100, 151; Steven Dudley, "Walking Through the Nightscapes of Bogotá," *NACLA* (Sept.-Oct. 1998): 12.

17. Murillo 84, 152–153.

18. Murillo 100–101; Dugan 84.

19. *Colombia, South America, 2008* [map]. "Political Map of Colombia." 2008. Central Intelligence Agency, *The World Factbook* <https://www.cia.gov/library/publications/the-world-factbook/geos/co.html>.

20. Murillo 27–28, 33–34.

21. Murillo 127, 135, 137, 142; Winifred Tate, "Repeating Past Mistakes: Aiding Counter-insurgency in Colombia," *NACLA* (Sept.-Oct. 2000): 16; Jason Hagen, "New Colombian President Promises More War," *NACLA* (July-Aug. 2002): 28; Giraldo 12; Dugas 81; "How They Voted: U.S. Congress," *The Republican* (Springfield, Massachusetts), 7 Sept. 2007, <http://www.masslive.com/>.

22. Murillo 39–40; Palacios 261; Malcolm Deas, "Violent Exchanges: Reflections on Political Violence in Colombia," in *The Legitimization of Violence*, ed. David E. Apter (New York: New York University Press, 1997), 356.

23. *Violentólogos* are scholars who focus on the phenomenon of violence in contemporary Colombia. Wolfgang S. Heinz, "Violencia política y cambio social en Colombia," in *Literatura colombiana hoy: Imaginación y barbarie*, ed. Karl Kohut (Madrid: Iberoamericana, 1994), 122–123; Tate 17; Hagen 26; Frances Robles, "Many Colombians Leave Miami Area, Return Home," *Miami Herald*, 22 Dec. 2003 <http://www.miami.com>.

24. Murillo 27, 103; Dugas 85; Gerardo Reyes, "Uribe 'empeñado en devolver la paz' a los colombianos," *El Nuevo Herald*, 1 Oct. 2004 <http://www.elherald.com>; Frances Robles, "Revision to Colombian Constitution Grants Military, Police Broad New Powers," *Miami Herald*, 12 Dec. 2003 <http://www.miami.com>. See Casto Ocando and Graciela Mrad, "El sueño americano defrauda a inmigrantes," *El Nuevo Herald*, 12 Oct. 2003: 1A; Robles.

25. Palacios 216; Rubén G. Rumbaut, "Origins and Destinies: Immigration, Race, and Ethnicity in Contemporary America," in *Origins and Destinies*, ed. Silvia Pedraza and Rubén G. Rumbaut (Belmont, CA: Wadsworth, 1996), 24; Saskia Sassen-Koob, "Formal and Informal Associations: Dominicans and Colombians In New York," *International Migration Review* 13 (1979): 316, 320; Luis Eduardo Guarnizo and Luz Marina Díaz, "Transnational Migration: A View From Colombia," *Ethnic and Racial Studies* 22.2 (March 1999): 397. For a more recent portrayal of the community-building efforts of Miami-based U.S.-Colombians, see Andrea Elliott, "Thousands Flee War in Colombia, Plan New Lives in U.S.," *Miami Herald*, 29 Aug. 2001. A detailed discussion of the key differences between the transnational activities of "old" and "new" U.S. migrants can be found in Peggy Levitt, *The Transnational Villagers* (Berkeley: University of California Press, 2001).

26. "The Colombian Diaspora in South Florida." Working paper, Colombian Studies Institute, Latin American and Caribbean Center, Florida International University, Miami, Florida, May 2001 <http://lacc.fui.edu/Publications/working_papers/working_paper_01.htm>; Juan Forero, "Prosperous Colombians Fleeing, Many to the U.S.," *New York Times on the Web*, 10 April 2001 <http://www.nytimes.com>; "Colombia's Diaspora," chart, *New*

York Times on the Web, 10 April 2001 <http://www.nytimes.com>; "Los colombianos en Estados Unidos," Embassy of Colombia, Washington, DC, 29 Oct. 2002 <http://www.colombiaemb.org/colombians_in_us.htm>; Palacios 214; Dugas 86; Guarnizo, Sánchez, and Roach 369; Guarnizo and Smith 19; Casto Ocando, "Recibirán una tarjeta consular los colombianos en EEUU," El Nuevo Herald, 24 March 2004: 2A.

27. Raúl Fernández and Bernardo Useche, "'¡No somos criminales; somos trabajadores!': La emigración latinoamericana a Estados Unidos," Deslinde, Revista del Centro de Estudios del Trabajo 40 (Sept.-Nov. 2006) <http://www.deslinde.org.co> 9. See also Marla Dickerson, "Placing Blame for Mexico's Ills," Los Angeles Times, 1 July 2006 <http://www.latimes.com>; Peter S. Goodman, "In Mexico, People Do Really Want to Stay: Chicken Farmers Fear U.S. Exports Will Send More Workers North for Jobs," Washington Post, 7 Jan. 2007: A01; Andrew Christie, "The Debate You're Not Hearing: Immigration and Trade," Common Dreams Newscenter, 8 April 2006 <http://www.commondreams.org>; Helen B. Marrow, "South America: Ecuador, Peru, Brazil, Argentina, Venezuela," in The New Americans: A Guide to Immigration Since 1965, ed. Mary C. Waters and Reed Ueda with Helen B. Marrow (Cambridge, MA: Harvard University Press, 2007), 597.

28. Suzanne Oboler, "South Americans," in Oxford Encyclopedia of Latinos and Latinas in the United States, ed. Suzanne Oboler and Deena J. González (New York: Oxford University Press, 2005), 146; Espitia 259, 261; Marrow 507.

29. As more recent government statistics on the U.S.-Colombian community reflect, an error in the 2000 Census resulted in widespread undercounts of the U.S.'s most rapidly increasing Latino populations. Because of the flawed wording contained in one key question, the 2000 Census ultimately reported a decrease of 7,000 persons, rather than the expected 35,000-person increase, within New York City's Colombian community. According to these flawed statistics, the Florida Colombian population numbers roughly 138,768, while the total U.S.-Colombian population is at 618,262. For this reason, I have elected to cite what I felt were the most reliable numerical estimates available from a variety of sources, rather than the 2000 U.S. Census statistics. Janny Scott, "A Census Query Is Said to Skew Data on Latinos," New York Times, 27 June 2001: 1; "Hispanic or Latino by Specific Origin," table, U.S. Census Bureau, PCT006 <http://www.factfinder.census.gov>; "Hispanic or Latino by Type," table, U.S. Census Bureau, QT-P9 <http://www.factfinder.census.gov>. For a critical account of the 2000 U.S. Census debacle and its potential effects on the Colombian and other U.S. Latino communities, see Suro 2002.

30. "Hispanic or Latino Origin for the United States, Regions, Divisions, States, and for Puerto Rico: 2000," table, U.S. Census Bureau, Census 2000 PHC-T-10, 22 Oct. 2001 <http://www.census.gov>; Rumbaut 21, 28–29, 32; Frederick M. Binder and David M. Reimers, "New York as an Immigrant City," in Origins and Destinies, ed. Silvia Pedraza and Rubén G. Rumbaut (Belmont, CA: Wadsworth, 1996), 125, 345; Michael Jones-Correa, Between Two Nations: The Political Predicament of Latinos in New York City (Ithaca: Cornell University Press, 1998) 125; Sassen-Koob; Douglas R. Gurak and Greta Gilbertson, "Household Transitions in the Migrations of Dominicans and Colombians to New York," International Migration Review 26 (1992): 22–45.

31. Sassen-Koob 317. The Colombian-born writer Jaime Manrique's 1993 novel Latin Moon in Manhattan, which is largely set in the Jackson Heights Colombian enclave, was among the few English-language accounts of Colombian immigrant life widely available until the late 1990s. However, since then, the rapid escalation of the Colombian conflict

and the subsequent rise in immigration rates have prompted more mainstream media attention. The 2004 release of the critically acclaimed film *María Full of Grace* (*María llena de gracias eres*) by the U.S. director Joshua Marston, a production that earned the lead actress Catalina Sandino Moreno an Oscar nomination for Best Actress, provided the U.S. public with a detailed artistic portrayal of the Colombian crisis and its impact on Colombian immigration practices. Like Manrique's novel, Marston's film highlights the vibrancy of the Queens-based Colombian community and its importance within the U.S.- Colombian popular imagination, as the constant presence of electronic signs and other forms of advertising promoting New York Colombian social events in Miami's most popular Colombian restaurants and gathering places attests. For example of recent print media coverage of the Colombian migrant experience, see Nina Bernstein and Adam B. Ellick, "The New Immigrant Dream: Arepas as Common as Bagels," *New York Times*, 6 Feb. 2007: A1; María Alejandra Chaparro, "Little Colombia: Teen Immigrants Make New Lives in the United States," *Hemisphere* 11.3 (2002): 8–11; Davis 2002; Elliot 2001; Elizabeth Mora-Mass, "Colombianos en Nueva York, del sueño americano a la pesadilla gringa," *ElTiempo.com*, 1 July 2001 <http://eltiempo.terra.com.co/01-07-2001/pano_pf_o.html>; "The Colombian Diaspora: Miami Nice," *Economist.com*, 3 May 2001 <http://www.economist.com>; Karl Penhaul, "The Lure of a Better Life," *U.S. News & World Report*, 8 Jan. 2001: 28; "Éxodo con visa," *Semana*, 6 Nov. 2000: 58–60; "Colombia's Other Import," editorial, *Palm Beach Post*, 6 April 2000: 16A; "Grave compromiso," editorial, *La Nación* (San José, Costa Rica), 23 May 2000: 13A; "Llegan más colombianos," *La Nación* (San José, Costa Rica), 22 May 2000: 18A; Larry Rohter, "Driven by Fear, Colombians Leave in Droves," *New York Times on the Web*, 5 March 2000 <http://www.nytimes.com>. Apart from the limited Spanish-language materials available on New York Colombians, Germán Castro Caycedo's 1989 book *El Hueco* appears to be the only general book-length account of Colombian migration to the United States from the period. In it, Castro Caycedo chronicles the processes through which undocumented Colombians enter the United States via Haiti, the Bahamas, and Mexico. More recent texts chronicling the U.S.-Colombian immigrant experience include Adriana Téllez Herrera's *"El sueño Americano." Colombianos que alcanzaron el éxito en Estados Unidos* (Bogotá: Intermedio, 2002) and Freddy Parado's *Justicia Made in U.S.A.: dramática historia de un inmigrante astropellado por el solo hecho de ser colombiano* (Bogotá: Planeta, 2002).

32. John Logan, "The New Latinos: Who They Are, Where They Are," Lewis Mumford Center for Comparative Urban and Regional Research, State University of New York at Albany, 2001; "The Colombian Diaspora in South Florida"; Mike Clary, "Colombians Flee Homeland to Seek Refuge in Miami," *Los Angeles Times*, 12 Oct. 1999: 1; Guarnizo 222–223.

33. Guarnizo 223; Michael W. Collier, "Colombian Migration to South Florida: A Most Unwelcome Reception." Working paper, Colombian Studies Institute, Latin American and Caribbean Center, Florida International University, Miami, Florida, May 2004 <http://digitalcommons.fiu.edu/laccwps/2/>.

34. Collier; for more detailed information regarding the South American "brain drain" phenomenon of the period, consult Oboler, "Los que llegaron," in addition to David L. McKee, "Some Specifics on the Brain Drain from the Andean Region," *International Migration/Migrations Internationales/Migraciones Internacionales* 21.4 (1983): 488–499.

35. Ong 1.

36. An important exception in this case is the valuable studies of South Florida's Colombian community currently being conducted under the auspices of Florida International University's Colombian Studies Institute, located in Miami, as well as the foundational sociological and political science research published by Espitia; Guarnizo and Espitia; Guarnizo and Díaz; Guarnizo, Sánchez, and Roach; Guarnizo; and Cristina Escobar, "Dual Citizenship and Political Participation: Migrants in the Interplay of United States and Colombian Politics," in *Latinos and Citizenship: The Dilemma of Belonging*, ed. Suzanne Oboler (New York: Palgrave Macmillan, 2006), 113–141.

37. "The Colombian Diaspora in South Florida"; Collier. Many thanks to Robert Franzino and Dan Ríos for their expertise and generosity in the creation of this map of greater Miami.

38. "The Colombian Diaspora in South Florida"; Elliott. "*Balsero/a*" is the colloquial Spanish word for Cuban immigrants who flee Cuba by raft or boat. While originally limited to the Cuban context, the term is increasingly applied to Miami-area Colombian immigrants, as well. See Ana María Jaramillo, "Mueren seis balseros colombianos en el Caribe," *El Tiempo.com*, 20 July 2001 <http://www.eltiempo.terra.com.co/20-07-2001/inte_pf_f.html>.

39. Roxana de la Riva, "Alvaro Nieto: 'Quiero trabajar por los colombianos,'" *La Prensa* (San Antonio, TX), 2 Feb. 2006: 10; Fernández and Useche; "Sueño americano," *Semana.com*, 14 May 2001 <http://semana.terra.com.co/993/actualidad/ZZZ30BVTMMC.asp>; María Peña, "Thousands of Colombians Continue Exodus to the U.S.," Efe News Services (U.S.), Global News Wire, 8 March 2002; Guarnizo and Espitia 375; Elsa Chaney, cited in Oboler, "South Americans," 149.

40. Guarnizo, Sánchez, and Roach 384; Escobar 113–114; Luis Eduardo Guarnizo and Marilyn Espitia, "Colombia," in *The New Americans: A Guide to Immigration Since 1965*, ed. Mary C. Waters and Reed Ueda with Helen B. Marrow (Cambridge, MA: Harvard University Press, 2007), 376; Falconi and Mazotti 8. An example of a more traditional conceptualization of transmigrant political dynamics can be found in Nancy Foner, "Second-Generation Transnationalism, Then and Now," in *The Changing Face of Home: The Transnational Lives of the Second Generation*, ed. Peggy Levitt and Mary Waters (New York: Russell Sage Foundation, 2002), 242–252.

41. Hall, "The Local and the Global" 36; Guarnizo and Espitia 371; and Marrow 602. Interestingly, U.S.-Cubans and U.S.-Colombians share various noteworthy historical parallels. See Oboler, "Los que llegaron," for further discussion of this topic.

42. "El elegido," *Semana*, 11 Nov. 2002: 104; Ocando 2004; see also Guarnizo and Smith; Alvarez.

CHAPTER 2

1. George Lipsitz, "World Cities and World Beat: Low-Wage Labor and Transnational Culture," *Pacific Historical Review* 68.2 (May 1999): 213–216 (emphasis in original); John Beverley and David Houston, "Una utopía degradada: notas sobre Miami," in *Heterotopías: narrativas de identidad en América Latina*, trans. Juan Pablo Dabove, ed. Juan Pablo Dabove and Carlos Jáuregui (Pittsburgh: ILLI, 2003), 426. For further analysis of black-Cuban dynamics in Miami, see Guillermo J. Grenier and Max J. Castro, "Triadic Politics: Ethnicity, Race, and Politics in Miami, 1959–1998," *Pacific Historical Review* 68.2 (May

1999): 273–292. As detailed by Grenier and Castro, the process of selective white flight in Miami has been largely distinguished by class differences: while working-class Anglos have largely left the city, white managers and executives have tended to remain in Miami (276).

2. George Yúdice, *The Expediency of Culture: Uses of Culure in the Global Era* (Durham: Duke University Press, 2003), 206; Beverley and Houston 419 (translation mine). See also Alejandro Portes and Alex Stepick, *City on the Edge: The Transformation of Miami* (Berkeley: University of California Press, 1993). Here, Portes and Stepick argue that Miami, which they term a "city on the edge," represents "the nation's very first full-fledged experiment in bicultural living in the contemporary era"(xi) and thereby constitutes an essential blueprint for the future of the "American" city.

3. Analogous to my usage of the term "U.S.-Colombian," I favor the term "U.S.-Cuban" here and elsewhere because I find the label "Cuban-American" somewhat problematic: as a geographic designator it is redundant and furthermore reinscribes the imbalance of power between North and South.

4. John Logan, "The New Latinos: Who They Are, Where They Are," Lewis Mumford Center for Comparative Urban and Regional Research, State University of New York at Albany, 2001; Teun A. van Dijk, "Principles of Critical Discourse Analysis," *Discourse & Society* 4.2 (1993): 255 (emphasis in original).

5. "Election 2000: Bush, Gore Locked in Unprecedented Fight for Control of the White House," Special Event, CNN (Cable News Network), 8 Nov. 2000. While the monolithic character of the Miami Cuban vote has certainly been exaggerated, its significance for George W. Bush's contested 2000 electoral vistory is not, as a reported 82 percent of the state's U.S.-Cuban community voted for Bush that year (Julian Borger, "Republican Grip Starts to Loosen in Little Havana," *The Guardian*, 2 Oct. 2004: 12). However, an influx of non-Cuban Latinos, in addition to generational differences within the U.S.-Cuban voting population itself, has had a considerable impact on voting behavior in the period since the 2000 election. See Kim Cobb, "Changing Mix of Latinos Stirs Florida Politics: Cuban-America Support for GOP Could Be Offset by Other Hispanics," *Houston Chronicle*, 28 Sept. 2004: A1; Abby Goodnough, "Hispanic Vote in Florida: Neither a Bloc Nor Lock," *New York Times*, 17 Oct. 2004: 31, and Carla Marinucci, "Cuban Americans' Key Role in Election 2004: Community No Longer Republican Monolith in Miami," *San Francisco Chronicle*, 3 Oct. 2004: A14.

6. Michel-Rolph Trouillot, *Silencing the Past: Power and the Production of History* (Boston: Beacon Press, 1995), 48.

7. It is essential to note here, however, that portrayals of the U.S.-Cuban community that reach beyond standard media depictions, specifically those that focus on the community's many working-class, poor, nonwhite, and/or non-Republican citizens, can be located in the fiction of authors such as Elías Miguel Muñoz, Achy Obejas, and Dolores Prida, as well as in the nonfiction of Ruth Behar, Tanya Katerí Hernández, Nancy Raquel Mirabal, Isabel Molina-Guzmán, José Esteban Muñoz, and María de los Angeles Torres, among others.

8. Karen Branch-Brioso, Tim Henderson, and Alfonso Chardy, "Los anglos, el poder verdadero," *El Nuevo Herald*, 3 Sept. 2000 <http://www.elherald.com/content/archivos/poder/docs/078386.htm>, as well as Karen Branch-Brioso, Tim Henderson, and Alfonso Chardy, "Sondeo rompe el mito del poder cubano en Miami-Dade," *El Nuevo Herald*, 3

Sept. 2000 <http://www.elherald.com/content/archivos/poder/docs/068672.htm>, and Karen Branch-Brioso, "El poder político en Miami es complejo," *El Nuevo Herald*, 4 Sept. 2000 <http://www.elherald.com/content/archivos/poder/docs/008125.htm>. See also Beverley and Houston 423, where the authors further underscore the myth of Cuban hegemony. As Beverley and Houston note, contemporary Miami narratives tend toward the uncritical celebration of the U.S.-Cuban subject, while failing to note such realities as Cubans' overrepresentation in low-paying service and construction jobs.

9. John L. Jackson, *Harlem World: Doing Race and Class in Contemporary Black America* (Chicago: University of Chicago Press, 2001), 31; see also Angharad Valdivia, "Is Penélope to J. Lo as Culture Is to Nature?" in *From Bananas to Buttocks: The Latina Body in Popular Film and Culture*, ed. Myra Mendible (Austin: University of Texas Press, 2007), 129–148.

10. Jackson 40.

11. Néstor García Canclini, *Transforming Modernity: Popular Culture in Mexico*, trans. Lidia Lozano (Austin: University of Texas Press, 1993), 15 (emphasis mine).

12. Arlene Dávila, *Latinos, Inc.: The Marketing and Making of a People* (Berkeley: University of California Press, 2001). For a related example of the ways in which U.S. Latinos engage in a variety of discriminatory practices against each other, see Robert Smith, "'Mexicanness' in New York: Migrants Seek New Place in Old Racial Order," *NACLA* (Sept.-Oct. 2001): 14–17.

13. A mere two years later, however, Latin(o) music sales began to exhibit a downward slide similar to that suffered by the mainstream U.S. music industry in recent years. Brook Larmer, "Latino America," *Newsweek*, 12 July 1999: 48–49; Achy Obejas, "Taking Rock Around the Globe: Shakira, Chao and 'Alterlatinos' Are Changing the Scene," *Chicago Tribune*, 12 Sept. 2002: C6; Keith Negus, *Music Genres and Corporate Cultures* (New York: Routledge, 1999), 134; Neda Ulaby, "U.S. Crossover Hits Elude Latin Alternative," *All Things Considered*, National Public Radio, 8 March 2006; Kate King, "Hispanic Buying Power, Entrepreneurship on the Rise," *CNN.com*, 1 Oct. 2007 http://www.cnn.com/2007/US/10/01/hispanics.economy/index.html; John Lannert, "Latin Sales Swell in First Half of '99," *Billboard*, 21 Aug. 1999: 8; Leila Cobo, "Latin Music Sales Plummet in 2007," Reuters.com, 10 Dec. 2007 <http://www.reuters.com/article/musicNews/idUSN1043099320071210>; Robert Walser, *Running With the Devil. Power, Gender and Madness in Heavy Metal Music* (Hanover, NH: Wesleyan University Press/University Press of New England, 1993), xi; Keith Negus, *Producing Pop: Culture and Conflict in the Popular Music Industry* (New York: E. Arnold, 1992), 79.

14. Frances R. Aparicio, "On Sub-Versive Signifiers: Tropicalizing Language in the United States," *Tropicalizations: Transcultural Representations of Latinidad*, ed. Frances R. Aparicio and Susana Chávez-Silverman (Hanover, NH: University Press of New England, 1997), 196.

15. Licia Fiol-Matta, "Pop *Latinidad*: Puerto Ricans in the Latin Explosion, 1999," *CENTRO Journal* 14, no. 1 (2002): 31.

16. Christopher John Farley with David E. Thigpen, "Christina Aguilera: Building a 21st Century Star," *Time*, 6 March 2000: 71.

17. Peter Watrous, " A Country Now Ready to Listen," *New York Times*, 27 June 1999: 27.

18. Néstor García Canclini, *Hybrid Cultures. Strategies for Entering and Leaving Modernity*, trans. Christopher L. Chiappari and Silvia L. López (Minneapolis: University of Minnesota Press, 1995), 69.

19. Helene A. Shugart, "Crossing Over: Hybridity and Hegemony in the Popular Media," *Communication and Critical/Cultural Studies* 4.2 (2007): 115–141.

20. Bacilos, "*Mi primer millón*," *Caraluna*, Warner Music Latina, 2002. Other Miami-based Colombian musicians are undoubtedly aware of the power that Emilio Estefan enjoys in Latin(o) music industry. During a Miami concert that I attended, Carlos Vives appeared, as he often does in interviews, keenly aware of the Cuban business community's influence. First, he publicly thanked Miami Cubans for their kind treatment of him; more notably, he then proceeded to insert Emilio Estefan's name in a call-and-response improvisation in between musical numbers (Carlos Vives, Concert, Miami Arena, Miami, FL, 6 Sept. 2000). A tongue-in-cheek reference to capital's role in the Miami industry comes from the popular U.S.-Cuban rapper and Miami native Pitbull, who cleverly titled his 2004 and 2005 albums *M.I.A.M.I. (Money Is a Major Issue)* and *M.I.A.M.I. (Money Is Still a Major Issue)*, respectively.

21. Timothy Mitchell, qtd. in Andrew Leyshon, David Matless, and George Revill, preface, *The Place of Music*, ed. Andrew Leyshon, David Matless, and George Revill (New York: Guilford Press, 1998), 17; Carlos G. Vélez-Ibáñez and Anna Sampaio, "Introduction: Processes, New Prospects, and Approaches," in *Transnational Latino Communities: Politics, Processes, and Cultures*, ed. Carlos Vélez-Ibáñez and Anna Sampaio (Lanham, MD: Rowman & Littlefield, 2002), 5.

22. John Lovering, "The Global Music Industry: Contradictions in the Commodification of the Sublime," in *The Place of Music*, ed. Andrew Leyshon, David Matless, and George Revill (New York: Guilford Press, 1998) 41.

23. Gregory W. Bush, "'Playground of the USA': Miami and the Promotion of Spectacle," *Pacific Historical Review* 68.2 (May 1999): 153–154.

24. Juan León, "Tropical Overexposure: Miami's 'Sophisticated Tropics' and the *Balsero*," in *Tropicalizations: Transcultural Representations of Latinidad*, ed. Frances R. Aparicio and Susana Chávez-Silverman (Hanover, NH: University Press of New England, 1997). 215.

25. Grenier and Castro 291.

26. George Yúdice, "La industria de la música en la integración América Latina—Estados Unidos," in *Las industrias culturales en la integración latinoamericana*, ed. Néstor García Canclini and Carlos Moneta (Buenos Aires: Eudeba, 2003), 139; Beverley and Houston 421. For an exceedingly problematic journalistic description of Miami's recent history, see James Kelly, "Trouble in Paradise," *www.time.com*, 23 Nov. 1981 <http://www.time.com/time/printout/0,8816,922693,00.html>.

27. Leyshon et al,11.

28. Yúdice, *Expediency* 204.

29. Ibid. 198.

30. Ibid. 199. As John Sinclair argues, however, the label "Latin Hollywood" is actually somewhat of a misnomer, given that Miami, unlike Hollywood, is the capital of Latin(o) American television and music production, not the film industry; see John Sinclair, "'The Hollywood of Latin America': Miami as Regional Center in Television Trade," *Television & New Media* 4.3 (2003): 12.

31. Katynka Z. Martínez, "American Idols With Caribbean Soul: Cubanidad and the Latin Grammys," *Latino Studies* 4 (2006): 383; Negus, *Music Genres* 140; M. Whitefield, cited in Robert Hanke, "'Yo Quiero Mi MTV!': Making Music Television for Latin Amer-

ica," in *Mapping the Beat: Popular Music and Contemporary Theory*, ed. Thomas Swiss, John Sloop, and Andrew Herman (Malden, MA: Blackwell, 1998), 240.

32. Associated Press, "Hispanics Set to Surpass Blacks in Buying Power in U.S.," *International Herald Tribune*, 1 Sept. 2006 <http://iht.com.bin/print_ipub.php?file=?/articles/ap/2006/09/01/business/NA_FIN_US_Hispanics_Buying_Power.php>.

33. Deborah Pacini Hernández, "Race, Ethnicity and the Production of Latin/o Popular Music," in *Global Repertoires: Popular Music Within and Beyond the Transnational Music Industry*, ed. Andreas Gebesmair and Alfred Smudits (Aldershot: Ashgate, 2001) 60; Negus, *Music Genres* 153; Yúdice, "La industria" 116, 121, 126, 134; Katynka Zazueta Martínez, "The 'Latin Explosion,' Media Audiences, and the Marketing of Latino Panethnicity: Latina Magazine and the Latin Grammys in a Post-Selena América" (Ph.D. diss., University of California, San Diego, 2003),154–155; Luis Clemens, "The Sound That Sells," *Marketing y Medios* (Dec. 2005) <www.marketingymedios.com/marketingymedios/magazine/article_display.jsp?vun_content_id=100>. *Billboard* magazine began to employ Soundscan technology in participating retailers in order to track Latin(o) music sales in 1993. However, as Katynka Zazueta Martínez explains, the average retail cost of the equipment necessary to be added to Soundscan's database is$5,000, rendering it cost-prohibitive to many family-run, independent music stores in the Latin(o) community. The overrepresentation of large chain stores (which tend to focus on Latin[o] pop music sales) in Soundscan figures thus promotes the erasure of working-class cites of consumption, as reflected in the Latin Grammy's continued slights of Mexican Regional music. This is not to suggest, however, that Mexican Regional's consumers are solely working class or that Latin(o) pop is exclusively consumed by Latin(o) America's middle and upper classes.

34. Yúdice, *Expediency* 203; Daniel Shoer Roth, "Miami, Capital de la Música," *El Nuevo Herald*, 12 June 1999: 1A; Howard Cohen, "There's Something About Miami," *Billboard*, 15 May 1999: 54.

35. James R. Curtis and Richard F. Rose, "'The Miami Sound': A Contemporary Latin Form of Place-Specific Music," in *The Sounds of People and Places: A Geography of American Folk and Popular Music* (3rd ed.), ed. George O. Carney (Lanham, MD: Rowman & Littlefield, 1994), 265–266.

36. Yúdice, "La industria" 140–141.

37. See Yúdice, *Expediency*; Sinclair 221, 224.

38. Negus, *Music Genres* 143–145. Another factor impacting the production and (in a more indirect sense) distribution of Latin(o) music is payola. Though certainly not new to the music industry as a whole, payola has emerged as endemic to the New York, Los Angeles, and Miami Latin(o) radio networks in particular. The pervasiveness of payola within Latin(o) radio, which increases recording promotion expenses by an additional 20 to 30 percent, has most notably impacted smaller recording studios and ultimately curtailed the range of new artists and genres accessible to audiences, even in the face of the boom's myriad crossover successes. Jordan Levin, "Payola Called Fixture in Latin Music," *Miami Herald*, 8 Dec. 2002: n.p.

39. Alex Aponte, "Miami, the Media Heavy," *Hispanic Business*, July–August 1998: 54; see also Sinclair.

40. Tammerlin Drummond, "Godfather of the Miami Sound," *Time*, 24 May 1999:78.

41. Curtis and Rose 269–270; Jordan Levin, "Miami's Potent Musical Mix," *Variety*, 10–16 June 1996: 49 (emphasis mine); Jordan Levin, "Grammy-Winning Producer Touts Heart Over High-Tech," *Variety*, 10–16 June 1996: 56.

42. Grammy Awards, CBS, 23 Feb. 2000.

43. Trouillot xix, 28; Ali Behdad, *A Forgetful Nation: On Immigration and Cultural Identity in the United States* (Durham, NC: Duke University Press, 2005), 176.

44. Pacini Hernández, 63–64.

45. Zazueta Martínez 139, 203; Pacini Hernández 64.

46. Zazueta Martínez 176; Mireya Navarro, "Latin Grammys Border Skirmish," *newyorktoday.com*, 13 Sept. 2000 <.../genListing.htm&categoryid=30&only+y&bfromind+1815&eeid=3066484&eetype=article&ren>; see Martínez, "American Idols."

47. Willie Colón, qtd. in Edgardo Soto Torres, "Willie Colón: gestor de la salsa acosado por el boicot," *Diálogo*, Nov. 1999: 20.

48. For a more comprehensive perspective of the issues involved in this long-running debate, see Peter Manuel, "Puerto Rican Music and Cultural Identity: Creative Appropriation of Cuban Sources From Danza to Salsa," *Ethnomusicology* 38.2 (1994): 249–280, and Marisol Berríos-Miranda, "'Con Sabor a Puerto Rico': The Reception and Influence of Puerto Rican Salsa in Venezuela," in *Musical Migrations: Transnationalism and Cultural Hybridity in Latin/o America*, ed. Frances R. Aparicio and Cándida Jáquez with María Elena Cepeda (New York: St. Martin's Press, 2003), 47–67.

49. In 1999, during the height of the Latin(o) music boom, Mexican regional music accounted for approximately 60 percent of U.S. Latino music sales (Zazueta Martínez 169); "Emilio Estefan tilda a Willie Colón de izquierdista," *El Universal*, 20 Oct. 2000 <http://www.el-universal.com.mx>; Navarro. In accordance with the Estefans' wishes, the 2001 Latin Grammys were scheduled to be held in Miami; however, amid protests from local U.S.-Cubans angered by the inclusion of Cuban musicians, the Latin Grammys were moved to Los Angeles a few weeks prior to the ceremonies. The 2001 ceremonies were ultimately canceled in the wake of the September 11 terrorist attacks on the United States. Los Angeles again became the site of the Latin Grammys in 2002, though by this time television ratings had fallen so much that plans for televising future ceremonies were uncertain. In the years immediately following, Miami and Los Angeles continued to alternate hosting privileges. However, by 2006 the Latin Grammys ceremonies had moved to New York City, followed by Las Vegas, Nevada (2007), and Houston, Texas (2008).

50. Zazueta Martínez 140, 171.

51. See Ed Morales, *Living in Spanglish: The Search for Latino Identity in America* (New York: St. Martin's Press, 2002), 216–218; Ed Morales, *The Latin Beat: The Rhythms and Roots of Latin Music From Bossa Nova to Salsa and Beyond* (Cambridge, MA: Da Capo Press, 2003), 259–263.

52. Celeste Fraser Delgado, "Los Producers," *miaminewtimes.com*, 6 Sept. 2001 <http://www.miaminewtimes.com/issues/2001-09-06/feature.htm/print.html>; Leila Cobo, "Santander, Estefan Resolve Legal Quarrel," *Billboard*, 6 April 2002: 8.

53. Howard Llewellyn, "Estefan, GVM, and Sony Launch Long-Awaited Latin Label Sunnyluna," *Billboard*, 11 May 2002: 42.

54. Morales, *The Latin Beat* 296, 315; Leila Cobo, interview with John Ystdie, *All Things Considered*, National Public Radio, 18 Sept. 2002; Carlos Agudelo, "New Colombian Sounds Coming to U.S. Market," *Billboard*, 15 Jan. 1983: 43.

55. One such early mention of a New York tour stop can be found in Enrique Fernández, "Topline Colombian," *Village Voice*, 1 Feb. 1983: 81–82, a feature on the *vallenato* great Lisandro Meza. Iván Cuesta's Maryland-based band has also gained a measure of success in the United States, having recorded an album for the Arhoolie music label (Iván Cuesta y sus Baltimore Vallenatos, *A Ti, Colombia*, Arhoolie, 1993).

56. Celeste Fraser Delgado, personal interview, 23 May 2002; "Richard Blair: un británico pachangero," *www.boomonline.com*, 3 June 2002 <http: www.boomonline.com/htmls/e_blair.html>; Miguel A. Sirgado, "Sidestepper: música colombiana de vibra suave," *El Nuevo Herald*, 15 Aug. 2003: 1C; Julienne Gage, "The British *Invasión*," *www.miaminewtimes.com*, 17 May 2007 <http://music.miaminewtimes.com/2007-05-17/music/the-british-invasi-oacute-n/print>; Simon Frith, "The Discourse of World Music," in *Western Music and Its Others: Difference, Representation, and Appropriation in Music*, ed. Georgina Born and David Hesmondhalgh (Berkeley: University of California Press, 2000) 309. A more industry-inspired perspective on Latin(o) music's recent growth and its relationship to (im)migrant demographics can be found in Cathleen Farrell and Valeria Escobari's article "¡Que le pongan salsa!" *Poder*, April 2002: 22–26.

57. Curtis and Rose 266. In their comprehensive discussion of the roots of the Miami Sound, the authors trace the genre's origins back to the U.S. -Cuban musician and recording executive Carlos Oliva.

58. See, for example, Fernández; Habell-Pallán; Raquel Z. Rivera, *New York Ricans from the Hip-Hop Zone* (New York: Palgrave Macmillan, 2003); Juan Flores, *From Bomba to Hip-Hop: Puerto Rican Culture and Latino Identity* (New York: Columbia University Press, 2000); John Storm Roberts, *The Latin Tinge: The Impact of Latin American Music on the United States* (2nd ed.) (New York and Oxford: Oxford University Press, 1999); Frances R. Aparicio, *Listening to Salsa: Gender, Latin Popular Music, and Puerto Rican Cultures* (Hanover, NH: Wesleyan University Press/University Press of New England, 1998); Ruth Glasser, *My Music Is My Flag: Puerto Rican Musicians and Their New York Communities, 1917–1940* (Berkeley: University of California Press, 1995); and Manuel H. Peña, *The Texas-Mexican Conjunto: History of a Working-Class Music* (Austin: University of Texas Press, 1985), among others.

59. Glasser, *My Music* 4, xix.

60. Timothy Taylor, qtd. in Heidi Feldman, *Black Rhythms of Peru: Reviving African Music Heritage in the Black Pacific* (Middletown, CT: Wesleyan University Press, 2006), 216. The phrase "Columbus Effect" is borrowed from Wilson Valentín-Escobar as he employs it in his own research on Latin(o) popular music. Wilson Valentín-Escobar, ""Between Salsa and Jazz: The Latin Scene in New York," Center for African and African American Studies, University of Michigan, Ann Arbor, Fall 1998; Wilson Valentín-Escobar, "Marketing Memory/Marketing Authenticity in Buena Vista Social Club Recordings," Latin American Studies Association International Congress, Hyatt Regency Hotel, Miami, 16 Mar. 2000. For a comprehensive analysis of the musical production and media representation of Susana Baca, see Feldman chapter 6.

61. Trouillot 114.

62. García Canclini, *Transforming* viii.

63. *Buena Vista Social Club*, DVD, directed by Wim Wenders (Lion's Gate, 1999); Frances R. Aparicio and Susana Chávez-Silverman, introduction, *Tropicalizations: Transcultural Representations of Latinidad*, ed. Frances R. Aparicio and Susana Chávez-Silverman (Hanover, NH: University Press of New England, 1997), 8–14.

64. Tanya Katerí Hernández, "The Buena Vista Social Club: The Racial Politics of Nostalgia," in *Latino/a Popular Culture*, ed. Michelle Habell-Pallán and Mary Romero (New York: New York University Press, 2002), 67.

65. Stuart Hall, "The Whites of Their Eyes: Racist Ideologies and the Media," in *Silver Linings: Some Strategies for the Eighties: Contributions to the Communist University of London*, ed. Communist University of London (London: Lawrence and Wishart, 1981) 38 (emphasis in original).

66. Valentín-Escobar, "Marketing."

67. García Canclini, *Transforming* 40.

68. Ibid. vii. García Canclini, *Hybrid* 5. In an analogous vein, Hall ("The Local and the Global," 38–39) notes that

> All the most explosive modern musics are crossovers. The aesthetics of modern popular music is the aesthetic of the hybrid, the aesthetics of the crossover, the aesthetics of the diaspora, the aesthetics of creolization. It is the mix of musics which is exciting to a young person who comes right out of what Europe is pleased to think of as some ancient civilization, and which Europe can control. The West can only control it if only they will stay there, if only they will remain simple tribal folks. The moment they want to get hold of, not the nineteenth-century technology to make all of the mistakes the West did for another hundred years, but to leap over that and get hold of some of the modern technologies to speak their own tongue, to speak of their own condition, then they are out of place, then the Other is not where it is. The primitive has somehow escaped from control.

69. Trouillot 96.

70. At a panel discussion for professional musicians at a Smithsonian Institution conference gathering, Jerry González remarked that the Buena Vista Social Club, despite high record sales, is not considered particularly musically innovative within professional circles, and he in fact criticized its simplification of Afro-Caribbean percussive techniques. I found his perspective as a professional musician to be of particular interest, given that his assessment of the mostly Afro-Cuban Buena Vista Club's music as "inauthentic" runs directly counter to that of most world music consumers. Jerry González, Música de las Américas: Salsa and Latin Jazz, panel discussion, Smithsonian Institution, S. Dillon Ripley Center, Washington, DC, 31 July 1999.

71. Valentín-Escobar, "Marketing."

72. Ruth Glasser, "Musical Darwinism," Música de las Américas: Salsa and Latin Jazz, panel discussion, Smithsonian Institution, S. Dillon Ripley Center, Washington, DC, 31 July 1999.

73. It appears that the majority of Buena Vista consumers are Anglos between thirty-five and fifty-five years of age, who initially learned of the group through newspapers, public radio, or the *Buena Vista* documentary feature. Largely because the decades-old *son* style that dominates the group's repertoire might be considered outdated by a U.S.

Latino audience with a median age of twenty-six, the album's distributors (World Circuit/ Nonesuch) focused on the world music market rather than a Latino consumer base. See Alisa Valdés-Rodríguez, "Who's Buying Cuban Phenom?" *Los Angeles Times*, 14 Aug. 1999 <http://www.picadillo.com/vdesign/articles/990814~1.HTML>.

74. Deborah Pacini Hernández, "Dancing With the Enemy: Cuban Popular Music, Race, Authenticity, and the World-Music Landscape," *Latin American Perspectives*, 25.3 (May 1998): 110–111, 122.

75. Reebee Garofalo, "Black Popular Music: Crossing Over or Going Under?" in *Rock and Popular Music: Politics, Policies, and Institutions*, ed. Tony Bennett, Simon Frith, Lawrence Grossberg, John Shepherd, and Graeme Turner (New York: Routledge, 1993), 231.

76. Reebee Garafalo, *Rockin' Out: Popular Music in the USA* (Boston: Allyn and Bacon, 1997), 11–12.

77. Kristen Baldwin, "The Best Next Thing," *Entertainment Weekly*, 31 March 2000: 22.

78. Juan M. Méndez, "Unbottled and Unleashed: Christina Aguilera," *Latina*, Dec. 1999: 81 (emphasis mine).

79. Pedro Cabán, "The New Synthesis of Latin American and Latino Studies," in *Borderless Borders: U.S. Latinos, Latin Amercians, and the Paradox of Interdependence*, ed. Frank Bonilla, Edwin Meléndez, Rebecca Morales, and María de los Angeles Torres (Philadelphia: Temple University Press, 1998), 203–204.

80. Baldwin 28.

81. Yúdice, *The Expediency* 208.

82. Suzanne E. Smith, *Dancing in the Street: Motown and the Cultural Politics of Detroit* (Cambridge, MA: Harvard University Press), 88, 163–164, 167.

83. Negus, *Producing Pop* 68–69.

84. Christopher John Farley, "Latin Music Pops," *Time*, 24 May 1999: 78; Angharad N.Valdivia, "Latinas as Radical Hybrid: Transnationally Gendered Traces in Mainstream Media," *Global Media Journal* 4.7 (2004) <http://lass.calumet.purdue.edu/gmj/refereed/htm>.

85. Frank Pellegrini, "America Goes Mucho Loco for Ricky," *time daily*, 3 May 1999 <http://www.pathfinder.com/time/daily/0,2960,24750,00.htm> (emphasis in original).

86. Ibid.

87. Chris Willman, "Marque Marc," *EW Magazine*, 8 Oct. 1999 <http://www.pathfinder.com/...r_ref+ON&mtype=0&list_size=25&direction.htm>.

88. Rodrigo Salazar, "An Icon Goes Pop!: *Ricky siempre será nuestro*," *Urban Latino* (June-July 2000): 46.

89. Farley 79; Willman; *Latin Beat*, ABC, 7 Sept. 1999.

90. Guy García, "Another Latin Boom, but Different," *New York Times*, 27 June 1999: 27.

91. Fiol-Matta 46 (emphasis in original).

92. The latter title ironically refers to Gloria Estefan's 1987 hit "The Rhythm Is Gonna Get You," a connection that leads one to wonder just how up-tempo the rhythm in question could possibly be, as it took twelve years to arrive.

93. See Aparicio and Chávez-Silverman 1–17.

CHAPTER 3

1. Daniel Mato, "On Global and Local Agents and the Social Making of Transnational Identities and Related Agendas in 'Latin' America," *Identities* 4.2 (1997): 168–169; Peggy Levitt, "Transnational Ties and Incorporation: The Case of Dominicans in the United States," in *The Columbia History of Latinos in the United States Since 1960*, ed. David G. Gutiérrez (New York: Columbia University Press, 2004), 241–242; Nina Glick Schiller and Georges Fouron, "Transnational Lives and National Identities: The Identity Politics of Haitian Immigrants," in *Transnationalism From Below*, ed. Michael Peter Smith and Luis Eduardo Guarnizo (New Brunswick, NJ: Transaction, 1998) 133.

2. Michael Peter Smith and Luis Eduardo Guarnizo, "The Locations of Transnationalism," introduction, *Transnationalism from Below*, ed. Luis Eduardo Guarnizo and Michael Peter Smith (New Brunswick, NJ: Transaction, 1998), 19; Luin Goldring, "The Power of Status in Transnational Social Fields," in *Transnationalism from Below*, ed. Michael Peter Smith and Luis Eduardo Guarnizo (New Brunswick, NJ: Transaction, 1998), 166; Larry Rohter, "Rock en Español Is Approaching Its Final Border," *New York Times*, 6 Aug. 2000, late ed.: 2.27. The ubiquitous MTV (Music Television) channel emerges as a prime example in this regard, just as the now-defunct "*Show de Cristina*" and the wildly popular Colombian soap opera "*Yo soy Betty, la Fea*" ("I'm Betty, the Ugly One") (now *Ugly Betty*, an award-winning ABC series) also come to mind. On a related note, NBC's $1.98 billion purchase of Telemundo, the U.S.'s second-largest Spanish-language television broadcaster, in 2002, is proving an interesting factor in NBC's future programming decisions. It is likely that NBC executives took note of the fact that throughout the spring of 2001, the highly successful *Friends* series was consistently beaten in the prime-time ratings in the Miami and Los Angeles markets by Telemundo's airing of the transnational Colombian hit. Andrew Ross Sorkin, "NBC Is Paying $1.98 Billion for Telemundo," *New York Times*, 12 Oct. 2001: C1.

3. Arjun Appadurai, *Modernity at Large: Cultural Dimensions of Globalization* (Minneapolis: University of Minnesota Press, 1996), 35; Ella Shohat and Robert Stam, *Unthinking Eurocentrism: Multiculturalism and the Media* (New York: Routledge, 1994), 6–7.

4. Smith and Guarnizo 10, 12; see Aihwa Ong, *Flexible Citizenship: The Cultural Logics of Transnationality* (Durham, NC: Duke University Press, 1999), for a more complete critique of this overly celebratory view of transnational dynamics.

5. Denis-Constant Martin, "The Choices of Identity," *Social Identities* 1.1 (1995): 7.

6. Stacy Takacs, "Alien-Nation: Immigration, National Identity and Transnationalism," *Cultural Studies* 13.4 (1999): 596 (emphasis in original).

7. Angharad N.Valdivia, "Latinas as Radical Hybrid: Transnationally Gendered Traces in Mainstream Media," *Global Media Journal* 4.7 (2004) <http://lass.calumet.purdue.edu/gmj/refereed/htm>. According to Valdivia, "radical hybrids" are those individuals or communities composed of "hybrids[s] of hybrids." She argues that the predilection toward representing Latino hybridity solely in the terms of a "brown race" ultimately elides the group's heterogeneity.

8. Chandra Talpade Mohanty, "Cartographies of Struggle: Third World Women and the Politics of Feminism," introduction, *Third World Women and the Politics of Feminism*, ed. Chandra Talpade Mohanty, Ann Russo, and Lourdes Torres (Bloomington: Indiana University Press, 1991), 28; Renato Rosaldo, "Cultural Citizenship, Inequality, and

Multiculturalism," in *Latino Cultural Citizenship. Claiming Identity, Space, and Rights*, ed. William V. Flores and Rina Benmayor (Boston: Beacon Press, 1997) 29. Recent scholarship addressing the topic of *Latinidad*, such as Suzanne Oboler's landmark ethnographic study *Ethnic Labels, Latino Lives: Identity and the Politics of (Re)Presentation in the United States* (Minneapolis: University of Minnesota Press, 1995), offers a more nuanced account of what I term the "epistemology of *Latinidad*"; see also Mérida M. Rúa, "Latinidades," in *Oxford Encyclopedia of Latinos and Latinas in the United States*, ed. Suzanne Oboler and Deena J. González (New York: Oxford University Press, 2005), 505–507. Aihwa Ong's notion of "flexible citizenship" also proves particularly useful to our understanding of Shakira's case. As she notes, "'flexible citizenship' refers to the cultural logics of capitalist accumulation, travel and displacement that induce subjects to respond fluidly and opportunistically to changing political-economic conditions" (6). For additional discussion of the material and symbolic links between identity documents and elite transnational citizenship, see Benedict Anderson, "Exodus," *Critical Inquiry* 20.2 (1994): 314–327.

9. Jillian Baéz, "'En mi imperio': Competing Discourses of Agency in Ivy Queen's Reggaetón," *CENTRO Journal* 18.1 (2006): 62–81.

10. George Lipsitz, "World Cities and World Beat: Low-Wage Labor and Transnational Culture," *Pacific Historical Review* 68.2 (May 1999): 215.

11. Renato Rosaldo, *Culture and Truth: The Remaking of Social Analysis* (Boston: Beacon Press, 1989), 198. Per this perspective, "authentic" U.S. identity is synonymous with the cultural "lack" most often expressed through one's (white, Anglo-Saxon) ethnoracial status, as well as the seemingly wholesale erasure of collective or individual genealogical memory.

12. Blanca G. Silvestrini, "'The World We Enter When Claiming Our Rights': Latinos and Their Quest for Culture," in *Latino Cultural Citizenship. Claiming Identity, Space, and Rights*, ed. William V. Flores and Rina Benmayor (Boston: Beacon Press, 1997), 44.

13. Mike Davis, *Magical Urbanism: Latinos Reinvent the U.S. Big City* (London: Verso, 2000), 77, 80–81.

14. Luis Eduardo Guarnizo and Luz Marina Díaz, "Transnational Migration: A View From Colombia," *Ethnic and Racial Studies* 22:2 (March 1999): 397; "Colombian Migration to South Florida"; Mato 192–193. For a more recent portrayal of the community-building efforts of Miami-based U.S.-Colombians, see Andrea Elliott, "Thousands Flee War in Colombia, Plan New Lives in U.S.," *Miami Herald*, 29 Aug. 2001.

15. See Luis Eduardo Guarnizo, Arturo Ignacio Sánchez, and Elizabeth M. Roach, "Mistrust, Fragmented Solidarity and Transnational Migration: Colombians in New York City and Los Angeles," *Ethnic and Racial Studies* 22.3 (March 1999): 367–396; Guarnizo and Díaz; Ong; Natalia Franco, "The Colombian Migration to South Florida: Expectations and Experiences" (master's thesis, Florida International University, 2002); John Britt Hunt, "Beyond the Drug Trafficker Stereotype: The Changing American Perceptions of Colombians" (master's thesis, Florida International University, 2002); and "Colombian Migration to South Florida.".

16. Glick Schiller and Fouron, "Transnational Lives" 141 (emphasis mine).

17. Regarding the often virulent strain of regionalism present within Colombia and its impact on Colombians in the United States, see Guarnizo and Díaz. For further discussion of the ways in which regionalism manifests itself within Colombian musical culture, see Peter Wade, *Music, Race and Nation: Música Tropical in Colombia* (Chicago: University of Chicago Press, 2000).

18. See Frances R. Aparicio, "The Blackness of Sugar: Celia Cruz and the Performance of (Trans)Nationalism," *Cultural Studies* 13.2 (1999): 223–236.

19. "Diosa coronada," *Semana*, 26 Feb. 2001: 27.

20. Leila Cobo, "A Rich Musical Tradition Swells Up and Out Into the World." *Miami Herald*, 25 July 1999: 5m, 7m.

21. Andrew Paxman, "Latinas Making Music: *Cantautoras* Shaking up Tune Industry," *Variety*, 31 Mar.-6 April 1997: 71; John Lannert, "Colombia's Shakira: I'm Here," *Billboard*, 15 June 1996: 1.

22. Wade, *Music, Race and Nation* 40–41, 43.

23. "Colombia," *New Grove Dictionary of Music and Musicians* (New York: Grove's Dictionaries, 1980).

24. Ed Morales, "*Colombia te canto*: The Redeeming Power of Music," *Hopscotch* 1.4 (1999): 43.

25. Jorge Arévalo-Mateus, "The Colombian Costeño Musicians of the New York Metropolitan Region: A Manifestation of Urban Vallenato" (master's thesis, Hunter College, CUNY, 1998, 52–56; also see Celeste Fraser Delgado, "Not for Export," www.miamisunpost.com, 23 Feb. 2006 <http://www.miamisunpost.com/archives/2006/02-23-06/entertainment%20industry.htm>. Queens is better known among the U.S. diaspora, however, for its annual Colombian Independence Day festivities, celebrated each July, which constitutes the largest Colombian party held in the United States. Miami hosts a similar event each year. Cities with smaller Colombian populations, such as San Francisco, have also staged Colombian arts festivals and the like, just as Colombian Independence Day parties have been held more recently in locales as diverse as Minneapolis, Minnesota, and Springfield, Massachusetts.

26. Interestingly, accounts of the Middle Eastern and Italian immigrant presence on the Coast cite the relative ease with which they were incorporated into *costeño* culture, in contrast to the more lengthy process of assimilation experienced by migrants from Colombia's own interior departments. See Oliverio Del Villar Sierra, "Significa resistir," in *Colombia: País de regiones*, ed. Fabio Zambrano F. (Bogotá: Cinep, 1998), 305.

27. Leila Cobo-Hanlon, "Barefoot Girl: Pop Diva Shakira Comes of Age," *L.A. Weekly*, 22 Nov. 1996: 51.

28. Cobo, "Rich," 5m, 7m.

29. Anna Cristina Báez, personal communication, 30 Nov. 2000.

30. Steve Dorfman, Luis R. Rigual, and Linda Marx, "The City's Most Fascinating Faces of 2000," *Miami Metro*, Dec. 2000: 31–36.

31. Leila Cobo, "Shakira x2," *azcentral.com*, 24 May 2005 <http://www.azcentral.com/ent/music/articles/0525shakira.html>.

32. *Mil gracias* to Annette Alonso for her astute observation in this regard. See Shakira, *Shakira, MTV Unplugged*, Videocassette, Sony Music, 2000; Suzanne Oboler, "Introduction: *Los que llegaron*: 50 Years of South American Immigration (1950–2000)—An Overview," *Latino Studies* 3 (2005): 42–52.

33. Simon Frith, "Towards an Aesthetic of Popular Music," in *Music and Society. The Politics of Composition, Performance, and Reception*, ed. Susan McClary and Richard Leppert (Cambridge: Cambridge University Press, 1987), 140.

34. Ibid. 141.

35. Bruce Orwall, "The Burden of Power: The U.S. in the 21st Century," *The Wall Street Journal*, 13 Feb. 2001: A1 (emphasis mine).

36. Andrew Leyshon, David Matless, and George Revill, preface, *The Place of Music*, ed. Andrew Leyshon, David Matless, and George Revill (New York: Guilford Press, 1998), 14.

37. Celeste Fraser Delgado, "Viva Colombia! Could Shakira End the Economic Slump?" *miaminewtimes.com*, 22 Nov. 2001 <http://ww.miaminewtimes.com/issues/2001-11-22/shake.html/print.html>.

38. Mark Kemp, "*Rock en español*: The Latin Invasion," *Paste* (April-May 2005): 83; Cobo, "Shakira x 2."

39. Christopher John Farley, "The Making of a Rocker," *Time*, Fall 2001: 17.

40. Juana Suárez, "Sites of Contention: Colombian Cultural Production at the Threshold of a New Millennium" (Ph.D. diss., Arizona State University, 2000), 82.

41. For a detailed analysis of the complex dynamics of Latino fandom and reception practices, see Frances R. Aparicio, *Listening to Salsa: Gender, Latin Popular Music and Puerto Rican Cultures* (Hanover, NH: Wesleyan University Press/University Press of New England, 1998); Jillian Báez, "Mexican (American) Women Talk Back: Audience Responses to Representations of Latinidad in U.S. Advertising," *Latina/o Communication Studies Today*, ed. Angharad N. Valdivia (New York: Peter Lang, 2008), 62–81; Dolores Inés Casillas, "Sounds of Belonging: A Cultural History of Spanish-Language Radio in the United States" (Ph.D. diss., University of Michigan, 2006); Rosa Linda Fregoso, *MeXicana Encounters: The Making of Social Identities on the Borderlands* (Berkeley: University of California Press, 2003); Dolores Inés Casillas and María Elena Cepeda, "How *Tejas* Arrived at *La Isla*: Jennifer López, Selena, and the Construction of a Latina Iconography," lecture, Puerto Rican Studies Association, Chicago, IL, 4 October 2002; María Elena Cepeda, "Survival Aesthetics: U.S. Latinas and the Negotiation of Popular Media," in *Latina/o Communication Studies Today*, ed. Angharad N. Valdivia (New York: Peter Lang, 2008), 237–256; Silvia Paz-Frydman, "The Latina Body and the Entertainment Industry: The Practices of Resistance, Hegemony, and Identity Construction" (Unpublished manuscript, Williams College, Williamstown, MA, 2006); Yeidy M. Rivero, "The Performance and Reception of Televisual 'Ugliness' in *Yo soy Betty la fea*," *Feminist Media Studies* 3.1 (2003): 65–82; Viviana Rojas, "The Gender of *Latinidad*: Latinas Speak About Hispanic Television," *Communication Review* 7 (2004): 125–153, and Angharad N. Valdivia, *A Latina in the Land of Hollywood and Other Essays on Media Culture* (Tucson: University of Arizona Press, 2000).

42. Dániza Tobar, "¡Una sirena única!: La *Next Big Thing* entró a la cancha," *Ocean Drive En Español* (Dec. 2001): 65.

43. Leyshon et. al., 14; John Lovering, "The Global Music Industry: Contradictions in the Commodification of the Sublime," in *The Place of Music*, ed. Andrew Leyshon, David Matless, and George Revill (New York: Guilford Press, 1998), 45.

44. Jon Weiderhorn, "Make Shakira Dance for You Whenever, Wherever," mtv.com, 5 Nov. 2001 <http://www.mtv.com.news/articles/1458520/20021105/shakira.jhtml?headlines=true>. For further discussion of the sociocultural significance of "Latina" Barbie dolls, see Frances Negrón-Muntaner, *Boricua Pop: Puerto Ricans and the Latinization of American Culture* (New York: New York University Press, 2004), 206–227.

45. Orwall A1.

46. "Diosa"; "No pienso sacrificar mi personalidad," *Semana*, 24 Sept. 2001: 117.

47. Angharad N. Valdivia with Ramona Curry, "Xuxa! Can Latin Americans Be Blonde or Can the United States Tolerate a Latin American?"; Angharad N. Valdivia, *A Latina in the Land of Hollywood*, 125–126.

48. Angharad Valdivia, "Is Penélope to J. Lo as Culture Is to Nature?" in *From Bananas to Buttocks: The Latina Body in Popular Film and Culture*, ed. Myra Medible (Austin, TX: University of Texas Press, 2007), 129–148; Chuck Arnold and Linda Trischitta, "*Bomba* shell," *People*, 11 Feb. 2002: 136; Tobar 66; Jane Desmond, "Embodying Difference: Issues in Dance and Cultural Studies," in *Everynight Life: Culture and Dance in Latin/o America*, ed. Celeste Fraser Delgado and José Esteban Muñoz (Durham: Duke University Press, 1997), 48, 50–51.

49. Deborah Parédez, "Remembering Selena, Re-remembering *Latinidad*," *Theatre Journal* 54 (2002): 82.

50. Fraser Delgado , "Viva Colombia!" (emphasis mine).

51. Celeste Rodas de Juárez, "Shakira: Música y amor," *Cosmopolitan en español*, Nov. 2001:

52. Suárez 81.

53. Dolores Inés Casillas, presentation, "From Colonial Hottentot to Post-Colonial 'Hottie': Jennifer López' Re(buttals) to White America," SCOR Conference, University of Michigan, Ann Arbor, February 13, 2000; Frances Negrón-Muntaner, "Jennifer's Butt," *Aztlán* 22 (Fall 1997): 189, 192.

54. Michel Foucault, *The History of Sexuality: An Introduction*, vol. I, trans. Robert Hurley (New York: Vintage Books, 1990), 157.

55. Adrian Deevoy, "Colombian Gold," *Maxim Blender* (April/May 2002): 100–107; Evan Wright, "Shakira," *Rolling Stone*, 11 April 2002: 68–76; 142; Lydia Martin, "Shakira Wants the World," *Latina* July 2001: 90–93, 13–-134.

56. Saidiya Hartman, "Seduction and the Uses of Power," in *Between Woman and Nation: Nationalisms, Transnational Feminisms, and the State*, ed. Norma Alarcón, Caren Kaplan, and Minoo Moallem (Durham, NC: Duke University Press, 1999): 123. Thanks to Margaret Crosby for pointing out to me the presence of military metaphors in many popular media articles about Shakira. It is worth noting, moreover, that while many articles on Shakira employ a metaphorical, militaristic vocabulary, all fail to mention the concrete impacts of the United States' involvement in Plan Colombia on the Colombian people, much less the millions of deaths, kidnappings, and displacements precipitated by decades of internal conflict.

57. For more on gender, rock music, and the ways in which journalists "authenticate" popular musicians, see Angela McRobbie and Simon Frith's essay "Rock and Sexuality" (1978), in *On Record: Rock, Pop, and the Written Word*, ed. Simon Frith and Andrew Goodwin (London: Routledge, 2000); Keith Negus, *Producing Pop: Culture and Conflict in the Popular Music Industry* (New York: E. Arnold, 1992); and Sheila Whiteley, ed., *Sexing the Groove: Popular Music and Gender* (New York: Routledge, 1997).

58. Eliseo Cardona, "Shakira: From Colombia to the World," *CDNOW*, 20 Sept. 2000 <http://www.cdnow.com>; "Diosa coronada" 27; James Clifford, "Diasporas," in *Internationalizing Cultural Studies: An Anthology*, ed. Ackbar Abbas and John Nguyet Erni (Malden, MA: Blackwell, 2005), 536; Ernesto Lechner, *Rock en Español: The Latin Alternative Rock Explosion* (Chicago: Chicago Review Press, 2005) xii (emphasis mine).

59. Sara Cohen, "Men Making a Scene: Rock Music and the Production of Gender," in *Sexing the Groove: Popular Music and Gender*, ed. Sheila Whiteley (London and New York: Routledge, 1997), 17; see also Barry Shank, *Dissonant Identities: The Rock 'n' Roll Scene in Austin, Texas* (Middleton, CT: Wesleyan University Press, 1994), as well as Will Straw, "Systems of Articulation, Logics of Change: Communities and Scenes in Popular Music," *Cultural Studies* 5.3 (1991): 368–388.

60. See Chandra Talpade Mohanty's canonical essay "Under Western Eyes: Feminist Scholarship and Colonial Discourses," in *Third World Women and the Politics of Feminism*, ed. Chandra Talpade Mohanty, Ann Russo, and Lourdes Torres (Bloomington: Indiana University Press, 1991), 51–80.

61. Rob Sheffield, "Shakira Sinks Her Colombian Flag," *Rolling Stone*, 31 Jan. 2002: 20 (emphasis in original).

62. Ibid. 20.

63. Frank Kogan, "River Deep, Freckle High," *! Voice* 26 Dec. 2001–1 Jan. 2002 <http://www.villagevoice.com/issues/0152/kogan.php>.

64. Aída Hurtado, "Relating to Privilege: Seduction and Rejection in the Subordination of White Women and Women of Color," in *Theorizing Feminism: Parallel Trends in the Humanities and Social Sciences*, ed. Anne C. Herrmann and Abigail J. Stewart (Hanover, NH: Wesleyan University Press, 1994), 144.

65. In this chorus, Shakira sings: "Underneath your clothes / There's an endless story / There's the man I chose / There's my territory / *And all the things I deserve / For being such a good girl honey*" ("Underneath Your Clothes, *Laundry Service*, Sony, 2001) (emphasis mine). Her partner de la Rúa also appears in the video for the hit single.

66. Tobar 66.

67. Ed Morales, "Fade to Blonde," *Urban Latino* (Dec.-Jan. 2001): 40 (emphasis mine).

68. Shakira, "*Se quiere se mata*," *Pies Descalzos*, Sony Discos, 1996. Having spoken with many of Shakira's listeners in the past several years, I have found that "*Se quiere se mata*" appears to be the song whose meaning is most highly contested among her fans. For example, one pro-choice U.S. Latina listener remarked to me that although she initially was a fan of Shakira's music, upon hearing "*Se quiere se mata*," she decided that she disagreed with what she interpreted as Shakira's overly conservative anti-abortion stance and, as a result, decided to stop listening to Shakira's albums. I would venture to speculate that this reading, which this particular listener formulated despite the inclusion of the song's lyrics in the album's liner notes, might be attributed in part to this listener's expectations regarding the type of political content (or lack thereof) to be found on a album of pop ballads directed at Latin(o) American teens, as well as to the power of Shakira's predominant media image as an apolitical female popular icon.

69. Norma Coates, "(R)evolution Now?: Rock and the Political Potential of Gender," in *Sexing the Groove: Popular Music and Gender*, ed. Sheila Whiteley (London and New York: Routledge, 1997), 58; Walser, *Running With the Devil* 110; Sheila Whiteley, "Challenging the Feminine: Annie Lennox, Androgyneity, and the Illusions of Identity," in *Women and Popular Music: Sexuality, Identity, and Subjectivity*, ed. Sheila Whiteley (New York: Routledge, 2000), 122. Many thanks to my students at the University of Michigan, Macalester College, and Williams College for sharing their invaluable insights regarding this song.

70. Shakira, *¿Dónde Están los Ladrones?*, advertisement, Columbia House Club Música Latina 1998: 1–2.

71. Shakira, "*Dónde están los ladrones?*" *Dónde están los ladrones*, Sony Discos, 1998 (emphasis mine).
72. "En la variedad está el placer," *Semana*, 5 Nov. 2001: 80.
73. Liliana Angélica Martínez, "Shakira es imparable," *ElTiempo.com*, 23 Feb. 2001 <http://eltiempo.terra.com.co/23-02-2001/rock_pf_3.html>; "La cantante Shakira, una buena noticia de Colombia," *El Tiempo.com*, 9 May 2001 <http://eltiempo.terra.com.co/09-05-2001/cult_pf_4.html>; Marcela Rodríguez, "Cartas a Shakira: orgullo nacional," *ElTiempo.com*, 6 May 2001 <http://www.eltiempo.terra.com.co/06-05-2001?cult_pf_6.html>.
74. Morales, "Colombia te canto" 34.
75. "Pastrana: 'Shakira, nuestra embajadora internacional," *ElTiempo.com*, 23 Feb. 2001 <http://www.eltiempo.terra.com.co/23-02-2001/rock_pf_5.html>.
76. Robert Alvarez, Jr., *Mangos, Chiles, and Truckers: The Business of Transnationalism* (Minneapolis: University of Minnesota Press, 2005),199.
77. George Yúdice, "Linking Cultural Citizenship and Transnationalism to the Movement for an Equitable Global Economy," *Latin American Studies Association FORUM* 37.1 (2006): 15–16.
78. Glick Schiller and Fouron, "Transnational Lives" 145, 153–154; Michael Peter Smith's work on the transnational community of Guanajuato, Mexico, and Napa, California, is an excellent case in point. See Suzanne Oboler, "South Americans," in *Oxford Encyclopedia of Latinos and Latinas in the United States*, ed. Suzanne Oboler and Deena J. González (New York: Oxford University Press, 2005),150; Michael Peter Smith, "Transnationalism, the State, and the Extraterritorial Citizen," *Politics & Society* 31.4 (2003): 476–502; Smith, "Power in Place."
79. Notably, by 1958, well before any other Latin American or Caribbean nation, Colombia permitted its citizens living in the United States to vote in Colombian presidential elections. The Colombian and the Dominican cases have thus foreshadowed key political shifts: by the year 2000, at least ten Latin American and ten Caribbean nations permitted some form of dual nationality. Peggy Levitt, "Transnational Ties and Incorporation: The Case of Dominicans in the United States," *Columbia History of Latinos in the United States Since 1960*, ed. David G. Gutiérrez (New York: Columbia University Press, 2004), 244.
80. Smith, "Power in Place," 14; Luis Eduardo Guarnizo, "On the Political Participation of Transnational Migrants: Old Practices and New Trends," in *E Pluribus Unum?: Contemporary and Historical Perspectives on Immigrant Political Participation*, ed. Gary Gerstle and John Mollenkopf (New York: Russell Sage Foundation, 2001), 237–238; Cristina Escobar, "Dual Citizenship and Political Participation: Migrants in the Interplay of United States and Colombian Politics," in *Latinos and Citizenship: The Dilemma of Belonging*, ed. Suzanne Oboler (New York: Palgrave Macmillan, 2006), 113–141; Luis Eduardo Guarnizo and Marilyn Espitia, "Colombia," *The New Americans: A Guide to Immigration Since 1965*, ed. Mary C. Waters and Reed Ueda with Helen B. Marrow (Cambridge, MA: Harvard University Press, 2007), 382.
81. Daniel Samper Pizano, "Sé lo que significa esto para mi tierra," *ElTiempo.com*, 23 Feb. 2001 <http://www. eltiempo.terra.com.co/23-02-2001/rock_pf.0.html>; Martínez, "American Idols" 382. *El Tiempo*, based in Bogóta, is one of Colombia's major newspapers; in this particular edition, no fewer than eight separate features were dedicated to coverage of Shakira's Grammy win.

82. Goldring 167. More specifically, Luin Goldring observes that "transnational social fields, and localities of origin in particular, provide a special context in which people can improve their social position and perhaps their power, make claims about their changing status and have it appropriately valorized, and also participate in changing their place of origin so that it becomes more consistent with their changing expectations and strategies" (167).

83. George Lipsitz, "The Lion and the Spider: Mapping Sexuality, Space and Politics in Miami Music," in *American Studies in a Moment of Danger*, ed. George Lipsitz (Minneapolis: University of Minnesota Press, 2001), 152–153; Daiva K. Stasiulis, "Relational Possibilities of Nationalisms, Racisms, and Feminisms," in *Between Woman and Nation: Nationalisms, Transnational Feminisms, and the State*, ed. Norma Alarcón, Caren Kaplan, and Minoo Moallem (Durham, NC: Duke University Press, 1999), 183.

84. Goldring 174.

85. Gordon Mathews, "Context and Consciousness in the Practice of Transnationality," *City & Society* 17.1 (2005): 45.

86. See Martin, as well as John Storey, *Inventing Popular Culture* (Malden, MA: Blackwell, 2005) 80.

CHAPTER 4

1. Aterciopelados, "*Florecita rockera*," *El Dorado*, RCA International, 1995. Aterciopelados also released an electronica remake of this track entitled "*Florecita rockera 2003*," which the group has frequently performed on tour. Though it retains the original lyrics, the 2003 recording is otherwise nearly indistinguishable from its 1995 punk-inspired predecessor, as it relies heavily on vocal effects, a slower tempo, prefabricated dance beats, and repetition. The character of this latest recording mirrors Aterciopelados's recent musical trajectory, which, unlike the band's economic and political practices, has grown less identifiably "Colombian" in recent years. To this end, "*Florecita rockera 2003*" arguably constitutes a more "globalized" product than its predecessor. Aterciopelados, concert, Bongo's Cuban Café/American Airlines Arena, Miami, Florida, 1 July 2001; Aterciopelados, "*Florecita rockera 2003*," *Evolución*, RCA International, 2002.

2. Juana Suárez, "Sites of Contention: Colombian Cultural Production at the Threshold of a New Millennium" (Ph.D. diss., Arizona State University, 2000), 74.

3. Sheila Whiteley, introduction, *Sexing the Groove: Popular Music and Gender*, ed. Sheila Whiteley (New York: Routledge, 1997), xix.

4. Suárez 93; Robert Walser, *Running With the Devil: Power, Gender and Madness in Heavy Metal Music* (Hanover, NH: Wesleyan University Press/University Press of New England, 1993), 131–132. See Leila Cobo, "A Rich Musical Tradition Swells Up and Out Into the World," *Miami Herald*, 25 July 1999: 5m, 7m, in addition to Peter Wade, *Music, Race and Nation: Música Tropical in Colombia* (Chicago: University of Chicago Press, 2000), 213–214, 217–220, 230.

5. Andrew Leyshon, David Matless, and George Revill, introduction, *The Place of Music*, ed. Andrew Leyshon, David Matless, and George Revill (New York: Guilford Press, 1998) 10. While the *rock en español* industry is not as centralized as the Latin(o) pop, tropical, or Mexican regional industry (important centers for the genre include several major Latin American cities and Los Angeles), Miami is still considered the central hub for Latin(o) music in the broadest sense.

6. Mario Rey, "Albita Rodríguez: Sexuality, Imaging, and Gender Construction in the Music of Exile," in *Queering the Popular Pitch*, ed. Sheila Whiteley and Jennifer Rycenga (New York: Routledge, 2006), 116.

7. Norma Coates, "(R)evloution Now?: Rock and the Political Potential of Gender," in *Sexing the Groove: Popular Music and Gender*, ed. Sheila Whiteley (London: Routledge, 1997), 55.

8. Whiteley, *Sexing the Groove* xvi. As Frances R. Aparicio and Susana Chávez Silverman state, "Latinization proper is exemplified by the appropriation and reformulation of cultural icons. . . . Latinization is limited to reformulations of cultural icons by the dominant sector: it is, thus, synonymous with commodification." Frances R. Aparicio and Susana Chávez-Silverman, introduction, *Tropicalizations: Transcultural Representations of Latinidad*, ed. Frances R. Aparicio and Susana Chávez-Silverman (Hanover, NH: University Press of New England, 1997), 3.

9. Pilar Riaño-Alcalá, "Urban Space and Music in the Formation of Youth Cultures: The Case of Bogotá, 1920–1980," *Studies in Latin American Popular Culture* 10 (1991): 102–103.

10. Larry Rohter, "Rock en Español Is Approaching Its Final Border," *New York Times*, 6 Aug. 2000, late ed.: 2.27; Néstor García Canclini, "Cultural Reconversion," trans. Holly Staver, in *On Edge: The Crisis of Contemporary Latin American Culture*, ed. George Yúdice, Jean Franco, and Juan Flores (Minneapolis: University of Minneapolis Press, 1992), 32.

11. Héctor Fernández L'Hoeste, "On How Bloque de Búsqueda Lost Part of Its Name: The Predicaments of Colombian Rock in the U.S. Market," in *Rockin' Las Americas: Rock Music and Rock Cultures Across Latin(o) America*, ed. Deborah Pacini Hernández, Héctor D. Fernández L'Hoeste, and Eric Zolov (Pittsburgh: University of Pittsburgh Press, 2004), 180. For a more complete account of rock's historical trajectory in Latin America than I am able to provide here, see Deborah Pacini Hernández, Héctor D. Fernández L'Hoeste, and Eric Zolov (eds.), *Rockin' las Américas: Rock Music and Rock Cultures Across Latin(o) America* (Pittsburgh: University of Pittsburgh Press, 2004), in particular Fernández L'Hoeste, "On How Bloque," as well as Ed Morales, *The Latin Beat: The Rhythms and Roots of Latin Music from Bossa Nova to Salsa and Beyond* (Cambridge, MA: Da Capo Press, 2003), which provides a clear account of what the author refers to as the "hidden history" of Latino influences in rock.

12. Eric Zolov, *Refried Elvis: The Rise of the Mexican Counterculture* (Berkeley: University of California Press, 1999); Andrés Caicedo, ¡*Que viva la música!* (Bogotá: Editorial Norma, 2001), 109.

13. Raymond L. Williams, "Andrés Caicedo's ¡*Que viva la música!*: Interpretation and the Fictionalized Reader," *Revista de Estudios Hispánicos* 17.1 (1983): 45. Ironically, in this instance Caicedo's protagonist conflates salsa (a hybrid genre that its widely associated with the New York City, U.S. Latino context, rather than strictly Latin American origins) with her native Colombian/Latin American culture.

14. Suárez 141.

5. Jody Berland, "Sound, Image and Social Space: Music Video and Media Reconstruction," in *Sound and Vision: The Music Video Reader*, ed. Simon Frith, Andrew Goodwin, and Lawrence Grossberg (London: Routledge, 1993), 26, 38.

16. Robert Hanke, "'Yo Quiero Mi MTV!': Making Music Television for LatinAmerica," in *Mapping the Beat: Popular Music and Contemporary Theory*, ed. Thomas Swiss,

John Sloop, and Andrew Herman (Malden, MA: Blackwell, 1998), 219, 221. MTV Latino is currently available, complete with programming geared toward local tastes, in all Latin American countries, with the exception of Brazil, where MTV Brazil reigns, and Cuba, where no version of MTV Latino is presently offered.

17. Suárez 141; Morales 304; Carmelo Esterrich and Javier H. Murillo, "Rock With Punk With Pop With Folklore: Transformations and Renewal in Aterciopelados and Café Tacuba," *Latin American Music Review* 21.1 (2000): 32–33; see also Deborah Pacini Hernández, "Race, Ethnicity and the Production of Latin/o Popular Music," in *Global Repertoires: Popular music within and beyond the transnational music industry*, ed. Andreas Gebesmair and Alfred Smudits (Aldershot: Ashgate, 2001), 57–72.

18. Pacini Hernández 69; Ella Shohat and Robert Stam, *Unthinking Eurocentrism: Multiculturalism and the Media* (New York: Routledge, 1994), 149; Suárez 73.

19. Wade, *Music, Race, and Nation* 214; Morales 305.

20. Fernández L'Hoeste 188–189; Morales 305.

21. Felix Contreras, "Defining Latin Alternative Music," *All Things Considered*, National Public Radio, 7 March 2006; see also Celeste Fraser Delgado, "Yo Quiero Mi MTV," *miaminewtimes.com*, 27 June 2006 <http://www.miaminewtimes.com/Issues/2002-10-24/music/music_print.html>.

22. Alisa Valdés-Rodríguez, "Latin American Rock Gets Its Green Card," *Boston Globe*, 4 Sept. 1998: D1.

23. John Beverley, "The Ideology of Postmodern Music and Leftist Politics," in *Against Literature*, ed. John Beverley (Minneapolis: University of Minneapolis Press, 1993) 139.

24. As Otto Santa Ana notes in his extensive study of U.S. media discourse, the use of water-based metaphors (i.e, "waves" of indocumented Latin Americans) pervades U.S. public discourse on immigration and is virtually exclusively pejorative in nature. In this light, the application of the "wave" metaphor in conjunction with mainstream media commentary on *rock en español* proves telling. See Otto Santa Ana with Juan Morán and Cynthia Sánchez, ""Awash Under a Brown Tide: Immigration Metaphors in California Public and Print Media Discourse," *Aztlán* 23.2 (Fall 1998): 137–177, as well as Otto Santa Ana, *Brown Tide Rising: Metaphors of Latinos in Contemporary American Public Discourse* (Austin: University of Texas Press, 2002).

25. Pacini Hernández, 59.

26. Holly Kruse, "Subcultural Identity in Alternative Music Culture," *Popular Music* 12.1 (1993): 35.

27. Celeste Fraser Delgado, "Velvet Offensive," *miaminewtimes.com*, 21 June 2001 <http://www.miaminewtimes.com/issues/2001-06-21/feature.html/printable_page>.

28. Jim Farber, "Ricky, Listen to These Numbers; Move Over Martin, Tell López the News . . . ," *Daily News* [New York], 4 March 2001, late ed.: 13.

29. Arlene Dávila, *Latinos, Inc.: The Marketing and Making of a People* (Berkeley: University of California Press, 2001), 36–37; Andrew Leyshon, David Matless, and George Revill, preface, *The Place of Music*, ed. Andrew Leyshon, David Matless, and George Revill (New York: Guilford Press, 1998), 12.

30. Coates 61.

31. See Jon Pareles, "Beyond Borders, Without Boundaries." *New York Times on the Web*, 12 July 2001 <http://www.nytimes.com/2001/07/12/arts/12NOTE.html>.

32. See Pareles; Andrés Zambrano D., "Aterciopelados' impulsa rock en español en E.U.," *ElTiempo*, 13 mayo 2001 <http://eltiempo.terra.com.co/13-05-2001/cult_pf_o.html>.

33. Dávila 101–102, 163.

34. Sara Cohen, "Men Making a Scene: Rock Music and the Production of Gender," in *Sexing the Groove: Popular Music and Gender*, ed. Sheila Whiteley (London: Routledge, 1997), 17; see also Barry Shank, *Dissonant Identities: The Rock'n'Roll Scene in Austin, Texas* (Middleton, CT: Wesleyan University Press, 1994); and Will Straw, "Systems of Articulation, Logics of Change: Communities and Scenes in Popular Music," *Cultural Studies* 5.3 (1991): 368–388.

35. Tim Padgett, "Tough as Males," *Time*, 3 Aug, 1998 <http://www.time.com/time/magazine/1998/int/980803/the_arts.music.tough_as_3.html>.

36. In popular Colombian speech, the term *"cachaca/o"* is employed in reference to individuals from the nation's interior; as such, it recalls the multiple stereotypes coastal/Caribbean Colombians attach to those from that region, such as rigidity, excessive order, and standoffishness. Conversely, an individual native to Colombia's coastal Caribbean region is referred to as a *"costeño/a,"* (or, in the pejorative extreme, a *"corroncho/a"*), someone who is stereotyped as lacking education and as lazy, loud, and disorganized. All of these terms are at times negative, and their shades of meaning are inevitably context bound. Furthermore, it has been my experience that coastal Colombians, perhaps because of the inferior position that they occupy within Colombia's cultural, ethnoracial, economic, and linguistic hierarchies, tend to be more invested in the maintenance and perpetuation of these regional labels than Colombians from the interior. For further clarification of the cultural import attributed to these Colombian regional signifiers, consult the discussion of Shakira's *costeña* identity in chapter 3.

37. Lydia Martin, "Breaking Tradition: Aterciopelados and Other Latin Rockers Bring a New Kind of Beat to Watcha Tour 2000," *www.herald.com*, 26 Aug. 2000 <http://www.herald.com/justgo/latingrammys/showarticle4.htm>.

38. "Artistas colombianos ganan cinco premios Grammy Latinos," *ElTiempo.com*, 31 Oct. 2001 <http://www.eltiempo.com/>.39. Coates 61; Marcia J. Citron, *Gender and the Musical Canon* (1993) (Urbana: University of Illinois Press, 2000), 166–167.

40. Citron 179–180.

41. Ibid. chapter 5.

42. Ibid. 182.

43. Christopher John Farley, "Sounds of Magical Realism," *Time*, 14 May 2001: 72; Fernández L'Hoeste 186–187; Fraser Delgado, "Velvet Offensive"; Lisa A. Lewis, *Gender Politics and MTV: Voicing the Difference* (Philadelphia: Temple University Press, 1990), 59; Angela McRobbie and Simon Frith, "Rock and Sexuality," in *On Record: Rock, Pop, and the Written Word*, ed. Simon Frith and Andrew Goodwin (London: Routledge, 1990); Lawrence La Fountain-Stokes, "Aterciopelados," *Claridad*, 11 July 1997: 22; Suárez 91. Notably, "El Dorado" is also the name of Bogotá's primary airport.

44. Súarez 68–69, 87. For an incisive discussion of the role of Latina(a) American women (specifically, *mexicanas* and Chicanas) in the punk genre, see Michelle Habell-Pallán, *Locomotion: The Travels of Chicana and Latina Popular Culture* (New York: New York University Press, 2005).

45. Fraser Delgado, "Velvet Offensive"; Farley 72; La Fountain-Stokes 22; Lewis 123; Aterciopelados, *"La estaca," El Dorado*, dir. Carlos Gaviria, MTV Latino, 1995; Sheila Whiteley, "Challenging the Feminine: Annie Lennox, Androgyneity, and the Illusions of Identity," in *Women and Popular Music: Sexuality, Identity, and Subjectivity*, ed. Sheila Whiteley (London: Routledge, 2000), 122; Helmi Järviluoma, Pirkko Moisala, and Anni Vilkko, "Not Only Vision—Analysing Sound and Music From the Perspective of Gender," in *Gender and Qualitative Methods*, ed. Helmi Järviluoma, Pirkko Moisala, and Anni Vilkko (Thousand Oaks, CA: Sage, 2003), 103–104. See also Jesús Martín-Barbero, "Latin America: Cultures in the Communication Media," *Journal of Communication* 43.2 (1993), 18–33.

46. Peter Wade, "Man the Hunter: Gender and Violence in Music and Drinking Contexts in Colombia," in *Sex and Violence: Issues in Representation and Experience*, ed. Peter Gow and Penelope Harvey (London: Routledge, 1994), 115–137; Cohen 30; Joel Streicker, "Policing Boundaries: Race, Class and Gender in Cartagena, Colombia," in *Blackness in Latin America and the Caribbean*, Vol. 1, ed. Norman E. Whitten, Jr., and Arlene Torres (Bloomington: University of Indiana Press, 1998), 279. However, as Jennifer Post notes, it is perhaps more theoretically fruitful and pragmatically accurate to conceptualize these literal and figurative spatial paradigms of gender and the public/private in terms of a continuum, rather than a rigid binary. See Jennifer C. Post, "Erasing the Boundaries Between Public and Private in Women's Performance Traditions," in *Cecilia Reclaimed: Feminist Perspectives on Gender and Music*, ed. Susan C. Cook and Judy S. Tsou (Urbana: University of Illinois Press, 1993), 36.

47. Lewis 123.

48. Ibid. 123.

49. Aterciopelados, *"Cosita seria," La pipa de la paz*, RCA International, 1996.

50. Lisa A. Lewis, "Being Discovered: The Emergence of Female Address on MTV," in *Sound and Vision: The Music Video Reader*, ed. Simon Frith, Andrew Goodwin, and Lawrence Grossberg (London: Routledge, 1993), 130; Nancy Morris, "The Myth of Unadulterated Culture Meets the Threat of Imported Media," *Media, Culture & Society* 24 (2002): 281. MTV Latino's status as the sole U.S.-based MTV global affiliate remains a point of interest on multiple counts: not only does it reflect the Miami industry's principal role in the transnational media's (re)invention of "Latin(o) America," but it also reveals a great deal regarding the MTV conglomerate's expectations about its viewership. Curiously, MTV Latino, unlike its English-language cousin, was virtually unavailable to Miami-area basic cable viewers by 2001, whereas myriad other Spanish-language channels were available to local consumers. When I contacted my cable provider in Miami to inquire about the channel's cancellation, I was surprised to learn that the channel purportedly wasn't popular enough among locals to warrant its continuation in the area.

51. Hanke 230–231.

52. Lewis, *Gender Politics* 156.

53. Ibid. 71; Joke Hermes, *Re-Reading Popular Culture* (Malden, MA: Blackwell, 2005), 11, 141.

54. Aterciopelados, *"El estuche," Caribe atómico*, RCA International, 1998.

55. Suárez 112.

56. Aterciopelados, *"El estuche," Caribe atómico*, dir. Marina Zurkow, MTV Latino, 1998; Lewis, "Being Discovered" 141.

57. Aterciopelados, *"Miss Panela," La pipa de la paz*, RCA International, 1996.

58. Aterciopelados, "*No necesito,*" *La pipa de la paz*, RCA International, 1996.
59. Carlos Vives, "*La casa en el aire*," *De Colecccción*, Polygram Colombia, 1995. A more traditional version of this Rafael Escalona classic, of slightly different word order, length, and musical arrangement, is performed by Colacho Mendoza and Ivo Díaz on *100 años de Vallenato*, CD #2, MTM, 1997.
60. Suárez 101.
61. Nicola Dibben, "Representations of Femininity in Popular Music," *Popular Music* 18.3 (1999): 333.
62. Esterrich and Murillo 37.
63. Aterciopelados, "*Baracunátana,*" *La pipa de la paz*, RCA International, 1996; the original *vallenato* version of this song, however, was composed by Leonidas Plaza.
64. In this vein, Víctor Uribe-Urán's study of domestic violence in colonial Colombia (then known as New Granada) references "*Baracunátana*" in its brief introductory discussion of gendered social mores in contemporary Colombia. (See Víctor Uribe-Urán, "Colonial *baracunátanas* and Their Nasty Men: Spousal Homicides and the Law in Late Colonial New Granada," *Journal of Social History* 35.1 [2001]: 43–72; see also Suárez 92). During a recent trip to Colombia, I experienced the popularity of "*Baracunátana*" firsthand in a bar in the interior city of Popayán; everyone, myself included, energetically shouted the chorus as it was played. I also noted that while nearly all of us had memorized the song's heavy slang, no one sitting at my table, which included a mixed group of Colombians from the interior and the Coast, actually understood all of it.
65. Esterrich and Murillo 38–39. In a similar way, Shakira's 2000 live *MTV Unplugged* recording of her hit "*Ciega, sordomuda*" (Blind, deaf, dumb) serves as yet another example of the ways in which stereotypically male folk genres are revoiced by women, as she refashions the Mexican *mariachi* genre from a feminine, if not necessarily feminist, perspective.
66. See Ed Morales, "*Colombia te canto*: The Redeeming Power of Music," *Hopscotch* 1.4 (1999): 34–49; Fraser Delgado, "Velvet Offensive"; "Aterciopelados se quedarán en Colombia, pese al conflicto armado," Efe News Services (U.S.), Spanish Newswire Services, 8 Feb. 2001.
67. Ana María Ochoa, "García Márquez, *Macondismo*, and the Soundscapes of Vallenato," *Popular Music* 24.2 (2005): 207–208, 213; Ella Shohat, *Taboo Memories, Diasporic Voices* (Durham, NC: Duke University Press, 2006), 4. (For a journalistic example of the tendency, see Farley, "Sounds of Magical Realism"). Originating in the Latin American literary boom of the 1960s, and partially inspired by the writings of the Colombian author Gabriel García Márquez, the label "magical realism" above all constitutes a publishing industry invention. With time, the literary concept of magical realism, which, loosely defined, encompasses writing that examines the supposedly extraordinary or fantastic nature of quotidian Latin American reality, has ceased to refer solely to literary production and is now utilized in the mainstream U.S. media as a catch-all signifier for all things "Latin(o) American," including music.
68. Jocelyn Guilbault, "On Redefining the 'Local' Through World Music," *The World of Music* 35.2 (1993): 33–34, 42.
69. "Artistas colombianos."
70. Suárez 80.

71. Fraser Delgado, "Velvet Offensive;" Andrea Echeverri, as qtd. in Bill Werde, "Crossover Dreams," *Village Voice*, 15 Aug. 2000: 59.

72. Rhett Butler, "And Our Winners Are ..." *Time*, Fall 2001: 29; Ernesto Lechner, *Rock en Español: The Latin Alternative Rock Explosion* (Chicago: Chicago Review Press, 2005), 38, 48.

73. Noah Adams and Gustavo Arellano, "Review: Andrea Echeverri's Self-Titled Debut Album," *Day to Day*, National Public Radio, 18 April 2005.

74. Andrea Echeverri, "Lactochampeta," *Andrea Echeverri*, Nacional Records, 2005.

75. *Champeta*, an Afro-Colombian music and dance style that first emerged in Cartagena, Colombia, in the 1970s, combines various Caribbean rhythms (such as *cumbia, compás, soca*, calypso, and reggae), along with numerous African musical genres (including *soukous, bikutsi*, highlife, *juju*, the Congolese rumba, and *mbaqanga*). It is also popularly known as *terapía criolla*, or "Creole therapy" (A. Romero, "Champeta Criolla," *World Music Central*, 26 Aug. 2004 <http://www.worldmusiccentral.org/article.php/20040528164253404>; Benyi Arregocés Carrere, "Champeta," *Fundación Cultural Son a Son*, 2000, 16 Aug. 2006 <http://www.radiorabel.com/ritmoy bailes/champeta.htm>. For an account of *champeta*'s grass-roots dissemination, see Deborah Pacini Hernández, "Sound Systems, World Beat and Diasporan Identity in Cartagena, Colombia," *Diaspora* 5.3 (1996): 429–466.

76. Jennifer Mannon, "Headbang in Bogotá: The Other Plan Colombia," *miaminewtimes.com*, 23 Nov. 2000 <http://www.miaminewtimes.com/issues/2000-11-23/music.html/printable_page> (emphasis mine).

77. Aparicio and Chávez-Silverman 14.

CHAPTER 5

1. Tomás Darío Gutiérrez, cited in Juanita Darling, "Colombia Strikes a New Note," *Los Angeles Times*, 25 September 1998: 1; *Lo mejor del vallenato, Volumen 1*, videocassette, Vedisco Records Inc., 1996.

2. Peter Wade, *Blackness and Race Mixture: The Dynamics of Racial Identity in Colombia* (Baltimore: Johns Hopkins University Press, 1993).

3. Ibid. 11 (emphasis mine).

4. Joel Streicker, "Policing Boundaries: Race, Class and Gender in Cartagena, Colombia," in *Blackness in Latin America and the Caribbean*, Vol. 1, ed. Norman E.Whitten, Jr., and Arlene Torres (Bloomington: University of Indiana Press, 1998), 283, 287. Streicker posits that older working-class males in Cartagena, one of the principal cities on the Colombian coast, pretend to wield authority over others (namely women and blacks) by means of their claim to a mythical past. By virtue of their real or imagined ties to a time when Cartagena was a more "respectable" city, these men thus exert considerable influence over what constitutes acceptable behavior among the popular classes.

5. Ana María Ochoa, "García Márquez, *Macondismo*, and the Soundscapes of *Vallenato*," *Popular Music*, 24.2 (2005): 213. For a related analysis that focuses on Colombian *cumbia* music, see also Héctor Fernández-L'Hoeste, "All Cumbias, the Cumbia: The Latin Americanization of a Tropical Genre," in *Imagining Our Americas: Toward a Transnational Frame*, ed. Snadhya Shukla and Heidi Tinsman (Durham, NC: Duke University Press, 2007), 338–364.

6. John Storey, *Inventing Popular Culture* (Malden, MA: Blackwell, 2005), 2, 13–14.

7. Peter Wade, "Racial Identity and Nationalism: A Theoretical View From Latin America," *Ethnic and Racial Studies* 24.5 (2001): 861. The disproportionate emphasis on Vives as the "savior" of contemporary Colombian popular music in the international context is particularly evident in Colombian media. See, for example, "Colombia se mueve," *Semana.com*, 29 Aug. 2004 <http://www.semana.com>.

8. Néstor García Canclini, *Transforming Modernity. Popular Culture in Mexico*, trans. Lidia Lozano (Austin: University of Texas Press, 1993), 13.

9. Fernando Ortiz, *La música afro-cubana* (Madrid: Ediciones Júcar, 1974). Frances Aparicio summarizes Fernando Ortiz's concept of musical metalepsis as "a cultural transvaloration of meaning by which a musical form assumes a cultural and social meaning different from that of its origins." Frances R. Aparicio, *Listening to Salsa: Gender, Latin Popular Music, and Puerto Rican Cultures* (Hanover, NH: University Press of New England, 1998), 24. It is in this sense that I employ the term "resematicization" here.

10. See John Fiske, *Understanding Popular Culture* (London and New York: Routledge, 1989), chapter 4.

11. Jane Desmond, "Embodying Difference: Issues in Dance and Cultural Studies," in *Everynight Life: Culture and Dance in Latin/o America*, ed. Celeste Fraser Delgado and José Esteban Muñoz (Durham, NC: Duke University Press, 1997), 39. In Colombia, as in other Latin American and Caribbean nations, racial nomenclature is extremely varied. For example, in Colombia individuals of mixed black and white heritage are known as *mulatos*, and those of mixed indigenous and black ancestry are referred to as *zambos*. Terms like *blanco* (white) and *negro* (black) occupy the opposite ends of the spectrum, while intermediary classifications such as *mestizo* (mized Indian/white), *claro* (light-skinned, lower class), and *moreno* (brown; located between *claro* and *negro*) are also commonly employed to describe positions along the racial continuum. Usage of these labels varies according to region and class, however, and this list reflects only the most basic terminologies. Peter Wade, "Patterns of Race in Colombia," *Bulletin of Latin American Research* 5.2 (1986): 1.

12. Jaime Arocha, "Inclusion of Afro-Colombians: Unreachable National Goal?" *Latin American Perspectives* 25.3 (1998): 70,78.

13. Aline Helg, "Race in Argentina and Cuba, 1880–1930: Theory, Policies, and Popular Reaction," in *The Idea of Race in Latin America, 1870–1940*, ed. Richard Graham (Austin: University of Texas Press, 1990), 37–38.

14. Jaime Arocha Rodríguez, "Afro-Colombia Denied," *NACLA* 25.4 (1992): 29.

15. Arocha, "Inclusion of Afro-Colombians," 71–72; "Las cadenas del racismo siguen sin romperse," *ElTiempo.com*, 26 Aug. 2001 <http://eltiempo.com>. As Mario Murillo notes, the percentage of Afro-Colombian citizens varies considerably, depending upon the source consulted. Mario A. Murillo, *Colombia and the United States: War, Unrest and Destablization* (New York: Seven Stories Press, 2004), 40.

16. Streicker 294; Peter Wade, *Race and Ethnicity in Latin America* (London: Pluto Press, 1997), 93–94. Note that the now highly commodified *cumbia* genre is also subsumed under the labels *música tropical* (tropical music) or the more telling *música caliente* (hot music). Among *costeños*, to be articulate is to be cultured (*tener cultura*); thus, when Afro-Colombians and members of the lower classes are labeled "lows," they are judged as inarticulate and are simultaneously systematically excluded from public discourse as part

of attempts to police or silence popular expression (Peter Wade, "Blackness and Cultural Syncretism in Colombia," in *Slavery and Beyond: The African Impact on Latin America and the Caribbean*, ed. Darién J. Davis [Wilmington, DE: Scholarly Resources, 1995], 135; Streicker 294–295, 298, 302). Paul Gilroy's concept of the Black Atlantic, a "modern political and cultural formation" alternatively defined as a "cultural system . . . which has encouraged a transnational identity based more on the shared experiences of displacement, exile, and oppression than on the specific experiences of slavery" further illuminates our understanding of the *vallenato*'s ethnoracial dynamics. The actor-musician Carlos Vives's actions during a soldout arena concert in his adopted hometown of Miami supply one pertinent, related example. At the concert's onset, Vives introduced himself to the audience with the words: "*No sé si les conté, pero vengo de Colombia*" ("I don't know if I told you, but I'm from Colombia"), provoking a deafening reaction from the overwhelmingly Caribbean and/or Colombian crowd. After identifying himself as a *colombiano*, he spoke of his birthplace, the Colombian Caribbean, thereby establishing his regional bearings. Finally, Vives proceeded to locate himself as a citizen of the greater Caribbbean, via frequent mentions of Puerto Rico, Cuba, and the Dominican Republic in conjunction with the Colombian coast. In this way, Vives engaged his audience in a exercise of self-naming that unconsciously (yet no less powerfully), recalled the dynamics of the Black Atlantic, as it simultaneously foregrounded the pan-Caribbean drive at the heart of *costeño* music. (Paul Gilroy, *The Black Atlantic. Modernity and Double Consciousness* [Cambridge, MA: Harvard University Press, 1993], 4; Deborah Pacini Hernández, "Sound Systems, World Beat and Diasporan Identity in Cartagena, Colombia," *Diaspora* 5.3 [1996]: 431).

17. Carlos Vives, concert, Miami Arena, Miami, Florida, 6 Sept. 2000. Most of the members of La Provincia, Vives's backup band, are from the Caribbean Guajira region—as Vives proclaimed, "*La Guajira reina aquí*"(The Guajira rules here). However, there are two musicians from other parts of the Coast (the percussionist and *gaita* player Mayte Montero, who is from Cartagena, and the accordionist Egidio Cuadrado, of Villanueva), as well as Vives himself, a native of Santa Marta. The regional divisions between the "Bogotá rockers" (as Vives called them) and the others were evident in Vives's introductions. He thereby separated the *bogotanos* from the *caribeños*, citing the former's uniqueness for their supposedly uncharacteristic interest in provincial Colombian music.

18. Arturo Arias Polo, "Carlos Vives: un cantautor con sonido propio," el herald.com, 18 Nov. 1999 <http://www.elherald.com/content/mon/digdocs/arte/viernes/046073.htm>; also see Norma Niurka, "Carlos Vives, el consentido de los dioses," elherald.com, 14 Sept. 2000 <http://www.elherald.com/content/today/galeria/viernes/02567393.htm>.

19. Ochoa 208.

20. Dick Hebdige, *Subculture: The Meaning of Style* (London and New York: Routledge, 1979). Other well-known Latin American genres, such as tango and *bachata*, among others, have demonstrated this pattern throughout their development and dissemination. See Marta Savigliano, *Tango and the Political Economy of Passion* (Boulder, CO: Westview Press, 1995), and Deborah Pacini Hernández, *Bachata: A Social History of Dominican Popular Music* (Philadelphia: Temple University Press, 1995).

21. Peter Wade, *Music, Race and Nation: Música Tropical in Colombia* (Chicago: University of Chicago Press, 2000) 215.

22. Ibid. 225.

23. Some contemporary representations of the *vallenato*, such as García Márquez's *Cien años de soledad* (1967) and the soap opera *Escalona* (1992), are linked by virtue of their roots in *costeño* orality as well as by the dialogic nature of their relationship to one another. Apart from their shared regional affiliations, *Cien años* and *Escalona* both possess, in varying degrees, what Raymond L. Williams terms "secondary orality." Williams cites García Márquez's work in particular as an example of secondary orality because of the incorporation of the *vallenato* as a key element. Secondarity orality, then, is located in recordings of the *vallenato* or other popular culture forms that were initially strictly oral in their manifestations. These works occupy a singular space as texts belonging both to oral and to "writing culture," as they appropriate elements of *costeño* orality in their writing. Raymond L. Williams, *The Colombian Novel, 1844-1987* (Austin: University of Texas Press), 87-88. This dialogue manifests itself on various levels, as exemplified in Vives's piece *"Que diera"* (What I would give) (*Tengo Fe*, EMI Latin, 1997), in which he sings:

A mí me dijeron	They told me
que iba a conocer a Gabito	that I was going to meet Gabito
que ese es hombre importante	that he's an important man
pa' la humanidad	to all of humanity
Me puse aquel traje	I put that suit on
que me regaló Enriquito	that Enriquito gave to me
pero al premio Nobel	but the Nobel Prize-winner
¡Hombre! le tocó viajar	Man! He had to travel

Upon inserting García Márquez (also known to Colombians as "Gabo" or the even more familiar "Gabito") into the lyrics of *"Que diera,"* Vives effectively establishes a dialogue among himself as a *costeño* performer, García Márquez and *Cien años de soledad*, the *Escalona* series in which Vives starred, and *vallenato* culture in general. While continuing the conversation between the *vallenato* and García Márquez that officially began with the publication of *Cien años*, in 1967, *"Que diera"* pays homage to García Márquez in the form of a reference to his 1982 Nobel Prize for Literature. The insertion of García Márquez into everyday *vallenato* discourse and, to a lesser extent, into the *Escalona* series, ultimately had a "purifying" effect on the genre (Ochoa 210). In an analogous vein, Vives's portrayal of Rafael Escalona in the popular *telenovela*, given the disparities between the two men in terms of subject position, almost certainly attracted a broader audience because of Vives's participation. See also Vives's interview with Julio Sánchez Cristo ("'La fama y el dinero son lo de menos,'" *Semana*, 2 Dec. 2002: 30-34), in which he describes any comparison between his music and García Márquez's novels as "pretentious," while simultaneously attributing the popularity of both men's work to stories that seem very local, despite their universality (34).

24. Wade, *Music, Race, and Nation* 218; Peter Wade, "Music, Blackness and National Identity: Three Moments in Colombian History," *Popular Music* 17.1 (1998): 6.

25. Alisa Valdés-Rodríguez, "Searching for Carlos Vives," latimes.com, 12 Sept. 2000 <http://www.calendarlive.com/music/latingrammy/lat_vives000912.htm>.

26. See Fernández L'Hoeste; Ed Morales, *The Latin Beat: The Rhythms and Roots of Latin Music From Bossa Nova to Salsa and Beyond* (Cambridge, MA: Da Capo Press, 2003), 261-262.

27. Deborah Pacini Hernández, "Bachata: From the Margins to the Mainstream," *Popular Music* 11.3 (1992): 362.

28. Daniel Samper Pizano and Pilar Tafur, *100 años de vallenato* (2nd ed.) (Colombia: MTM Limitada, 1997), 17–18.

29. Jorge Duany, "Popular Music in Puerto Rico: Toward an Anthropology of Salsa" *Latin American Music Review* 5.2 (1984): 189.

30. Consuelo Araújo de Molina, *Vallenatología. Orígenes y fundamentos de la música vallenata* (Bogotá: Ediciones Tercer Mundo, 1973), 30; Wade, *Blackness* 284.

31. Rocío Cárdenas Duque, *Música Caribeña. Tres países y un sólo ritmo. Ensayos* (Cali: Centro Editorial, Universidad del Valle, 1992), 112–113.

32. "Los ritmos del vallenato," *El Tiempo-Caribe*, 17 April 1999: 5; Ochoa 209.

33. Morales, *Latin Beat* 261; see also Frances R. Aparicio, "The Blackness of Sugar: Celia Cruz and the Performance of (Trans)Nationalism," *Cultural Studies* 13.2 (1999): 223–236.

34. Heidi Feldman, *Black Rhythms of Peru: Reviving African Musical Heritage in the Black Pacific* (Middletown, CT: Wesleyan University Press, 2006), 218–219; Martin F. Manalansan IV, *Global Divas: Filipino Gay Men in the Diaspora* (Durham, NC: Duke University Press, 2003). It is worth noting, as Martin F. Manalansan IV asserts, that not all forms of global cosmopolitanism are equally valorized. Andrew Leyshon, David Matless, and George Revill, preface, *The Place of Music*, ed. Andrew Leyshon, David Matless, and George Revill (New York: Guilford Press, 1998), 5.

35. "Colombia," *The New Grove Dictionary of Music and Musicians* (6th ed.) (New York: Grove's Dictionaries, 1980), 574.

36. Paúl Bolaño Saurith, "Caja, guacharaca y acordeón," *El Tiempo-Caribe*, 17 April 1999: 5.

37. "Colombia," 574; Luis L. Moya and Luis A. Del Castillo Cadavid, "What Is Vallenato?" 3 March 1998 <http://www.grupofantasia.com/vallenato.htm>; Wade, "Black Music and Cultural Syncretism" 131.

38. Moya and Del Castillo Cadavid. *Vallenato* historians maintain that the accordion reached the Colombian coast sometime during the mid-1800s and possibly as late as 1890. The instrument likely arrived via contraband, courtesy of German and Italian sailors. Originally invented in 1829 by Kirl Dimian, a German, the *vallenato* accordion possesses thirty-one keys on the right side intended for melody-making and twelve left-handed, or bass, keys designed for marking rhythm. Thus, the accordion's design makes it possible for one person to perform melodies and mark time simultaneously, making it a logical option for sailors and others in isolated locales. See Bolaño Saurith 5; Cárdenas Duque 113; José Portaccio Fontalvo, *Colombia y su Música, Volumen I* (Bogotá: Logos Diagramación, 1995), 103.

39. Cárdenas Duque 113; Samper Pizano and Tafur 172.

40. Javier Ocampo López, *Música y folclor de Colombia* (Bogotá: Plaza y Janés, 1976); Moya and Del Castillo Cadavid; Ochoa 209.

41. Ocampo López 100. As Tricia Rose argues, "self-naming" in musical discourse functions as a strategy for countering marginalization and competition in a hostile world and as a means of re-inventing one's destiny, at least in a figurative sense, and redefining the self. Tricia Rose, *Black Noise: Rap Music and Black Culture in Contemporary America* (Hanover, NH: Wesleyan University Press/University Press of New England, 1994), 36, 87–88.

42. Duany 192, 202.

43. Rose 3; Aparicio, *Listening to Salsa*, 195; Joke Hermes, *Re-Reading Popular Culture* (Malden, MA: Blackwell, 2005), 140.

44. George Lipsitz, *Time Passages: Collective Memory and American Popular Culture* (Minneapolis: University of Minnesota Press, 1990), 213.

45. Storey 85; Pacini Hernández, "Sound Systems" 436.

46. Wade, *Music, Race, and Nation* 47–48; Wade, "Music, Blackness and National Identity" 7–8. Contemporary accounts of the Andean *bambuco* genre offer a clear example of the case in point. By the early nineteenth century, urban variations of the numerous popular genres began to appear, most notably the *bambuco* music originating in the interior, which was largely performed by string ensembles. Javier Ocampo López further describes *bambuco* as a polyrhythmic genre performed in 3/4 or 6/8 time and characterized by its tendency to begin in a minor key yet end with major tones. While overwhelmingly associated with the interior Andean region, in time the *bambuco* came to symbolize what was thought of as "authentic Colombian music," both at home and abroad. Much like the persistent representation of whiteness as the unmarked norm, foregrounding the Andean *bambuco* in such terms ultimately served to undermine the legitimacy of other national popular musics, which were subsequently rendered somehow "less Colombian." See Wade, *Music, Race, and Nation* 47–48, 51–52; Ocampo López 73, 76––77; José Ignacio Perdomo Escobar, *Historia de la música en Colombia* (Bogotá: Editorial ABC, 1963), 308–309 (emphasis mine). For an alternative account of the *bambuco* as a predominantly African rather than Andean (indigenous/mestizo) genre, see Rafael Campo Miranda, *Crónicas didácticas sobre el folclor musical de Colombia* (Barranquilla: Editorial Mejoras, 1999), 122–123.

47. Wade, "Colombian History" 9.

48. Carlos Vives, "*Carito*," *Déjame entrar*, EMI Latin, 2001; Wade, "Racial Identity and Nationalism" 849. According to Wade, *mestizaje* has historically been understood as the overarching link between Latin American and Caribbean nations. However, this "international *mestizaje*" also assumes a hierarchical bent, in accordance with the degree of race mixture and closeness to whiteness within each respective nation.

49. Wade, *Race and Ethnicity* 38.

50. This is not an uncommon practice in Latin America, however. As Joel Streicker postulates, Latin American elites wishing to avoid the stigma brought on by the quantification of the non-European populations were responsible for the elimination of this practice. Wade, *Race and Ethnicity* 69–70; Peter Wade, "The Cultural Politics of Blackness in Colombia," *American Ethnologist* 22.2 (1995): 342; Streicker 284, 299–300.

51. Streicker 278, 285–286; Wade, *Blackness and Race Mixture* 3.

52. Wade, "Patterns," 12–13. Wade outlines the three primary sources of Colombia's coastal *mestizaje*: first, the presence of a permanently settled, albeit small, white population in the region increased the likelihood of miscegenation. Second, greater access to the Atlantic coast, coupled with the Spaniards' subsequent efforts to concentrate coastal settlements in order to facilitate their administration, led to increased cohabitation. Finally, the large population of *libres*, or free peoples of both indigenous and African descent, while inhabiting more isolated coastal zones, did work in towns and on large farms or *haciendas*, thus rendering miscegenation more likely. In short, *La Costa*'s political economy expedited race mixture among its populations. High rates of miscegenation

on the coast, however, belie the long history of *cimarronismo* (slave flight) and *palenques* (runaway slave settlements) in the region. See Wade, "Cultural Politics" 345–346, 350–351.

53. Wade, *Race and Ethnicity* 3.
54. Wade, *Race and Ethnicity* 28, 30, 106–107; See Wade, "Cultural Politics," as well.
55. Wade, *Race and Ethnicity* 93–94.
56. Wade, *Blackness and Race Mixture* 90, 282–283; Fiske 73; García Canclini, as cited in Aparicio, *Listening to Salsa* 33.
57. Raymond Williams, as cited in Wade, *Race and Ethnicity* 86–87.
58. Wade, "Music" 1.
59. Wade, "Music, Blackness and National Identity" 3–4 (emphasis mine); see also Stuart Hall, "Old and New Identities, Old and New Ethnicities," in *Culture, Globalization and the World-System: Contemporary Conditions for the Representation of Identity*, ed. Anthony D.King (Minneapolis: University of Minneapolis Press, 1997) 58.
60. García Canclini 15.
61. Wade, *Music, Race and Nation* 38–39.
62. Ibid. See also pages 42–47 of the same volume for the most comprehensive English-language treatment of *costeño* identity to date. In this section, Wade outlines what he classifies as the four principal ideological fields upon which *costeño* identity is founded. He also highlights the seemingly incongruous nature of the Coast's sum characteristics, which have in turn rendered the region ripe for competing representations.
63. Pacini Hernández, "Bachata: From the Margins" 363.
64. Fiske 192–193; Bourdieu, as cited in García Canclini 17.
65. Celeste Fraser Delgado, "What Rock and Roll Owes the Blues, Carlos Vives Owes Vallenato," *miaminewtimes.com*, 20 Dec. 2001 <http://www.miaminewtimes.com/issues/2001-12-20/music.html/print/html>; see also Ken Dermota, "Colombia's 'Elvis' Popularizes New Folk," *Christian Science Monitor*, 20 Aug. 1995: 14; Dániza Tobar, "Carlos Vives: el dueño de la parranda," *Ocean Drive en Español*, Dec. 2001: 82–85. Of these articles, Fraser Delgado's is best at teasing out the multiple similarities between Vives and Elvis, as she compares the blues great Robert Johnson, who allegedly sold his soul to the Devil in order to obtain supernatural guitar skills, to the *vallenato* legend Francisco el Hombre, who defeated the Devil in an accordion duel by playing the Lord's Prayer backwards.
66. Carlos Vives, "*Décimas*," *Déjame entrar*, EMI Latin, 2001. A *décima* is a poetic stanza consisting of ten octosyllabic lines; it also refers to a type of rural Cuban ballad.
67. "Tengo derecho a soñar," *Semana.com*, 31 March 2007 <http://www.semana.com>; "'Quiero serle fiel a la música colombiana,'" *Semana.com*, 3 March 2002 <http://www.semana.com>; "Colombia se mueve."
68. Lipsitz 114. Lipsitz defines songs that engender communal affiliation as "songs with references to familiar folk tales or sagas or to everyday speech or street-corner games [that] tended to include listeners in a community of improvisation and elaboration. The songs came from life and blended back into it. As the members of the audience remembered and repeated, they ritualistically confirmed the commonality of everyday experience."
69. Frith 312; Desmond 41–42; Gilroy 99; also see George Lipsitz, *Dangerous Crossroads: Popular Music, Postmodernism, and the Poetics of Place* (London: Verso, 1994), chapter 3.

70. Carlos Vives, "*Malas lenguas*," *Tengo fe*, EMI Latin, 1997.

71. Leandro Díaz is considered among the foremost composers and performers of the vallenato genre. Though no one is certain whether or not such an individual ever actually existed, Francisco "El Hombre" Moscote is a *vallenato* legend on the Atlantic coast and is believed by many to be the finest accordion player ever known. The lyrics to one of Díaz's most famous compositions, "La Diosa Coronada," were incorporated by García Márquez into his 1985 novel *El amor en los tiempos del cólera* (Love in the time of cholera). The association with García Márquez's renowned literary masterpiece, which could be read as a movement away from the *vallenato*'s oral framework, in turn marked a formative moment in the genre's more welcoming reception among Colombian elites.

72. Cárdenas Duque 111; Wade, "Racial Identity and Nationalism" 860; see also Samper Pizano and Tafur 172–177 for a more balanced discussion of the *vallenato*'s recent commercial success.

73. Cárdenas Duque 111.

74. Carlos Vives and La Provincia, "*La celosa*," *Clásicos de la Provincia*, PolyGram Discos, 1993.

75. For more on this recurrent theme in Latin American and Caribbean music, see Frances R. Aparicio, "Ethnifying Rhythms, Feminizing Cultures," in *Music and the Racial Imagination*, ed. Ronald Radano and Philip V. Bohlman (Chicago: University of Chicago Press, 2000), 95–112.

76. At a Miami concert that I attended, Vives appeared eager to allow the audience to determine what songs his band played and simultaneously to transform the cavernous concert hall into a more intimate space. In fact, at one point in the concert he forcefully insisted that the audience members tell the band what they wanted to hear next; when he began to sing the opening bars of "*La celosa*," the crowd cheered its approval, prompting Vives to laugh and chide the audience for favoring "the most trampy, sexist songs." Despite the apparent contradictions between my own subject position and the content of "*La celosa*," Vives's rendering is among my favorite *vallenatos*. Michel de Certeau's concept of the "reader [or in this case, listener] as poacher" elucidates the ways in which many Latinas negotiate the incongruities between theoretical feminist discourses and popular pleasures. Thus, to read and/or listen as a "poacher" entails claiming what is most "useful" and leaving the rest behind. Michel de Certeau, *The Practice of Everyday Life*, trans. Steven Rendall (Berkeley: University of California Press, 1984).

77. Frances R. Aparicio, "La Lupe, La India, and Celia: Toward a Feminist Genealogy of Salsa Music," in *Situating Salsa: Global Markets and Local Meaning in Latin Popular Music*, ed. Lise Waxer (London: Routledge, 2002), 137.

78. Wade, *Race and Ethnicity* 17; bell hooks, "Postmodern Blackness," in *Cultural Theory and Popular Culture: A Reader* (2nd ed.), ed. John Storey (Athens: University of Georgia Press, 1998); Aparicio, "Feminist Genealogy" 139; for more on the impact of salsa *romántica*'s feminization, see 135–146 of the same essay. See also Enrique Fernández, "Topline Colombian," *Village Voice*, 1 Feb. 1983: 81.

79. Aparicio, *Listening to Salsa* 174.

80. Stuart Hall, "Notes on Deconstructing 'the Popular,'" in *People's History and Socialist Theory*, ed. Raphael Samuel (London: Routledge and Kegan Paul, 1981), 235;

Ali Behdad, *A Forgetful Nation: On Immigration and Cultural Identity in the United States* (Durham, NC: Duke University Press, 2005). Consult Fernández L'Hoeste, "All Cumbias, the Cumbia" for a cogent analysis of this tendency in contemporary Colombian popular music, and *cumbia* music in particular.

CHAPTER 6

1. Felicity Schaeffer-Grabiel, "Beyond and Back: Locating Chicanas and Latinas Within Transnational Feminist Theories" (roundtable presentation, American Studies Association Annual Meeting, Atlanta, GA, 11 Nov. 2004); Emory Elliot, "Diversity in the United States and Abroad: What Does It Mean When American Studies Is Transnational?," *American Quarterly* 59.1 (2007): 9. Notably, a growing number of American Studies scholars, including Mae M. Ngai, Emory Elliott, and Winfried Fluck, among others, have also publicly acknowledged the centrality of Ethnic Studies' role in the ongoing transnationalization of American Studies. See Elliot; Mae M. Ngai, "Transnationalism and the Transformation of the 'Other': Response to the Presidential Address," *American Quarterly* 57.1 (2005): 59–65, and Winfried Fluck, "Inside and Outside: What Kind of Knowledge Do We Need?: A Response to the Presidential Address," *American Quarterly* 59.1 (2007): 23–32.

2. Ella Shohat, *Taboo Memories, Diasporic Voices* (Durham, NC: Duke University Press, 2006), 4; David W. Noble, *Death of a Nation: American Culture and the End of Exceptionalism* (Minneapolis: University of Minnesota Press, 2002), xxiv; Juan Flores, "Latina/o Studies: New Contexts, New Concepts," in *Critical Latin American and Latina/o Studies*, ed. Juan Poblete (Minneapolis: University of Minnesota Press, 2003), 192–193; Frances R. Aparicio, "Gendered Transculturations in *Six Feet Under*: Implications for Rethinking Latin American, American, Latino/a and Gender Studies" (lecture, The Future of Ethnic Studies in/as American Studies, Williams College, Williamstown, MA, 12 March 2005). For a lucid critique of Women's and Postcolonial Studies in the U.S. context, related topics that fall beyond the scope of this chapter, see Shohat, *Taboo Memories*.

3. José David Saldívar, *Border Matters: Remapping American Cultural Studies* (Berkeley: University of California Press, 1997), 10. Although I employ the labels "Arab" and "Middle Eastern" throughout my analysis, I am keenly aware of their failure to adequately capture the broad spectrum of national and regional affiliations, political circumstances, and lexical preferences of the communities I discuss. As Lisa Suhair Mujaj has cogently argued, labels such as "Middle Eastern" permit Arab Americans to locate themselves within existing categorizations, yet ultimately prove problematic in that they foreground geography over culture, underscore the relative invisibility of Arabs vis-à-vis other ethnoracial communities, and potentially contribute to the group's political, cultural, and religious fragmentation. Lisa Suhair Majaj, "Arab-Americans and the Meanings of Race," *Postcolonial Theory and the U.S.: Race, Ethnicity, and Literature*, ed. Amritjit Singh and Peter Schmidt (Jackson: University of Mississippi Press, 2000) 334. For further discussion on the problematics of these labels in the broader American context, see Ignacio Klich and Jeffrey Lesser, "Introduction: 'Turco' Immigrants in Latin America," *The Americas* 53.1 (1996): 2–5; Nadine Naber, "Ambiguous Insiders: An Investigation of Arab-AmericanIinvisibility," *Ethnic and Racial Studies* 23.1 (2000): 37–61; and Steven Salaita, "Ethnic Identity

and Imperative Patriotism: Arab Americans Before and After 9/11," *College Literature* 32.2 (2005), 146–169.

4. Shakira, *Shakira: En vivo y en privado*, DVD, Sony Music International, 2004. Kibbeh (or Kibbe, as it is also spelled in English) are small balls of minced lamb meat, bulgur, and spices, served raw, fried, or boiled. In her self-description, Shakira refers to the raw version, which is also known in Latin America as "quibbe naye." The dish is familiar in much of Latin America and the Spanish-speaking Caribbean, particularly in areas with high concentrations of Middle Eastern immigrants. While prepared in numerous forms, kibbeh are considered the national dish of many countries of the Levant, including Lebanon, Syria, Palestine, and Iraq. Plantains, a larger member of the banana family, are served in various preparations throughout the Americas but particularly in the Caribbean.

5. Jillian Báez, "'*En mi imperio*': Competing Discourses of Agency in Ivy Queen's Reggaetón," *CENTRO Journal* 18.1 (2006): 67; Susan McClary and Robert Walser, "Start Making Sense: Musicology Wrestles With Rock," in *On Record: Rock, Pop, and the Written Word*, ed. Simon Frith and Andrew Goodwin (London: Routledge, 2000), 278; Andrew Goodwin, *Dancing in the Distraction Factory: Music Television and Popular Culture* (Minneapolis: University of Minnesota Press, 1992) 2, 24–25, 56–57. For a timely discussion of the growing import of convergence phenomena in contemporary media culture, see Henry Jenkins, *Convergence Culture: Where New and Old Media Collide* (New York: New York University Press, 2006).

6. Susan McClary, *Feminine Endings: Music, Gender and Sexuality* (Minneapolis: University of Minnesota Press, 1991), 161 (emphasis in original).

7. Jody Berland, "Sound, Image and Social Space: Music Video and Media Reconstruction," in *Sound and Vision: The Music Video Reader*, ed. Simon Frith, Andrew Goodwin, and Lawrence Grossberg (London: Routledge, 1993), 25.

8. Goodwin, *Dancing in the Distraction Factory*, 8. A notable exception to this tendency is the work of Carol Vernallis, *Experiencing Music Video: Aesthetics and Cultural Context* (New York: Columbia University Press, 2004).

9. See, for example, the foundational work of Lisa A. Lewis, *Gender Politics and MTV: Voicing the Difference* (Philadelphia: Temple University Press, 1990) 59; Angela McRobbie and Simon Frith, "Rock and Sexuality," in *On Record: Rock, Pop, and the Written Word*, ed. Simon Frith and Andrew Goodwin (London: Routledge, 2000); Sheila Whiteley, ed., *Sexing the Groove: Popular Music and Gender* (New York: Routledge, 1997); McClary and Walser, "Start Making Sense!," 277–292; and Suzanne G. Cusick, "On a Lesbian Relationship With Music: A Serious Effort Not to Think Straight," in *Queering the Pitch: The New Gay and Lesbian Musicology* (2nd ed.), ed. Elizabeth Wood and Philip Brett (London and New York: Routledge, 2006), 67–85.

10. McClary 151–152.

11. Jon Pareles, "The Shakira Dialectic," *New York Times*, 13 Nov. 2005 <http://www.nytimes.com>.

12. "Live Earth Artist: Shakira," 27 July 2007 *msn.com* <http://www.liveearth.msn.com/artists/shakira?ocid=T001MSN43A03001&photoidx=4>.

13. Damarys Ocaña, "Has Shakira Sold Out?" *Latina*, Sept. 2006: n.p.

14. Saul Austerlitz, *Money for Nothing: A History of Music Video From the Beatles to the White Stripes* (New York: Continuum, 2006); Steven Levy, "Ad Nauseam: How MTV Sells Out Rock & Roll," *Rolling Stone*, 8 Dec. 1983: 33. Important departures from this tendency

include the work of Rana A. Emerson, "'Where My Girls At?'": Negotiating Black Womanhood in Music Videos," *Gender & Society* 16.1 (2002): 115–135, and Báez, as well as Sheila Whiteley and Jennifer Rycenga, eds., *Queering the Popular Pitch* (London and New York: Routledge, 2006); Lisa A. Lewis, "Being Discovered: The Emergence of Female Address on MTV," in *Sound and Vision: The Music Video Reader*, ed. Simon Frith, Andrew Goodwin, and Lawrence Grossberg (London: Routledge, 1993), 134–135.

15. Lewis, *Gender Politics and MTV*; Lisa A. Lewis, "Consumer Girl Culture: How Music Video Appeals to Girls," in *Television and Women's Culture: The Politics of the Popular*, ed. Mary Ellen Brown (London: Sage, 1990), 89–101; Lewis, "Being Discovered."

16. Lewis, "Being Discovered" 131.

17. Ibid.134.

18. Goodwin 105, 107.

19. Notable exceptions include Austerlitz; Jack Banks, *Monopoly Television: MTV's Quest to Control the Music* (Boulder, CO: Westview Press, 1996); Gary Burns, "Pop Up Video: The New Historicism," *Journal of Popular Film and Television* 32.2 (2004): 74–83; Gary Burns, "Visualizing 1950s Hits on 'Your Hit Parade,'" *Popular Music* 17.2 (1998): 139–153; Gary Burns, "'Where the Action Is': Dick Clark's Precursor to Music Video," *Journal of Popular Film and Television* 25.1 (1997): 31–38; Gary Burns, "Formula and Distinctiveness in Movie-Based Music Videos," *Popular Music and Society* 18.4 (1994): 7–18; Gary Burns, "How Music Video Has Changed, and How It Has Not Changed," *Popular Music and Society* 18.3 (1994): 67–80; Emerson; Robert Hanke, "'Yo Quiero Mi MTV!': Making Music Television for Latin America," in *Mapping the Beat: Popular Music and Contemporary Theory*, ed. Thomas Swiss, John Sloop, and Andrew Herman (Malden, MA: Blackwell, 1998), 219–245; Heather McIntosh, "Music Video Forerunners in Early Television Programming: A Look at WCPO-TV's Innovations and Contributions in the 1950s," *Popular Music and Society* 27.3 (2004): 259–273; Tricia Rose, "Never Trust a Big Butt and a Smile," in *Feminist Television Criticism: A Reader*, ed. Charlotte Brundson, Julia D'Acci, and Lynn Spigel (New York and Oxford: Oxford University Press, 1997), 300–317; Vernallis; and Sheila Whiteley, "Challenging the Feminine: Annie Lennox, Androgyneity, and the Illusions of Identity," in *Women and Popular Music: Sexuality, Identity, and Subjectivity*, ed. Sheila Whiteley (London and New York: Routledge, 2000), 119–135.

20. Angharad N. Valdivia, "Latinas as Radical Hybrid: Transnationally Gendered Traces in Mainstream Media," *Global Media Journal* 4.7(2004) <http://lass.calumet.purdue.edu/gmj/refereed/htm>.

21. Austerlitz 22; Goodwin 29. For further information regarding the precursors of music video in the U.S. context, see Austerlitz; Burns, "'Where the Action Is'"; Goodwin; and McIntosh.

22. Goodwin 28–30; Vernallis 141; Martin Lister and others, eds., *New Media: A Critical Introduction* (London: Routledge, 2003), 9–10, 20. Historical and/or journalistic portrayals of music video as the "new media" of its era can be found in Austerlitz, as well as Levy.

23. Austerlitz 22–23; see also Goodwin 25–27.

24. See, for example, Austerlitz; Goodwin; and Lawrence Grossberg, "The Media Economy of Rock Culture: Cinema, Postmodernity and Authenticity," in *Sound and Vision: The Music Video Reader*, ed. Simon Frith, Andrew Goodwin, and Lawrence Grossberg (London: Routledge, 1993), 185–209.

25. Vernallis 91.

26. Sue Wise, "From Butch God to Teddy Bear? Some Thoughts on My Relationship With Elvis Presley," in *Feminist Praxis: Research, Theory and Epistemology in Feminist Sociology*, ed. Liz Stanley (London: Routledge, 1990), 142 (emphasis mine).

27. Ella Shohat and Robert Stam, "From the Imperial Family to the Transnational Imaginary: Media Spectatorship in the Age of Globalization," in *Global/Local: Production and the Transnational Imaginary*, ed. Rob Wilson and Wimal Dissanayake (Durham, NC: Duke University Press, 1996), 147.

28. Louise L'Estrange Fawcett, "Lebanese, Palestinians, and Syrians in Colombia," in *The Lebanese in the World: A Century of Emigration*, ed. Albert Hourani and Nadim Shehadi (London: I. B. Tauris, 1992), 365, 368.

29. Albert Hourani and Nadim Shehadi, "Introduction," *The Lebanese in the World: A Century of Emigration*, ed. Albert Hourani and Nadim Shehadi (London: I. B. Tauris, 1992), 9; Klich and Lesser 1–2; Nadine Naber, "Ambiguous Insiders: An Investigation of Arab American Invisibility," *Ethnic and Racial Studies* 23.1 (2000): 37–61; Suhair Majaj 326.

30. Suhair Majaj 323; Naber 37–61.

31. Klich and Lesser 8.

32. Louise Fawcett and Eduardo Posada-Carbó, "Arabs and Jews in the Development of the Colombian Caribbean 1850–1950," in *Arab and Jewish Immigrants in Latin America: Images and Realities*, ed. Ignacio Klich and Jeffrey Lesser (London: Frank Cass, 1998), 59; L'Estrange Fawcett 363; Hourani and Shehadi 4–5.

33. Fuad Khuri, cited in Hourani and Shehadi 9. Further discussion of the unique prejudices faced by Middle Eastern immigrants in Colombia can be found in L'Estrange Fawcett and in Fawcett and Posada-Carbó.

34. Fawcett and Posada-Carbó 59; Marco Palacios, *Between Legitimacy and Violence: A History of Colombia, 1875–2002*, trans. Richard Stoller (Durham, NC: Duke University Press, 2006), 54; L'Estrange Fawcett 363, 369–370, 372–375.

35. Caitlin Habib, "The Two Sides of Shakira," *Urban Latino* 58 (2005): 39.

36. Rob Tannenbaum, "Miss Universe," *Blender* (July 2005): 72.

37. Shakira, concert, T. D. Banknorth Arena, Boston, Massachusetts, 5 Sept. 2006.

38. Sergio de León, "Shakira Welcomed Home in Colombia," abcnews.com, 25 Nov. 2006 <http://abcnews.go.com/Entertainment/wireStory?id=2656785&CMP=OTC-RSS-Feeds0312/>; Martha Guarín R., "Mi tierra se merece lo mejor: Shakira," *El Heraldo* (Barranquilla, Colombia), 16 Nov. 2006 <http://elheraldo.com.co/anteriores/06-11-16/sociales/noti3.htm/>.

39. Shakira, *Laundry Service*, Sony Music, 2001.

40. Licia Fiol-Matta, "Pop *Latinidad*: Puerto Ricans in the Latin Explosion, 1999," *CENTRO Journal* 14.1 (2002): 29.

41. Tannenbaum 80; Pareles; Aaron Gell, "Love in the Time of Shakira," *Elle* (April 2006): 304, 306.

42. Adel Iskandar, "'Whenever, Wherever!': The Discourse of Orientalist Transnationalism in the Construction of Shakira," *The Ambassadors* 6.2 (2003) <http://ambassadors.net/archives/issue14/selected_studies4.htm>.

43. Shohat and Stam 146.

44. A particularly explicit model of this tendency appears in Aaron Gell's 2006 article "Love in the Time of Shakira," whose title references García Márquez's famed novel *El amor en los tiempos del cólera* (Love in the time of cholera) (1985). Further examples can

be found in Pareles and in Jesús Rodríguez, "Ciclón Shakira," *EP/El País Semanal* (Madrid, Spain), 28 May 2006.

45. Shakira, interview by Katie Couric and Matt Lauer, *Today Show*, NBC, April 28, 2007.

46. Goodwin 103.

47. Chon Noriega, introduction to *I, Carmelita Tropicana: Performing Between Cultures* (Boston: Beacon Press, 2003), xii.

48. Javier Lorbada, "Shakira: 'Estar en este cuerpo no es nada fácil,'" *MTV Magazine* (Spain) 15 (July-Aug. 2005): 54.

49. Tannenbaum.

50. Tannenbaum 80.

51. Goodwin 51–52.

52. Tannenbaum.

53. Pareles.

54. Báez.

55. Tannenbaum 77 (emphasis in original).

56. Goodwin; Berland 25.

57. Goodwin 12; Berland 25. Also see Keith Negus, *Producing Pop: Culture and Conflict in the Popular Music Industry* (New York: E. Arnold, 1992), 64–67.

58. Goodwin 41–42. For further details regarding the singular nature of the production and promotional dynamics behind the *Fijación Oral, Volumen I*, and *Oral Fixation, Volume II*, albums, see Leila Cobo, "Shakira x 2," *azcentral.com*, 24 May 2005 <http://www.azcentral.com/ent/music/articles/0525shakira.html>.

59. Kobena Mercer, "Monster Metaphors: Notes on Michael Jackson's *Thriller*," in *Sound and Vision: The Music Video Reader*, ed. Simon Frith, Andrew Goodwin, and Lawrence Grossberg (London: Routledge, 1993), 95.

60. See Vernallis 3–26. I employ the verb "play" in this context rather loosely, and with the understanding that what Shakira and Sanz are actually undertaking is a representation of the roles that they play in the song upon which the video is based—in short, a multilayered performance. This is not to suggest, however, that any of these performances can be interpreted or even exist independently of Shakira and Sanz's media-driven star texts. Shakira featuring Alejandro Sanz, "*La Tortura*," *Fijación oral, Volumen I*, dir. Michael Haussman, 2005.

61. Julian Dibbell, qtd. in Jane Desmond, "Embodying Difference: Issues in Dance and Cultural Studies," in *Everynight Life: Culture and Dance in Latin/o America*, ed. Celeste Fraser Delgado and José Esteban Muñoz (Durham, NC: Duke University Press, 1997), 49.

62. Vernallis 97, 127; see Goodwin 90–92, 94.

63. Gell 308.

64. Lewis, "Being Discovered" 135.

65. Báez.

66. Iskandar.

67. See Frances R. Aparicio and Susana Chávez-Silverman, introduction, *Tropicalizations: Transcultural Representations of Latinidad*, ed. Frances R. Aparicio and Susana Chávez-Silverman (Hanover, NH: University Press of New England, 1997).

68. Iskandar.

69. Kaja Silverman, *Male Subjectivity at the Margins* (London: Routledge, 1992), 204 (emphasis mine). Many thanks to Roger Rothman for suggesting this fruitful connection.

70. McClary 152.

71. Shakira featuring Alejandro Sanz, "La tortura," Fijación oral, Volumen I, EPIC, 2005.

72. Ocaña.

73. Goodwin 107–108.

74. See, for example, Báez; Juan Flores, *From Bomba to Hip-Hop: Puerto Rican Culture and Latino Identity* (New York: Columbia University Press, 2000); and Raquel Z. Rivera, *New York Ricans From the Hip-Hop Zone* (New York: Palgrave Macmillan, 2003).

75. Vernallis 191.

76. Berland 27; Vernallis 71.

77. Goodwin 64, 116; Mercer 97–89.

78. Ella Shohat, "Ethnicities-in-Relation: Toward a Multicultural Reading of American Cinema," in *Unspeakable Images: Ethnicity and the American Cinema*, ed. L. D. Friedman (Urbana: University of Illinois Press, 1991), 237; Mario Rey, "Albita Rodríguez: Sexuality, Imaging and Gender Construction in the Music of Exile," in *Queering the Popular Pitch*, ed. Sheila Whiteley and Jennifer Rycenga (London: Routledge, 2006), 120.

79. Pareles.

80. Shakira, featuring Wycleff Jean, "Hips Don't Lie," *Oral Fixation, Volume II*, EPIC, 2006.

81. The journalist Celeste Fraser-Delgado has chronicled the rising popularity among Miami residents in recent years of Barranquilla carnival celebrations, which are markedly more commercialized and pan-Latino in nature than the original *costeño* festivities. Nonetheless, both *carnavales* have assumed a more transnational dimension, as at least two recent carnival queens (who are traditionally selected from among the ranks of Barranquilla's most elite families) have been U.S. residents. As Fraser Delgado notes, however, the likelihood that the traditional carnival celebrations will migrate to Miami is slight, given the ready availability of cheap airline tickets that enable the wealthier *costeño* natives to return for the real thing. See Fraser Delgado, "Not for Export."

82. Rafael Pérez-Torres, "Brown Transnationalisms: Consuming Latino Identities in a Postmodern Era" (lecture, American Studies Association Annual Meeting, Oakland, CA, 12 Oct. 2006).

83. Shakira, featuring Wycleff Jean. Consult Vernallis, chapter 3, for a detailed discussion of the role of supporting characters in music video.

84. Shakira, featuring Wycleff Jean.

85. Shakira, featuring Wycleff Jean. Two such examples of the union of immigrant advocacy and popular art in Wycleff Jean's work include his April 2006 televised performances with Shakira at the *Latin Billboard Awards* and the *Today Show*. Altering the final lyrics of "Hips Don't Lie" as he instructed the *Today Show* audience "No fights/Immigrant rights, baybee," for both performance Jean donned similar tank tops reading "Immigration Rights, Mayo 10," a reference to the upcoming marches a few days later. In these televised performances as well as others, Jean strategically combined bilingual Spanish/English iconography and additional references to Colombia and/or Colombian flags. Shakira, featuring Wycleff Jean, *The Today Show*, NBC, 28 April 2007; Shakira, featuring Wycleff Jean, Latin Billboard Awards, *Telemundo*, 27 April 2007.

86. Shakira, featuring Wycleff Jean, "Hips Don't Lie," *Oral Fixation, Volume II*, EPIC, 2006.

87. Valdivia; Klich and Lesser, "Introduction: Images and Realities of Arab and Jewish Immigrants in Latin America," ix; Armando Vargas, "Migration, Literature, and the Nation: Majar Literature in Brazil" (Ph.D. diss., University of California, Berkeley, 2006).

88. Klich and Lesser; Ignacio Klich and Jeffrey Lesser, "Introduction: Images and Realities of Arab and Jewish Immigrants in Latin America," in *Arab and Jewish Immigrants in Latin America: Images and Realities*, ed. Ignacio Klich and Jeffrey Lesser (London: Frank Cass, 1998), ix.

89. Salaita 146–169.

AFTERWORD

1. Bloque, *"Descarga,"* Bloque, Luaka Bop, 1998; Julio Sánchez Cristo, "La fama y el dinero son lo de menos," *Semana*, 2 Dec. 2002, 30–34; Carlos Vives, *"La tierra del olvido,"* La tierra del olvido, Polygram Discos, 1995; Amy Kaplan, "Violent Belongings and the Question of Empire Today: Presidential Address to the American Studies Association, October 17, 2003," *American Quarterly* 56.1 (2004): 7, 10; Simon Frith, "The Discourse of World Music," in *Western Music and Its Others: Difference, Representation, and Appropriation in Music*, ed. Georgina Born and David Hesmondhalgh (Berkeley: University of California Press, 2000), 312, 314, 317.

2. Here I reference the September 2001 kidnapping and murder of Consuelo Araújonoguera by FARC rebels. As Colombia's ex-Minister of Culture and wife of the Nation's Attorney General, Araújonoguera was nationally beloved for her support of Colombia's traditional musical genres, particularly the *vallenato*. "Recuperado cuerpo de Consuelo Araújonoguera," *ElTiempo.com*, 30 Sept. 2001 <http://ww.eltiempo.terra.com.co/30-09-2001/ulti_pf_1.html>.

3. See Peter Wade, *Music, Race and Nation: Música Tropical in Colombia* (Chicago: University of Chicago Press, 2000), for further discussion of the Colombian government's recent efforts to instrumentalize *costeño* popular expression, in addition to Robert Alvarez, Jr., *Mangos, Chiles, and Truckers: The Business of Transnationalism* (Minneapolis: University of Minnesota Press, 2005), for a grounded analysis of the state-sponsored management of transnationalism.

4. Néstor García Canclini, *Transforming Modernity. Popular Culture in Mexico*, trans. Lidia Lozano (Austin: University of Texas Press, 1993), 113.

5. Dick Hebdige, *Subculture: The Meaning of Style* (London: Routledge, 1979), 75–76.

6. Andrew Leyshon, David Matless, and George Revill, preface, *The Place of Music*, ed. Andrew Leyshon, David Matless, and George Revill (New York: Guilford Press, 1998) 8.

7. Winfried Fluck, "Inside and Outside: What Kind of Knowledge Do We Need? A Response to the Presidential Address," *American Quarterly* 59.1 (2007): 30–31.

References

Abbas, Ackbar, and John Nguyet Erni, eds. *Internationalizing Cultural Studies: An Anthology*. Malden, MA: Blackwell, 2005.

Abu-Lughod, Lila. "Writing Against Culture." *Recapturing Anthropology*. Ed. Richard Fox. Santa Fe, NM: School of American Research Press, 1991. 137–162.

Adams, Noah, and Gustavo Arellano. "Review: Andrea Echeverri's Self-Titled Debut Album." *Day to Day*. National Public Radio. 18 April 2005.

Agudelo, Carlos. "New Colombian Sounds Coming to U.S. Market." *Billboard*, 15 Jan. 1983: 43.

Alvarez, Jr., Robert R. *Mangos, Chiles and Truckers: The Business of Transnationalism*. Minneapolis: University of Minnesota Press, 2005.

Amnistía Internacional. *Violencia política en Colombia. Mito y realidad*. Madrid: Editorial Amnistía Internacional, 1994.

Anderson, Benedict. "Exodus." *Critical Inquiry* 20.2 (1994): 314–327.

Aparicio, Frances R. "On Sub-Versive Signifiers: Tropicalizing Language in the United States." *Tropicalizations: Transcultural Representations of Latinidad*. Ed. Frances R. Aparicio and Susana Chávez-Silverman. Hanover, NH: Dartmouth/University Press of New England, 1997. 194–212.

———. *Listening to Salsa: Gender, Latin Popular Music, and Puerto Rican Cultures*. Hanover, NH: University Press of New England, 1998.

———. "The Blackness of Sugar: Celia Cruz and the Performance of (Trans)Nationalism." *Cultural Studies* 13.2 (1999): 223–236.

———. "Ethnifying Rhythms, Feminizing Cultures." *Music and the Racial Imagination*. Ed. Ronald Radano and Philip V. Bohlman. Chicago: University of Chicago Press, 2000. 95–112.

———. "La Lupe, La India, and Celia: Toward a Feminist Genealogy of Salsa Music." *Situating Salsa: Global Markets and Local Meaning in Latin Popular Music*. Ed. Lise Waxer. London: Routledge, 2002. 135–160.

———. "Gendered Transculturations in *Six Feet Under*: Implications for Rethinking Latin American, American, Latina/o and Gender Studies." Lecture. The Future of Ethnic Studies in/as American Studies, Williams College, Williamstown, MA, 12 March 2005.

Aparicio, Frances R., and Susana Chávez-Silverman. Introduction. *Tropicalizations: Transcultural Representations of Latinidad*. Ed. Frances R. Aparicio and Susana Chávez-Silverman. Hanover, NH: Dartmouth/University Press of New England, 1997.

Aparicio, Frances R., and Cándida Jáquez. Introduction. *Musical Migrations: Transnationalism and Cultural Hybridity in Latin/o America*. Ed. Frances R. Aparicio and Cándida Jáquez with María Elena Cepeda. New York: St. Martin's Press, 2003.

Aponte, Alex. "Miami, the Media Heavy." *Hispanic Business* (July-August 1998): 50ff.

Appadurai, Arjun. *Modernity at Large: Cultural Dimensions of Globalization*. Minneapolis: University of Minnesota Press, 1996.
Araújo de Molina, Consuelo. *Vallenatología. Orígenes y fundamentos de la música vallenata*. Bogotá: Ediciones Tercer Mundo, 1973.
Arévalo-Mateus, Jorge. "The Colombian Costeño Musicians of the New York Metropolitan Area: A Manifestation of Urban Vallenato." Master's thesis. Hunter College, CUNY, 1998.
Arias Polo, Arturo. "Carlos Vives: un cantautor con sonido propio." *Elherald.com*, 18 Nov. 1999 <http://www.elherald.com/content/mon/digdocs/arte/viernes/046073.htm>.
Arnold, Chuck, and Linda Trischitta. "Bomba shell." *People*, 2 Feb. 2002: 134–136.
Arocha, Jaime. "Inclusion of Afro-Colombians: Unreachable National Goal?" *Latin American Perspectives* 25.3 (1998): 70–89.
Arocha Rodríguez, Jaime. "Afro-Colombia Denied." *North American Congress on Latin America (NACLA)* 25.4 (1992): 28–31.
Arregocés Carrere, Benyi. "Champeta." *Fundación Cultural Son al Son*. 2000. <http:/www.radiorabel.com/ritmosybailes/champeta.htm>.
"Artistas colombianos ganan cinco premios Grammy Latinos." *ElTiempo.com*, 31 Oct. 2001 <http://www.eltiempo.com/>.
Associated Press. "Hispanics Set to Surpass Blacks in Buying Power in U.S." *International Herald Tribune*, 1 Sept. 2006 <http://iht.com/bin/print_ipub.php?file=/articles/ap/2006/09/01/business/NA_FIN_US_Hispanics_Buying_Power.php>.
Aterciopelados. "La estaca." *El Dorado*. Dir. Carlos Gaviria. MTV Latino. 1995.
———. "Baracunátana." *La pipa de la paz*. RCA International, 1996.
———. *Colombia conexión*. El Dorado. RCA International, 1995.
———. "Cosita seria." *La pipa de la paz*. RCA International, 1996.
———. "Cosita seria." *La pipa de la paz*. RCA International, 1996.
———. "Miss Panela." *La pipa de la paz*. RCA International, 1996.
———. "No necesito." *La pipa de la paz*. RCA International, 1996.
———. "El estuche." *Caribe atómico*. RCA International, 1998.
———. "El estuche." *Caribe atómico*. Dir. Marina Zurkow. MTV Latino. 1998.
———. "Florecita rockera 2003." *Evolución*. RCA International, 2002.
"Aterciopelados se quedarán en Colombia, pese al conflicto armado." Efe News Services (U.S.). Spanish Newswire Services [cited 8 Feb. 2001].
Austerlitz, Saul. *Money for Nothing: A History of Music Video From the Beatles to the White Stripes*. New York: Continuum, 2006.
Báez, Anna Cristina. Personal communication. 30 Nov. 2000.
Báez, Jillian. " 'En mi imperio': Competing Discourses of Agency in Ivy Queen's Reggaetón." *CENTRO Journal* 18.11 (2006): 62–81.
———. "Mexican (American) Women Talk Back: Audience Responses to Representations of Latinidad in U.S. Advertising." *Latina/o Communication Studies Today*. Ed. Angharad N. Valdivia. New York: Peter Lang, 2008. 257–282.
Baldwin, Kristen. "The Best Next Thing." *Entertainment Weekly*, 31 March 2000: 20–28.
Ballvé, Marcelo. "The Battle for Latino Media." *North American Congress on Latin America (NACLA)* 37.4 (Jan.-Feb. 2004): 20–25.
Banks, Jack. *Monopoly Television: MTV's Quest to Control the Music*. Boulder, CO: Westview Press, 1996.

Bayton, Mavis. "Feminist Musical Practice: Problems and Contradictions." *Rock and Popular Music: Politics, Policies, Institutions*. Ed. Tony Bennett, Simon Frith, Lawrence Grossberg, John Shepherd, and Graeme Turner. London: Routledge, 1993. 177–192.

Behdad, Ali. *A Forgetful Nation: On Immigration and Cultural Identity in the United States*. Durham, NC: Duke University Press, 2005.

Bennett, Tony, Simon Frith, Lawrence Grossberg, John Shepherd and Graeme Turner, eds. *Rock and Popular Music: Politics, Policies, Institutions*. London: Routledge, 1993.

Bergquist, Charles, Ricardo Peñaranda, and Gonzalo Sánchez, eds. *Violence in Colombia, 1990–2000: Waging War and Negotiating Peace*. Lanham, MD: SR Books, 2001.

Berland, Jody. "Sound, Image and Social Space: Music Video and Media Reconstruction." *Sound and Vision: The Music Video Reader*. Ed. Simon Frith, Andrew Goodwin, and Lawrence Grossberg. London: Routledge, 1993. 25–43.

Bernstein, Nina, and Adam Glick. "The New Immigrant Dream: Arepas as Common as Bagels." *New York Times*, 6 Feb. 2007: A1.

Berríos-Miranda, Marisol. " 'Con Sabor a Puerto Rico': The Reception and Influence of Puerto Rican Salsa in Venezuela." *Musical Migrations: Transnationalism and Cultural Hybridity in Latin/o America*. Ed. Frances R. Aparicio and Cándida Jáquez with María Elena Cepeda. New York: St. Martin's Press, 2003. 47–67.

Beverley, John. "The Ideology of Postmodern Music and Leftist Politics." *Against Literature*. Minneapolis: University of Minneapolis Press, 1993. 124–142.

Beverley, John, and David Houston. "Una utopía degradada: notas sobre Miami." Trans. Juan Pablo Dabove. *Heterotropías: Narrativas de identidad en América Latina*. Ed. Juan Pablo Dabove and Carlos Jáuregui. Pittsburgh: ILLI, 2003. 419–445.

Binder, Frederick M., and David M. Reimers. "New York as an Immigrant City." *Origins and Destinies*. Ed. Silvia Pedraza and Rubén G. Rumbaut. Belmont, CA: Wadsworth, 1996. 334–345.

Bloque. "*Descarga.*" *Bloque*. Luaka Bop, 1998.

Blow. DVD. Directed by Ted Demme. New Line Home Video, 2001.

Bolaño Saurith, Paúl. "Caja, guarcharaca, y acordeón." *El Tiempo-Caribe*, 17 April 1998: 5.

Borger, Julian. "Republican Grip Starts to Loosen in Little Havana." *Guardian* (London, England), 5 Oct. 2004: 12.

Branch-Brioso, Karen. "El poder político en Miami es complejo." *El Nuevo Herald*, 4 Sept. 2000 <http://www.elherald.com/content/archivos/poder/docs/008125.htm>.

Branch-Brioso, Karen, Tim Henderson, and Alfonso Chardy. "Los anglos, el poder verdadero." *El Nuevo Herald* 3 Sept. 2000 <http://www.elherald.com/content/archivos/poder/docs/078386.htm>.

———. "Sondeo rompe el mito del poder cubano en Miami-Dade." *El Nuevo Herald*, 3 Sept. 2000 <http://www.elnuevoherald.com/content/archivos/poder/docs/086872.htm>.

Braun, Herbert. *Our Guerrillas, Our Sidewalks: A Journey Into the Violence of Colombia*. Lanham, MD: Rowman & Littlefield, 2003.

Burns, Gary. "Formula and Distinctiveness in Movie-Based Music Videos." *Popular Music and Society* 18.4 (1994): 7–18.

———. "How Music Video Has Changed, and How It Has Not Changed." *Popular Music and Society* 18.3 (1994): 67–80.

———. "'Where the Action Is': Dick Clark's Precursor to Music Video." *Journal of Popular Film and Television* 25.1 (1997): 31–38.

———. "Visualizing 1950s Hits on 'Your Hit Parade.'" *Popular Music* 17.2 (1998): 139–153.
———. "Pop Up Video: The New Historicism. *Journal of Popular Film and Television* 32.2 (2004): 74–83.
Bush, Gregory W. "'Playground of the USA': Miami and the Promotion of Spectacle." *Pacific Historical Review* 68.2 (May 1999): 153–172.
Bushnell, David. *The Making of Modern Colombia: A Nation in Spite of Itself.* Berkeley: University of California Press, 1993.
Butler, Rhett. "And Our Winners Are . . ." *Time*, Fall 2001: 29.
Cabán, Pedro. "The New Synthesis of Latin American and Latino Studies." *Borderless Borders: U.S. Latinos, Latin Americans, and the Paradox of Interdependence.* Ed. Frank Bonilla, Edwin Meléndez, Rebecca Morales and María de los Angeles Torres. Philadelphia: Temple University Press, 1998. 195–215.
Cabrera, Carlos Augusto. E-mail forwarded to the author containing the article "Para los colombianos, los eventos culturales importantes son de la Costa Caribe." Bernardo Bejarano González. *ElTiempo.com*, 14 July 2002.
Caicedo, Andrés. *¡Que viva la música!* Bogotá: Editorial Norma, 2001.
Campo Miranda, Rafael. *Crónicas didácticas sobre el folclor musical de Colombia.* Barranquilla: Editorial Mejoras, 1999.
Cárdenas Duque, Rocío. *Música caribeña. Tres países y un sólo ritmo. Ensayos.* Cali: Centro Editorial/Universidad de Valle, 1992.
Cardona, Eliseo. "Shakira: From Colombia to the World." *CDNOW*, 20 Sept. 2000 <http://www.cdnow.com>.
Casillas, Dolores Inés. "From Colonial Hottentot to Post-Colonial 'Hottie': Jennifer López' Re(butt)als to White America." Students of Color of Rackham Conference. University of Michigan, Ann Arbor, Michigan, 13 Feb. 2000.
———. "Sounds of Belonging: A Cultural History of Spanish-Language Radio in the United States." Ph.D. diss., University of Michigan, Ann Arbor, 2006.
———. "A Morning Dose of Latino Masculinity: U.S. Spanish-Language Radio and the Politics of Gender." *Latina/o Communication Studies Today.* Ed. Angharad N. Valdivia. New York: Peter Lang, 2008. 161–186.
Casillas, Dolores Inés, and María Elena Cepeda. "How *Tejas* Arrived at *La Isla*: Jennifer López, Selena, and the Construction of a Latina Iconography." Puerto Rican Studies Association. Congress Plaza Hotel, Chicago, 5 Oct. 2002.
Castro Caycedo, Germán. *El Hueco.* Bogotá: Planeta, 1989.
Cepeda, María Elena. "Columbus Effect(s): The Politics of Crossover and Chronology within the Latin(o) Music 'Boom.'" *Discourse* 23.1 (2001): 242–267.
———. "Shakira as the Idealized, Transnational Citizen: A Case Study of *Colombianidad* in Transition." *Latino Studies* 1.2 (2003): 210–232.
———. "Survival Aesthetics: U.S. Latinas and the Negotiation of Popular Media." *Latina/o Communication Studies Today.* Ed. Angharad N. Valdivia. New York: Peter Lang, 2008. 237–256.
Chaparro, María Alejandra. "Little Colombia: Teen Immigrants Make New Lives in the United States." *Hemisphere* 11.3 (2002): 8–11.
Chernick, Marc W. "The Paramilitarization of the War in Colombia." *NACLA*, March-April 1998: 28–33.

Christie, Andrew. "The Debate You're Not Hearing: Immigration and Trade." *Common Dreams News Center*, 8 April 2006 <http://www.commonsdreams.org>.

Citron, Marcia J. *Gender and the Musical Canon*. Urbana: University of Illinois Press, 2000.

Clary, Mike. "Colombians Flee Homeland to Seek Refuge in Miami." *Los Angeles Times*, 12 Oct. 1999: 1.

Clemens, Luis. "The Sound that Sells." *Marketing y Medios*, December 2005 <www.marketingymedios.com/marketingymedios/magazine/article_display.jsp?vun_content_id=100>.

Click, Melissa A., and Michael W. Kramer. "Reflections on a Century of Living: Gendered Differences in Mainstream Popular Songs." *Popular Communication* 5.4 (2007): 241–262.

Clifford, James. "Diasporas." *Internationalizing Cultural Studies: An Anthology*. Ed. Ackbar Abbas and John Nguyet Erni. Malden, MA: Blackwell, 2005. 524–558.

Coates, Norma. "(R)evolution Now? Rock and the Political Potential of Gender." *Sexing the Groove: Popular Music and Gender*. Ed. Sheila Whiteley. London: Routledge, 1997. 50–64.

Cobb, Kim. "Changing Mix of Latinos Stirs Florida Politics: Cuban-American Support for GOP Could Be Offset by Other Hispanics." *Houston Chronicle*, 28 Sept. 2004: A1.

Cobo, Leila. "A Rich Musical Tradition Swells Up and Out Into the World." *Miami Herald*, 25 July 1999: 5m, 7m.

———. "Santander, Estefan Resolve Legal Quarrel." *Billboard*, 6 April 2002: 8.

———. Interview With John Ydstie. *All Things Considered*. National Public Radio. 18 Sept. 2002.

———. "Shakira x 2." *azcentral.com*, 24 May 2005 <http://www.azcentral.com/ent/music/articles/0525shakira.html>.

———. "Latin Music Sales Plummet in 2007." *reuters.com*, 10 Dec. 2007 <http://www.reuters.com/article/musicNews/idUSN1043099320071210>.

Cobo-Hanlon, Leila. "Barefoot Girl: Pop Diva Shakira Comes of Age." *L.A. Weekly*, 22 Nov. 1996: 51.

Cocaine Cowboys. DVD. Directed by Billy Corben. Magnolia Pictures, 2005.

Cohen, Howard. "There's Something About Miami." *Billboard*, 15 May 1999: 51–57.

Cohen, Sara. "Men Making a Scene: Rock Music and the Production of Gender." *Sexing the Groove: Popular Music and Gender*. Ed. Sheila Whiteley. London and New York: Routledge, 1997. 17–36.

Collier, Michael W. "Colombian Migration to South Florida: A Most Unwelcome Reception." Working paper. Colombian Studies Institute, Latin American and Caribbean Center. Florida International University, Miami, Florida. May 2004 <http://digitalcommons.fiu.edu/laccwps/2/>.

"Colombia." *The New Grove Dictionary of Music and Musicians*. 6th ed. New York: Grove's Dictionaries, 1980.

Colombia, South America, 2008 [map]. 1:200. "Political Map of Colombia." 2008. Central Intelligence Agency. The World Factbook <https://www.cia.gov/library/publications/the-world-factbook/geos/co.html>.

"Colombia se mueve." *Semana.com*, 29 August 2004 <http:www.semana.com>.

"Colombia's Diaspora." Chart. *New York Times on the Web*, 10 April 2001 <http://www.nytimes.com>.

"Colombia's Other Import." Editorial. *Palm Beach Post*, 6 April 2000: 16A.

"The Colombian Diaspora: Miami Nice." *Economist.com*, 3 May 2001 <http://www.economist.com>.

"The Colombian Diaspora in South Florida." Working paper. Colombian Studies Institute, Latin American and Caribbean Center. Florida International University, Miami, Florida. May 2001 <http://lacc.fiu.edu/Publications/working_paper_01.htm>.

Colón, Willie. "The Latin Grammys: Is There No End to the Egotism of the Miami Mafia?" Trans. Octavio Romano. Fwd. by Wilson Valentín-Escobar. 18 Sept. 2000 <http://www.egroups.com/group/AztlanNet>.

"Conéctese con una causa—Migraciones." *conexioncolombia.com*, 20 Aug. 2006 <http://www.conexioncolombia.com/conexioncolombia/content/page.jsp?ID=887>.

"Conexión Colombia." *Semana*, 11 Nov. 2002: 17.

Contreras, Feliz. "Defining Latin Alternative Music." *All Things Considered*. National Public Radio, 7 March 2006.

Cunin, Elizabeth. "El caribe visto desde el interior del país: estereotipos raciales y sexuales." *Revista de Estudios Colombianos* 30 (2006): 6–14.

Curtis, James R., and Richard F. Rose. "'The Miami Sound': A Contemporary Latin Form of Place-Specific Music." *The Sound of People and Places: A Geography of American Folk and Popular Music*. Ed. George O. Carney. 3rd ed. Lanham, MD: Rowman & Littlefield, 1994. 263–273.

Cusick, Suzanne G. "On a Lesbian Relationship With Music: A Serious Effort Not to Thnk Straight." *Queering the Pitch: The New Gay and Lesbian Musicology*. 2nd ed. Ed. Elizabeth Wood and Philip Brett. London: Routledge, 2006. 67–85.

Darling, Juanita. "Colombia Strikes a New Note." *Los Angeles Times*, 25 Sept. 1998: A1.

Das Gupta, Monica. *Unruly Immigrants: Rights, Activism and Transnational South Asians Politics in the United States*. Durham, NC: Duke University Press, 2006.

Dávila, Arlene. *Latinos, Inc.: The Marketing and Making of a People*. Berkeley: University of California Press, 2001.

Dávila, José. "Bush Whacked by Ricky Martin." *miaminewtimes.com*, 17 May 2007 <http://www.music.miaminewtimes.com/2007-05-17/music/bush-whacked-by-ricky-martin/print>.

Davis, Martha Ellen. "An Antidote to Crisis." *Hemisphere* 11.3 (2002): 4–7.

Davis, Mike. *Magical Urbanism: Latinos Reinvent The U.S. Big City*. London: Verso, 2000.

Deas, Malcolm. "Violent Exchanges: Reflections on Political Violence in Colombia." *The Legitimization of Violence*. Ed. David E. Apter. New York: New York University Press, 1997. 350–404.

De Certeau, Michel. *The Practice of Everyday Life*. Trans. Steven Rendall. Berkeley: University of California Press, 1984.

Deevoy, Adrian. "Colombian Gold." *Maxim Blender* April-May 2001: 100–107.

De Genova, Nicholas, and Ana Y. Ramos-Zayas. *Latino Crossings: Mexicans, Puerto Ricans, and the Politics of Race and Citizenship*. London: Routledge, 2003.

De la Riva, Roxana. "Alvaro Nieto: 'Quiero trabajar por los colombianos.'" *La Prensa* (San Antonio, TX). 2 Feb. 2006: 10.

De León, Sergio. "Shakira Welcomed Home in Colombia. *abcnews.com*, 15 Nov. 2006 <http://abcnews.go.com/Entertainment/wireStory?id=2656785&CMP=OTC-RSSFeeds0312/>.

Del Villar Sierra, Oliverio. "Significa resistir." *Colombia: País de regiones*. Ed. Fabio Zambrano F. Vol. 1. Bogotá: Cinep, 1998. 302–305.

Dermota, Ken. "Colombia's 'Elvis' Popularizes New Folk." *Christian Science Monitor*, 28 Aug. 1995: 14.

Desmond, Jane. "Embodying Difference: Issues in Dance and Cultural Studies." *Everynight Life: Culture and Dance in Latin/o America*. Ed. Celeste Fraser Delgado and José Esteban Muñoz. Durham, NC: Duke University Press, 1997. 33–64.

Dibben, Nicola. "Representations of Femininity in Popular Music." *Popular Music* 18.3 (1999): 331–355.

Dickerson, Marla. "Placing Blame for Mexico's Ills." *Los Angeles Times*, 1 July 2006 <http://www.latimes.com>.

"Diosa coronada." *Semana*, 26 Feb. 2001: 25–29.

Dolinsky, Lewis. "The True State of Colombia." *San Francisco Chronicle*, 22 April 2001 <http://www.sfgate.com/chronicle>.

Domínguez, Virginia R. "For a Politics of Love and Rescue." *Cultural Anthropology* 15.3 (2000): 361–393.

Dorfman, Steve, Luis R. Rigual, and Linda Larx. "The City's Most Fascinating Faces of 2000." *Miami Metro* (December 2000): 31–36.

Drummond, Tammerlin. "Godfather of the Miami Sound." *Time*, 24 May 1999: 78.

Duany, Jorge. "Popular Music in Puerto Rico: Toward an Anthropology of Salsa." *Latin American Music Review* 5.2 (1984): 186–216.

Dudley, Steven. "Walking Through the Nightscapes of Bogotá." *North American Congress on Latin America (NACLA)* (Sept.-Oct. 1999): 10–14.

———. *Walking Ghosts: Murder and Guerrilla Politics in Colombia*. New York: Routledge, 2004.

Dugas, John C. "Colombian Attitudes Toward the United States After 9/11." *America: Sovereign Defender or Cowboy Nation*? Ed. Vladmir Shlapentokh, Joshua Woods, and Eric Shiraev. Hants, Great Britan/Burlington, VT: Ashgate, 2005. 69–88.

Echeverri, Andrea. "Lactochampeta." *Andrea Echeverri*. Nacional Records, 2005.

"Election 2000: Bush, Gore, Locked in Unprecedented Fight for Control of the White House." Special Event. CNN. Miami. 8 Nov. 2000.

"El elegido." *Semana*, 11 Nov. 2002: 104.

Elliot, Andrea. "Thousands Flee War in Colombia, Plan New Lives in U.S." *Miami Herald*, 29 Aug. 2001 <http://www.miami.com/herald/content/news/local/broward/digdocs/079752.html>.

Elliot, Emory. "Diversity in the United States and Abroad: What Does It Mean When American Studies Is Transnational?" *American Quarterly* 59.1 (2007): 1–22.

"Emilio Estefan tilda a Willie Colón de izquierdista." *El Universal*, 20 Oct. 2000 <http://www.el-universal.com.mx>.

Emerson, Rana A. "'Where My Girls At?': Negotiating Black Womanhood in Music Videos." *Gender & Society* 16.1 (2002): 155–135.

"En la variedad está el placer." *Semana*, 5 Nov. 2001: 80–81.

Escobar, Cristina. "Dual Citizenship and Political Participation: Migrants in the Interplay of United States and Colombian Politics." *Latinos and Citizenship: The Dilemma of Belonging.* Ed. Suzanne Oboler. New York: Palgrave Macmillan, 2006. 113–141.

Espitia, Marilyn. "The Other 'Other Hispanics': South American-Origin Latinos in the United States." *Columbia History of Latinos in the United States Since 1960.* Ed. David G. Gutiérrez. New York: Columbia University Press, 2004. 257–280.

Esterrich, Carmelo, and Javier H. Murillo. "Rock With Punk With Pop With Folklore: Transformations and Renewal in Aterciopelados and Café Tacuba." *Latin American Music Review* 21.1 (2000): 31–44.

"Éxodo con visa." *Semana,* 6 Nov. 2000: 58–60.

Falconi, José Luis, and José Antonio Mazzotti, eds. Introduction. *The Other Latinos: Central and South Americans in the United States.* Cambridge, MA: Harvard University Press, 2007.

Farber, Jim. "Ricky, Listen to These Numbers; Move Over Martin, Tell López the News . . ." *Daily News* [New York], 4 March 2001: 13.

Farley, Christopher John. "Latin Music Pops." *Time,* 24 May 1999: 74–79.

———. "Sounds of Magic Realism." *Time,* 14 May 2001: 72.

———. "The Making of a Rocker." *Time,* Fall 2001: 16–18.

Farley, Christopher John, with David E. Thigpen. "Christina Aguilera: Building a 21st Century Star." *Time,* 6 March 2000: 71–72.

Farrell, Cathleen, and Valeria Escobar. "¡Que le pongan salsa!" *Poder* (April 2002): 22–26.

Fast, Susan. *In the Houses of the Holy: Led Zeppelin and the Power of Rock Music.* Oxford: Oxford University Press, 2001.

Fawcett, Louise, and Eduardo Posada-Carbó. "Arabs and Jews in the Development of the Colombian Caribbean, 1850–1950." *Arab and Jewish Immigrants in Latin America: Images and Realities.* Ed. Ignacio Klich and Jeffer Lesser. London and Portland, OR: Frank Cass, 1998. 57–591.

Feldman, Heidi. *Black Rhythms of Peru: Reviving African Musical Heritage in the Black Pacific.* Middleton, CT: Wesleyan University Press, 2006.

Fernández, Enrique. "Topline Colombian." *Village Voice,* 1 Feb. 1983: 81–82.

Fernández, Raúl. *From Afro-Cuban Rhythms to Latin Jazz.* Berkeley: University of California, 2006.

Fernández, Raúl, and Bernardo Useche. "'¡No somos criminales; somos trabajadores!': La emigración latinoamericana a Estados Unidos." *Deslinde: Revista del Centro de Estudios del Trabajo* 40 (Sept.-Nov. 2006) <http://deslinde.org.co>.

Fernández L'Hoeste, Héctor D. "On How Bloque de Búsqueda Lost Part of Its Name: The Predicaments of Colombian Rock in the U.S. Market." *Rockin' Las Americas: Rock Music and Rock Cultures Across Latin(o) America.* Ed. Deborah Pacini Hernández, Héctor D. Fernández L'Hoeste, and Eric Zolov. Pittsburgh: University of Pittsburgh Press, 2004. 179–199.

———. "Del vallenato propio y ajeno: Hacia una reconfiguración del imaginario colombiano y mexicano." *Revista de Estudios Colombianos* 27–28 (2005): 73–77.

———. "All Cumbias, the Cumbia: The Latin Americanization of a Tropical Genre." *Imagining Our Americas: Toward a Transnational Frame.* Eds. Sandhya Shukla and Heidi Tinsman. Durham, NC: Duke University Press, 2007. 338–364.

Fiol-Matta, Licia. "Pop *Latinidad*: Puerto Ricans in the Latin Explosion, 1999." *CENTRO Journal* 14.1 (2002): 27–51.

Fiske, John. *Understanding Popular Culture*. London and New York: Routledge, 1989.

Flores, Juan. *From Bomba to Hip-Hop: Puerto Rican Culture and Latino Identity*. New York: Columbia University Press, 2000.

———. "Latina/o Studies: New Contexts, New Concepts." *Critical Latin American and Latina/o Studies*. Ed. Juan Poblete. Minneapolis: University of Minnesota Press, 2003. 191–205.

Fluck, Winfried. "Inside and Outside: What Kind of Knowledge Do We Need?: A Responsse to the Presidential Address." *American Quarterly* 59.1 (2007): 23–32.

Foner, Nancy. "Second-Generation Transnationalism, Then and Now." *The Changing Face of Home: The Transnational Lives of the Second Generation*. Ed. Peggy Levitt and Mary Waters. New York: Russell Sage, 2002. 242–252.

Forero, Juan. "Prosperous Colombians Fleeing, Many to the U.S." *New York Times on the Web*, 10 April 2001 <http://www.nytimes.com>.

Foucault, Michel. *The History of Sexuality: An Introduction*. Vol. 1. Trans. Robert Hurley. New York: Vintage Books, 1990.

Franco, Natalia. "The Colombian Migration to South Florida: Expectations and Experiences." Master's thesis, Florida International University, 2002.

Fraser Delgado, Celeste. "Velvet Offensive." *miaminewtimes.com*, 21 June 2001 <http://www.miaminewtimes.com/issues/2001-06-21/feature.html/printable_page>.

———. "Los Producers." *miaminewtimes.com*, 6 Sept. 2001 <http://www.miaminewtimes.com/issues/2001-09-06/feature.html/print.html>.

———. "Viva Colombia! Could Shakira End the Economic Slump?" *miaminewtimes.com*, 22 Nov. 2001 <http://www.miaminewtimes.com/issues/2001-11-22/shake.html/print.html>.

———. "What Rock and Roll Owes the Blues, Carlos Vives Owes Vallenato." *miaminewtimes.com*, 20 Dec. 2001 <http://www.miaminewtimes.com/issues.2001-12-20/music.html/print/html>.

———. Personal Interview. 23 May 2002.

———. "Yo Quiero Mi MTV." *miaminewtimes.com*, 24 Oct. 2002 <http://www.miaminewtimes.com/Issues/2002-10-24/music/music_print.html>.

———. "Not for Export." *www.miamisunpost.com*, 23 Feb. 2006, <http://www.miamisunpost.com/archives/2006/02-23-06/entertainment%20industry.htm>.

Fregoso, Rosa Linda. *MeXicana Encounters: The Making of Social Identities on the Borderlands*. Berkeley: University of California Press, 2003.

Frith, Simon. "Towards an Aesthetic of Popular Music." *Music and Society: The Politics of Composition, Performance, and Reception*. Ed. Susan McClary and Richard Leppert. Cambridge: Cambridge University Press, 1987. 133–149.

———. "The Discourse of World Music." *Western Music and Its Others: Difference, Representation, and Appropriation in Music*. Ed. Georgina Born and David Hesmondhalgh. Berkeley: University of California Press, 2000. 305–322.

Frith, Simon, and Andrew Goodwin, eds. *On Record: Rock, Pop and the Written Word*. London: Routledge, 2000.

Frith, Simon, Andrew Goodwin, and Lawrence Grossberg, eds. *Sound and Vision: The Music Video Reader*. London: Routledge, 1993.

Gage, Julienne. "The British *Invasión*." miaminewtimes.com, 17 May 2007 <http://www.music.miaminewtimes.com/2007-01-17/music/the-british-invasi-0acute-n/print>.
García, Guy. "Another Latin Boom, but Different." *New York Times*, 27 June 1999: 25ff.
García Canclini, Néstor. "Cultural Reconversion." Trans. Holly Staver. *On Edge: The Crisis of Contemporary Latin American Culture*. Ed. George Yúdice, Jean Franco, and Juan Flores. Minneapolis: University of Minneapolis Press, 1991. 29–43.
——. *Transforming Modernity. Popular Culture in Mexico*. Trans. Lidia Lozano. Austin: University of Texas Press, 1993.
——. *Hybrid Cultures. Strategies for Entering and Leaving Modernity*. Trans. Christopher L. Chiappari and Silvia L. López. Minneapolis: University of Minneapolis Press, 1995.
García Márquez, Gabriel. *Cien años de soledad*. Madrid: Ediciones Cátedra, 1997.
——. "Valledupar, la parranda del siglo." *RevistaCambio.com*, 5 April 2001 <http://www.revistacambio.com/web/interior.php?idp=8&ids=40&ida=240.htm>.
Garofalo, Reebee. "Black Popular Music: Crossing Over or Going Under?" *Rock and Popular Music: Politics, Policies, Institutions*. Ed. Tony Bennett, Simon Frith, Lawrence Grossberg, John Shepherd, and Graeme Turner. London: Routledge, 1993. 231–248.
——. *Rockin' Out: Popular Music in the USA*. Boston: Allyn and Bacon, 1997.
Gell, Aaron. "Love in the Time of Shakira." *Elle*, April 2006: 304–309, 345.
Ghitis, Frida. "The Colombian Miracle." *Arkansas Democrat-Gazette* (Little Rock), 8 July 2008 <http://www.2.arkansasonline.com>.
Gilroy, Paul. *The Black Atlantic: Modernity and Double Consciousness*. Cambridge, MA: Harvard University Press, 1993.
Giraldo, Javier. *Colombia: The Genocidal Democracy*. Monroe, ME: Common Courage Press, 1996.
Glasser, Ruth. *My Music Is My Flag: Puerto Rican Musicians and Their New York Communities, 1917–1940*. Berkeley: University of California Press, 1995.
——. "Musical Darwinism." Música de las Américas: Salsa and Latin Jazz Panel Discussion. Smithsonian Institution. S. Dillon Ripley Center, Washington, DC, 31 July 1999.
Glick-Schiller, Nina. "Transnational Urbanism as a Way of Life: A Research Topic Not a Metaphor." *City & Society* 17.1 (2005): 49–64.
Glick Schiller, Nina, and Georges Eugene Fouron. "Transnational Lives and National Identities: The Identity Politics of Haitian Immigrants." *Transnationalism From Below*. Ed. Michael Peter Smith and Luis Eduardo Guarnizo. New Brunswick, NJ: Transaction, 1998. 130–161.
——. *Georges Woke Up Laughing: Long-Distance Nationalism and the Search for Home*. Durham, NC: Duke University Press, 2001.
Goldring, Luin. "The Power of Status in Transnational Social Fields." *Transnationalism from Below*. Ed. Michael Peter Smith and Luis Eduardo Guarnizo. New Brunswick, NJ: Transaction, 1998. 165–195.
Goodman, Peter S. "In Mexico, People Do Really Want to Stay: Chicken Farmers Fear U.S. Exports Will Send More Workers North for Jobs." *Washington Post*, 7 January 2007: A01.
Goodnough, Abby. "Hispanic Vote in Florida: Neither a Bloc Nor Lock." *New York Times*, 17 Oct. 2004: 31.
Goodwin, Andrew. *Dancing in the Distraction Factory: Music Television and Popular Culture*. Minneapolis: University of Minnesota Press, 1992.

"Grave compromiso." Editorial. *La Nación* (San José, Costa Rica), 23 May 2000: 13A.
Grenier, Guillermo J., and Max J. Castro. "Triadic Politics: Ethnicity, Race, and Politics in Miami, 1959–1998." *Pacific Historical Review* 68.2 (May 1999): 273–292.
Grewal, Inderpal. *Transnational America: Feminisms, Diasporas, Neoliberalisms*.Durham, NC: Duke University Press, 2005.
Grossberg, Lawrence. "The Media Economy of Rock Culture: Cinema, Postmodernity and Authenticity." *Sound and Vision: The Music Video Reader*. Ed. Simon Frith, Andrew Goodwin, and Lawrence Grossberg. London: Routledge, 1993. 185–209.
Guarín R., Martha. "Mi tierra se merece lo mejor: Shakira." *El Heraldo* (Barranquilla, Colombia), 16 Nov. 2006 <http//: elheraldo.com.co/anteriores/06-11-16/sociales/noti3.htm/>.
Guarnizo, Luis Eduardo. "On the Political Participation of Transnational Migrants: Old Practices and New Trends." *E Pluribus Unum? Contemporary and Historical Perspectives on Immigrant Political Incorporation*. Ed. Gary Gerstle and John Mollenkopf. New York: Russell Sage Foundation, 2001. 213–263.
Guarnizo, Luis Eduardo, and Marilyn Espitia. "Colombia." *The New Americans: A Guide to Immigration Since 1965*. Ed. Mary C. Waters and Reed Ueda with Helen B. Marrow. Cambridge, MA: Harvard University Press, 2007. 371–385.
Guarnizo, Luis Eduardo, and Luz Marina Díaz. "Transnational Migration: A View From Colombia." *Ethnic and Racial Studies* 22.3 (1999): 397–421.
Guarnizo, Luis Eduardo, Arturo Ignacio Sánchez, and Elizabeth M. Roach. "Mistrust, Fragmented Solidarity and Transnational Migration: Colombians in New York City and Los Angeles." *Ethnic and Racial Studies* 22.3 (1999): 367–396.
Guilbault, Jocelyn. "On Redefining the 'Local' Through World Music." *The World of Music* 35.2 (1993): 33–47.
Gurak, Douglas, and Greta Gilbertson. "Household Transitions in the Migrations of Dominicans and Colombians to New York." *International Migration Review* 26 (1992): 22–45.
Gutiérrez, David G. *The Columbia History of Latinos in the United States Since 1960*. New York: Columbia University Press, 2004.
Habell-Pallán, Michelle. *Locomotion: The Travels of Chicana and Latina Popular Culture*. New York: New York University Press, 2005.
Habib, Caitlin. "The Two Sides of Shakira." *Urban Latino* 58 (July 2005): 39–42.
Hagen, Jason. "New Colombian President Promises More War." *North American Congress on Latin America (NACLA)* (July–Aug. 2002): 24–29.
Hall, Stuart. "Encoding/decoding." *Culture, Media, Language: Working Papers in Cultural Studies, 1972–79*. London: Hutchinson, 1980. 128–138.
———. "Notes on Deconstructing 'The Popular.'" *People's History and Socialist Theory*. Ed. Raphael Samuel. London: Routledge and Kegan Paul, 1981. 227–240.
———. "The Whites of Their Eyes: Racist Ideologies and the Media." *Silver Linings: Some Strategies for the Eighties: Contributions to the Communist University of Londond*. Ed. Communist University of London. London: Lawrence and Wishart, 1981. 28–52.
———. "What Is This 'Black' in Black Popular Culture?" *Black Popular Culture*. Ed. Gina Dent. Seattle: Bay Press, 1992. 21–36.
———. "Old and New Identities, Old and New Ethnicities." *Culture, Globalization and the World System. Contemporary Conditions for the Representation of Identity*. Ed. Anthony D. King. Minneapolis: University of Minnesota Press, 1997. 43–68.

———. "Cultural Identity and Diaspora." *Theorizing Diaspora: A Reader*. Eds. Jana Evans Braziel and Anita Mannur. Malden, MA: Blackwell, 2003. 233–246.

Hanke, Robert. "'Yo Quiero Mi MTV!': Making Music Television for Latin America." *Mapping the Beat: Popular Music and Contemporary Theory*. Ed. Thomas Swiss, John Sloop, and Andrew Herman. Malden, MA: Blackwell, 1998. 219–245.

Hartman, Saidiya. "Seduction and the Uses of Power." *Between Woman and Nation: Nationalisms, Transnational Feminisms, and the State*. Ed. Norma Alarcón, Caren Kaplan, and Minoo Moallem. Durham, NC: Duke University Press, 1999. 111–141.

Hayden, Thomas, and Karen Schoemer. "¿Se Habla Rock and Roll? You Will Soon." *Newsweek*, 8 Sept. 1997: 70–71.

Hebdige, Dick. *Subculture: The Meaning of Style*. London and New York: Routledge, 1979.

Heinz, Wolfgang S. "Violencia política y cambio social en Colombia." *Literatura colombiana hoy: Imaginación y barbarie*. Ed. Karl Kohut. Madrid: Iberoamericana, 1994. n.p.

Helg, Aline. "Race in Argentina and Cuba, 1880–1930: Theory, Policies, and Popular Reaction." *The Idea of Race in Latin America, 1870–1940*. Ed. Richard Graham. Austin: University of Texas Press, 1990. 37–69.

Hermes, Joke. *Re-Reading Popular Culture*. Malden, MA: Blackwell, 2005.

Hernández, Tanya Katerí. "The Buena Vista Social Club: The Racial Politics of Nostalgia." *Latina/o Popular Culture*. Ed. Michelle Habell-Pallán and Mary Romero. New York: New York University Press, 2002. 61–72.

"Hispanic or Latino by Specific Origin." Table. U.S. Census Bureau, PCT006 <http://www.factfinder.census.gov>.

"Hispanic or Latino by Type." Table. U.S. Census Bureau, QT-P9 <http://www.factfinder.census.gov>.

"Hispanic or Latino Origin for the United States, Regions, Divisions, States, and for Puerto Rico: 2000." Table. U.S. Census Bureau, Census 2000 PHC-T-10. 22 Oct. 2001 <http://www.census.gov>.

hooks, bell. *Yearning: Race, Gender and Cultural Politics*. Boston: South End Press, 1990.

———. "Postmodern Blackness." *Cultural Theory and Popular Culture: A Reader*. 2nd ed. Ed. John Storey. Athens: University of Georgia Press, 1998. 417–424.

Hourani, Albert, and Nadim Shehadi. Introduction. *The Lebanese in the World: A Century of Emigration*. Ed. Albert Hourani and Nadim Shehadi. London: I. B. Tauris, 1992.

Hunt, John Britt. "Beyond the Drug Trafficker Stereotype: The Changing American Perceptions of Colombians." Master's thesis. Florida International University, 2002.

Hurtado, Aída. "Relating to Privilege: Seduction and Rejection in the Subordination of White Women and Women of Color." *Theorizing Feminism: Parallel Trends in the Humanities and Social Sciences*. Ed. Anne C. Hermann and Abigail J. Stewart. Hanover, NH: Wesleyan University Press, 1994. 136–154.

Iskandar, Adel. "'*Whenever, Wherever!*'": The Discourse of Orientalist Transnationalism in the Construction of Shakira." *The Ambassadors* 6.2 (July 2003) <http://ambassadors.net/archives/issue14/selected_studies4.htm>.

Jackson, John L. *Harlem World: Doing Race and Class in Contemporary Black America*. Chicago: University of Chicago Press, 2001.

Jaramillo, Ana María. "Mueren seis balseros colombianos en el Caribe." *El Tiempo.com*, 20 July 2001 <http://www.eltiempo.terra.com.co/20-07-2001/inte_pf_f.html>.

Järviluoma, Helmi, Pirkko Moisala, and Anni Vilkko. "Not Only Vision—Analysing Sound and Music From the Perspective of Gender." *Gender and Qualitative Methods.* Ed. Helmi Järviluoma, Pirkko Moisala, and Anni Vilkko. Thousand Oaks, CA: Sage, 2003. 84–106.

Jenkins, Henry. *Convergence Culture: Where New and Old Media Collide.* New York: New York University Press, 2006.

Jones-Correa, Michael. *Between Two Nations: The Political Predicament of Latinos in New York City.* Ithaca: Cornell University Press, 1998.

Kaplan, Amy. "Violent Belongings and the Question of Empire Today: Presidential Address to the American Studies Association, October 17, 2003." *American Quarterly* 56. 1(2004): 1–18.

Kaplan, E. Ann. *Rocking Around the Clock: MTV Postmodernism and Consumer Culture.* New York: Methuen, 1987.

Kelly, James. "Trouble in Paradise." *time.com,* 23 Nov. 1981 <http://www.time.com/time/printout/0,8816,922693,00.html>.

Kemp, Mark. "*Rock en español*: The Latin Invasion." *Paste* April-May 2005: 78–83.

King, Kate. "Hispanic Buying Power, Entrepreneurship on the Rise." *CNN.com,* 1 Oct. 2007 <http://www.cnn.com/2007/US/10/01/hispanics.economy/index.html.>

Klich, Ignacio, and Jeffrey Lesser. "Introduction: 'Turco' Immigrants in Latin America." *The Americas* 53.1 (1996): 1–14.

———. "Introduction: Images and Realities of Arab and Jewish Immigrants in Latin America." *Arab and Jewish Immigrants in Latin America: Images and Realities.* Ed. Ignacio Klich and Jeffrey Lesser. London: Frank Cass, 1998. vii–xiiii.

Kogan, Frank. "River Deep, Freckle High." *!Voice,* 26 Dec. 2001–7 Jan. 2002 <http: //www.villagevoice.com/issues/0152/kogan.php>.

Kruse, Holly. "Subcultural Identity in Alternative Music Culture." *Popular Music* 12.1(1993): 33–41.

La arepa colombiana en Nueva York/The Colombian Arepa in New York. DVD. Directed by Roberto Arévalo. Atlanta, GA: Beyond Documentary, 2007 [1991].

"La cantante Shakira, una buena noticia de Colombia." *ElTiempo.com,* 9 May 2001 <http://eltiempo.com.terra.com.co/09-05-2001/cult_pf_4.html>.

La Fountain-Stokes, Lawrence. "Aterciopelados." *Claridad,* 11 July 1997: 22.

Lannert, John. "Colombia's Shakira: I'm Here." *Billboard,* 15 June 1996: 1.

———. "Latin Sales Swell in First Half of '99." *Billboard,* 21 Aug. 1999: 8.

Larmer, Brook. "Latino America." *Newsweek,* 12 July 1999: 48–58.

"Las cadenas del racismo siguen sin romperse." *ElTiempo.com,* 26 Aug. 2001 <http://www.eltiempo.com>.

Latin Beat. ABC. 7 Sept. 1999.

"Latin U.S.A." *Newsweek,* 12 July 1999: 48–61.

Lechner, Ernesto. *Rock en Español: The Latin Alternative Rock Explosion.* Chicago: Chicago Review Press, 2005.

León, Juan. "Tropical Overexposure: Miami's 'Sophisticated Tropics' and the *Balsero*." *Tropicalizations: Transcultural Representations de Latinidad.* Ed. Frances R. Aparicio and Susana Chávez-Silverman. Hanover, NH: Dartmouth/University Press of New England, 1997. 213–228.

L'Estrange Fawcett, Louise. "Lebanese, Palestinians, and Syrians in Colombia." *The Lebanese in the World: A Century of Emigration*. Ed. Albert Hourani and Nadim Shehadi. London: I. B. Tauris, 1992. 361–377.

Levin, Jordan. "Grammy-Winning Producer Touts Heart Over High-Tech." *Variety* 10–16 June 1996: 56.

———. "Miami's Potent Musical Mix." *Variety*, 10–16 June 1996: 49.

———. "Payola Called Fixture in Latin Music." *Miami Herald* 8 Dec. 2002: n.p.

Levitt, Peggy. *The Transnational Villagers*. Berkeley: University of California Press, 2001.

———. "Transnational Ties and Incorporation: The Case of Dominicans in the United States." *The Columbia History of Latinos in the United States Since 1960*. Ed. David G. Gutiérrez. New York: Columbia University Press, 2004. 229–256.

Lewis, Lisa A. "Consumer Girl Culture: How Music Video Appeals to Girls." *Television and Women's Culture: The Politics of the Popular*. Ed. Mary Ellen Brown. London: Sage, 1990. 89–101.

———. *Gender Politics and MTV: Voicing the Difference*. Philadelphia: Temple University Press, 1990.

———. "Being Discovered: The Emergence of Female Address on MTV." *Sound and Vision: The Music Video Reader*. Ed. Simon Frith, Andrew Goodwin, and Lawrence Grossberg. London: Routledge, 1993. 129–151.

Levy, Steven. "Ad Nauseam: How MTV Sells Out Rock & Roll." *Rolling Stone*, 8 Dec. 1983: 30–37, 74, 76, 78–79.

Leyshon, Andrew, David Matless, and George Revill. Introduction. *The Place of Music*. Ed. Andrew Leyshon, David Matless, and George Revill. New York: Guilford Press, 1998.

Lipsitz, George. *Time Passages: Collective Memory and American Popular Culture*. Minneapolis: University of Minnesota Press, 1990.

———. *Dangerous Crossroads: Popular Music, Postmodernism, and the Poetics of Place*. London: Verso, 1994.

———. "World Cities and World Beat: Low-Wage Labor and Transnational Culture." *Pacific Historical Review* 68.2 (1999): 213–231.

———. "The Lion and the Spider: Mapping Sexuality, Space and Politics in Miami Music." *American Studies in a Moment of Danger*. Minneapolis: University of Minneapolis Press, 2001.

Lister, Martin, Jon Dovey, Seth Giddings, Iain Grant, and Kieran Kelley, eds. *New Media: A Critical Introduction*. London: Routledge, 2003.

"Live Earth Artist: Shakira." msnPRESENTS, *www.msn.com*, 27 July 2007 <http://liveearth.msn.com/artists/shakira?ocid=T001MSN43A03001&photoidx=4>.

Livingstone, Grace. *Inside Colombia: Drugs, Democracy and War*. New Brunswick, NJ: Rutgers University Press, 2004.

"Llegan más colombianos." *La Nación* (San José, Costa Rica), 22 May 2000: 18A.

Llewellyn, Howard. "Estefan, GVM, and Sony Launch Long-Awaited Latin Label Sunnyluna." *Billboard*, 11 May 2002: 42.

Logan, John. "The New Latinos: Who They Are, Where They Are." Lewis Mumford Center for Comparative Urban and Regional Research. State University of New York at Albany, 2001.

Lo mejor del vallenato, Volumen 1. Videocassette. Vedisco Records 1996.

Lorbada, Javier. "Shakira: Estar en este cuerpo no es nada fácil." *MTV Magazine* (Spain) (July-Aug. 2005): 52–56.

"Los colombianos en Estados Unidos." Embassy of Colombia, Washington, DC. 20 Oct. 2002 <http://www.colombiaemb.org/colombians_in_us.htm>.

"Los ritmos del vallenato." *El Tiempo-Caribe*, 17 April 1998: 5.

Lovering, John. "The Global Music Industry: Contradictions in the Commodification of the Sublime." *The Place of Music*. Ed. Andrew Leyshon, David Matless, and George Revill. New York: Guilford Press, 1998. 31–56.

Manalansan IV, Martin F. *Global Divas: Filipino Gay Men in the Diaspora*. Durham, NC: Duke University Press, 2003.

Mannon, Jennifer. "Headbang in Bogotá: The Other Plan Colombia." *miaminewtimes*, 23 Nov. 2000 <http://www.miaminewtimes.com/issues/2000-11-23/music html/printable_page>.

Manrique, Jaime. *Latin Moon in Manhattan*. New York: St. Martin's Press, 1993.

Manuel, Peter. "Puerto Rican Music and Cultural Identity: Creative Appropriation of Cuban Sources from Danza to Salsa." *Ethnomusicology* 38.2 (1994): 249–280.

Marinucci, Carla. "Cuban Americans' Key Role in Election 2004; Community No Longer Republican Monolith in Miami." *San Francisco Chronicle*, 3 Oct. 2004: A14.

Marrow, Helen B. "South America: Ecuador, Peru, Brazil, Argentina, Venezuela." *The New Americans: A Guide to Immigration Since 1965*. Ed. Mary C. Waters and Reed Ueda with Helen B. Marrow. Cambridge, MA: Harvard University Press, 2007. 593–611.

Martin, Denis-Constant. "The Choices of Identity." *Social Identities* 1.1 (1995): 5–20.

Martin, Lydia. "Breaking Tradition: Aterciopelados and Other Latin Rockers Bring a New Kind of Beat to Watcha Tour 2000." *www.herald.com*, 26 Aug. 2000 <http://www.herald.com/justgo/latingrammys/showarticle4.html>.

———. "Shakira Wants the World." *Latina* July 2001: 90–93, 133–134.

Martín Barbero, Jesús. "Latin America: Cultures in the Communication Media." *Journal of Communication* 43.2 (1993): 18–30.

Martínez, Katynka Z. "American Idols With Caribbean Soul: Cubanidad and the Latin Grammys." *Latino Studies* 4 (2006): 381–400.

Martínez, Liliana Angélica. "Shakira es imparable." *ElTiempo.com*, 23 Feb. 2001 <http://eltiempo.terra.com.co/23-02-2001/rock_pf_3.html>.

Mathews, Gordon. "Context and Consciouness in the Practice of Transnationality." *City & Society* 17.1 (2005): 35–48.

Mato, Daniel. "On Global and Local Agents and the Social Making of Transnational Identities and Related Agendas in 'Latin' America." *Identities* 4.2 (1997): 167–212.

McClary, Susan. *Feminine Endings: Music, Gender, and Sexuality*. Minneapolis: University of Minnesota Press, 1991.

McClary, Susan, and Robert Walser. "Start Making Sense! Musicology Wrestles With Rock." 1988. *On Record: Rock, Pop, and the Written Word*. Ed. Simon Frith and Andrew Goodwin. London: Routledge, 2000. 277–292.

McClintock, Anne. "Family Feuds: Gender, Nationalism, and the Family." *Feminist Review* 44 (1993): 61–80.

McGovern, James P. *The Suffering Continues: Internally Placed People in Colombia*. Report Prepared for the Congressional Human Rights Caucus, 110th Cong., 2nd sess., 21 July 2008.

McGovern, Jim. "Recognizing 2007 as the Year of the Internally Displaced in Colombia." H. Res. 426, 110th Cong., 1st sess. *Congressional Record*, 11 July 2007 <http://www.govtrack.us/congress/bill.xpd?bill=hr110-426>.

McIntosh, Heather. "Music Video Forerunners in Early Television Programming: A Look at WCPO-TV's Innovations and Contributions in the 1950s." *Popular Music and Society* 27.3 (2004): 259-273.

McKee, David L. "Some Specifics on the Brain Drain From the Andean Region." *Internationational Migration/Migrations Internationales/Migraciones Internacionales* 21.4 (1983): 488-499.

McRobbie, Angela, and Simon Frith. "Rock and Sexuality." *On Record: Rock, Pop, and the Written Word*. Ed. Simon Frith and Andrew Goodwin. London: Routledge, 1990. 371-389.

Me duele el corazón/My Heart Aches. DVD. Directed by Roberto Arévalo. Atlanta, GA: Beyond Documentary, 2007 [n.d.].

Méndez, Juan M. "Unbottled and Unleashed: Christina Aguilera." *Latina*, Dec. 1999: 78-81.

Mercer, Kobena. "Monster Metaphors: Notes on Michael Jackson's *Thriller*." *Sound and Vision: The Music Video Reader*. Ed. Simon Frith, Andrew Goodwin, and Lawrence Grossberg. London: Routledge, 1993. 93-108.

Mirabel, Manuel 'Guajiro,' and Amadito Valdés. *Buena Vista Social Club*. DVD. Directed by Wim Wenders. Lion's Gate, 1999.

Miyoshi, Masao. "A Borderless World? From Colonialism to Transnationalism and the Decline of the Nation-State." *Critical Inquiry* 19.4 (1993): 726-751.

Mohanty, Chandra Talpade. "Cartographies of Struggle: Third World Women and the Politics of Feminism." Introduction. *Third World Women and the Politics of Feminism*. Ed. Chandra Talpade Mohanty, Ann Russo, and Lourdes Torres. Bloomington: Indiana University Press, 1991.

———. "Under Western Eyes: Feminist Scholarship and Colonial Discourses." *Third World Women and the Politics of Feminism*. Ed. Chandra Talpade Mohanty, Ann Russo, and Lourdes Torres. Bloomington: Indiana University Press, 1991. 51-80.

Molina-Guzmán, Isabel. "Gendering Latinidad Through the Elián News Discourse About Cuban Women." *Latino Studies* 3(2005): 179-204.

Molina-Guzmán, Isabel, and Angharad N. Valdivia. "Brain, Brow or Bootie: Iconic Latinas in Contemporary Popular Culture." *Communication Review* 2 (2004): 205-221.

Morales, Ed. "*Colombia te canto*: The Redeeming Power of Music." *Hopscotch* 1.4 (1999): 34-49.

———. "Fade to Blonde." *Urban Latino*, Dec.-Jan. 2001: 38-41.

———. *Living in Spanglish: The Search for Latino Identity in America*. New York: St. Martin's Press, 2002.

———. *The Latin Beat: The Rhythms and Roots of Latin Music From Bossa Nova to Salsa and Beyond*. Cambridge, MA: Da Capo Press, 2003.

Mora-Mass, Elizabeth. "Colombianos en Nueva York, del sueño americano a la pesadilla gringa." *ElTiempo.com*, 1 July 2001 <http://eltiempo.terra.com.co/01-07-2001/pano_pf_0.html>.

Morris, Nancy. "The Myth of Unadulterated Culture Meets the Threat of Imported Media." *Media, Culture & Society* 24 (2002): 278-289.

Moya, Luis L., and Luis A. Del Castillo Cadavid. "What Is Vallenato?" 3 March 1998 <http://www.grupofantasia.com/vallenato.htm>.

Murillo, Mario A. *Colombia and the United States: War, Unrest and Destabilization*. New York: Seven Stories Press, 2004.

Naber, Nadine. "Ambiguous Insiders: An Investigation of Arab American Invisibility." *Ethnic and Racial Studies* 23.1 (2000): 37–61.

Navarro, Mireya. "Latin Grammys Border Skirmish." newyorktoday.com, 13 Sept. 2000. 14 Sept. 2000 <.../genListing.htm&categoryid=30&only+y&bfromind+1815&eeid=3066484&eetype=article&ren>.

Negrón-Muntaner, Frances. "Jennifer's Butt." *Aztlán* 22 (1997): 181–194.

———. *Boricua Pop: Puerto Ricans and the Latinization of American Culture*. New York: New York University Press, 2004.

Negus, Keith. *Producing Pop: Culture and Conflict in the Popular Music Industry*. London: Hodder. Arnold, 1992.

———. *Music Genres and Corporate Cultures*. London: Routledge, 1999.

"New Girl In Town." *Newsweek*, 26 Nov. 2001: n.p.

Ngai, Mae M. "Transnationalism and the Transformation of the 'Other': Response to the Presidential Address." *American Quarterly* 57.1 (2005): 59–65.

Niurka, Norma. "Carlos Vives, el consentido de los dioses." *Elherald.com*, 14 Sept. 2000 <http://www.elherald.com/content/today/galeria/viernes/02567393.htm>.

Noble, David W. *Death of a Nation: American Culture and the End of Exceptionalism*. Minneapolis: University of Minnesota Press, 2002.

"No peace." *The Economist*, 11 Oct. 1997: 38.

"No pienso sacrificar mi personalidad." *Semana*, 24 Sept. 2001: 116–117.

Noriega, Chon. Introduction. *I, Carmelita Tropicana: Performing Between Cultures*. Boston: Beacon Press, 2000.

Obejas, Achy. "Taking Rock Around the Globe: Shakira, Chao and 'Alterlatinos' Are Changing the Scene." *Chicago Tribune*, 12 Sept. 2002: C6.

Oboler, Suzanne. *Ethnic Labels, Latino Lives. Identity and the Politics of (Re)Presentation in the United States*. Minneapolis: University of Minneapolis Press, 1995.

———. "Introduction: *Los que llegaron*: 50 Years of South American Immigration (1950–2000)—An Overview." *Latino Studies* 3 (2005): 42–52.

———. "South Americans." *The Oxford Encyclopedia of Latinos and Latinas in the United States*. Ed. Suzanne Oboler and Deena J. González. Oxford and New York: Oxford University Press, 2005. 146–158.

Ocampo López, Javier. *Música y folclor de Colombia*. Bogotá: Plaza y Janés, 1976.

Ocaña, Damarys. "Has Shakira Sold Out?" *Latina*, Sept. 2006: n.p.

Ocando, Casto. "Recibirán una tarjeta consular de identidad los colombianos en EEUU." *El Nuevo Herald*, 24 March 2004: 2A.

Ocando, Casto, and Graciela Mrad. "El sueño americano defrauda a inmigrantes." *El Nuevo Herald*, 12 Oct. 2003: 1a.

Ochoa, Ana María. "García Márquez, *Macondismo*, and the Soundscapes of *Vallenato*." *Popular Music* 24.2 (2005): 207–222.

Ong, Aihwa. *Flexible Citizenship: The Cultural Logics of Transnationality*.Durham, NC: Duke University Press, 1999.

Oppenheimer, Andrés. "Uribe's Counteroffense Working—at Least at Home." *Miami Herald*, 22 April 2007 <http://miamiherald.com>.

Ortiz, Fernando. *La música afrocubana*. Madrid: Ediciones Júcar, 1974.

Orwall, Bruce. "The Burden of Power: The U.S. in the 21st Century." *The Wall Street Journal*, 13 Feb. 2001: A1ff.

Pacini Hernández, Deborah. "Bachata: From the Margins to the Mainstream." *Popular Music* 11.3 (1992): 359–364.

———. *Bachata: A Social History of Dominican Popular Music*. Philadelphia: Temple University Press, 1995.

———. "Sound Systems, World Beat and Diasporan Identity in Cartagena, Colombia." *Diaspora* 5.3 (1996): 429–466.

———. "Dancing With the Enemy: Cuban Popular Music, Race, Authenticity, and the World-Music Landscape." *Latin American Perspectives* 25.3 (May 1998): 110–125.

———. "Race, Ethnicity and the Production of Latin/o Popular Music." *Global Repertoires: Popular Music Within and Beyond the Transnational Music Industry*. Ed. Andreas Gebesmair and Alfred Smudits. Aldershot: Ashgate, 2001. 57–72.

Pacini Hernández, Deborah, Héctor Fernández L'Hoeste, and Eric Zolov, eds. *Rockin' Las Americas: Rock Music and Rock Cultures Across Latin(o) America*. Pittsburgh: University of Pittsburgh Press, 2004.

Padgett, Tim. "Tough as Males." *Time*, 3 Aug.1998 <http://www.time.com/time/magazine/1998/int/980803/the_arts.music.tough_as_3.html>.

Palacios, Marco. *Between Legitimacy and Violence: A History of Colombia, 1875–2002*. Trans. Richard Stoller. Durham, NC: Duke University Press, 2006.

Parado, Freddy. *Justicia Made in U.S.A.: dramática historia de un inmigrante atropellado por el sólo hecho de ser colombiano*. Bogotá: Planeta, 2002.

Parédez, Deborah. "Remembering Selena, Re-membering *Latinidad*." *Theatre Journal* 54 (2002): 63–84.

Pareles, Jon. "Beyond Borders, Without Boundaries." *New York Times on the Web*, 12 July 2001 <http://www.nytimes.com/2001/07/12/arts/12NOTE.html>.

———. "The Shakira Dialectic." *New York Times*, 13 Nov. 2005 <http://www.nytimes.com>.

"Pastrana: 'Shakira, nuestra embajadora internacional.'" *ElTiempo.com*, 23 Feb. 2001 <http://www.eltiempo.terra.com.co/23-02-2001/rock_pf_5.html>.

Paxman, Andrew. "Latinas Making Music: *Cantautoras* Shaking Up Tune Industry." *Variety*, 31 March-6 April 1997: 71.

Paz-Frydman, Silvia. "The Latina Body and the Entertainment Industry: The Practices of Resistance, Hegemony, and Identity Construction." Unpublished manuscript, Williams College, Williamstown, MA, 2006.

"Peace in Colombia? This Year, Next Year, Sometime . . ." *The Economist*, 10 April 1999: 31. 14 Nov.

Pellegrini, Frank. "America Goes Mucho Loco for Ricky." *time daily*, 13 May 1999 <http://www.pathfinder.com/time/daily/0,2960,24750,00.htm>.

Peña, Manuel H. *The Texas-Mexican Conjunto: History of a Working-Class Music*. Austin: University of Texas Press, 1985.

Peña, María. "Thousands of Colombians Continue Exodus to the U.S." Efe News Services (U.S.), Global News Wire, 8 March 2002.

Penhaul, Karl. "The Lure of a Better Life." *U.S. News & World Report*, 8 Jan. 2001: 28.

Perdomo Escobar, José Ignacio. *Historia de la música en Colombia*. Bogotá: Editorial ABC, 1963.

Pérez-Torres, Rafael. "Brown Transnationalisms: Consuming Latino Identities in a Postmodern Era." Lecture. American Studies Association, Oakland, CA, 12 Oct. 2006.

Portaccio Fontalvo, José. *Colombia y su música. Volumen I.* Bogotá: Logos Diagramación, 1995.

Portes, Alejandro, and Alex Stepick. *City on the Edge: The Transformation of Miami.* Berkeley: University of California Press, 1993.

Portes, Alejandro, and Rubén Rumbaut. *Legacies: The Story of the Immigrant Second Generation.* Berkeley: University of California Press, 2001.

Post, Jennifer. "Erasing the Boundaries Between Public anmd Private in Women's Performance Traditions." *Cecilia Reclaimed: Feminist Perspectives on Gender and Music.* Ed. Susan C. Cook and Judy S. Tsou. Urbana: University of Illinois Press, 1993. 35–51.

Pratt, Mary Louise. *Imperial Eyes: Travel Writing and Transculturation.* London: Routledge, 1992.

"'Quiero serle fiel a la música colombiana." *Semana.com*, 3 March 2002 <http://www.semana.com>.

Rakow, Lana. "Feminist Approaches to Popular Culture: Giving Patriarchy its Due." *Cultural Theory and Popular Culture: A Reader.* 2nd ed. Ed. John Storey. Athens: University of Georgia Press, 1998. 275-291.

"Recuperado cuerpo de Consuelo Araújonoguera." *ElTiempo.com*, 30 Sept. 2001 <http://ww.eltiempo.terra.com.co/30-09-2001/ulti_pf_1.html>.

Rey, Mario. "Albita Rodríguez: Sexuality, Imaging and Gender Construction in the Music of Exile." *Queering the Popular Pitch.* Ed. Sheila Whiteley and Jennifer Rycenga. London: Routledge, 2006. 115-129.

Reyes, Gerardo. "Uribe 'empeñado en devolver la paz' a los colombianos." *El Nuevo Herald*, 1 Oct. 2004 <http://www.elnuevoherald.com>.

Riaño-Alcalá, Pilar. "Urban Space and Music in the Formation of Youth Cultures: The Case of Bogotá, 1920-1980." *Studies in Latin American Popular Culture* 10 (1991): 87–106.

"Richard Blair: Británico pachangero." *www.boomonline.com*, 3 June 2002 <http://www.boomonline.com/htmls/e_blair.html>.

Rivera, Raquel Z. *New York Ricans From the Hip-Hop Zone.* New York: Palgrave Macmillan, 2003.

Rivero, Yeidy M. "The Performance and Reception of Televisual 'Ugliness' in 'Yo soy Betty la fea.'" *Feminist Media Studies* 3.1 (2003): 65–82.

Roberts, John Storm. *The Latin Tinge: The Impact of Latin American Music on the United States.* 2nd ed. New York: Oxford University Press, 1999

Robles, Frances. "Revision to Colombian Constitution Grants Military, Police Broad New Powers." *Miami Herald*, 12 Dec. 2003 <http://www.miami.com>.

———. "Many Colombians Leave the Miami Area, Return Home." *Miami Herald*, 22 Dec. 2003 <http://www.miami.com>.

Robinson, Linda. "Watch Out: The Rhythm Is Gonna Get You, Too." *U.S. News & World Report*, 24 May 1999: 61.

Rodas de Juárez, Celeste. "Shakira: Música y amor." *Cosmopolitian en español*, Nov. 2001: 67–69.

Rodríguez, Jesús. "Ciclón Shakira." *EP/El País Semanal* (Madrid, Spain), 28 May 2006: 48–54.

Rodríguez, Marcela. "Cartas a Shakira: orgullo nacional." *ElTiempo.com*, 6 May 2001 <http://www.eltiempo.terra.com.co/06-05-2001/cult_pf_6.html>.

Rohter, Larry. "Driven by Fear, Colombians Leave in Droves." *New York Times on the Web*, 5 March 2000 <http://www.nytimes.com>.

———. "Rock en Español Is Approaching Its Final Border." *New York Times*, 6 Aug. 2000: 2.27.

Rojas, Cristina. *Civilization and Violence: Regimes of Representation in Nineteenth-Century Colombia*. Minneapolis: University of Minnesota Press, 2002.

Rojas, Viviana. "The Gender of *Latinidad*: Latinas Speak About Hispanic Television." *Communication Review* 7(2004): 125–153.

Roldán, Mary. *Blood and Fire: La Violencia in Antioquia, Colombia, 1946–1953*. Durham, NC: Duke University Press, 2002.

Romero, A. "Champeta Criolla." *World Music Central*, 26 Aug. 2004 <http://www.worldmusiccentral.org/article/php/20040528164253404>.

Roque Ramírez, Horacio N. "Rafa Negrón's Pan Dulce and the Queer Sonic *latinaje o* San Francisco." *CENTRO Journal* 24.1 (2007): 274–313.

Rosaldo, Renato. *Culture and Truth: The Remaking of Social Analysis*. Boston: Beacon Press. 1989.

———. "Cultural Citizenship, Inequality, and Multiculturalism." *Latino Cultural Citizenship. Claiming Identity, Space, and Rights*. Ed. William V. Flores and Rina Benmayor. Boston: Beacon Press, 1997. 27–38.

Rose, Tricia. *Black Noise: Rap Music and Black Culture in Contemporary America*. Hanover, NH: Wesleyan University Press/University Press of New England, 1994.

———. "Never Trust a Big Butt and a Smile." *Feminist Television Criticism: A Reader*. Ed. Charlotte Brundson, Julia D'Acci, and Lynn Spigel. New York: Oxford University Press, 1997. 300–317.

Ross Sorkin, Andrew. "NBC Is Paying $1.98 Billion for Telemundo." *New York Times*, 12 Oct. 2001: C1.

Rúa, Mérida M. "Latinidades." *Oxford Encyclopedia of Latinos and Latinas in the United States*. Ed. Suzanne Oboler and Deena J. González. New York: Oxford University Press, 2005. 505–507.

Rumbaut, Rubén. "Origins and Destinies: Immigration, Race and Ethnicity in Contemporary America." *Origins and Destinies*. Ed. Silvia Pedraza and Rubén G. Rumbaut. Belmont, CA: Wadsworth, 1996. 21–42.

Salaita, Steven. "Ethnic Identity and Imperative Patriotism: Arab Americans Before and After 9/11." *College Literature* 32.2 (2005): 146–169.

Salazar, Rodrigo. "An Icon Goes Pop!: *Ricky siempre será nuestro*." *Urban Latino* June-July 2002: 46.

Saldívar, José David. *Border Matters: Remapping American Cultural Studies*. Berkeley: University of California Press, 1997.

Samper Pizano, Daniel. "Sé lo que significa esto para mi tierra." *ElTiempo.com*, 23 Feb. 2001 <http://eltiempo.terra.com.co/23-02-2001/rock_pf_0.html>.

Samper Pizano, Daniel, and Pilar Tafur. *100 años de vallenato*. 2nd ed. Colombia: MTM Limitada, 1997.

Sánchez Cristo, Julio. "'La fama y el dinero son lo de menos.'" *Semana*, 2 Dec. 2002: 30–34.
Sandino Moreno, Catalina, Virginia Ariza, and Yenny Paola Vega. *María Full of Grace*. DVD. Directed by Joshua Marston. HBO Films, 2004.
Santa Ana, Otto. *Brown Tide Rising: Metaphors of Latinos in Contemporary American Public Discourse*. Austin: University of Texas Press, 2002.
Santa Ana, Otto, with Juan Morán and Cynthia Sánchez. "Awash Under a Brown Tide: Immigration Metaphors in California Public and Print Media Discourse." *Aztlán* 23.2 (Fall 1998): 137–177.
Sassen-Koob, Saskia. "Formal and Informal Associations: Dominicans and Colombians In New York." *International Migration Review* 13 (1979): 314–332.
Savigliano, Marta. *Tango and the Political Economy of Passion*. Boulder, CO: Westview Press, 1995.
Scarface. [1983]. DVD. Directed by Brian De Palma. Universal Studios, 2006.
Schaeffer-Grabiel, Felicity. "Beyond and Back: Locating Chicanas and Latinas Within Transnational Feminist Theories." Roundtable Presentation. American Studies Association Annual Meeting, Atlanta, 11 Nov. 2004.
———. "Planet-Love.com: Cyberbrides in the Americas and the Transnational Routes of U.S. Masculinity." *Signs: Journal of Women in Culture and Society* 31 (2006): 331–356.
Scott, Janny. "A Census Query Is Said to Skew Data on Latinos." *New York Times*, 27 June 2001: 1.
Shakira. "¿Dónde Están los Ladrones?" Advertisement. Columbia House Club Música Latina: 1–2, 1998.
———. *Shakira, MTV Unplugged*. Videocassette. Sony Music, 2000.
———. *Laundry Service*. DVD. Sony Music, 2001.
———. *Shakira: En vivo y en privado*. DVD. Sony Music International, 2004.
———. "La tortura." *Fijación oral, Volumen I*. Dir. Michael Haussman. MTV. 2005.
———. "Hips Don't Lie." *Oral Fixation, Volume II*. Dir. Sophie Muller. MTV. 2006.
———. Concert. TD Banknorth Arena, Boston, Massachusetts. 5 Sept. 2006.
———. Interview. By Katie Couric and Matt Lauer, *Today Show*, NBC, 28 April 2007.
Shakira, Featuring Alejandro Sanz. "La Tortura." *Fijación oral, Volumen I*, EPIC. Dir. Michael Haussman, 2005.
Shakira, Featuring Wycleff Jean. Latin Billboard Awards, Telemundo, 27 April 2007.
———. *The Today Show*. NBC, 28 April 2007.
Shank, Barry. *Dissonant Identities: The Rock'n'Roll Scene in Austin, Texas*. Middleton, CT: Wesleyan University Press, 1994.
Sheffield, Rob. "Shakira Sinks Her Colombian Flag." *Rolling Stone*, 31 Jan. 2002: 20.
Shoer Roth, Daniel. "Miami, Capital de la Música." *El Nuevo Herald*, 12 June 1999: 1A.
Shohat, Ella. *Taboo Memories, Diasporic Voices*. Durham, NC: Duke University Press, 2006.
———. "Ethnicities-in-Relation: Toward a Multicultual Reading of American Cinema." *Unspeakable Images: Ethnicity and the American Cinema*. Ed. L. D. Friedman. Urbana: University of Illinois Press, 1991. 215–250.
Shohat, Ella, and Robert Stam. *Unthinking Eurocentrism: Multiculturalism and the Media*. London: Routledge, 1994.

———. "From the Imperial Family to the Transnational Imaginary: Media Spectatorship in the Age of Globalization." *Global/Local: Cultural Production and the Transnational Imaginary.* Ed. Rob Wilson and Wimal Dissanayake. Durham, NC: Duke University Press, 1996. 145–170.

Shugart, Helene A. "Crossing Over: Hybridity and Hegemony in the Popular Media." *Communication and Critical/Cultural Studies* 4.2 (2007): 115–141.

Shultz, Cara Lynn. "Shakirattack: With Legions of Loyal Fans in Latin America, Singer Shakira Is Taking the U.S. by Storm—and Loving It." *Teen People*, March 2002: 86–87.

Silverman, Kaja. *Male Subjectivity at the Margins.* London: Routledge, 1992.

Silvestrini, Blanca G. "'The World We Enter When Claiming Our Rights': Latinos and Their Quest for Culture." *Latino Cultural Citizenship. Claiming Identity, Space, and Rights.* Ed. William V. Flores and Rina Benmayor. Boston: Beacon Press, 1997. 39–53.

Simonett, Helena. *Banda: Mexican Musical Life Across Borders.* Middletown, CT: Wesleyan University Press, 2001.

Sinclair, John. "'The Hollywood of Latin America': Miami as Regional Center in Television Trade." *Television & New Media* 4.3 (2003): 211–229.

Sirgado, Miguel A. "Sidestepper: música colombiana de vibra suave." *El Nuevo Herald*, 15 Aug. 2003: 1C.

Slobin, Mark. "Micromusics of the West: A Comparative Approach." *Ethnomusicology* 36 (Winter 1992): 1–87.

———. "Music in Diaspora: The View From America." *Diaspora* 3.3 (1994): 243–250.

Smith, Michael Peter. "Transnationalism, the State, and the Extraterritorial Citizen." *Politics & Society* 31.4 (2003): 467–502.

———. "Power in Place/Places of Power: Contextualizing Transnational Research." *City & Society* 17.1 (2005): 5–34.

Smith, Michael Peter, and Luis Eduardo Guarnizo. "The Locations of Transnationalism." Introduction. *Transnationalism from Below.* Ed. Michael Peter Smith and Luis Eduardo Guarnizo. New Brunswick, NJ: Transaction, 1998.

Smith, Robert. "'Mexicanness' in New York: Migrants Seek New Place in Old Racial Order." *NACLA*, Sept.-Oct. 2001: 14–17.

Smith, Suzanne E. *Dancing in the Street: Motown and the Cultural Politics of Detroit.* Cambridge, MA: Harvard University Press, 1999.

Soto Torres, Edgardo. "Willie Colón: gestor de la salsa acosado por el boicot." *Diálogo*, Nov. 1999: 20.

Stack, John F., Jr. "The Ethnic Citizen Confronts the Future: Los Angeles and Miami at Century's End." *Pacific Historical Review* 68.2 (1999): 309–316.

Stasiulis, Daiva K. "Relational Possibilities of Nationalisms, Racisms, and Feminisms." *Between Woman and Nation: Nationalisms, Transnational Feminisms, and the State.* Ed. Norma Alarcón, Caren Kaplan, and Minoo Moallem. Durham, NC: Duke University Press, 1999. 182–218.

Storey, John. *An Introduction to Cultural Theory and Popular Culture.* 2nd ed. Athens: University of Georgia Press, 1998.

———. *Inventing Popular Culture.* Malden, MA: Blackwell, 2003.

Straw, Will. "Systems of Articulation, Logics of Change: Communities and Scenes in Popular Music." *Cultural Studies* 5.3 (1991): 368–388.

Streicker, Joel. "Policing Boundaries: Race, Class and Gender in Cartagena, Colombia." *Blackness in Latin America and the Caribbean*. Vol 1. Ed. Norman E. Whitten, Jr., and Arlene Torres. Bloomington: Indiana University Press, 1998. 278–308.

Suárez, Juana. "Sites of Contention: Colombian Cultural Production at the Threshold of a New Millenium." Ph.D. diss., Arizona State University, 2000.

"Sueño americano." *Semana.com*, 14 May 2001 <http://semana.terra.com.co/993/actualidad/ZZZ30BVTMMC.asp>.

Suhair Majaj, Lisa. "Arab Americans and the Meanings of Race." *Postcolonial Theory and the U.S.: Race, Ethnicity, and Literature*. Ed. Amritjit Singh and Peter Schmidt. Jackson: University of Mississippi Press, 2000. 320–337.

Suro, Roberto. *Counting the "Other Hispanics": How Many Colombians, Dominicans, Ecuadorians, Guatemalans and Salvadorans Are There in the United States?* Washington, DC: Pew Hispanic Center, 2002.

Takacs, Stacey. "Alien-Nation: Immigration, National Identity and Transnationalism." *Cultural Studies* 13.4 (1999): 591–620.

Tannenbaum, Rob. "Miss Universe." *Blender*, July 2005: 72–80.

Tate, Winifred. "Repeating Past Mistakes: Aidiing Counterinsurgency in Colombia." *NACLA*, Sept.-Oct. 2002: 19.

Téllez Herrera, Andrea. "El sueno Americano." *Colombianos que alcanzaron el éxito en Estados Unidos*. Bogotá: Intermedio, 2002.

"Tengo derecho a soñar." *Semana.com*, 31 March 2007 <http://www.semana.com>.

Tobar, Dániza. "Carlos Vives: el dueño de la parranda." *Ocean Drive en Español*, Dec. 2001: 82–85.

———. "Una sirena única!: La Next Big Thing entró a la cancha." *Ocean Drive en Español*, Dec. 2001: 64–67.

Torres-Saillant, Silvio. "Pitfalls of Latino Chronologies: South and Central Americans." *Latino Studies* 5 (2007): 489–502.

Trouillot, Michel-Rolph. *Silencing the Past: Power and the Production of History*. Boston: Beacon Press, 1995.

Ulaby, Neda. "U.S. Crossover Hits Elude Latin Alternative." *All Things Considered*. National Public Radio. 8 March 2006.

Uribe-Urán, Víctor. "Colonial *baracunátanas* and Their Nasty Men: Spousal Homicides and the Law in Late Colonial New Granada." *Journal of Social History* 35.1 (2001): 43–72.

Valdés-Rodríguez, Alisa. "Latin American Rock Gets Its Green Card." *Boston Globe*, 4 Sept. 1998: D1.

———. "Who's Buying Cuban Phenom?" *Los Angeles Times*, 14 Aug. 1999 <http://www.picadillo.com/vdesign/articles/990814~1.HTML>.

———. "Searching for Carlos Vives." *latimes.com*, 12 Sept. 2000 <http://www.calendarlive.com/music/latingrammy/la_vives000912.htm>.

Valdivia, Angharad N. *A Latina in the Land of Hollywood and Other Essays on Media Culture* (Tucson: University of Arizona Press, 2000).

———. "Latina/o Communication and Media Studies Today: An Introduction." *Communication Review* 7 (2004): 107–112.

———. "Latinas as Radical Hybrid: Transnationally Gendered Traces in Mainstream Media." *Global Media Journal* 4.7 (2004) <http: lass.calumet.purdue.edu/gmj/refereed/htm>.

———. "Is Penélope to J.Lo as Culture Is to Nature?" *From Bananas to Buttocks: The Latina Body in Popular Film and Culture*. Ed. Myra Mendible. Austin: University of Texas Press, 2007. 129–148.

Valdivia, Angharad N., ed. *Latina/o Communication Studies Today*. New York: Peter Lang, 2008.

Valdivia, Angharad N., with Ramona Curry. "Xuxa!: Can Latin Americans Be Blonde or Can the United States Tolerate a Latin American?" *A Latina in the Land of Hollywood and Other Essays on Media Culture*. Ed. Angharad N.Valdivia. Tucson: University of Arizona Press, 2000. 125–147.

Valentín-Escobar, Wilson. "Between Salsa and Jazz: The Latin Scene in New York." Center for African and African-American Studies. University of Michigan, Ann Arbor. Fall 1998.

———. "Marketing Memory/Marketing Authenticity in Buena Vista Social Club Recordings." Paper presented at XXII Latin American Studies Association International Congress, Hyatt Regency Hotel, Miami, 16 Mar. 2000.

van Dijk, Teun A. "Principles of Discourse Analysis." *Discourse & Society* 4.2 (1993): 249–283.

Vargas, Armando. "Migration, Literature, and the Nation: Majar Literature in Brazil." Ph.D. diss., University of California at Berkeley, 2006.

Vélez-Ibáñez, Carlos, and Anna Sampaio. "Introduction: Processes, New Prospects, and Approaches." *Transnational Latina/o Communities: Politics, Processes, and Cultures*. Ed. Carlos Vélez-Ibáñez and Anna Sampaio. Lanham, MD: Rowman & Littlefield, 2002.

Vernallis, Carol. *Experiencing Music Video: Aesthetics and Cultural Context*. New York: Columbia University Press, 2004.

Vila, Pablo. *Crossing Borders, Reinforcing Borders: Social Categories, Metaphors and Narrative Identities on the U.S.-Mexico Frontier*. Austin: University of Texas Press, 2000.

Vives, Carlos. "La tierra del olvido." *La tierra del olvido*. Polygram Discos, 1995

———. "Malas lenguas." *Tengo fe*. EMI Latin, 1997.

———. Concert. Miami Arena, Miami, Florida. 6 Sept. 2000.

———. "Carito." *Déjame entrar*. EMI Latin, 2001.

———. "Décimas." *Déjame entrar*. EMI Latin, 2001.

Vives, Carlos, and La Provincia. "La celosa." *Clásicos de la Provincia*. PolyGram Discos, 1993.

Wade, Peter. "Patterns of Race in Colombia." *Bulletin of Latin American Research* 5.2 (1986): 1–19.

———. *Blackness and Race Mixture: Racial Dynamics in Colombia*. Baltimore: Johns Hopkins University Press, 1993.

———. "Man the Hunter: Gender and Violence in Music and Drinking Contexts in Colombia." *Sex and Violence: Issues in Representation and Experience*. Ed. Peter Gow and Penelope Harvey. London : Routledge, 1994. 115–137.

———. "Blackness and Cultural Syncretism in Colombia." *Slavery and Beyond: The African Impact on Latin America and the Caribbean*. Ed. Darién J. Davis. Wilmington, DE: Scholarly Resources, 1995.

———. "The Cultural Politics of Blackness in Colombia." *American Ethnologist* 22.2 (1995): 342–358.

———. *Race and Ethnicity in Latin America*. London: Pluto Press, 1997.

———. "Music, Blackness and National Identity: Three Moments in Colombian History." *Popular Music* 17.1 (1998): 1–19.
———. *Music, Race and Nation: Música Tropical in Colombia*. Chicago: University of Chicago Press, 2000.
———. "Racial Identity and Nationalism: A Theoretical View From Latin America." *Ethnic and Racial Studies* 24.5 (2001): 845–865.
Walser, Robert. *Running With the Devil: Power, Gender, and Madness in Heavy Metal Music*. Hanover, NH: Wesleyan University Press/University Press of New England, 1993.
Watrous, Peter. "A Country Now Ready to Listen." *New York Times*, 27 June 1999: 25ff.
Waxer, Lise. Rev. of *Music, Race and Nation: Música Tropical in Colombia*, by Peter Wade. *Journal of Popular Music Studies* 13.2 (2001): 235–239.
Weiderhorn, "Make Shakira Dance for You Whenever, Wherever." *mtv.com*, 5 Nov. 2001 <http://www.mtv.com.news/articles/1458520/20021105/shakira.jhmtl?headlines=true>.
Werde, Bill. "Crossover Dreams." *Village Voice*, 15 Aug. 2000: 59.
Whiteley, Sheila. Introduction. *Sexing the Groove: Popular Music and Gender*. Ed. Sheila Whiteley. London: Routledge, 1997.
———. "Challenging the Feminine: Annie Lennox, Androgyneity, and Illusions of Identity." *Women in Popular Music: Sexuality, Identity, and Subjectivity*. Ed. Sheila Whiteley. London: Routledge, 2000. 119–135.
Whiteley, Shiela, and Jennifer Rycenga, eds. *Queering the Popular Pitch*. London: Routledge, 2006.
Wierderhorn, Jon. "Make Shakira Dance for You Whenever, Wherever." *mtv.com*, Nov. 2002 <http://www.mtv.com.news/articles/1458520/20021105/shakira.jhtml?headlines=true>.
Williams, Raymond L. "Andrés Caicedo's ¡Que viva la música!: Interpretation and the Fictionalized Reader." *Revista de Estudios Hispánicos* 17.1 (1983): 43–54.
———. *The Colombian Novel, 1844–1987*. Austin: University of Texas Press, 1991.
Willman, Chris. "Marque Marc." *EW Magazine*, 8 Oct. 1999 <http://www.pathfinder.com/…r_ref+ON&mtype=0&list_size=25&direction.htm>.
Wise, Sue. "From Butch God to Teddy Bear?: Some Thoughts on My Relationship With Elvis." *Feminist Praxis: Research, Theory, and Epistemology in Feminist Sociology*. Ed. Liz Stanley. London: Routledge, 1990. 134–144.
Wright, Evan. "Shakira." *Rolling Stone*, 11 April 2002: 68–76, 142.
Youngers, Coletta. "U.S. Entanglements in Colombia Continue." *NACLA*, March-April 1998: 34–35, 47.
Yúdice, George. *The Expediency of Culture: Uses of Culture in the Global Era*. Durham, NC: Duke University Press, 2003.
———. "La industria de la música en la integración América Latina-Estados Unidos." *Las industrias culturales en la integración latinoamericana*. Ed. Néstor García Canclini and Carlos Moneta. Buenos Aires: Eudeba, 2003. 115–161.
———. "Linking Cultural Citizenship and Transnationalism to the Movement for an Equitable Global Economy." *Latin American Studies Association FORUM* 37.1 (2006): 15–16.
Zambrano D., Andrés. "Aterciopelados impulsa rock en español en E.U." *ElTiempo.com*, 13 May 2001 <http://eltiempo.terra.com.co/13-05-2001/cult_pf_0.html>.
Zapata Olivella, Delia. "La cumbia: Síntesis musical de la nación colombiana." *Revista colombiana del folclor* 3.7 (1962): 189–204.

Zazueta Martínez, Katynka. "The 'Latin Explosion,' Media Audiences, and the Marketing of Latino Panethnicity: *Latina* Magazine and the Latin Grammys in a Post-Selena América." Ph.D. diss., University of California, San Diego, 2003.

Zentella, Ana Celia. *Growing Up Bilingual*. Malden, MA: Blackwell: 1997.

Zolov, Eric. *Refried Elvis: The Rise of the Mexican Counterculture*. Berkeley: University of California Press, 1999.

Discography

Aterciopelados. "*Mujer gala.*" *Con el corazón en la mano*. RCA International, 1993.
———. *Con el corazón en la mano*. RCA International, 1993.
———. "*Colombia conexión.*" *El Dorado*. RCA International, 1995.
———. "*La estaca.*" *El Dorado*. RCA International, 1995.
———. "*Florecita rockera.*" *El Dorado*. RCA International, 1995.
———. *El Dorado*. RCA International, 1995.
———. "*Baracunátana.*" *La pipa de la paz*. RCA International, 1996.
———. "*Chica difícil.*" *La pipa de la paz*. RCA International, 1996.
———. "*Cosita seria.*" *La pipa de la paz*. RCA International, 1996.
———. "*Miss Panela.*" *La pipa de la paz*. RCA International, 1996.
———. "*No necesito.*" *La pipa de la paz*. RCA International, 1996.
———. *La pipa de la paz*. RCA International, 1996.
———. "*El estuche.*" *Caribe atómico*. RCA International, 1998.
———. *Caribe atómico*. RCA International, 1998.
———. "*El álbum.*" *Gozo poderoso*. RCA International, 2000.
———. *Gozo poderoso*. RCA International, 2000.
———. "*Florecita rockera 2003.*" *Evolución*. RCA Internacional, 2002.
———. *Evolución*. RCA Internacional, 2002.
Bacilos. *Bacilos*. Warner Music Latina, 2000.
———. "*Mi primer millón.*" *Caraluna*. Warner Music Latina, 2002.
———. *Caraluna*. Warner Music Latina, 2002.
———. *Sin Vergüenza*. Warner Music Latina, 2004.
Bloque. "*Descarga.*" *Bloque*. Luaka Bop, 1998.
Bloque. *Bloque*. Luaka Bop, 1998.
Cuesta, Iván, y sus Baltimore Vallenatos. *A ti, Colombia*. Arhoolie, 1993.
Durán, Alejo. *Recuerdos vallenatos: 16 grandes éxitos*. Discos Fuentes, 1996.
———. *Álbum de oro*. Discos Victoria, 1997.
Echeverri, Andrea. "*Lactochampeta.*" *Andrea Echeverri*. Nacional Records, 2005.
Echeverri, Andrea. *Andrea Echeverri*. Nacional Records, 2005.
Estefan, Gloria. *Abriendo puertas*. Sony Music, 1995.
Mendoza, Colacho, and Ivo Díaz. "*La casa en el aire.*" *100 años de vallenato*. CD #2. MTM, 1997.
Shakira. "*Un poco de amor.*" *Pies descalzos*. Sony Discos, 1996.
———. *Pies descalzos*. Sony Discos, 1996.
———. "*Ciega, sordomuda.*" *¿Dónde están los ladrones?* Sony Discos, 1998.
———. "*¿Dónde están los ladrones?*" *¿Dónde están los ladrones?* Sony Discos, 1998.
———. *¿Dónde están los ladrones?* Sony Discos, 1998.

———. "Ciega, sordomuda." *Shakira, Unplugged*. Sony Discos, 2000.
———. *Shakira, Unplugged*. Sony Discos, 2000.
———. "Underneath Your Clothes." *Laundry Service*. Sony Music, 2001.
———. *Laundry Service*. Sony Music, 2001.
———. *En vivo y en privado*. Sony Music International, 2004.
———. *Fijación oral, Volumen I*. EPIC, 2005.
———. *Oral Fixation, Volume II*. EPIC, 2005.
Shakira, featuring Alejandro Sanz. "La tortura." *Fijación oral, Volumen I*. EPIC, 2005.
Shakira, featuring Wycleff Jean. "Hips Don't Lie." *Oral Fixation, Volume II*. EPIC, 2006.
Sidestepper. *Logozo*. Apartment 22, 1999.
———. *More Grip*. Palm Pictures, 2000.
———. *3 a.m. (In Beats We Trust)*. Palm Pictures, 2003.
Vives, Carlos. "La celosa." *Clásicos de la provincia*. PolyGram Discos, 1993.
———. *Clásicos de la provincia*. PolyGram Discos, 1993.
———. *El rock de mi pueblo*. EMI International, 2004.
———. *Escalona: Un canto a la vida*. PolyGram Colombia, 1994.
———. *Escalona, Volumen 2*. PolyGram Colombia, 1994.
———. "La casa en el aire." *De colección*. PolyGram Colombia, 1995.
———. *De colección*. PolyGram Colombia, 1995.
———. "La tierra del olvido." *La tierra del olvido*. PolyGram Discos, 1995.
———. *La tierra del olvido*. PolyGram Discos, 1995.
———. "Malas lenguas." *Tengo fe*. EMI Latin, 1997.
———. "Que diera." *Tengo fe*. EMI Latin, 1997.
———. *Tengo fe*. EMI Latin, 1997.
———. *El amor de mi tierra*. EMI Latin, 1999.
———. "Carito." *Déjame entrar*. EMI Latin, 2001.
———. "Décimas." *Déjame entrar*. EMI Latin, 2001.
———. *Déjame entrar*. EMI Latin, 2001.

Index

Abu-Lughod, Lila, 5, 171n17
Accordion, 50, 104, 119, 127, 206n38
Adams, Noah, 109
African-American, 35, 55, 129, 139, 158
Afro-Caribbean, 54, 116–117, 119–124, 127, 129, 160. *See also* Afro-Colombian
Afro-Colombian, 111, 116, 119–120, 123, 129, 160, 203–204n16. *See also* Afro-Caribbean
Aguilera, Christina, 39–40, 46, 56–58, 72–73
Alvarez, Robert Jr., 173n33, 180n42, 216n3
American Studies, 13–14, 17, 19–20, 135, 158, 162, 168; and the transnational, 20, 134–136, 143, 168
Anderson, Benedict, 172n29, 190n8
Anglos, 35, 37, 39, 53, 55–58, 69, 71, 73, 75, 79, 90, 94–95, 117, 144
Anthony, Marc, 52, 58
Aparicio, Frances, 38, 176n4, 186n58, 191n18, 192n41, 197n8, 203n9, 206n33, 209n77, 209n79, 214n67. *See also* Tropicalization
Appadurai, Arjun, 8, 10
Arab American, 144
Arab American Studies, 135, 163
Araújo de Molina, Consuelo, 119
Araújonoguera, Consuelo, 165, 216n2
Area Studies, 6, 13, 135, 163; and transnationalism, 17, 143
Arévalo, Roberto, 175–176n4
Arévalo-Mateus, Jorge, 68, 175n4
Arnaz, Desi, 46. *See also* Latin music boom; Martin, Ricky
Arroyo, Joe, 51, 61
Asian American Studies, 135
Aterciopelados, 13, 15–16, 51, 69, 72, 87–88, 92–95, 98–110, 141, 148, 196n1,

201n64. *See also* Buitrago, Héctor; Echeverri, Andrea
Austerlitz, Saul, 212n19, 212n21, 212n22, 212n24
Autodefensas Unidas de Colombia (AUC), 22–23, 28; as terrorist organization, 23–24. *See also* Paramilitaries, Colombian
Authenticity, 94–95, 129, 160; musical, 117, 126, 128, 131–132, 159

Baca, Susana, 52, 186n60
Bacilos, 41
Báez, Jillian, 137, 172n25, 211–212n14, 215n74
Balseros: Colombian, 32; Cuban, 161–162, 180n38; Haitian, 161–162
Banks, Jack, 212n19
Bambuco, 10, 207n46
Barranquilla, 30, 65–66, 68, 92, 127, 146, 157, 160, 163, 171n18; Arab community of, 136, 145; and carnival, 61, 68, 159–160, 215n81; and immigration 68, 143, 145; Jewish community of, 145
Behar, Ruth, 181n7
Behdad, Ali, 47
Benavides, Iván, 51
Berland, Jody, 137
Berríos Miranda, 185n48
Bernstein, Nina, 179n31
Betancourt, Ingrid, 21
Beverley, John, 182n8
Billboard, 56, 58, 108, 157, 184n33
Blades, Rubén, 58
Blair, Richard, 51
Blender, 78
Bloque, 51, 93, 164

| 245

Bogotá, 15, 30, 32, 65, 69, 88–89, 92, 98–101; youth of, 89–90
Bolaño Saurith, Paúl, 206n38
Bolero, 92, 118, 131
Buena Vista Social Club, 53–54, 60, 187n70, 187–188n73. *See also* Cooder, Ry
Buitrago, Elías Pellet, 68
Buitrago, Héctor, 98–99, 103, 107, 108. *See also* Aterciopelados; Echeverri, Andrea
Burns, Gary, 212n19, 212n21

Cachaco, 96, 124, 199n36. *See also* Colombia; *Costeño/a*
Caicedo, Andrés, 11, 90–91
Caja vallenata, 50, 119–120
Cali, 30, 50, 90
Campo Mirando, Rafael, 207n46
Cárdenas Duque, Rocío, 129, 206n39
Caribbean, 35, 42, 63, 65, 68, 92, 112, 117, 119, 121–122, 127, 136, 159, 161; and Middle Eastern community, 136; musical history of, 129, 131, 158
Carrilera, 10, 92, 99
Cartagena, 68, 123, 127, 204n17. *See also* La Costa; *Costeño/a*
Casillas, Dolores Inés, 76, 172n25, 192n41
Castaño, Carlos, 23
Castro, Max J., 180–181n1
Castro Caycedo, Germán, 179n31
Census, U.S., 29, 32, 178n29
Cepeda, María Elena, 192n41
Champeta, 10, 109, 202n75
Chaparro, María Alejandra, 179n31
Chávez-Silverman, Susana, 197n8, 214n67. *See also* Tropicalization
Chernick, Mark, 176n14
Citizenship, 2–3, 15, 34, 63–64, 85; cultural, 2, 64
Citron, Marcia, 97
Click, Melissa A., 170n10
Clifford, James, 14,
Coates, Norma, 89
Cobb, Kim, 181n5
Cobo, Leila, 66, 196n4, 214n58
Cohen, Sara 96
Collier, Michael W., 33

Colombia: Caribbean Coast, 14, 16, 105, 110, 123, 143, 145, 148, 159, 204n16; and 1886 Constitution, 115–116; and 1991 Constitution, 2, 34, 116, 125; and Catholicism, 81, 92, 97, 99; and coffee, 28, 30–31; and contemporary crisis, 1, 10, 14, 18, 20, 41, 167–168, 176n11; "Dirty War" in, 20–21; and disappearances, 21; and displacement, 17, 21; and drug-trafficking, 13, 103; and gender roles, 88–89, 97, 105–106; homicide rate 20–21, 27; human rights in, 20–21, 26–27; military, 20, 23–24; and military aid, 24; and the political moment, 14, 115, 167–168; and race, 43, 111–112, 117, 122, 124, 127, 145, 167–168, 203n11; and refugees, 21; regionalism, 65, 86, 89, 92, 106,121–122;and stereotypes, 18, 80; and *La Violencia*, 22, 30; youth, 90–91
Colombianidad, 4, 15, 17, 63–64, 85, 113, 115, 126, 133
Colombian Studies, 19, 168
"Columbus Effect," 52–55, 60. *See also* Valentín-Escobar, Wilson
Colón, Willie, 48–49
Colonialism, 12, 57, 134–135
Commodification, Musical 79, 117, 126, 129, 132
Cooder, Ry, 53–54, 60, 126. *See also* Buena Vista Social Club
Costa, La, 65, 117–120, 123, 143, 207–208n52. *See also Costeño/a*
Costeño/a, 65, 96, 112–113, 116–117, 121–124, 128–130, 136, 145, 165, 199n36, 203n16. See also *Cachaco*; Colombia
Cross-media approach, 7, 13, 16; to music video, 137, 143, 162
"Cross-over," 40, 44–45, 49, 58, 60, 71, 81, 148–149; and "race music," 58; and U.S. music industry, 37–38, 55, 57. *See also* Latin Grammys; Music industry, Latin(o); Music industry, U.S.
Cuba, 42, 53–54
Cubans, 19, 36, 48, 54–55
Cuesta, Iván, y sus Baltimore Vallenatos, 51, 186n55

Cultural Studies, 6, 126, 140
Cumbia, 10, 50, 69, 92–93, 122, 124, 127, 158, 202n75, 203n16
Curry, Ramona, 73
Curtis, James R., 44. *See also* "Miami Sound"
Cusick, Susan G., 211n9

Das Gupta, Monisha, 173n33
Dávila, Arlene, 38, 60, 95, 174n46
Dávila, José, 173n36
Davis, Martha Ellen, 169n2
Davis, Mike, 179n31
Deas, Malcolm, 26
de Certeau, Michel, 209n76
De Genova, Nicholas, 174n46
de la Rúa, Antonio, 81
Del Villar Sierra, Oliverio, 191n26
Dermota, Ken, 208n65
Diaspora: Colombian, 10, 12, 17, 34, 112, 114, 126, 133; Caribbean, 161; Latino, 54; South American, 19
Díaz, Diomedes, 131
Díaz, Leandro, 120, 129, 209n71
Díaz, Luz Marina, 180n36, 190n15, 190n17
Domínguez, Virginia, 12
Dominicans, 19
Drug traffickers, Colombian, 20, 23–24
Dugas, John C., 170n13
Durán Alejo, 111–114, 120, 130

Echeverri, Andrea, 11, 13, 15–16, 51, 79, 87–110, 133, 148, 165, 167–168. *See also* Aterciopelados; Buitrago, Héctor
El exterior, 18, 84, 145, 175n2
Ellick, Adam B., 179n31
Elliot, Emory, 134–135, 210n1
Elliott, Andrea, 177n25, 179n31, 190n14
ELN (National Liberation Army), 22–24, 27–28. *See also* FARC; Guerrillas
El Tiempo, 97, 195n81
Emerson, Rana A., 211–212n14, 212n19
Escalona, Rafael, 104, 117, 120, 201n59
Escobar, Cristina, 180n36
Escobari, Valeria, 186n56
Espitia, Marilyn, 170n8, 173n33, 180n36

Estefan, Emilio, 15, 37, 40–41, 43, 44–46, 48–50, 52, 60, 69, 118, 183n20. *See also* Estefan, Gloria; Latin Grammys; "Miami Sound"; Santander, Kike
Estefan, Gloria, 15, 37, 46–48, 50, 52, 69, 71, 131, 188n92. *See also* Estefan, Emilio; Latin Grammys; "Miami Sound"; Santander, Kike
Esterrich, Carmelo, 106
Ethnic Studies, 6, 13–14, 17, 19, 35, 135, 143, 162–163, 168; and transnationalism, 17, 134, 143

FARC (Revolutionary Armed Forces of Colombia), 21–24, 27–28, 165, 216n2. *See also* ELN; Guerrillas, Colombian
Farley, Christopher, 201n67
Farrell, Cathleen, 186n56
Fast, Susan, 138
Feldman, Heidi, 186n60
Feminist theory, U.S.: and music video, 137, 143; and popular culture studies, 11; and single-axis framework, 5; and transnationalism, 137, 143, 153
Fernández, Enrique, 186n55, 209n80
Fernández, Raúl, 29, 176n4, 186n58
Fernández L'Hoeste, Héctor, 170n9, 197n11, 202n5, 205n26, 210n80
Fiol-Matta, Licia, 60, 148
Fiske, John, 203n10
Flores, Juan, 186n58, 215n74
Florida, South, 31–32, 34, 36, 41, 164. *See also* Miami
Fluck, Winfried, 210n1
Folk culture, 4, 16, 119; Colombian, 112–113
Foner, Nancy, 180n40
Fortou, Emilio, 68
Foucault, Michel, 76, 78
Fouron, Georges Eugene, 64, 173n33
Franco, Natalia, 190n15
Francisco el Hombre, 129, 208n65, 209n71
Fraser Delgado, Celeste, 49, 107, 191n25, 201n66, 215n81
Fregoso, Rosa Linda, 172n25
Freud, Sigmund, 16, 134–135, 150–151
Frith, Simon, 70, 165, 193n57, 208n69, 211n9

Index | 247

Gaita, 120, 204n17
García Canclini, Néstor, 37, 54, 167
García Márquez, Gabriel, 148, 201n67, 205n23, 209n71, 213n44
Garofalo, Reebee, 55
Gell, Aaron, 213n44
Gender: in Colombian popular music, 11; in Latin(o) America, 167; in Latin American popular music studies, 12; and nationalism, 9, 11–12; in popular music scholarship, 11
Gilroy, Paul, 204n16
Giraldo, Javier, 24
Glasser, Ruth, 52, 176n4, 186n58
Glick Schiller, Nina, 64, 171n21, 173n33
Globalization, 16, 34, 63, 84, 86, 89, 108, 148, 158
Goldring, Luin, 196n82
González, Elián, 36. *See also* Cubans; U.S.-Cubans
González, Jerry, 187n70
González, Rubén, 52
Goodnough, Abby, 181n5
Goodwin, Andrew, 140, 212n21, 212n23, 212n24
Grammys, 39, 52, 84–85; and categorization of Latin music, 47
Grenier, Guillermo J., 180–181n1
Grewal, Inderpal, 173n39
Grossberg, Lawrence, 212n24
Grupo Niche, 51
Guacharaca, 50, 120
Guarnizo, Luis Eduardo, 10, 62, 173n33, 173n34, 175n1, 180n36, 180n42, 190n15, 190n17
Guerrillas, Colombian, 18, 20–21, 23–24, 28, 41; as "internal enemy," 23–24; and peace negotiations, 27. *See also* ELN; FARC
Gutiérrez, Tomás Darío, 111

Habell-Pallán, Michelle, 170n9, 172n25, 176n4, 186n58, 199n44
Hall, Stuart, 6, 134, 171n24, 174n52, 187n68, 208n59
Hanke, Robert, 212n19

Heinz, Wolfgang, 26–27
Hermes, Joke, 4,
Hernández, Rafael, 47, 52
Hernández, Tanya Katerí, 53, 181n7
Hernández, Victoria, 52
Hip-hop, 3, 58. *See also* Rap
Hispanic, 56–57
hooks, bell, 12
Houston, David, 182n8
Hunt, John Britt, 190n15
Hurtado, Aída, 81

Identity: Arab American, 162–163; bicultural, 55, 58, 73; Colombian, 13, 15–16, 80, 112, 114, 116, 122–124, 126, 133, 160, 164–165; discourses on, 101; ethnoracial, 13, 122, 126; hybrid, 126, 133, 149–150, 160; and gender, 13, 16; Latin(o) American, 86, 93, 145–146, 162–163; Latino, 60, 136, 162–163; Middle Eastern, 162–163; politics of, 38, 70, 148; and Spanish language, 161; transnational, 13, 16, 62, 93, 126, 166–167; U.S.-Colombian, 164–165; U.S. Latino, 86
Iglesias, Enrique, 41
Immigration: Colombian, 27–30, 32–37, 190n15; European, 116; and Miami, 30–35, 41; and political asylum, 32; political vs. economic, 28; transnational, 13, 34; and visas, 29, 31–32
Immigration, Middle Eastern, 143–144, 163, 191n26
Indigenous peoples, Colombian, 112, 116, 120, 123–125, 129. *See also* Afro-Colombian
Iskandar, Adel, 155–156

Jackson, Michael, 71, 139
Jackson Heights, 149–150; *See also* Manrique, Jaime; Queens
Jaramillo, Ana María, 180n38
Järviluoma, Helmi, 171n19
Jean, Wycleff, 150, 157–162, 215n80, 215n83, 215n84, 215n85, 215n86
Jenkins, Henry, 211n5
Juanes, 93

248 | Index

Kelly, James, 175n1, 183n26
Kibbeh, 211n4
Klich, Ignacio, 143, 210n3
Kogan, Frank, 80–81
Kramer, Michael W., 170n10

Latina, 56, 73, 79
Latin Academy of Recording Arts and Sciences (LARAS), 47–49, 85. *See also* Estefan, Emilio; Latin Grammys; Miami
Latin American Studies, 14, 17, 19–20, 135, 162–163, 168; and notions of race, 143; and the transnational, 134–136
Latin(a/o) American, 169n7
Latinas: and corporality, 75–76, 98, 146; and hypersexuality, 75, 96
"Latin Beat," 39–41
Latin Grammys, 47–49, 56, 70, 79, 84–85, 108, 184n33, 185n49; for Best New Artist, 54, 56; as "Gramilios," 48; and Mexican Regional Music, 184n33. *See also* Estefan, Emilio; Latin Academy of Recording Arts and Sciences; Miami
Latinidad, 15, 19, 37, 63–64, 70, 80, 85, 95; as marketing tool, 62–63, 85; as social identity, 62–63; and U.S. Latino identity, 56, 60
Latinization, 42, 89, 197n8
Latin music boom, 15, 17, 37–39, 43, 46, 55, 60, 63, 66, 73, 80, 89, 95, 149, 167; and Mexican regional music, 185n49; as transnational phenomenon, 88
Latino Studies, 6, 17, 19, 135, 168; as transnational field, 20, 134–135
Lebanon, 143; and immigration quotas, 145; migrants of, 144–145; and transnational identity, 145
Lechner, Ernesto, 79–80
León, Juan, 42
Lesser, Jeffrey, 143, 210n3
L'Estrange Fawcett, Louise, 213n33
Levin, Jordan, 184n38
Levitt, Peggy, 177n25, 195n79
Levy, Steven, 142, 212n22
Lewis, Lisa A., 211n9, 211–212n14

Lipsitz, George, 35, 86, 121, 208n68, 208n69
Livingston, Grace, 176n10
López, Jennifer, 39–40, 46, 58, 73, 76, 80, 94
Los Angeles, 30, 54, 69; and Latin Grammys, 48; and music industry, 45
Lovering, John, 72
Lowe, Lisa A., 100–101, 140

Macondismo, 107, 112, 148
Magical realism, 107, 201n67
Manalansan, Martin F. IV, 169n5, 173n33, 206n34
Manrique, Jaime, 149–150, 178n31
Manuel, Peter, 185n48
Manzanera, Phil, 50–51, 103
Marianismo, 76, 96
Marinucci, Carla, 181n5
Martin, Denis-Constant, 196n86
Martin, Ricky, 39, 41, 46–47, 58–59, 71, 80, 94
Martín Barbero, Jesús, 169n6, 200n45
Mato, Daniel 169–170n7
Matthews, Gordon, 86
McClary, Susan, 7, 137, 211n9
McIntosh, Heather, 212n19, 212n21
McKee, David L., 179n34
McRobbie, Angela, 193n57, 211n9
Media, Colombian, 84, 127; and Colombian identity, 8; globalized, 43–44, 61, 129, 141; hypodermic models of, 6, 140; Latino-centered, 39, 59; mainstream, 39, 44, 52, 58–59, 71, 73, 79, 95–96, 107, 110, 127, 149; "old" vs. "new," 142; and popular music, 89, 96; transnational, 7, 76, 84, 97
Media Studies, 6, 14, 140
Media, United States, 35, 37, 76, 79, 84; and division of labor, 94; and representation of Colombia, 24
Medellín, 30, 92, 122
Mercer, Kobena, 154
Merengue, 93–94; as *vallenato* rhythm, 119
Mestizaje, 111, 113, 115–116, 119, 122–123, 133, 207n48, 207n52
Meza, Leandro, 186n55

Index | 249

Mía, 59
Miami, 1, 35–36, 41–43, 50–51, 54, 57, 64, 69, 84–85, 95, 164, 179n31; and ethnoracial identity, 37; as "instant city," 42; and Latin Grammys, 47, 49; as "Latin Hollywood," 41, 43, 45, 110, 183n30; and mainstream media, 141; Miami Beach, 32, 45, 76; Miami-Dade County, 31–33, 35–37, 41; and multicultural citizenry, 3, 35; as music center, 2, 3, 13–14, 16, 19, 38, 41–45, 48, 52, 71–72, 89, 196n5; as pan-Latino space, 57, 65; and political right, 42
Miami Herald, 36, 96
Miami New Times, 49, 107
"Miami Sound," 43, 45–46, 50–52. See also Estefan, Emilio; Estefan, Gloria
Miami Vice, 43, 141
Middle Eastern Studies, 17, 162–163; and the transnational, 135
Mirabal, Nancy Raquel, 181n7
Miyoshi, Masao, 16
Moisala, Pirkko, 171n19
Moisés y la Gente del Camino, 120
Molina Guzmán, Isabel, 172n25, 181n7
Morales, Ed, 169n1, 185n51, 197n11, 201n66, 205n26
Mora-Mass, Elizabeth, 179n31
MTV Latino, 44, 101, 197–198n16, 200n50. See also Latin music boom; Miami; Music industry, Latin(o); Music industry, U.S.; Music video
MTV United States, 70, 140, 152, 162, 189n2; and advertising, 139; audience for, 154; and gender, 140; history of, 139, 141–142
MTV Unplugged: Latin America, 70–71; U.S., 70–71
Muñoz, Elías Miguel, 181n7
Muñoz, José Esteban, 181n7
Murillo, Javier, 106
Murillo, Mario, 21, 24
Music industry, Latin(o), 34, 37–38, 43, 46–47, 52, 110, 118; Colombian, 126; historical chronologies of, and payola, 184n38; marketing, 44. See also "Cross-over"; Miami

Music industry, U.S., 3, 38, 40, 43–44, 95, 108; marketing strategies, 73, 94, 149, 152; and record keeping, 93; role of women in, 136; transnational, 148. See also "Cross-over"
Music, Latin(o), 40, 42, 53, 62; and Latin Grammys, 48; vs. Latin music, 5; and relationship to ethnoracial identity, 57
Music video, 16–17, 62, 89, 91, 99–103, 110, 111, 135, 137, 142–143, 149, 154; and class, 143; and ethnoracial identity, 135–136, 153, 157; feminist critiques of, 155–157; and gender, 101–102, 110, 135–136, 139, 143, 153–154, 157; and language, 153; in Latin America, 88; Latin(a) American, 136, 162; and national identity, 153; and sexuality, 135–136, 139, 143, 153–154; study of, 137, 139–141, 143. See also MTV Latino; MTV United States
Music, world, 55, 112, 119, 128
Musical ImagiNation, 8, 10, 121, 131, 167–168

Naber, Nadine, 144, 210n3
National Academy of Recording Arts and Sciences (NARAS), 44, 47. See also Latin music boom; Music industry, Latin(o)
Nationalism: methodological, 6; relationship to gender and race, 12;
Native American Studies, 135
Negrón Muntaner, Frances, 76, 176n4, 192n44
Negus, Keith, 38, 193n57, 214n57
New Orleans, 30, 127
New York, 19, 54, 70, 85; and Colombian community, 30; and metropolitan area, 30; and music industries, 45
New York Times, 39, 54, 138
Ngai, Mae M., 210n1
Niurka, Norma, 204n18
Nuevo Herald, El, 36–37
Núñez, Rafael, 169n1

Obejas, Achy, 181n7
Oboler, Suzanne, 5, 169n7, 179n34, 180n41, 191n32, 195n78
Ocampo López, Javier, 207n46

Ochoa, Ana María, 106
Ochoa, Luis Fernando, 69
Oliva, Carlos, 186n57
Ong, Aihwa, 31, 173n33, 189n4, 190n8, 190n15
Orientalism, 155–156
Orwall, Bruce, 73

Pacini Hernández, Deborah, 47, 126, 170n9, 197n11, 198n17, 198n25, 202n75, 204n16, 204n20
Padgett, Tim, 96
Palacios, Marco, 22, 172n28
Parado, Freddy, 179n31
Paramilitaries, Colombian, 20–23, 28; and drug traffickers, 23; and landowners, 23; as terrorist organization, 23–24. See also *Autodefensas Unidas de Colombia* (AUC)
Parédez, Deborah, 75, 172n25
Pareles, John, 199n32, 213n41, 214n44
Pastrana, Andrés, 1, 24, 26–27, 84
Paz-Frydman, Silvia, 192n41
Peña, Manuel H., 186n58
Penhaul, Karl, 179n31
People en Español, 77
Perdomo Escobar, José Ignacio, 207n46
Pérez-Torres, Rafael, 160
Plan Colombia, 24–25, 110
Plantains, 211n4
Pop music, 3, 79, 152, 158; and gender, 137–138; history of women in, 136
Popular culture, Colombian, 99, 103–104; and transnational framework, 13
Popular music, Colombian, 41–42; 65–66, 98–99, 112, 117, 158
Portaccio Fontalvo, José 206n38
Portes, Alejandro, 170n8, 181n2
Posada-Carbó, Eduardo, 213n33
Post, Jennifer, 200n46
Pratt, Mary Louise, 172n29
Presley, Elvis, 126, 208n65
Prida, Dolores, 136, 181n7
Punk, 87, 91–92, 98–99

Queens: and Barranquilla carnival, 68; and Colombian community, 30, 179n31, 191n25. *See also* Immigration; New York

Quiñones, John, 39–40

Radio Caracol, 90
Ramos-Zaya, Ana Y., 174n46
Rap, 121, 158, 161–162; and MTV United States, 139
Reggae, 65–66
Reggaetón, 152
Regional music, Mexican, 49. *See also* Estefan, Emilio; Latin Grammys
Riaño-Alcalá, Pilar, 89–90
Rivera, Raquel Z., 176n4, 186n58, 215n74
Rivero, Yeidy M., 192n41
Roach, Elizabeth M., 175n1, 180n36, 190n15
Rock music, 3, 65, 79; in Colombian context, 11, 87, 92, 93, 98–99, 110, 127; criticism, 97; relationship to gender and race, 79–80, 88–89, 96, 110, 136–139, 142; and Grammy categorization, 47; as musical "scene," 96; as U.S.-European musical genre, 79, 92, 95–96, 139. *See also* Grammys; *Rock en español*
Rock en español, 2, 11–12, 16, 62, 66, 69, 79–80, 89–96, 158; as alternative music, 16, 94–95, 108, 138; and gender, 88–89, 99; marketing of, 88; and media, 88
Rockera, 79, 87, 89. *See also* Echeverri, Andrea; *Rock en español*; Shakira
Rodríguez, Jesús, 213–214n44
Rohter, Larry, 179n31
Rojas, Viviana, 192n41
Rolling Stone, 78, 80
Rosaldo, Renato, 190n11
Rose, Richard F., 44. *See also* "Miami Sound"
Rose, Tricia, 207n43, 212n19
Ross-Sorkin, Andrew, 189n2
Rúa, Mérida M, 174n50, 190n8
Rumbaut, Rubén, 170n8
Rycenga, Jennifer, 211–212n14

Salaita, Steven, 163, 210n3
Saldívar, José David, 6, 135–136
Salsa, 3, 10, 47, 51, 61, 69, 90–93, 121, 197n13; and contested Cuban origins, 49; and gender, 132; *romántica*, 131–132, 209n78

Index | 251

Sánchez, Arturo Ignacio, 175n1, 180n36, 190n15
Sandino, Amparo, 120, 131
Sandino Moreno, Catalina, 179n31
Samper, Daniel Pizano, 129, 209n74
Santa Ana, Otto, 198n24
Santa Marta, 68, 117, 127–128, 204n17
Santander, Kike, 49–50 52, 118
Sanz, Alejandro, 150, 154–157
Savigliano, Marta, 204n20
Schaeffer-Grabiel, Felicity, 134, 172n25
Semana, 79, 126, 179n31, 203n7
September 11, 2001, 16, 29, 34, 66, 75, 146, 163; and War on Terror, 146
Shakira, 7–9, 11, 13, 16–17, 50, 60–61, 63–86, 88, 93, 96, 98, 105, 107, 128, 133, 135–136, 138, 141, 145–146, 148, 150–163, 165, 167–168, 194n68; and English, 71,73; and fans, 72, 138–139; and media, 145–146, 148; as *rockera*, 68–69,72, 76,79; and sexuality, 75–76, 78–79, 151; as transnational citizen, 64, 69, 84–86, 165
Shank, Barry, 194n59, 199n34
Sheffield, Rob, 80
Shohat, Ella, 5, 135, 210n2
Shohat, Ella, and Robert Stam, 7
Sidestepper, 51
Silverman, Kaja, 156
Simon, Paul, 126
Sinclair, John, 170n8, 183n30
Síndici, Oreste, 169n1
Slobin, Mark, 170n12
Smith, Michael Peter, 20, 62, 173n33, 180n42, 195n78
Smith, Robert, 182n12
Smith, Suzanne E., 57
Smits, Jimmy, 46
Sony Discos, 44, 69, 71, 83, 117–118. See also Latin music boom; Latin(o) music industry
Soundscan, 44, 184n33
South Beach 43, 72, 75. See also Miami
Soraya, 11, 93
Stack, John F., Jr., 169n7
Stepick, Alex, 181n2

Storey, John, 170n14, 172n29, 196n86
Storm Roberts, John, 52, 186n58
Straw, Will, 194n59, 199n34
Streicker, Joel, 173n39
Suárez, Juana, 72, 76, 98, 108, 169n3
Suhair Mujaj, Lisa, 210n3
Suro, Roberto, 175n4, 178n29

Tafur, Pilar, 129, 209n72
Takacs, Stacy, 62
Talpade-Mohanty, Chandra, 194n60
Telemundo, 62, 189n2
Television, Music (MTV), 91, 136; in Latin America (MTV Latino), 91, 93, 103. See also Music video
Téllez Herrera, Andrea, 179n31
Time, 40, 56–57, 59, 108
Tobar, Dániza, 208n65
Torres, María de los Angeles, 181n7
Totó la Momposina, 11, 51
Transnationalism, 13, 61–62, 64, 84–86, 89, 162; and communal networks, 20; and community-building practices, 20; "from above," 10, 34; "from below," 10, 84, 167; and nation-state, 61, 216n3; relationship gender and race, 12; and research, 14, 20, 133, 136–137
Tropicana, Carmelita, 136, 150
Trouillot, Michel-Rolph, 54
Tropicalization, 6, 53, 60, 156
Troyano, Alina, 150. See also Tropicana, Carmelita

Univisión, 62
Uribe-Urán, Víctor, 201n64
Uribe Vélez, Alvaro, 27, 29, 34
U.S.-Colombian, 19, 31–32, 34; vs. Colombian-American, 4–5; and *desconfianza*, 18; and remittances, 28; studies, 19–20, 168; and Temporary Protected Status (TPS), 34; and transnationalism, 28, 63–64, 85, 136. See also U.S. Latinos
U.S.-Cuban, 31, 34–37, 136, 181n3; as anti-Castro, 48; and ethnic enclave, 43; and media, 36

U.S. Latinos, 31, 34–40; as consumers, 56; and media presence, 38; "new," 14, 19, 29, 35, 167, 175n4; as "Other" Latinos/Hispanics, 29; population, 44, 73; as "radical hybrids," 63, 189n7; and spending power, 44

Useche, Bernardo, 29

Valdés-Rodríguez, Alisa, 187–188n73

Valdivia, Angharad, 63, 73, 141, 172n25, 182n9, 189n7, 192n41

Valentín-Escobar, Wilson, 52, 54, 186n60. *See also* "Colombus Effect"

Valledupar, 119–120, 128

Vallenato, 3–4, 10, 12, 16, 18, 50–51, 69, 90, 93, 103–106, 111–133, 204n16, 205n23; and gender, 105–106, 112, 130–132; Golden Age of, 118; as oral tradition, 120–121, 209n71; as regional genre, 118; resemanticization of, 113, 122, 126, 133; as transnational genre, 118, 133

Van Djik, Teun, 7

Vernallis, Carol, 211n8, 212n19, 214n60, 215n83

Vila, Pablo, 174n46

Vilkko, Anni, 171n19

Village Voice, 80

Violence, 18, 20–21, 24, 26, 28, 41, 112, 168; and Colombian drug-trafficking, 13; and politics, 21, 26, 113; and *vallenato*, 115, 126. *See also* Colombia

Vives, Carlos, 13, 50–51, 60, 93, 104–105, 113–120, 122, 125–131, 133, 141, 164–168, 183n20, 204n16, 209n76

La Voz de Barranquilla, 68

Wade, Peter, 10–11, 16, 111, 114–115, 117, 124, 171n21, 172n28, 190n17, 196n4, 203n11, 203–204n16, 207nn46–52, 208nn52–56, 208nn58–59, 208nn61–63, 208n63, 216n3

Wall Street Journal, 73

Walser, Robert, 101, 211n956

War on drugs, 26, 28, 63, 69

War on terror, 146

Watrous, Peter, 39, 54

Waxer, Lise, 10–11,

Wenders, Wim, 53. *See also* Buena Vista Social Club

Whiteley, Sheila, 82, 88, 193n57, 211–212n14, 212n19

Williams, Raymond, 124

Williams, Raymond L., 205n23

Wise, Sue, 143

Youth, Latino, 38, 95: relationship to Spanish language, 57; and U.S. music industry, 38, 94–95

Yúdice, George, 174n52, 184n33

Zambrano, Juan Vicente, 50.

Zapata, Juan Carlos, 34

Zapata Olivella, Delia, 173n41

Zazueta Martínez, Katynka, 184n33

Zentella, Ana Celia, 169n4

Zolov, Eric, 170n9, 197n11

Zuleta, Emiliano, 120

Zuleta, Iván, 131

Zuluaga, Tulio, 111–112

Index | 253

About the Author

MARÍA ELENA CEPEDA is Assistant Professor of Latina/o Studies at Williams College. Her research and teaching centers on contemporary media, popular culture, language politics, transnational identity, and community-based pedagogical approaches.